Reflections from the Frontline

Developing Country Negotiators in the WTO

Editors

PRADEEP S. MEHTA
ATUL KAUSHIK
RASHID S. KAUKAB

CUTS International

Academic Foundation
New Delhi

First published in 2012
by

ACADEMIC FOUNDATION
4772-73 / 23 Bharat Ram Road, (23 Ansari Road),
Darya Ganj, New Delhi - 110 002 (India).
Phones : 23245001 / 02 / 03 / 04.
Fax : +91-11-23245005.
E-mail : books@academicfoundation.com
www.academicfoundation.com

in association with:

CUTS International

37-39, Rue de Vermont, 1202 Geneva, Switzerland
Ph: +41.22.734.6080; Fx:+41.22.734.3914
E-mail: geneva@cuts.org, Website: www.cuts-grc.org

Supported by:

REGERINGSKANSLIET
Ministry for Foreign Affairs
Sweden

FRIEDRICH EBERT STIFTUNG

Reflections from the Frontline: Developing Country Negotiators in the WTO
Editors: Pradeep S. Mehta, Atul Kaushik and Rashid S. Kaukab

ISBN 13: 9788171889266
ISBN 10: 8171889263

Printed and bound in India.

Reflections

"The picture this book provides is one of active participation and deep involvement of developing countries in the life of the World Trade Organisation across all its activities. It speaks of their negotiating positions, of their ideas and efforts to shape the future of the organisation. I recommend it for anyone seeking to understand how the WTO has evolved in the last decade and where we are today".

Pascal Lamy
Director General, WTO

This is an enlightening book for people to read, particularly for those whose are familiar with the practice of GATT and WTO negotiations. The summary of the experience of the previous negotiations as well as during the Doha Round is very comprehensive, objective and in great depth. The description of developing country coalitions and the proposal for future South-South cooperation are very relevant and pragmatic. I fully share the view that Doha Round should not and cannot simply be thrown away. It might be a good idea to suspend the negotiation for a year or two for Members to draw lessons and consider positively how to move forward. The suggestions for handling negotiations in post Doha period are also good food for thought and I do hope Members would give them serious considerations.

Sun Zhenyu
Ambassador of China to the WTO

As a Chief Negotiator for India at the WTO, I am extremely happy that CUTS is bringing out this publication. The negotiations at the WTO are extremely complex and it is essential that developing country negotiators read up on the history of each negotiating position, understand the dynamics of developing country and developed country negotiating positions and work ceaselessly to develop coalitions. This calls for constant interaction especially at the finishing stages of negotiations on any issue. Any lapse at this stage would be irrevocable. I am sure that this publication will be of great benefit to future negotiations.

Gopal Pillai
Former Home Secretary, Government of India

Reflections from the Frontline: Developing Countries Negotiators in the WTO is a highly timely and relevant publication. It will serve as the indispensable compass in navigating our way through the very choppy, transformative and uncharted waters of the contemporary global trade regime. It is fully comprehensive in describing the developments and major issues of the multilateral rules-based trading system, while providing sound analysis of the trends. It will help both to understand policy and to guide policy. CUTS are once again to be congratulated.

Jean-Pierre Lehmann
Professor, IMD, Founding Director, The Evian Group @ IMD, Lausanne Switzerland
Senior Fellow, Fung Global Institute, Hong Kong

The role of developing countries in the multilateral trading system of the WTO has evolved rapidly in the decade and a half since the conclusion of the Uruguay Round. With the Doha Round in a moribund state and policy-makers around the world struggling to revive the talks or pursue alternative strategies for liberalisation and reform, this book makes a valuable contribution to understanding and appreciating developing country group dynamics that have so powerfully influenced the Geneva deliberations in the early years of the 21st Century.

Andrew L Stoler
Executive Director, Institute for International Trade
Adelaide, Australia

This is an invaluable book for all who are interested in trade policy and specifically in trade negotiations. It is an informative, real-time account of the Doha Round by some of the key developing country players who have been involved. These reflections from the frontline remind us of much that is unprecedented – and perhaps ultimately problematic – about the Doha Round: the scope and sweep of its subject matter, the high ambition, the fact that so much of the action is not in fact at the "frontline" but, to continue the imagery, in the hinterland, traditionally reserved for domestic policy making, and the veritable alphabet soup of geographic and issue based groups that emerged in Geneva, both assisting and sometimes complicating the negotiations. A genuine contribution of these reflections is that they contain, explicitly and otherwise, important lessons begging to be learnt about multilateral trade negotiations in a dramatically changed global context…

Ransford Smith
Former Jamaican Ambassador to the WTO
Commonwealth Deputy Secretary-General

Contents

III. Developing Country Coalitions

Foreword

In contrast to the long period when GATT was rightly considered as a *"rich men's club"*, it is remarkable how much, since WTO's establishment, developing countries have become increasingly aware of their interest and responsibility in strengthening and defending a fair and rule-based multilateral trading system. This change did not take place in a *vacuum*. It was evolving at the same time as the world witnessed a turning point of truly gigantic historic proportions. China, whose endless accession process would only conclude after WTO's foundation, rapidly grew into the leading trading nation, dominating trade in manufactures. India's accelerated economic growth, its role in services trade, the explosion in Brazil's agricultural exports, the unprecedented development of trade among emerging economies, all these trends created a completely different landscape from what had characterised the relatively weak participation of developing countries in past negotiating rounds.

This is not to say that these countries had accepted a passive position in negotiations. On the contrary, since the Tokyo Round and afterwards they had insisted in claiming priority treatment for the so-called *"unfinished business agenda"* of past GATT rounds: full incorporation of agriculture and textiles into the rule-based system, tariff peaks and tariff escalation, abuse of anti-dumping and countervailing duties, more balanced approach to intellectual property rights in the light of public health problems, concrete expression for the special and differential treatment principle, with particular consideration of LDCs' situation, among other issues.

It is only in this sense that the round launched in Doha in late 2001 could deserve to be named the Doha Development Agenda: because of its promise to place development at the centre of the multilateral trading system, finally tackling, once and for all, the eternal *unfinished agenda* of past disappointments and unfulfilled expectations. Developing countries were urged to be equal participants in the DDA to ensure that their interests and concerns are fully addressed. The decade-long DDA negotiations – as documented in this volume – demonstrate that developing countries have made important strides towards their equal participation. But it has been neither easy nor smooth.

Developing countries have traditionally faced several formidable challenges in their active and effective participation in the WTO. These range from their own very limited technical, financial and institutional capacities *vis-à-vis* the expanding and evolving WTO agenda that now cover issues that go far beyond measures at the border, to uneven power relationships and processes that put them at a disadvantage compared with developed countries. They had also discovered that in a trade liberalization oriented system they needed a positive approach to negotiations. It was not enough to know what one did not want to be brought into the system. Equally indispensable was to know what one should want as the outcome of the negotiations. In other words, they needed a pro-active agenda of forward-looking proposals. Time had come to equip themselves with sound substantive knowledge and good negotiating tactics and strategies to ensure that the WTO negotiations take place among more-or-less equal partners. Ten years of DDA present a fascinating story of this effort by developing countries with many successes.

Let me mention one or two successes. In agriculture negotiations, a coalition of developing countries with varied interests has emerged as a formidable force balancing its process and content. Though the formation of this coalition started with a reactive agenda, over the years it took several proactive and progressive steps on several issues to highlight linkages between trade in agriculture and development. Another example is a remarkable achievement by a group of small and vulnerable countries to establish themselves as a special group by bringing together diverse economies from among the Caribbean states and Central America and, at the same time, without asking more concessions than least developed countries are expected to achieve from the DDA negotiations.

Substance is at the heart of DDA negotiations. Complex issues are involved whether it is the traditional market access negotiations dealing with tariffs and non-tariff barriers to trade or the negotiations to improve and develop rules including in new areas. Agriculture, industrial products, services, intellectual property, fisheries, trade and environment, all are part of the negotiations, interwoven in a complex web of economics, public policy and law. Understanding and analysing the issues and their interlinkages, particularly in the context of their development implications is needed to present proposals to take the negotiations forward while responding to proposals by the other participants.

In my paper titled: Integration of Developing Countries into the Multilateral Trading System, published in the book: The Uruguay Round and Beyond *Essays in Honor of Arthur Dunkel*, (Jagdish Bhagwati and Mathias Hirsch, ed., The University of Michigan Press, Ann Arbor, 1999) while analysing the future of the multilateral trading system, I had argued: "It is clear that the practice of working out the rules, principles and details of trade agreements along like-minded countries, to be brought subsequently to the multilateral forum, and the sectoral approach (i.e. negotiations on basic telecommunications) is likely to intensify in future."

I was not surprised by the manner in which the events unfolded during the course of DDA negotiations. However and more than that, I am happy to note that in a surprisingly short period, developing countries have made extraordinary progress in acquiring substantive capacities on all issues. They were helped in improving their learning curves by the more resourceful among them and often with assistance from development partners. As a matter of objective justice it should be recognized the noteworthy contribution in this respect from UNCTAD not only in helping with giving shape to a pro-active development agenda but also in providing valuable assistance and training in the accession process of many developing countries that are now active participants in the negotiations. It is no surprise then, as this volume attests, that most of the proposals in almost all areas of DDA negotiations have been put forward by developing countries.

Substantive capacities alone do not guarantee success. These have to be complemented by negotiating skills, tactics and strategies. DDA has also witnessed a visible improvement in the quality of negotiating skills and strategies of developing countries. One key aspect of this improvement relates to the number, role and performance of coalitions and alliances of developing countries. They have mastered the art of combining forces in a flexible and pragmatic manner to achieve common interests where possible. Their alliances range from formal, large, multi-issue groupings to informal, small, issue-based coalitions, each conscious of its niche as well as limitations. This volume includes several examples of developing country coalitions and offers deep insights into their functioning.

Many concerns have been raised on the slow progress of DDA negotiations and one of the reasons, as argued by many experts, is the 'single undertaking' nature of negotiations. In my paper, referred to above, I had also said that developing countries were among the main proponents of the 'single undertaking" because they wished to pre-empt a recurrence of the situation in earlier multilateral rounds where the initiatives to liberalise the agriculture sector had simply been permitted to die during the course of the negotiations. Now, several calls have been made to reform the process of WTO negotiations by considering the 'variable geometry' approach toward negotiating contentious issues. The possibility of adopting a new approach to expedite the conclusion of the Doha Round is there in the Doha Declaration itself. It was also evident in a recent call made by Pascal Lamy to discuss an 'LDC Plus Package' at the forthcoming WTO Ministerial Conference to be held in Geneva in December 2011.

Without going into the merits and demerits of 'single undertaking' and/or 'variable geometry' let me underline that if a different modality on negotiations is adopted then developing countries, particularly emerging economies like Brazil, China, India (but without creating a new group of 'emerging economies' in DDA negotiations) will have a much larger role to play to take forward the development dimensions of DDA negotiations and to do *ex ante* evaluation of each and every clause of the final Doha text in respect to their possibility on 'delivering on development'.

In my opinion, this is *the* immediate challenge of developing countries and the multilateral trading system. And addressing this challenge requires significant negotiating skills, not just by trade ministry officials and negotiators but that of a large and diverse number of state and non-state actors dealing with trade and development. This unique collection of essays will serve a long way in addressing this challenge.

In many ways CUTS' history is a fascinating mirror of the profound transformation of the multilateral trading system and the decisive role of developing countries in that process. From a relatively small and modest organisation mainly devoted to consumer protection issues, CUTS has grown to become the uncontested privileged place of discussion about the future of the trading system among specialists of all origins and orientations.

CUTS should be congratulated for conceiving the idea of a publication to document, record and present the experience of developing country negotiators and then bringing that to fruition. This is preserving the history of multilateral trade negotiations as it unfolds based on first-hand accounts of those who are in the thick of it. This also collates valuable experiences and insights that can be used by their peers and successors to continue improving the participation of developing countries in the negotiations. Finally, this offers important lessons that can be learnt from the last ten years of DDA negotiations to fine-tune the substance and process of the negotiations for their successful and development-oriented conclusion as a significant contribution to overcome the most dangerous challenge faced by the global economy in our time.

Rubens Ricupero
Director, Economics
Armando Alvares Penteado Foundation (FAAP)
Brazil

Preface

Participation of developing countries in the multilateral trading system was invigorated with the establishment of the WTO. The WTO came up with a stronger and clearer legal framework for the conduct of international trade, including a more effective and reliable dispute settlement mechanism. Disciplines were also reinforced in areas such as agriculture which are of great interest to developing countries. While the Agreement Establishing the WTO allows for decisions by voting, the decision-making remained based on consensus to follow a healthy convention established during the GATT days.

Six years after its establishment, WTO members launched a new round of negotiations, whose stated goal was to foster development of developing and least developed members, hence the title "Doha Development Agenda". Negotiations are based on the concept of "Single Undertaking" or nothing-is-agreed-until-everything-is-agreed, where all tracks have to culminate in acceptance by all negotiating parties. Given that majority of members are developing countries it is not surprising that there is greater participation by these countries, individually or as part of various coalitions/alliances. Together they have made substantive proposals in the various areas of the negotiations and have also constructively engaged with their developed country partners in various formats of the negotiations.

Despite the drawn out Doha negotiations that have now dragged on for 10 years, and even though the negotiations have now come to a grinding halt, the performance of developing countries has been phenomenal. Many issues of their interest were successfully brought to the forefront of the negotiations. For example, in the agriculture negotiations, the G-20 coalition of developing countries has made several proposals on advancing the reform process of agriculture trade disciplines in all the three pillars of the negotiation while the G-33 coalition has strongly defended defensive interests of developing countries through proposals on Special Products and Special Safeguard Mechanism. Similarly, in Non-Agriculture Market Access (NAMA) negotiations, the NAMA 11 coalition of developing countries has constructively worked to facilitate the implementation of the Doha mandate regarding lesser obligations by developing countries. Another coalition of Small Vulnerable Economies has also made considerable achievements in the on-going Agriculture and NAMA negotiations where draft modalities include criteria to define this set of countries as well as special flexibilities which should be available to them.

The above stated accomplishments are just some of the examples of what developing countries continue to achieve in the on-going negotiations; however, despite these achievements, developing countries are faced with a multitude of challenges.

Dealing with negotiations at the multilateral level requires resources that often most of them do not have. They are often represented by a few delegates burdened with the task of covering many organisations, and not just the WTO, in Geneva. Although they are offered capacity building and trade related technical assistance, experience has shown that actual negotiations require much more than classroom theory. Moreover often delegates without a trade or economics background are posted by many developing countries who take more than the required time to come up to speed to the Geneva calculus. This works to the detriment of their countries' interests in the negotiations.

To illustrate the complexity of negotiations and the need for sustained preparations and engagement, let me quote here from a chapter on the negotiations on TRIPs written by B. K. Zutshi, former ambassador of India to the GATT who was engaged deeply in the Uruguay Round of talks.

"A crucial change in the situation occurred during the negotiations between 1991 and 1992. While India's position on most of the issues remained unchanged, most developing countries had, under bilateral pressure, substantially changed their negotiating position in regard to most of the contentious issues in the TRIPs Agreement. This was particularly true of patents. The developing countries' position had also changed on account of developments not directly related to the negotiations such as the collapse of the Berlin wall, developments in the former USSR and substantial liberalisation undertaken by the developing countries unilaterally and autonomously. In addition, the developing countries were keen to conclude the Round, and for that purpose were prepared to make concessions to the developed countries in new areas of services and TRIPS against better access to developed countries' markets in the area of trade in goods, in particular liberalisation of trade in agriculture.

"... the TRIPS Agreement that was finally accepted did impose several restrictions which the developing countries had opposed. This was due to a number of factors that accentuated the already existing unequal bargaining power between developed and developing countries.

In addition, there was a growing perception that failure of the TRIPs negotiations could result in a failure of the Uruguay Round itself, which, in turn, was perceived as opening the way for a possible breakdown of the existing multilateral trading system. At the end of the day, it was the assessment of developing countries that they needed a multilateral trading system, based on principles of nondiscrimination, much more then the developed countries and if inclusion of TRIPs in the system was the price for that, they would have to pay it". Zutshi, B. K. 1998. 'Bringing TRIPs into the Multilateral Trading System', in Bhagwati and Hirsch (eds). The Uruguay Round and Beyond – Essays in Honor of Arthur Dunkel. Springer: Berlin, pp. 37-50.

Let us not forget that it is the TRIPs agreement, which ensures the interest of trading powers like the USA and European Union and holds their commitment to the multilateral trading system. Even though IPRs are dealt with by the World Intellectual Property Organisation, the WTO is effectively the stronger institution due to its dispute settlement and cross retaliation provisions. If the TRIPs agreement was not a part of the WTO acquis, many scholars and analysts feel that the USA would walk out of the system.

Alas, though one can find much written on the subject by rich country negotiators and scholars, not much has been written by developing country negotiators on these nuances and history of trade negotiations in their full splendour.

Recognising this chasm, and the challenges faced by developing country negotiators, CUTS conceived the idea of documenting the achievements and experiences of developing country negotiators in the WTO Doha Round negotiations.

This publication is, therefore, a unique, valuable and timely contribution that draws from first hand experiences of developing country ambassadors and negotiators who have over the years successfully engaged their developed country counterparts. It provides authentic and substantive accounts of their experiences since the commencement of the WTO DDA negotiations and will be useful in enhancing the negotiating abilities of their peers and successors. The publication captures developing countries' perspective of negotiating mandates, the progress of the negotiations from inception to date including key moments, and most importantly, lessons to be drawn from the experience of applying different strategies and tactics. The publication will also be useful in preserving the history of these important events for future reference and posterity.

The publication comes at a crucial time when WTO Members are engaged in preparations for the 8th Ministerial Conference to be held in Geneva, Switzerland in December 2011. An important task for the Ministerial Conference will be to chart a forward course for DDA that continues to be stalemated, and also to address fundamental issues of WTO reforms. The analyses and lessons drawn by experienced developing country negotiators in various chapters of this publication provide valuable insights to better understand the complexities of substantive negotiations and role of developing country coalitions with a view to charting a viable way forward. Our message is clear: DDA is critical for global prosperity and for the development of developing and least-developed countries and we must strive for its successful conclusion with development at the centre of the negotiations.

Let me express my gratitude to our supporters in this endeavour: Ministry of Foreign Affairs of Sweden and the Geneva office of Friedrich Ebert Stiftung (FES), for their generous support; sixteen current and former developing country ambassadors and negotiators for contributing excellent chapters to the publication; Vinod Rege for going through all the chapters and writing the introductory chapter, and the staff of CUTS Geneva Resource Centre: R. Badrinath, Atul Kaushik, Rashid S. Kaukab, Julian Mukiibi and several others for their hard work in accomplishing this task within the allocated limits of resources and time. I would also like to thank all the reviewers for their valuable comments. All have been acknowledged in a Note on acknowledgements.

October 2011

Pradeep S. Mehta
Secretary General
CUTS International

Note on Contributors

Dr Manzoor Ahmad is an expert in international trade and customs with many years of experience at national and international level. Previously he served as Pakistan's Ambassador to the WTO before which he was head of Pakistan Customs among others. While at the WTO, he played a key role in negotiations on trade facilitation.

Ambassador Roberto Azevêdo is the Permanent Representative of Brazil to the WTO. He has previously served in the Brazilian Foreign Ministry as Undersecretary for Economic Affairs and Director of the Department for Economic Affairs.

Professor Arsene M. Balihuta is currently a Senior Presidential Adviser on Public Private Partnership in Uganda. Previously he was the Executive Chairman, Uganda Development Corporation; before which he served as Uganda's Ambassador and Permanent Representative to the WTO, UN and Switzerland during which time he chaired the WTO Africa Group. He has also served as an Associate Professor at the Faculty of Economics and Management, Makerere University Uganda.

Braz Baracuhy is the WTO agriculture negotiator and G-20 coordinator in the Permanent Mission of Brazil to the WTO.

Ujal Singh Bhatia was India's Ambassador and Permanent Representative to the WTO between 2004 and 2010. He joined the Indian Administrative Service in 1974 and served in a number of senior positions in the Central and State governments. He was involved in a number of regional and multilateral negotiations on trade issues. He has retired from the government now and writes and speaks frequently on trade and economic issues.

Ambassador Dian Triansyah Djani is Indonesia's Ambassador/Permanent Representative to the United Nations, WTO and other International Organisations in Geneva, Switzerland. He is a career diplomat having served at the Indonesian Missions in New York and Geneva, as Director for Multilateral Trade and Industry in charge of WTO issues in the Ministry of Foreign Affairs, and as Director General of ASEAN Cooperation. He serves as Vice President of the UN Human Rights Council, and held several other posts at UN Bodies, including President of the UNCTAD Trade and Development Board (2009).

Ambassador Erwidodo is the Ambassador/Deputy Permanent Representative in charge of WTO at the Indonesian Mission in Geneva before which he was Director General of the Agency for Trade Research and Development, Ministry of Trade, Indonesia. At the WTO, he coordinates the G-33 at Ambassadors' level. He was Chair of WTO Committee on Trade and Development (2010) and chairs the Council for Trade in Services (2011). He received his Ph.D in agricultural economics from Michigan State University, USA.

Guillermo Valles Galmés is a former Ambassador of Uruguay to the WTO where he chaired for five years the Negotiating Group on Rules. Prior to this, he was for four years Deputy Foreign Minister of Uruguay and has served in several bilateral and multilateral diplomatic missions in Latin American, European, Asian and UN posts.

Ambassador Faizel Ismail is currently the Ambassador and Permanent Representative of South Africa to the WTO. He chaired the WTO Committee on Trade and Development Special Session for two years 2004-2006. He has published two books: *Mainstreaming Development in the WTO* and *Reforming the World Trade Organisation (CUTS International, 2007 and 2009)*.

Deny Wachyudi Kurnia is a career diplomat who served at the Indonesian posts in Canberra, Australia and Brussels, Belgium. He joined the Indonesian Mission in Geneva in 2007 and coordinates the G-33 work at the Experts level. He chairs the WTO Committee on Sanitary and Phytosanitary Measures (2011). He holds a Master's degree in International Relations from Monash University, Australia.

Ambassador Matern Y.C. Lumbanga, is currently Tanzania's Ambassador Extraordinary and Plenipotentiary to the WTO as well as to the United Nations and other International Organisations in Geneva. He has served as Coordinator of the LDC Group to the WTO prior to which he served the Tanzanian Government in many senior positions, including as a Permanent Secretary in various Ministries and later became the Chief Secretary to "the Head of Public Service and Secretary to the Cabinet" of the United Republic of Tanzania.

Nelson Ndirangu is currently the Programme Director, Programme Management Unit (PMU) of the ACP MTS Programme. Previously he was Kenya's lead negotiator in the WTO and coordinated the African Group in the DDA where he particularly spearheaded negotiations on NAMA, Development and TRIPs and Public Health.

Guilherme Patriota is a career diplomat with the Brazilian Foreign Service since 1983. He currently works as Special Adviser to the President on international affairs. He has taken part in several multilateral negotiations on science and technology, trade, intellectual property and on economic and social affairs. He served his country in diplomatic missions in New York, Geneva, Montevideo, Washington and Wellington.

Vinod Rege is a former Director of GATT (now WTO). In a career spanning nearly fifty years, at national and international level, he has specialised in the study of trade and development issues of developing countries and in international trade law; areas in which he has written extensively. Currently he provides expert assistance on WTO Doha Round negotiations to the Geneva group of Commonwealth developing countries.

Sir Ronald Sanders is a former Ambassador to the WTO for Antigua and Barbuda. More recently, he has been a member of the Commonwealth Eminent Persons Group tasked with recommending strengthening the 54-nation Commonwealth. He has negotiated trade and investment agreements with the UK, China, the US and the EU. A member of the Executive Board of UNESCO, he has also served on the Board of Directors of private sector companies in the US and several Caribbean countries.

Ambassador Shree Baboo Chekitan Servansing is the Ambassador and Permanent Representative of the Republic of Mauritius to the UN and other International Organisations in Geneva, including the WTO. He has served as Chair of the WTO Committee on Trade and Environment (CTE) and Chair of the Committee on Trade and Development (CTD). In this capacity, he also chaired the Dedicated Session of the CTD on Aid for Trade and the Work Programme on Small Economies. He is also the Coordinator of the ACP Group in Geneva and in this capacity represents ACP interests in the DDA negotiations including in most of the restricted meetings.

Guillermo Malpica Soto is Director General of Services and Investment Negotiations at the Mexican Ministry of the Economy since 2008. Earlier, he was Economic Counsellor at the Permanent Mission of Mexico to the WTO in Geneva, and has been working for more than ten years in services negotiations issues.

Manuel Antonio J. Teehankee is the former Ambassador and Permanent Representative of the Republic of the Philippines to the WTO and Chair of the WTO Committee on Trade and Environment sitting in Special Session. Previously he also chaired the regular Committee on Trade and Environment and the Working Group on Trade and Transfer of Technology. He is a lawyer by training and was formerly Undersecretary of the Department of Justice and Government Corporate Counsel from 2001 to early 2004. As head of the Philippine Mission, he was active in various disputes involving the Philippines before the WTO.

Acknowledgements

This publication is the outcome of the efforts and contributions of many. It may not be possible to list all of them but the following must be mentioned.

Authors of seventeen chapters in the publication (for their short introduction, kindly see the Note on Contributors in this publication);

Members of the Experts Committee, Ambassador Dr Magda Shahin Director, Trade-related Assistance Centre, American Chamber of Commerce in Egypt, and Mr Huang Rengang, Deputy Director General, WTO Affairs Department, Ministry of Commerce, People's Republic of China;

Several CUTS colleagues reviewed various drafts of the chapters including Bipul Chatterjee, Deputy Executive Director, CUTS International, Archana Jatkar, Coordinator and Deputy Head, CUTS CITEE, Simi T.B., Assistant Policy Analyst, CUTS CITEE, Joseph George, Research Associate, CUTS CITEE, Natasha Nayak, Policy Analyst, CUTS CCIER, and Suparna Kumar, Senior Fellow, CUTS Institute for Regulation and Competition;

Madhuri Vasnani, Publications Officer, CUTS International for overseeing the publication with support from Julien Grollier, Research Associate CUTS GRC, and the layout team at Jaipur;

CUTS GRC staff Atul Kaushik, former Director, and Rashid S. Kaukab, Associate Director and Research Coordinator, Julian Mukiibi, Programme Officer, Josiane Rufener, Administrative Officer, and CUTS GRC interns Iulia Andrea Toma, Yaru Wu and Adeline Sozanski who worked under the strategic direction of Ramamurti Badrinath, Director CUTS GRC;

Finally, this publication would not have been possible without the generous support of the Ministry of Foreign Affairs, Sweden, and Friedrich Ebert Stiftung (FES), Geneva Office.

Abbreviations and Acronyms

ABS	Access and Benefit Sharing
ACP	African, Caribbean, and Pacific
ACTA	Anti-Counterfeiting Trade Agreement
ACWL	Advisory Centre on WTO Law
ADA	Anti-Dumping Agreement
AfT	Aid for Trade
AGMs	Ambassadorial Group Meetings
AGOA	African Growth and Opportunity Act
AIE	Agents Importers Exporters
AITIC	Agency for International Trade Information and Co-operation
AMS	Aggregate Measure of Support
AoA	Agreement on Agriculture
APEC	Asia-Pacific Economic Co-operation
ASCM	Agreement on Subsidies and Countervailing Measures
ASEAN	Association of Southeast Asian Nations
AU	African Union
AVEs	Ad valorem equivalents
BOP	Balance of Payments
BSA	Business Software Alliance
CAP	Common Agricultural Policy
CARICOM	Caribbean Community and Common Market
CBD	Convention on Biological Diversity
CDP	Committee for Development Policy (United Nations Department of Economic and Social Affairs, Development Policy and Analysis Division)
CEPAL	UN Economic Commission for Latin America and the Caribbean
CIEL	Centre for International Environmental Law
CIPIH	WHO Commission on Intellectual Property Rights, Innovation and Public Health
CoA-SS	Committee on Agriculture Special Session
COMTD-SS	WTO Committee on Trade and Development Special Session
CRTA	Committee on Regional Trade Agreement
CSEND	Centre for Socio-Eco-Nomic Development
CTD	Committee on Trade and Development
CTD-SS	Committee on Trade and Development Special Session
CTE	Committee on Trade and Environment
CTE-SS	Committee on Trade and Environment Special Session
CTG	Council for Trade in Goods
CTS	Council for Trade in Services

DAC	Disproportionately affected countries
DCNT	Draft Consolidated Negotiating Text
DDA	Doha Development Agenda
DDAGTF	Doha Development Agenda Global Trust Fund
DFID	UK Department for International Development
DFQFMA	Duty-free quota-free market access
DG	Director General
DSB	Dispute Settlement Body
DSM	Dispute Settlement Mechanism
DSU	Dispute Settlement Understanding
DTIS	Diagnostic Trade Integrated Study
EBA	Everything But Arms
EC	European Communities
ECA	Economic Commission for Africa
ECLAC	Economic Commission for Latin America and the Caribbean
ECOSOC	United Nations Economic and Social Council
EEZ	Exclusive Economic Zone
EIF	Enhanced Integrated Framework
EMC	Electromagnetic Compatibility
EMIT	Group on Environmental Measures and International Trade
ENTs	Economic Needs Tests
EPAs	Economic Partnership Agreements
EPPs	Environmentally Preferable Products
ESM	Emergency Safeguard Mechanism
EU	European Union
EVI	Economic Vulnerability Index
FANs	Friends of Antidumping Negotiations
FAO	Food and Agriculture Organisation
FIPs	Five Interested Parties
FTAs	Free Trade Agreements
GATS	General Agreement on Trade in Services
GATT	General Agreement on Tariffs and Trade
GC	General Council
GDP	Gross Domestic Product
GIs	Geographical Indications
GNI	Gross National Income
GNS	Group of Negotiations on Services
GRULAC	Group of Latin American and Caribbean Countries
GSP	Generalised System of Preferences
HAI	Human Assets Index
HKMD	Hong Kong Ministerial Declaration
HS	Harmonised Commodity Description and Coding System
ICTSD	International Centre for Trade and Sustainable Development
IF	Integrated Framework
IFIs	International Financial Institutions
IFPMA	International Federation of Pharmaceutical Manufacturers & Associations

IIAs	International Investment Agreements
IISD	International Institute for Sustainable Development
IMF	International Monetary Fund
IMPACT	International Medical Products Anti-Counterfeiting Taskforce
IP	Intellectual Property
IPRs	Intellectual Property Rights
ITC	International Trade Centre
ITPGR	International Treaty on Plant Genetic Resources
ITTC	WTO Institute for Training and Technical Co-operation
IUU	Illegal, Unreported and Unregulated
LDC	Least Developed Country
LTFR	Less Than Full Reciprocity
MA	Market Access
MEAs	Multilateral Environmental Agreements
MFN	Most Favoured Nation
MTS	Multilateral Trading System
NAFTA	North American Free Trade Agreement
NAMA	Non-Agricultural Market Access
NFIDCs	Net Food-Importing Developing Countries
NGMA	Negotiating Group on Market Access
NGO	Non-Governmental Organisation
NGR	Negotiating Group on Rules
NGTF	Negotiating Group on Trade Facilitation
NT	National Treatment
NTB	Non-Trade Barrier
NTCs	Non-Trade Concerns
NTMs	Non-Tariff Measures
OECD	Organisation for Economic Co-operation and Development
OECS	Organisation of Eastern Caribbean States
OTDS	Overall Trade-Distorting Domestic Support
PIC	Prior Informed Consent
PPMs	Process and Production Methods
PRSPs	Poverty Reduction Strategy Papers
PSI	Pre-Shipment Inspection
PUC	Product Under Consideration
QUNO	Quaker United Nations Office
R&D	Research and Development
RAMs	Recently Acceded Members
RoO	Rules of Origin
RTAs	Regional Trade Agreements
SACU	Southern African Customs Union
SAPs	Structural Adjustment Programmes
SAR	South African Republic
SAT	Substantially All Trade
S&D	Special and Differential
SCM	Subsidies and Countervailing Measures
SIDS	Small Island Developing States

SPs	Special Products
SPS	Sanitary and Phytosanitary
SSG	Special Agricultural Safeguard
SSM	Special Safeguard Mechanism
STO	Specific Trade Obligation
SVE	Small, Vulnerable Economy
TA&CB	Technical Assistance & Capacity Building
TBT	Technical Barriers to Trade
TF	Trade Facilitation
TFC	Trade Facilitation Committee
TK	Traditional Knowledge
TNC	Trade Negotiations Committee
TPA	US Trade Policy Authority
TPG	Tropical Products Group
TPMs	Technological Protection Measures
TPRB	Trade Policy Review Body
TRIMs	Trade-Related Investment Measures
TRIPs	Trade-Related Aspects of Intellectual Property Rights
TRTA	Trade-Related Technical Assistance
TRQs	Tariff Rate Quotas
UK	United Kingdom of Great Britain and Northern Ireland
UN	United Nations
UNCTAD	United Nations Conference on Trade and Development
UNEP	United Nations Environment Programme
UNESCO	United Nations Educational, Scientific and Cultural Organisation
US	United States of America
USTR	United States Trade Representative
WCO	World Customs Organisation
WHO	World Health Organisation
WIPO	World Intellectual Property Organisation
WTI	World Trade Institute
WTO	World Trade Organisation
WWF	World Wildlife Fund

Introduction

1 Developing Countries in WTO Negotiations: Moving From the Margins to the Middle

Vinod Rege
Former Director of GATT

Introduction

This chapter has two objectives. First, it hopes to provide future negotiators, trade policy officials, business leaders and research scholars insight into how negotiations on trade and economic relations take place among countries in the legal framework established by the World Trade Organisation (WTO). This background information should help them in understanding and appreciating the points and views expressed by developing country ambassadors and senior negotiators in the experiences presented here. Second, it provides a basis for further analysis and discussion on the steps taken by developing countries to strengthen their bargaining positions, through consultations in regional and interregional groups and issue-based coalitions, aimed at improving further their effective participation in WTO activities and in the negotiations held under its auspices.

Part One of this chapter introduces the reader to the WTO's rule-based multilateral trading system.

Part Two is devoted to the description of how the Doha Development Round was launched, the reasons for the initial reluctance of developing countries to agree to the launching of the negotiations and the reasons it has not been possible to conclude the Round even though more than ten years have passed since it was launched.

Part Three provides an overview of the results that have been achieved in the negotiations on the liberalisation of trade in agricultural and non-agricultural products, trade in services, rule making and other areas. It also describes briefly the main reasons for the present deadlock in the negotiations.

Part Four describes the changing pattern of the strategy and tactics adopted by developing countries to strengthen their bargaining positions *vis-à-vis* developed countries and the strategy applied by them in the present Doha Round of Negotiations in pursuing both their common and diverse interests through consultations in regional and interregional groups and in issue-based coalitions, followed later by consultations in wider groups consisting of all WTO developing country members. It also provides an assessment of the extent to which the strategy has been effective in achieving its aims and describes the lessons the experience of its application has for the future.

Part Five describes the proposals that are under consideration for concluding the negotiations in the Doha Round, which were to be completed in three years but would be soon entering the eleventh year. It also makes some observations on the possible impact that the unsatisfactory experience of the Doha Round would have on how negotiations are arranged in the WTO in future.

Part One

Main Features of the Multilateral Trading System: Its Role and Functions

The WTO rule-based multilateral trading system has evolved gradually over a period of nearly six decades and is in the process of continuous evolution. The first steps toward adopting rules that should govern trade in goods were taken in 1948 when the General Agreement on Tariffs and Trade (GATT) was adopted. Since then, a number of associate agreements, clarifying the rules of the GATT, taking into account the experience of their operation to make them more responsive to the trade and development needs of developing countries have been adopted. In 1995, the scope and the coverage of the rules, which applied until then only to trade in goods, was broadened to include trade in services and trade-related aspects of intellectual property. For overseeing the operation of the new broadened system, a new organisation, the WTO, was established. As a result, the GATT ceased as a separate entity and became an integral part of the WTO system.[1]

How a Change in Approach Adopted by Developing Countries in Trade Policies Influenced their Membership in the WTO

In the years following the establishment of the GATT in 1948, until about the middle of the 1970s, a large number of developing countries were skeptical about how far the rule-based system created by it could assist them in promoting economic development. This was largely because these countries were, during that period, pursuing policies for the promotion of economic development by encouraging industries to produce products that were being imported, by granting them protection through tariffs or other measures. These import-substitution policies reflected an approach toward economic development that was vastly different from the approach of the GATT, which called on countries to promote economic growth by following open and liberal trade policies and exposing domestic industries to foreign competition to enable them to remain competitive for selling in the international markets.

By about the beginning of the 1980s, the attitude of developing countries, however, changed when, the limitations of import-substitution policies started being felt and increasing numbers of countries started combining import-substitution policies with those aimed at promoting export-oriented growth by following open and liberal trade policies. Since these policies were broadly consistent with the GATT's philosophy and approach, an increasing number of developing countries started becoming members of the organisation. Thus, over two thirds of the 153 countries that are at present members of WTO are developing countries. In addition, about 20 developing countries are currently negotiating for accession.

Role of the WTO

The WTO as an organisation is responsible for continuous surveillance to monitor the extent to which the rules of the multilateral trading systems created by it are adhered to by its member countries. It is also open to a country that considers that another country with which it is trading is in breach of its obligation under the rules, to bring the matter for settlement to the Dispute Settlement Body (DSB), if efforts to find mutually acceptable solutions through consultations on a bilateral or multilateral basis fail to produce desired results. The decisions of the DSB are binding; the country found in breach of the obligation is required to withdraw the measures that were found to be inconsistent with the rules.

In addition to providing a legal framework for the conduct of international trade and for the settlement of disputes, the multilateral trading system urges member countries to hold negotiations. The primary objective behind holding such negotiations on a periodic basis is to promote further liberalisation of trade by securing more reductions in tariffs and the removal of non-tariff barriers to trade. They also present an opportunity for securing improvements in the existing rules as well as for developing rules covering new subject areas.

Eight rounds of multilateral trade negotiations have been held in the period between the establishment of the GATT in 1948 and the founding of the WTO in 1995 (Table 1). The first five Rounds dealt almost exclusively with tariffs. Starting with the Kennedy Round (1964–67) attention began to shift toward addressing non-tariff measures which, with gradual reductions in tariffs, were increasingly considered to be providing more serious barriers for the development of trade.

Table 1: The GATT Trade Rounds

Year	Place/Name	Subjects Covered	Number of Countries
1947	Geneva	Tariffs	23
1949	Annecy	Tariffs	13
1951	Torquay	Tariffs	38
1956	Geneva	Tariffs	26
1960–1961	Geneva (Dillon Round)	Tariffs	26
1964–1967	Geneva (Kennedy Round)	Tariffs and anti-dumping measures	62
1973–1979	Tokyo (Tokyo round)	Tariffs, non-tariff measures, and adoption of decision on General Enabling Clause	102
1989–1994	Punta-del Este (Uruguay Round)	Tariffs, non-tariff measures, rules, services, intellectual property, dispute settlement, textiles, agriculture, creation of WTO	123

Most of these barriers arise as a result of differences among countries in applying the laws and regulations that countries adopt at the national level to imported products. In order to ensure uniformity in practices, the Kennedy Round adopted agreements that stipulated the broad principles and rules countries should follow in determining the value of imported goods for the purpose of levying customs duties and in applying anti-dumping measures. These agreements were reviewed in the Tokyo Round and new ones were adopted in such areas as subsidies and countervailing measures, technical barriers to trade, government procurement and import licensing procedures.

In the Uruguay Round, most of these agreements were reviewed and modified taking into account the experience of their application. In addition, a new agreement on safeguard measures, elaborating on the provisions in the GATT dealing with emergency safeguard situations created by sudden increases in imports was adopted.

The Uruguay Round brought about one far-reaching change in relation to these agreements. Prior to the Round, membership of these agreements was voluntary. This had resulted in a large number of developing countries choosing not to become members on the grounds that they would be unable to accept the additional procedural and other obligations they imposed. The Marrakesh Agreement, establishing the WTO changed this situation by providing that since the WTO system was a "single undertaking" all agreements negotiated under its auspices should be treated as "multilateral agreements" and would be binding on all of its member countries. This rule, however, does not apply to the "plurilateral" agreements. Such agreement can be negotiated among a limited number of countries only after obtaining prior approval from all member countries. There are at present only two agreements that are plurilateral: the Agreement on Government Procurement and the Agreement on Information Technology.

Special Provisions Relating to Developing Countries

The WTO multilateral system recognises that the developing countries, particularly those that are least developed, may not be able to derive full benefits from the rule-based system unless positive efforts are taken to secure for them a share in the growth of international trade that is commensurate with their needs for economic development. To assist developing counties derive full benefits from the system in promoting economic development, over the years, a number of special provisions have been added to the legal instruments.

These provisions can be broadly grouped into the following three categories:

- Principles, guidelines and rules that should be taken into account in the conduct of negotiations;
- Grant of preferential access to imports from developing countries by developed countries; and
- Extension of special and differential (S&D) treatment to developing countries in the application of the rules.

How Work in the WTO is Organised

The main responsibility for overseeing the work of the organisation lies with the Ministerial Conference. The Marrakesh Agreement establishing the WTO provides that member countries must meet at the Ministerial level at least every second year to review the work undertaken during the previous two years and to adopt a programme of work for the next two years. Between meetings of the Ministerial Conference, the General Council is responsible for carrying out the functions of the WTO. The DSB considers disputes and the Trade Policy Review Body (TPRB) reviews the trade policies of individual countries. Three subsidiary councils for trade in goods, trade-related aspects of intellectual property and trade in services operate under the guidance of the General Council. There are also a number of permanent committees, like those on trade and development, trade and environment, budget finance and administration that report directly to the General Council. The committees that monitor the implementation of agreements – such as those on customs valuation, technical barriers to trade, sanitary and phytosanitary measures and anti-dumping practices – report to the Council of Trade in Goods, which, in turn, reports to the General Council.

In addition, working groups are often established for study and analysis in specific subject areas, like trade and finance or trade and investment. Some 40 councils, committees, sub-committees and working groups function under the auspices of the WTO. The membership of these bodies is open-ended and as such all WTO members can attend their meetings.

Decisions by Consensus

All decisions in the WTO are taken by consensus – from the level of the committees and working groups to that of the councils and General Council as well as at the Ministerial Conference. Consensus does not mean that unanimity is required for decisions to be taken. In fact, consensus is reached when there appears to be broad support among members for a decision and those who are not in favour agree not to express their opposition when it is being adopted.

Consultations in Green Room Meetings

From the early days of the GATT it was recognised that in order to prepare for arriving at consensus, meetings might have to be arranged among limited numbers of key delegations with differing views on the subjects under discussion. These meetings were initially held in the conference room of the Director-General, which has green wallpaper. They, therefore, came to be called "green room" meetings, a term that has stuck even though they are not always held there and are convened not only by the Director-General, but also by the chairmen of the particular councils or committees seeking consensus. Such meetings may also be convened outside Geneva during or at the same time as Ministerial Conferences.

The procedures followed to develop consensus through consultations on a limited country basis, have, in the past, been a matter of controversy. Considerable efforts have been made in recent years to improve the procedures for arranging such meetings. In order to ensure that attendance is representative of developing countries belonging to different regions and to ensure fair and equitable representation of developing countries, the chairpersons of the regional and interregional groups of developing countries, which have come into existence in Geneva (such as the African, Caribbean and the Pacific (ACP), the African countries, the Least Developed Countries (LDCs) and Small and Vulnerable Economies (SVE) Groups are invited to nominate two or three of their members, who have expertise in the subjects and issues to be discussed, to take part in the meeting.

Institutional Framework for Overseeing How Negotiations are Launched and their Progress

The decisions to launch new Rounds of negotiations are taken in Ministerial Conferences based on preparatory work which may take place over three to four years.

Since the GATT years it has been the practice to establish a separate institutional framework to oversee the work on negotiations whenever a decision is taken to launch a new Round. The declarations launching the negotiations generally provide for the establishment of a Trade Negotiations Committee consisting of all WTO member countries, which guides and supervises progress. The WTO Director-General has chaired this leading body since the Uruguay Round. Separate negotiating groups are constituted for negotiations in subject areas included in the agenda for negotiations. In the present ongoing Doha Round, separate negotiating groups have been established for negotiations on agricultural products, non-agricultural products, trade in services, trade facilitation, and in rules-based areas. Ambassadors, chosen on the basis of their knowledge and expertise of the issues under negotiations, generally chair these negotiating groups.

The Secretariat

The WTO Secretariat is headed by the Director-General, who is elected for a term of four years by the member countries. The Director-General selects Deputy Directors-General (currently four) from different regions on the basis of their experience, knowledge and expertise in WTO law and practice. The Secretariat is divided into divisions headed by Directors.

The role of the Secretariat is however limited compared with those of other international organisations like the International Monetary Fund (IMF) and World Bank. Its primary role is to provide members with technical and logistical support. This includes organising meetings of governing bodies, preparing background papers that are requested by the committees and councils and reports on the discussions in the meetings. It has very little formal authority to take initiatives.[2] Neither the Secretariat nor the Director-General have any authority to suggest a new subject be taken up for discussion or that a particular case be brought before the WTO Dispute Settlement Body for examination, even when, in their view, a country is in breach of the rules.

Part Two

Present Ongoing Doha Development Round of Negotiations: The Development So Far and the Reasons for Deadlock

Pre-Launch Period

With this broad overview of the crucial role that the WTO system plays in international trade relations and the way the system works, we shall now turn to why the developing countries were reluctant about the launching of a new round, how they were persuaded to agree to the new round being launched in Doha in 2001 and the reasons it has not been possible even after ten years to conclude it.

With the establishment of the WTO at the conclusion of the Uruguay Round, the developing countries found they would have to adopt the legislative and administrative framework at the national level that is necessary for the implementation not only of the provisions of GATT and its associated agreements, but also those of the General Agreement on Trade in Services (GATS) and the Agreement on Trade-Related Aspects of Intellectual Property Rights (TRIPs). They also found that they would need time to adjust to the new situation created by their further integration into the multilateral trade system. However, at the first Ministerial meeting in Singapore (December 1996), some of the developed countries proposed that a fresh round of negotiations covering new subject areas be held in the near future. The US proposed that the agenda include negotiations on the subject of government procurement, while the EU pushed for the inclusion of trade facilitation. The EU also wanted trade and investment and trade and competition policy to be included on the agenda, although the US voiced concerns about both of these issues. A large number of developing countries mounted strong resistance to the demands. In the end, WTO members agreed to set up working groups to examine whether these subjects could be taken up for negotiations. These four subject areas have come to be known as the "Singapore issues."

Geneva Ministerial Meeting (1998)

At the next Ministerial meeting, which was held in Geneva in May 1998 to celebrate the 50th anniversary of the multilateral trading system, developing countries offered more resistance to these proposals. Most voiced serious concerns about the inclusion of the Singapore issues in the agenda for negotiations. Led by India, several developing countries insisted that they were unable to meet the obligations imposed by the WTO agreements. It was, therefore, necessary to examine the problems they were encountering in implementing the agreements and whether any improvements were needed in the provisions for S&D treatment before any decision was taken for launching of the negotiations.

Seattle Ministerial Meeting (1999)

The serious differences that existed among participating countries, particularly the opposition of developing countries to the Singapore issues, also resulted in no agreements being reached on the launching of negotiations and its agenda at the Seattle Ministerial meeting in 1999.

Even though no decision could be taken for launching the new round, the WTO member countries decided to commence negotiations for liberalisation of trade in agricultural products and of trade in services early in 2001. This decision was taken because the Agreement on Agriculture (AoA) and GATS imposed an obligation on WTO members to start negotiations for further liberalisation of trade in the areas covered by them within five years of their coming into operation (i.e. before January, 01, 2001).

Launch of the Round and Initial Developments

A new Round of negotiations, covering a range of subjects, was ultimately launched at the Ministerial meeting held in Doha in November 2001 with a view to completion not later than January, 01, 2005.

Developed countries, seeking to win over the opposition, promised to put in place all possible measures in the Round to facilitate the promotion of economic development. It has, therefore, come to be called a "Development Round." The agenda for the Round lays down some broad guidelines on how the development dimensions should be taken into account in further liberalisation of trade in goods and services and in the adoption of new rules. In particular, it provides that developed countries should give priority to reductions in tariffs and other barriers affecting the trade of developing countries. It further stipulates that S&D treatment should be extended to developing countries by requiring them to reduce tariffs and other barriers to trade applied by them, based on the principle of making a contribution that is "less than full reciprocity."

Cancún Ministerial Meeting (2003)

The agenda, however, included the four Singapore issues, despite opposition by developing countries. These issues were included only for study and analysis and the decision on whether they should be taken up for negotiations in the Round was left to be determined at the next Ministerial meeting. At the next Ministerial meeting, which was held in Cancún, members failed to reach a decision on whether these subjects should be taken up for negotiations in the Round, as the developing countries continued to resist negotiations being held on these subjects. However, as a result of consultations held subsequently in Geneva, agreement was reached in July 2004 to drop from the negotiations three of the four Singapore issues– namely, trade and investment, trade and competition policy, and transparency in government procurement – and to take up in the Round only the subject of trade facilitation. It was included in the agenda for negotiations on the basis of a firm commitment by developed countries to provide technical assistance to developing countries for building up their capacities to apply the new rules that may be adopted for facilitating trade.

Hong Kong Ministerial Meeting (2005)

The compromise solution enabled WTO member countries to agree on a broad framework governing the modalities that could be applied in the negotiations for liberalisation of trade in agricultural and non-agricultural products and in the various subject areas taken up for negotiations at the Hong Kong Ministerial meeting held in 2005. Box 1 lists the main subject areas on which negotiations are being held, taking into account the decisions reached at the Hong Kong Ministerial meeting.

Box 1: Main subject areas included in the Doha Agenda

Agriculture

Continuation of the negotiations commenced in early 2000, in accordance with the aims of the provisions of the Agreement on Agriculture for:

- Securing substantial improvement in market access;
- Phasing out of all types of export subsidies; and
- Substantial reduction in domestic trade distorting support

Market access for non-agricultural products

Commencement of the negotiations for:

- Reduction and, where appropriate, elimination of tariffs including tariff peaks and high tariff, and tariff escalation; and
- Removal of non-tariff measures.

Services

- Continuation of the negotiations launched in January 2001 in accordance with the provisions of GATS.

Trade-related aspects of intellectual property

Negotiations shall aim to:

- Find solutions to the problems faced by countries with insufficient or no manufacturing capacities in making effective use of compulsory licensing under the TRIPs Agreement;
- Complete negotiations for the establishment of a multilateral system for notification and registration of geographical indications for wines and spirits; and
- Examine the relationship between the TRIPs Agreement and the Convention on Biological Diversity and issues relating to the protection of traditional knowledge and folklore.

Trade and environment

- Negotiations on improving the relationship between WTO rules and specific trade obligations set out in the multilateral environmental agreements;
- Negotiations for the liberalisation of trade in environmental goods and services;
- Continuation of the work on the effect of environmental measures on market access;
- Examination of the relevant provisions of the TRIPS Agreement and of the labelling requirements for environmental purpose.

WTO rules

- Clarification of the rules of the Agreement on Anti-dumping Practices and of the Agreement on Subsidies and Countervailing Measures;
- Clarification and improvements in the WTO discipline on use of fishery subsidies;
- Improvements in WTO rules applying to regional trade agreements.

Trade facilitation

The aim of the negotiations shall be to clarify and improve relevant aspects of:

- Article V relating to transit trade;
- Article VIII on fees and on formalities in connection with importation and exportation;
- Article X, which provides for the publication and administration of regulations with a view to expediting the movement, release, and clearance of goods in transit.

Source: Doha Ministerial Declaration 2001 WT/MIN(01)Dec. 1, November 20, 2001 and Hong Kong Ministerial Declaration 2005 WT/MIN/105, December 22, 2005.

Developments in the Negotiations: Slow Pace

After the Hong Kong Ministerial meeting, serious negotiations restarted on the modalities (or rules or procedures) that should be adopted in negotiations for further liberalisation of trade in agricultural and non-agricultural products, trade in services, trade facilitation, and improvements in the rules relating to the application of the Agreement on Anti-dumping Practices and on other rules-based subjects included on the agenda for the Round.

Shift of Negotiations to Small Ministerial Groups – 2006

But the negotiations proceeded at a very slow pace and there were periods when they had to be formally suspended or were subject to long pauses, owing to differences and deadlocks. In early 2006, ministers from the Group of Six G-6 member countries (Australia, Brazil, the EU, India, Japan and the US) began meeting in an attempt to advance the negotiations, particularly on modalities for negotiations on agricultural and non-agricultural products. But these meetings contributed little to resolving the issues on which differences existed and by July 2006 Pascal Lamy, Director-General of the WTO, who chaired these meetings, decided to suspend the negotiations. The following year another attempt to take the negotiations forward (this time by a smaller group of four ministers from Brazil, the EU, India and the US) collapsed in June.

Mini Ministerial Meeting – July 2008

Expressing frustration at the lack of progress in these efforts to find solutions to the problems, the Director-General decided to end the meetings of small groups of ministers and to commence the negotiations in Geneva on a multilateral basis at the level of ambassadors. By mid-June 2008 it appeared that this multilateral process had resulted in a broad consensus on the modalities for negotiations on agricultural and non-agricultural products. Director-General Lamy, therefore, decided to call for a mini-ministerial meeting in Geneva from July, 21-29, 2008, and ministers from some 39 countries were invited to participate.

The US Presidential election, which was due to be held in November 2008, was another factor that influenced the decision to hold the Ministerial meeting. Some delegations were apprehensive that unless the package containing agreements on modalities was accepted before that date, the new US Administration might re-open negotiations on some of the issues. But even though there appeared to be broad consensus on most of the issues, the meeting collapsed on the last day, owing to serious differences on a few technical issues, mainly in the area of modalities for negotiations on agricultural products. The failure of the meeting signalled that revival of the negotiations would be possible only after the new US Administration took over in January 2009 and elections in some of the other countries, notably India, were complete. However, these hopes were shattered when the world economy went into recession as a result of the global financial crisis.

Impact of the Financial Crisis

In late 2008 the attention of world leaders shifted from completing the Doha Round to finding solutions to the serious situations created by the global financial crisis. In order to help agricultural producers and manufacturing industries affected by the decline in economic activity, countries started taking trade protectionist measures. The WTO Director-General, the heads of the World Bank and the IMF and a number of leading economists emphasised that one of the ways to deal with the economic downturn was to curb protectionism by completing the Round of trade negotiations as quickly as possible. World leaders agreed in principle. The need to revive the trade negotiations was emphasised at every important meeting attended by heads of state or trade ministers to consider measures to deal with the financial crisis. But, it was clear that most countries lacked the political will to take measures that would commit them to further liberalise their trade and open up their economies to foreign competition until there were clear signs of an economic revival.

Part Three

Brief Overview of the Results of the Negotiations and Present State of Play

With this description of how the negotiating process has worked so far and the political and economic factors that have been responsible for the inordinate delay in completing the negotiations, we shall now turn to providing a synopsis of the progress achieved thus far on:

A. market access: agriculture and non-agricultural (industrial) products and services;
B. rules: trade facilitation, TRIPs and other rules (anti-dumping, subsidies and regional arrangements); and
C. cross-cutting areas: S&D treatment, preference erosion, trade and environment and review of dispute settlement.

A broad picture of the present state of play in each of the subject areas mentioned above is provided first. This is followed by the explanation of the issues on which differences still exist and which have created crisis situation in the negotiations. It is expected that the summary of the results would be found useful in appreciating fully the points and views by ambassadors in the following chapters on how the negotiations developed and the strategy and tactics adopted by the developing countries for achieving their negotiating goals and objectives.

Market Access: Agriculture and Non-Agricultural Products and Services

General

The modalities for negotiations envisaged that negotiations for the liberalisation of trade in agricultural and non-agricultural products should take place on the basis of a formula that would provide for cuts across the board on all tariffs. In the area of trade in services, however, it was agreed that the negotiations should take place on the basis of request and offer procedures.

Agricultural Products[3]

The negotiations in the agricultural sectors have focused on three pillars: tariffs, domestic trade distorting subsidies and export subsidies.

Tariffs

There is now general consensus that tariffs should be reduced on the basis of a "tiered formula" that provides for higher percentage reductions in tariffs that are high. By applying this formula the developed countries are expected to make an overall average reduction in tariffs of 54 percent; the percentage reduction that developing countries are expected to make is 34 percent.

LDCs are exempted from making any tariff reductions. SVEs have the flexibility of not applying the formula, if they make reductions in tariffs so as to ensure that the average level of tariffs is reduced by 24 percent.

Sensitive Products

It is open to developed countries to exclude from tariff reductions or make less than formula cuts, on the grounds that they are import sensitive, by designating four percent of the tariff lines as sensitive products. Developing countries have a right to designate one third more of such tariff lines.

Special Products

In addition to sensitive products developing countries have a right to self designate 12 percent of tariff lines as special products on which they consider the existing level of protection is necessary for ensuring food and livelihood security and for promoting rural development. No cuts may be made on five percent of such tariff lines. However, countries would have to ensure that the average tariff cuts on these products is not less than 10 to 14 percent instead of the average level of reductions of 34 percent, which they have to make on the rest of their tariffs. The SVEs have flexibility to designate as many products as special products as they wish so long as they maintain the average level of 24 percent cuts on all tariffs.

Special Safeguard Measures

Developing countries have a further right to apply special safeguard measures if either a specified surge in imports (volume trigger), or, on a shipment by shipment basis, a fall of the import price goes below a specified reference price (price trigger). Specifically, an additional tariff may be applied if the volume of the average level of imports exceeds average imports in the preceding year by a specified percentage or if the prices fall below a trigger of 85 percent of the average monthly most-favoured nation (MFN) import price for that product in the most recent three-year period. Such special safeguard measures could be applied on the basis of the volume and price triggers without having to establish that increased imports are causing injury to the domestic producers as is required at present under the Agreement on Safeguards. Thus, in the case of an increase in volume of 110 percent, the current bound rate can be increased by 25 percent or 25 percentage points. In the case of increase in volume of 115 percent the current bound rate can be increased by 40 percent or 40 percentage points whichever is higher; and where there is an increase of 135 percent or above the additional duty payable is 50 percent or 50 percentage points above, whichever is higher.

These additional duties would be applied by developing countries in the post Doha Round period by using as a base the lower bound rates that would result from the application of the reductions agreed in the round to the existing (Uruguay Round) bound rates. There is a difference of opinion on whether the rate resulting from additional duties imposed under special safeguard measures could exceed the present bound rates. The developed countries, particularly the US, hold the view that the resulting rates should in no case exceed the bound rates resulting from the reductions agreed in the Uruguay Round and on the basis of which reductions would be made in the present round of negotiations. The developing countries maintain that any such restrictions on the level of duties would frustrate the basic objective of the special safeguard measures and have opposed the inclusion of such provisions on the rules relating to the application of such measures. There are also differences among developed and developing countries on the scale mentioned above of additional duties that can be levied on the basis of volume triggers. These differences were one of the main reasons for the breakdown of the mini-ministerial meeting held in July 2008.

Trade Distorting Subsidies

Domestic Subsidies

As regards trade distorting domestic subsidies granted by developed countries, it is agreed that where final bound rate of Aggregate Measures of Support (AMS) is greater than USD40bn it should be reduced by 70 percent, (EU); by 60 percent, where the final AMS is greater than USD15bn (Japan and the US) and where the total AMS is less than USD15bn, it is to be reduced by 45 percent. Developing countries granting such subsidies are expected to reduce their subsidies by 30 percent.

With respect to blue box subsidies, the definition of such subsidies is being changed to include not only subsides aimed at reducing production of agricultural crops or of livestock, but also certain types of programmes that do not limit their production. The use of these broadened subsidies would however be limited to 2.5 percent of the value of total average production in the period 1995 to 2000. In the case of developing countries, the limit would be five percent. Also there would be caps on the use of such subsidies on a product-by-product basis.

Export Subsidies

On export subsidies, there is general consensus that the developed countries should eliminate them by the end of 2013. Developing countries granting such subsidies are expected to eliminate them by the end of 2016.

Special Provisions for Cotton

In view of the importance of cotton in the trade of LDCs, it is agreed that reductions in domestic trade subsidies should be made by countries granting such subsidies on the basis of a formula that would result in subsidies being reduced at a rate that is higher than that at which subsidies would be reduced by them on other products. Tentative agreements have also been reached for the elimination of export subsidies on cotton by a date which was earlier than the date agreed for their elimination on other agricultural products.

Non-Agricultural (Industrial) Products[4]

Tariffs

In the area of non-agricultural products the main focus of negotiations was on securing reductions in tariffs and removal of non-tariff measures. It is agreed that tariffs on industrial products should be reduced on the basis of Swiss formula. The extent of reductions that would result from the formula depends on the coefficient used. For example, a tariff of 10 would be reduced to 4.4, if a coefficient of eight is used. The resulting rate would remain high at 7.1 if a higher coefficient of 25 is used.

It is agreed that developed countries should apply a coefficient of eight. As regards the developing countries, they were pressing for a coefficient of 30 and above, in order to ensure that the principle that they should be required to make contributions that are less than full reciprocity is fully observed. Under the compromise solution that is under consideration, these countries have the option of using one of the three coefficients: 20, 22 or 25. The flexibility available to exclude tariff lines from tariff reductions or tariff bindings or to make less than tariff reductions varies according to the coefficient used. Countries using 20 as a coefficient, could make less than a formula cut on 14 percent tariff lines, if imports in such lines do not exceed 16 percent of total non-agricultural imports; those using 22 as a coefficient could make less than a formula cut on 10 percent of tariff lines, if they do not exceed 10 percent of total non-agricultural imports. And countries using 25 as a coefficient would not have any flexibility for exclusion of products from tariff reductions.

LDCs and SVEs

As in the case of agricultural products, LDCs would not be required to make reductions in their tariffs. It was also agreed that SVEs need not cut their tariffs by applying the formula, but could make reductions in tariffs in such a way as to ensure that the average does not exceed a particular percentage level if they agree to bind all of their tariffs. The scale that has been adopted for this purpose requires countries in this Group to make lower percentage reductions, if a large proportion of their tariff lines are at present unbound and they agree to bind their entire tariff lines. Thus, a country in the group that has less than 20 percent of tariffs bound would be required to make only a five percent average reduction on 95 percent of its tariff lines, if the country undertakes to bind all of its tariff lines. At the other end of the scale are countries that have more than 50 percent tariffs bound against further increases at preset. These countries are required to make overall average reductions of 30 percent on the condition that they bind the remaining tariff lines.

Countries with Low Binding Coverage

It is further agreed that some 12 developing countries, other than SVEs, that have a high proportion of their tariffs unbound, need not apply the formula, but could make reductions in tariffs in such a way that the average level of their tariffs does not exceed 30 percent, provided that countries with present bindings of less than 15 percent increase their binding coverage to 75 percent, while those between 15 and 35 percent raise their bindings to 80 percent.

Sectoral Negotiations
The Doha mandate for negotiations in the area of non-agricultural products envisages that in certain sectors negotiations should also take place for reductions in tariffs "over and above what would be achieved by the formula modality" and where possible for their total elimination. It is however agreed that participation in such negotiations should be on a "non-mandatory basis." The developing countries participating in such negotiations would be provided S&D treatment by, *inter alia*, providing them with more time to reduce or eliminate tariffs.

In pursuance of this mandate proposals have been tabled, mainly by developed countries, for negotiations on the above basis in the following sectors: bicycles and related parts, electronics and electrical products, fish and fish products, forest products, gems and jewelry, hand tools and machinery, health care, sports equipment, toys and textiles, and clothing and footwear.[5] All of the developing countries with the exception of six have so far shown a reluctance to participate in these negotiations.[6] These countries particularly those at higher stages of development are under pressure from developed countries to participate in negotiations on at least two or three sectors.

Non-Tariff Measures
In the area of non-tariff measures there is a broad agreement on adopting a Ministerial Decision for the establishment of a horizontal mechanism for finding solutions through consultations and conciliations to the problems countries may encounter as a result of such barriers.

The other proposals under negotiations aim at adopting issue-based specific agreements to clarify the provision of the Agreement on Technical Barriers to Trade on a product-by-product basis. The main features of such an Agreement on Labelling Requirements for Textiles Clothing and Footwear and Travel Goods appear to be generally acceptable to the countries that have taken an active interest in the negotiations. The proposals for developing such agreements in other subject areas, such as fireworks, electronic goods and automotive parts are at different stages of negotiation. It is, however, expected that it may be possible to conclude the negotiations in these subject areas in a short period of time, once the present deadlock on the issue of sectorals is resolved.

However, there are wide differences of view on the proposal made by the EU on the desirability of adopting an agreement on "export taxes," which would require countries to reduce taxes they levy on exports and bind them against further increases. The Agreement would also prohibit imposition of new taxes on exports.

Trade in Services[7]

Liberalisation of Trade
As noted earlier, the negotiations in the area of services are taking place on the basis of request and offer procedures. In order to intensify negotiations in this area, procedures were adopted subsequently for countries to make requests on a plurilateral basis and separate sector-wise groups have been constituted for negotiations among countries making such requests and those to which such requests have been made. In addition, in July 2008, a Ministerial meeting called a "Signalling Conference" was held. At the

conference, countries on which requests on a plurilateral basis were made for liberalisation were requested to indicate the steps that they were taking to meet the gaps between the requests made on them and their offers.

The most recent report submitted by the Chairman of the Negotiating Group on Services indicates that in most of the service sectors, the gap between the requests and the offers made is significant. The lack of progress is largely attributable to the fact that negotiations in this area are closely linked to progress in other areas of negotiations, particularly in the negotiations in agriculture and non-agricultural products and as such progress in improvements of offers made would be possible if and when solutions are found to the problems that have arisen in the negotiations in these areas.

A number of developing countries, particularly those that have been able to develop trade in services during the last few years, are taking an active interest in the negotiations and have tabled offers indicating sectors in which they are prepared to undertake further commitments for liberalisation. Most of them however consider that the offers made by developed countries in sectors in which they have export interest, particularly for services that could be provided through Mode 4 – movement of natural persons – are far from satisfactory and would need improvement.

It is agreed that the LDCs would not be required to undertake any liberalisation commitments in the Round. They are, however, pressing that developed countries give priority to liberalisation of trade in sectors in which they have trade interests. They have also suggested that developed countries should also extend preferential access to their service products and service providers. Negotiations are at present being held for the adoption of a decision granting waivers from their MFN obligations to enable developed countries to provide such treatment to them.

Rule Based Areas

In addition to negotiations for improvements in market access, simultaneous negotiations are taking place aimed at ensuring that domestic regulations which countries adopt in relation to the licensing and the qualification requirements for service providers do not cause barriers to trade. The negotiations that have taken place so far have resulted in narrowing the differences on the provisions included in the Draft text on Discipline on Domestic Regulations.

Other rule-based areas in which negotiations are going on at present include inclusion of provisions on emergency safeguard measures, government procurement and the use of subsidies in the GATS.

Rules: Trade Facilitation, Anti-Dumping and Countervailing Measures, Fisheries Subsidies and Regional Trade Agreements

Trade Facilitation[8]

The main objective of the Agreement on Trade Facilitation that is being negotiated at present is to expedite clearance of goods through customs by urging governments to publish the rules and regulations they apply to goods imported and exported and by requiring customs administration to reduce the time it takes for clearance of goods by calling on them, *inter alia,* to inspect physically only those goods that pose "high risk" by applying risk assessment techniques.

The Agreement would recognise that the customs administrations in LDCs and developing countries at lower stages of development may lack technical competence to apply immediately all of its rules. It, therefore, provides that before the Agreement becomes operational, they should notify separately the WTO Secretariat of the provisions that they would require time to implement and those for which they would need technical assistance to develop capacities for their application. One of the features of the Agreement would be that it would impose obligations on developed countries to provide such assistance. It would also provide that a developing country would be required to abide by the obligation of the provisions for which it has requested technical assistance, only after it has notified the Secretariat that it has developed the necessary competence.

As a result of the intensive negotiations that have taken place, there seems to be broad agreement on most of the provisions. However, there are still some differences on some of the provisions in the Agreement. Nevertheless, it is expected that it may not be difficult to resolve them in future negotiations, as both developed and developing countries consider that the adoption of the Agreement would be a "win-win" situation for all of them.

Anti-dumping Measures[9]

Under the GATT rules anti-dumping and countervailing duties are permitted to be levied, in addition to customs duties, only if, after investigations undertaken on the basis of a complaint made by domestic industry, it is established that increased volume of dumped or subsidised imports is causing material injury to the industry. While in the years prior to the establishment of the WTO developed countries, mainly the US, the EU, Canada and Australia were the major users of anti-dumping measures, the post WTO period has witnessed emerging economies, such as India, Brazil, Argentina, Mexico and others becoming major users . The increasing use of anti-dumping measures made some countries (which have in later years come to be known as Friends of Anti-Dumping Measures) press for a revision of the rules, that would, while permitting the use of such measures in appropriate situations, prevent them from being used for protective purposes. The Doha Round mandate, therefore, calls on member countries to clarify and improve the rules taking into account the need to avoid the unwarranted use of anti-dumping or countervailing measures, while at the same time ensuring that "the basic concepts, principles and effectiveness of the instruments, where such measures are warranted is preserved."

In the negotiations that have taken place a number of proposals for modifications in the text of the anti-dumping (AD) Agreement have been made. Important among these are:

- improving the rules of the AD Agreement relating to the calculation of margin of dumping by abolishing the practice of so called "zeroing"
- making a rule that anti-dumping duties levied should be lower than the margin of dumping (lesser duty rule) mandatory
- adopting stricter rules for the termination of anti-dumping duties (sunset reviews)

- adopting rules to prevent circumvention by exporters of the imposition of anti-dumping duties

While there appears to be a convergence of views on some of the legal texts that have been developed for modifications in the rules of the AD Agreement, on others, there is still a wide gap among the negotiating positions taken by different participants. Nevertheless, it is expected that it may be possible to find compromise solutions in a relatively short period, if the stalemate that has blocked the negotiations on the liberalisation of trade is resolved.

As far as developing countries are concerned, the ACP and African Group have also tabled – based on the work done in the Commonwealth Group of Developing Countries – a proposal for establishing a separate facility in the WTO for providing technical assistance to developing countries for *inter alia* building the technical capacities of their investigation authorities to apply the anti-dumping measures according to the rules of the Agreement. The facility would also be responsible for providing technical assistance to more than 50 developing countries and LDCs that so far have not been able to establish a legislative and institutional framework for applying trade remedy measures. This assistance would be for establishing such a framework, where possible, by putting in place regional investigating authorities for investigations of complaints from the member countries that belong to regional economic groupings.

***Countervailing Measures*[10]**

The agenda for the Doha Round calls also on member countries to clarify the provisions of the Agreement on Subsidies and Countervailing Measures. In pursuance of this mandate a few proposals have been made for modifications in the rules relating to subsidies. A number of these have been put forward by developing countries. These include the following two:

- Some of the developing countries – those whose per capita incomes are less than USD 1,000 and a few others – are allowed to use export subsidies. The right to grant such subsidies is contingent on the "export competiveness" of the products receiving subsidies. India and other countries benefiting from the right to use such subsidies have made proposals for reducing the rigour of the existing rules for determination whether the products have attained competitiveness.
- Brazil has made proposals calling for review of the rules relating to export credit guarantees to take into account the inequitable situation the present rules embody, which put developing countries at a disadvantage *vis-à-vis* developed countries in providing finance for export sales of large capital goods, owing to the differences *inter alia* in interest rate structures in developed and developing countries

Taking into account the difference among participants on the proposals mentioned above and other proposals that have been tabled, the Chairman of the Negotiating Group on Rules has refrained from circulating any legal text modifying the relevant provisions in the Agreement on Subsidies and Countervailing Measures and has only submitted a report highlighting different views expressed by the participants.

Fisheries Subsidies[11]

The Doha agenda also calls on countries to clarify and improve the existing WTO discipline on fisheries subsidies. The decisions to include fisheries subsidies in the agenda for negotiations was greatly influenced by the recognition that the increasing use of such subsidies was leading to overfishing and thus to the depletion of overall fish stocks. It was considered that unless steps were taken to control overfishing by further disciplining the use of subsidies, the alarming rates at which certain fish stocks were depleting would threaten employment opportunities and livelihoods in many countries, particularly in a large number of developing countries, where fishing provides a main source of subsistence and livelihood to millions of fishermen and women.

On the basis of the intensive negotiations that were held, the Chairman of the Negotiating Group circulated in 2007 a legal text providing *inter alia* that subsidies granted for the following purposes should be prohibited with a view to controlling both over capacity in the fishing sector and overfishing:

- acquisition/construction/renewal of vessels;
- operating costs;
- port infrastructure predominantly for fishing and related activities;
- income and price support; and
- onward transfer of access rights to fisheries.

In addition to prohibiting such general subsides, the proposed text also contains provisions prohibiting the use of subsides for fishing patently exploited stocks and provisions making actionable any non-prohibited subsidy that harms stocks in which another member has identified fishing interests.

The scope of the prohibition listed above is moderated by general exceptions. For developing countries, in addition to general exceptions, S&D treatment would be provided, consisting of further exceptions. Such exceptions include:

- Exemption of all LDCs (without any conditions) from all prohibition of subsidisation
- Exemption in the case of developing countries for:
    - All subsidies granted for subsistence (artisanal) fisheries, and
    - All subsides for commercial fisheries (with the exception of construction and operating subsidies for large vessels fishing outside the members EEZ)

The access to general exceptions as well as those provided under S&D treatment would, however, be conditional on implementing certain fisheries management obligations. These obligations would require countries to establish and implement fisheries management systems based on internationally recognised best practices, including science-based stock assessments.

Though there appears to be general consensus among both developed and developing countries on the need to discipline the grant of subsidies for development of fisheries, there is at the moment no convergence on the list of prohibitions, general exceptions and the provisions on S&D treatment.

Regional Trade Agreements[12]

The Doha Round mandate also calls on countries to clarify and improve disciplines applicable to regional trade arrangements under the existing GATT rules. The mandate further provides that in such negotiations, the development aspects should also be taken into account.

The work in this area has attained importance as an increasing number of countries both developed and developing are entering into preferential trade arrangements with their trading partners. The rules of GATT envisaged the formation of such free trade areas and customs unions as exception to its main rule requiring countries to extend MFN treatment in trade relations with one another. The "spaghetti bowl" that has formed with the proliferation of preferential arrangements is increasingly threatening the basis of the WTO system.

Against this background, priority was given in the work in this area to the negotiations on establishment in the WTO of "Transparency Mechanisms for Regional Trade Arrangements." The Decision calls on countries to notify to the WTO as soon as negotiations commence for the adoption of such arrangements, including *inter alia* the foreseen timetable for entry into force. The Decision lays down procedures that should be followed for the examination of the regional arrangements after the negotiations are completed and notified to the WTO. This Decision, which was adopted by the General Council in December 2005, is currently being reviewed by the Negotiating Group on Rules in the light of the experience of its operation.

In addition, two broad issues related to the adoption of such preferential arrangements are being examined by the Negotiating Group. GATT Article XXIV provides that parties to free trade arrangements must remove barriers on "substantially all trade" (SAT) among themselves within a reasonable period. The negotiations aim at developing criteria for measurement of SAT, both at the entry of the arrangement and after the expiry of the transitional period in order to ensure that the requirements have been fulfilled.

Proposals have been made by developing countries for the extension of S&D treatment to them, particularly in arrangements involving developed and developing countries. These include provisions of longer periods of time for developing countries than that available to developed countries for removal of tariffs and other barriers to trade and extension of S&D treatment to developing countries in meeting the criteria prescribed by GATT Art. XXIV for determining whether barriers have been removed on substantially all trade by allowing them to remove tariffs and other barriers on a lesser percentage of trade than that on which they would be reduced by developed countries.

Cross-Cutting Issues: Trade and Environment, TRIPs, Dispute Settlement Mechanism, Special and Differential Treatment and Preference Origin

Trade and Environment[13]

The objective of the negotiations in this area are first to clarify the relationship between WTO rules and the specific trade obligations (STOs) set out in the multilateral environmental agreements (MEAs) and to develop procedures for the regular exchange of information between the WTO Secretariat and the Committees established under the

MEAs. Second, the negotiations seek to adopt procedures for securing reductions and elimination of tariffs and non tariffs barriers applicable to environmental goods and for further liberalisation of trade in environmental services.

As regards the first objective, the negotiations that have taken place so far have resulted in broad agreement on Draft Decisions on the procedures that should be followed for cooperation between the WTO Secretariat and the MEA Secretariats and for exchange of documents and information between them.

The main responsibility for coordinating and overseeing the work in this area would be with the WTO Committee on Trade and Environment (CTE). The Decision calls on the CTE to establish flexible and expeditious procedures of a conciliatory and non-judicial nature to assist member countries in settling differences regarding the relationship between STOs imposed by multilateral environmental agreements and those imposed by WTO rules.

The decision also envisages broadening the technical assistance activities of the Secretariat to assist developing countries, particularly LDCs in the implementation of STOs that the MEAs lay down. It is also proposed that the CTE should establish a group of two experts on trade and environment, to be elected every three years, who would be available to provide such assistance.

With respect to the second mandate of the Group, the WTO Secretariat has prepared a consolidated list of six categories of goods that could be treated as environmental goods (environmental credible universe of products) for the purpose of further negotiations on reductions or eliminations of tariffs during the round. Discussions are at present being held on the modalities that could be adopted for negotiations on further reductions of tariffs on such environmental products over and above the levels of reductions that would be made under the modalities that would be used for reductions on agricultural and non-agricultural products. Consideration is at present being given to the adoption of a hybrid modality, which would combine the elements of the various proposals that have been tabled. This hybrid modality may consist of the following components:

i) an agreed core list comprised of environmental goods, on which all countries would make commitments to reduce tariffs;
ii) a complimentary self-selected list under which developed countries would individually select a number of environmental products for tariff elimination and developing countries would be encouraged to participate; and
iii) request and offer procedures as a complement of the core list that would include products identified through request and offer procedures, the outcome of which would be multilateralised on a MFN basis.
iv) Environmental projects, including products covered by the environmental projects could be included by countries in either the common core list of products or the complimentary self-selected list or request offer list.

Trade Related Intellectual Property Rights (TRIPs)[14]

The Doha Round Mandate calls on countries to complete the negotiations that were going on prior to its launching for the establishment in the WTO of a "multilateral system of notification and registration of geographical indications (GIs) of wines and spirits of those members participating in the system." These negotiations have resulted in broad agreement on the text of the Register on GIs for wines.

Negotiations are also taking place simultaneously for the coverage on the Register on GIs, to be broadened to include in it all products (not just wines and spirits) and for modifications of the rules of the TRIPs Agreement to require persons or companies applying for patents to disclose the origin of genetic resources and associated traditional knowledge on which they are based. The negotiations on these two issues are taking place on the basis of a draft modalities text that has been co-sponsored by over 100 countries, including both developed and developing countries.

Dispute Settlement[15]

The Doha Declaration mandates that negotiations should also take place for improvements in the Dispute Settlement Understanding. However, it provides that negotiations in this subject area "should be based on the work done earlier" and would not be covered by the single undertaking rule.

The negotiations on this are taking place in the Special Session of the Dispute Settlement Body (DSB). The negotiations that have taken place so far have enabled the Special Session to develop on the basis of proposals made by different delegations legal texts for modifications or clarifications of the provisions in the Dispute Settlement Understanding (DSU). These include:

- improvement in the rights of third parties in participating in the proceedings of panels and the Appellate Body;
- improvements in the procedures for appointment of panels with a view to ensuring that persons with expertise in the subject under dispute are selected;
- authority of the Appellate Body to "remand" the case to panels for further examination when it considers that it is unable to complete the legal analysis owing to lack of sufficient relevant factual information;
- treatment of mutually agreed solutions reached during the dispute settlement procedures; and
- enhanced transparency by opening panel and Appellate Body hearings to the public, making access to submissions made by parties to the dispute public and ensuring to them timely access to panel and Appellate Body reports.

Some proposals have been made by developing countries for the extension of special and differential treatment to them. For instance, it is proposed that as developing countries are not able to take full advantage of their rights to invoke dispute settlement procedures because of the high litigation costs involved, a dispute settlement fund for developing countries should be established. The procedures should also authorise the Appellate Body, in cases where a developing country wins, to require the losing party to pay litigation costs. One of the other proposals made by them suggests that rules should authorise developing countries to take "retaliatory action" on a group basis, where the country found to be in breach of the rules fails to modify the offending measure to bring it into conformity with the rules.

On all of the issues, both the concepts and legal texts have been exhaustively discussed. The progress made in developing a convergence of views however varies considerably.

***Special and Differential (S&D) Treatment*[16]**

The Doha Declaration provides that in order to ensure that full attention is paid to the development dimension, priority should be given to finding solutions to the problems they encountered in implementing the rules of the various agreements that constitute the WTO system by *inter alia* making provisions for S&D treatment in various Agreements "more precise, effective and operational." In pursuance of these provisions, nearly 80 proposals were submitted by developing countries for changes in the rules, which in their view could facilitate the implementation of the various Agreements by them.[17] Of these, 28 proposals on legal texts for modifications of the rules were agreed in principle at the Hong Kong Ministerial meeting. Since Hong Kong, work on other proposals is continuing, but so far very little progress has been made and only on six proposals have areas of divergence been reduced.

In order to ensure that provisions in the various agreements are implemented effectively, it is also agreed to establish a mechanism for analysis and review of the implementation of the provisions for S&D treatment in various WTO Agreements. The reviews under the mechanism will take place at least twice a year in the special sessions of the Committee on Trade and Development. Monitoring of the S&D provisions under the mechanism shall take place on the basis of the submissions made by member countries as well as reports received from different WTO bodies. It is recognised that the mechanism is not a negotiating body. It is however envisaged that this should not prevent it from making proposals for initiating negotiations in other GATT bodies on S&D provisions. There is broad agreement on the legal text of the mechanisms.

***Preference Erosion*[18]**

One of the reasons a large number of developing countries initially had shown reluctance to support the proposals for launching of new Round of negotiations was that reductions of duties on a MFN basis could result in an erosion of the preferential advantage they enjoy in the markets of developed countries, which extend to them preferential access on a non-reciprocal basis and thus adversely affect their trade with these countries. To reduce the adverse impact of MFN reductions on the trade of countries that have benefited from preferential tariff access over a long period, separate negotiated lists have been prepared of agricultural and non-agricultural products for which preference-receiving countries consider that existing preferential margins provide them meaningful trade advantages.

In relation to the products included in the above lists, the preference-giving countries are expected to spread tariff reductions over a longer period. In the case of agricultural products included on the list, no reductions in tariffs would be made for 10 years. Tariff cuts would commence only after that year and should be implemented over five years in equal installments. The provisions for staggering over a long period would, however, apply to those products included on the list in which total trade from preference-receiving countries is greater than USD50,000 or three percent of the preference-receiving countries' total agricultural trade for the developed country concerned.

In the case of non-agricultural products, separate lists of products on which reductions would be staged over a longer period have been prepared for the EU and the US. On products included in these lists, reductions would be staged over a period of nine years instead of five years. The reductions on these products would also commence two years after the first reduction is made on all products.

In addition to providing longer periods for staging reductions in tariffs, the preference-giving developed countries are urged to enhance their technical assistance to preference-receiving countries, particularly to LDCs, to help them build up their competitive position by *inter alia* removing some of the supply constraints they encounter.

Reasons for the Present Deadlock

Right from the beginning of the negotiations it was generally accepted that the most crucial subjects in the negotiations are those relating to the liberalisation of trade in agricultural and non-agricultural products. Once the differences among participants on the modalities that could be used for securing liberalisation in these two subject areas are resolved, it will be possible to find compromise solutions to meet the gap in views in trade in services and other rule-based areas of negotiations and to complete them in a period of a further six months or so.

Problems in trade negotiations often arise if, during the period of negotiations, there is a change in the government and a new party comes into power, particularly in countries that are major players in the negotiations. The possibility that a change in government, particularly in the US, might affect the progress in the negotiations made the Director-General, as we have noted in Part Two, convene a mini-Ministerial meeting in July 2009 before the US election. The meeting failed because of the differences of views among participants mainly on the agricultural area, particularly on the rules governing the application of special safeguard measures.

Since then the new US administration, which came to power after the elections, has, after reviewing the approach adopted by the previous administration, raised new issues. It has argued that in the case of agricultural products, the analysis made by their agricultural producers shows that their trade may not benefit significantly in the markets of the emerging economies, where there is a potential for the development of trade, as reductions would be made in many cases only in bound rates of tariffs, which are significantly higher than the present applied rates. Products on which applied tariffs would be cut would be relatively few. Further flexibility, which is provided to exclude 12 percent of tariff lines from tariff reductions, by designating them as special products, could in practice enable developing countries to exclude from tariff reductions main agricultural commodities, such as wheat, maize, soybean and sugar, in which a number of developed countries have export interest. This is particularly the case as the rules do not put any quantitative limits on the volume of trade that could be excluded. Therefore, the US has suggested that before the negotiations on modalities are completed, it would be necessary for countries to announce the products they want to exclude or make less than the formula cut in tariff reductions in the agricultural sector and engage in negotiations on a bilateral basis with their trading partners to ensure that there is a balance between advantages and obligations. These proposals are being resisted strongly by developing countries, particularly emerging economies. They have maintained that the modalities clearly recognise that the developing countries have a right to self designate in the agriculture sector the tariff lines they would like to treat as special products. The proposal for notifying such tariff lines with a view to entering into consultations with trade partners was not consistent with the agreements reached in the negotiations.

Recent developments, however, suggest that more than these differences in the negotiations in the agricultural sector, the main stumbling block in the negotiations are the differences that have arisen in the negotiations in the industrial sector. The US and the EU are insisting that the developing countries at higher stages of development, particularly emerging economies, such as Brazil, China and India, must in the industrial sector, complement the reductions they would be making on the basis of the formula by participating in the negotiations for complete elimination of tariffs in at least a few sectors.

The proposal has met with strong opposition from these developing countries. They have maintained that the mandate for the Doha Round clearly recognises that the participation in sector negotiations was non-mandatory and, as such, they were not under any obligation to participate in such negotiations. Moreover, by agreeing to a coefficient between 20 to 25, which were considerably lower than the coefficient of 30 they were demanding, they were reducing their tariffs in the industrial sector at much higher rates and making a contribution that was more than they were expected to make under the rule, which stipulates that they should make a contribution in the Round that was "less than full reciprocity."

The emerging economies, Brazil, China and India, against whom the proposal is mainly directed, maintain that in sectors where developed countries want to eliminate tariffs – such as chemicals, electronic products and machinery - they will be making substantial reductions in tariffs under the formula. Their assessment shows that their domestic industries in these sectors, given the present stage of their development, would not be able to withstand the competition that would result from any reductions in tariffs that would be greater than that resulting from the application of the formula. They have further indicated that they are not also looking to secure in the round any further liberalisation of trade from developed countries than that which would result from the application of the formula and, as such, they are not interested in participating in sectoral negotiations.[19]

These issues are further discussed in Part Five, which examines the strategy that could be adopted for concluding the Doha Round negotiations. These negotiations, which were scheduled to be concluded in three years, will soon be entering the tenth year, with no signs of being concluded in the near future.

Part Four

Building Common Approach through Regional and Interregional Groups and Issue-Based Alliances and Coalitions

The approach developing countries have adopted in the Round was greatly influenced by the experience of their co-operation in the earlier years. We will, therefore, begin by providing a brief description of the mechanism that was adopted in the earlier GATT years, before describing the pragmatic and changed approach they have adopted in the ongoing Doha Development Round of negotiations.

Earlier Years: The Role of the Informal Group

Developing countries have found that because of their weak bargaining positions, resulting from their lack of political clout and lower stage of economic development, they have to strengthen their bargaining position by forming groups, alliances and coalitions. Right from the establishment of the GATT in 1948, when only a few developing countries were its members, and later as its membership started increasing gradually, these countries developed the practice of meeting informally before important GATT meetings to exchange views and consider whether common positions could be developed on some of the issues that were to be discussed.

A major step towards establishing an institutional framework for consultations among developing country members of GATT was taken in the early 1960s when the Informal Group of Developing Countries was established following the establishment of the Non-Aligned Movement in the UN and the formation of the Group of 77 in UNCTAD. This Informal Group provided a useful forum for consultations and for taking joint positions. One of its major weaknesses was, and still is, that it does not have any support for carrying out research on issues under discussion. Therefore, it had to rely on a few of its members that had the necessary expertise to undertake research and prepare background papers. The result was that the work of the Group came to be dominated by four members – Brazil, Egypt, India, and the former Yugoslavia – and a few others, like Argentina, Pakistan and Uruguay. This domination by the Big Four, as they were called then, was resented by the other members, who considered that the group was submitting papers to the GATT committees and negotiating groups on behalf of the Informal Group, without providing adequate opportunity to other members to comment and to express their views.

This simmering dissatisfaction with the way in which the work of the Group was conducted, was to explode when in 1982, during the discussions for launching of a new round (the Uruguay Round) of negotiations, the US proposed that a new subject, trade in services, be included in its agenda. Initially, most of the members of the Group agreed to the view taken by the countries that were playing the leading role in the work of the Group and agreed to the joint statements made on behalf of the Group opposing its inclusion. Gradually, however, as a result of persuasion and in some cases pressures, by US and other developed countries that were in favour of the subject being included in the agenda and the "informal information meetings" that were arranged by them in pursuance of the decisions taken by the GATT Council, a number of members decided to change their hard-line positions. The resulting rift made Brazil, Egypt, India and the former Yugoslavia and six other countries take an unprecedented step to circulate a paper emphasising their continued opposition to the inclusion of the subject of services in the agenda for negotiations, ignoring the past practice of bringing it to the attention of the other members of the Group, before submitting it to any GATT forum. It is important to note that the hard-line approach that the ten countries were adopting was greatly influenced by their view that the studies on which information sessions were based were far from adequate to establish that the GATT type of rules could be applied to trade in services. They were further influenced in taking such a hard-line attitude by the fact that even some of the member countries of the EU were sceptical at that time about the feasibility of bringing trade in services under GATT discipline and its then Ambassador had indirectly in informal discussions expressed support for the concerns that were being expressed by them.

The Emergence of the Group of 10 and the Café-Au-Lait Group

The controversy and strong reaction that the circulation of the paper by the ten countries created, (which came to be known as Group of 10), made Jamaica and Colombia take a lead in constituting a new Group, in which some 20 members of Informal Group, who were now willing to support inclusion of trade in services on the agenda of the new round and some nine developed countries (other than the Quad countries of Canada, the EU, Japan and the US) agreed to participate. As the Group was chaired by the Ambassador of Colombia, a country whose main export crop was coffee and co-chaired by the Ambassador of Switzerland, which is famous for its milk products, the Group came to be known as the Café-au-Lait Group. The membership of the Group increased to 48 countries by the time of the Ministerial meeting to launch the Round was held in Punta-del Este in Uruguay.

The Group of 10 G-10 continued to hold its hard-line position opposing the inclusion of trade in services up to the Punta-del Este Ministerial meeting where they agreed to go along with the consensus on its inclusion. The decision of the member countries of the G-10 to not change their positions prior to the meeting, when they were realising that they were being increasingly isolated, was influenced by two factors. First, the negotiators found that it would be embarrassing for them to change their strong positions opposing the inclusion of trade in services, after having convinced the constituencies in their own countries that inclusion of services in the agenda for negotiations would not be in the national interest of developing countries. They were no doubt becoming increasingly conscious that the new studies that were coming out indicated some change in their hard-line position may be necessary and were looking for an opportunity and time to change their position gradually and without embarrassment. They expected that they would have such time as the Ambassador of the EU with whom they were in close touch continued to assure them on a personal and confidential basis, that a number of member countries of the EU were not in favour of inclusion of trade in services in the agenda of the Ministerial meeting and, as such, the EU would not be able to support the proposal. However, they were taken by surprise when, just four weeks before the Ministerial meeting, news came that the member countries of the EU had agreed to support the inclusion of services in the negotiating agenda.

After the Ministerial meeting the G-10 ceased to exist. The Café au Lait Group continued during the Uruguay Round as "Friends of Services," with slightly different membership.

However, it failed to make any significant impact on the developments of the negotiations and served mainly as a "club" for periodic exchanges of views on the issues under discussion in the area of services.[20]

As regards the Informal Group of developing countries, the misunderstandings caused by the rift between major players were gradually forgotten and the Group continued to be used by developing countries as a forum for exchange of views on issues of interest and concern to all of its members during the Uruguay Round.

Cairns Group

Another Group that was to play an important role in the Uruguay Round was the Cairns Group. Like the Café au Lait Group it was also a group consisting of both developed and developing countries. The Group came into existence at a meeting arranged by Australia at the Ministerial level at Cairns, a few weeks before the Ministerial meeting that launched the Uruguay Round. In addition to developed agricultural exporting countries, like Australia, Canada and New Zealand, developing agricultural exporting countries from Latin America, such as Argentina, Brazil, Chile and Uruguay and Asian countries like Fiji, Indonesia, Malaysia, and Thailand were its members. Its main aim was to secure further liberalisation of trade in agricultural products, particularly change in the common agricultural policy of the EU, which by its protectionist policies was increasingly becoming self sufficient in agricultural production and was distorting international markets by disposing the resulting high-priced excess domestic production in international markets at low prices by granting export subsidies. Even though US had not become a member of the Group, at the political level it was supporting the approach adopted by the Cairns Group of countries as it wanted to secure changes in the EU's agricultural policy. The research and analytical work undertaken by the Australian government helped the Group greatly in building up common positions on the approach that member countries could adopt. Through such technical preparation and by taking advantage of the rift between the US and the EU, the Group was able to exert considerable influence in the negotiations on the development of new rules against application of quantitative restrictions to imports of agricultural products and on reductions in the use of trade-distorting subsidies for such products.[21]

Doha Round

The years that followed the establishment of the WTO witnessed countries that were playing leading roles in the work of the Informal Group, such as Brazil, India and others making further rapid economic progress. As the gap in economic development between these developing countries, which had come to be known as emerging economies, and other developing countries widened, it started to become increasingly difficult for developing countries as a whole to adopt common and unified positions on issues under discussions and negotiations in the WTO. Consciously or unconsciously, therefore, they realised that their political unity and solidarity could be maintained only if it was recognised that because of the differences in the stages of development reached by the various members of the Group, there may be cases when countries may have different positions. Even though it may be possible for them to agree on a common approach in negotiations with developed countries at a broad policy level, differences among them could emerge at more detailed level. In such cases, efforts would need to be made to see whether these differing interests could be reconciled in adopting common positions. Furthermore, in the few cases where they could not be reconciled, member countries would have, in order to maintain the political unity and solidarity of the Group, to show respect for one another's' positions, accept these diverging interests and where possible support them.

Box 2 below provides a synopsis of the main regional and interregional Groups and coalitions on which developing countries are at present relying for preparatory work and for consultations on the approach which they could adopt in the negotiations on various subjects included in the agenda of the Doha Round.

Box 2: Groups and Coalitions that are used by Developing Countries for Consultations and Coordination of their Positions

Criteria based Regional and Interregional Groups	**Issue based Alliances and Coalitions**
ACP Group Africa Group Group of Commonwealth Developing Countries Group of Least Developed Countries (LDC Group) Group of Small and Vulnerable Economies (SVE Group)	**Agriculture products** Group of 20 Group of 33 Cotton 4 **Non agricultural products** NAMA Group of 11 Para 6 Countries
Apex Bodies with wider membership Informal Group of Developing Countries Group of 90 Group of 110 **Note: Annex I lists countries which are members of the various Groups and Coalitions**	

In evolving this institutional framework the developing countries appear to have been influenced not only by their past experience, but also by the findings of academic studies. Box 3 provides an overview of the main recommendations in some of these studies.

Box 3: Findings of the analytical studies on the guidelines that should be followed in fostering greater coordination in policy formulation by developing countries

- It must be recognised that the historical and political considerations that unite developing countries as a group can be maintained and further strengthened only if the members recognise that because of the differences in levels of development reached by them, their trade interests may in certain cases diverge. The members of the Group must in such cases show understanding and tolerance of the differing positions taken and, where possible, indicate their willingness to support the approach adopted.

Contd...

- In forming a coalition to ensure its effectiveness and sustainability it would be necessary to ensure that the members have a "shared and internally consistent agenda." The agenda must also be supported by research and analysis that would enable the members to review their positions from time to time taking into account developments in the negations. It would be also necessary to ensure that view points of smaller members are not ignored in formulating the collective agenda.

- Besides having a shared agenda, it is necessary to see, that in order to ensure that the coalition makes its impact felt in the negotiations, it has "external weight." The factors that influence or determine the external weight include the number of members, their share in world trade and the political importance of some of the member countries.

- The main negotiating strategy of the coalition should be to engage in constructive dialogue with countries with which it is negotiating with a view to reaching solutions that are acceptable to both parties. This should not however rule out the need to adopt "blocking strategies" in certain situations. Some influence can be exercised by using blocking strategies in the pre-negotiating period, particularly to block the inclusion of new subjects for rule making in the agenda for future negotiations. It can be also used with advantage, during the negotiations, to put a break on the negotiating process, in order to bring to the attention of the general public that the reasonable demands made by the coalition are not being respected by the countries with which it is negotiating.

- It should be recognised, that in the period soon after the formation of coalitions, some members may leave because of the pressures exerted on them by developed countries. Also, there would be cases where a member is able to support the general approach adopted by the coalition, but has a different position on some specific issue. In such cases, the coalition should allow the member to express its views in the negotiations or to join other coalitions of which members take similar views.

- It is important for a coalition to meet regularly and at frequent intervals at the expert level as well as at the level of Ambassadors in order to create on the part of all members a feeling of involvement and ownership of the approaches adopted and to avoid a feeling that it is being driven by a few countries with political weight. Holding of meetings of the coalition at the Ministerial level further strengthens the unity among the members of the coalition.

- It is desirable for different coalitions to hold meetings periodically for exchange of information among themselves and where possible for coordination of their negotiating approach. In this context, it is important to note that the ACP, the Africa Group, the Commonwealth Group of Developing Countries and the LDC Groups have overlapping and coordinated agendas and often hold joint workshops for adopting a coordinated approach on important issues.

- Judicious use of media to bring to the attention of the public the views and opinions of countries help in building up the image of the coalition and thus could enhance its weight in the negotiations.

Source: Narlikar, A. 2005. International Trade and Developing Countries Bargaining Coalitions in the GATT and WTO. London: Rutledge.

Development of a Common Approach through Coordination in Regional Groups

Criteria-Based Regional and Interregional Groups

ACP and African Groups

For African and ACP countries, the Geneva groups provided a forum for discussions on adopting, when possible, common positions. The cohesiveness of the two groups, resulting from the fact that most of their member countries are either at the middle or lower stages of development, enabled them to submit to the various WTO Negotiating Groups a number of submissions indicating broadly their negotiating positions and take, in certain cases, joint positions on some of the issues. In the area of tariffs, for instance, in the early period of negotiations, the ACP Group made a submission explaining why the member countries would need a greater degree of flexibility in reducing their tariffs. In support, they had referred to a number of empirical studies, which had brought out that the liberalisation measures taken by them in the earlier years under structural adjustment programmes, in which they were required to reduce tariffs on an across- the-board basis, had instead of promoting industrialisation and increasing employment, resulted in de-industrialisation and increased unemployment. The submissions, therefore, emphasised that the extent to which the tariffs should be reduced and their coverage should be left to be determined by them.

Both these groups had been active in the work on problems that developing countries encountered in applying at the national level the provisions of the multilateral agreements (the so-called implementation issues), and were responsible for submitting most of the proposals for modifications of the rules of these agreements to make them more responsive to the needs of developing countries. Since the launch of the Doha Round, both of these groups have either on their own or jointly submitted papers, indicating their positions on the issues under negotiation on agricultural and non-agricultural products. Members of these groups also have been taking an active interest by submitting some proposals in the area of trade facilitation and in some of the areas covered by the Negotiations on Rules, such as anti-dumping and fisheries subsidies and in the negotiations that are taking place in the area of trade-related aspects of intellectual property.

Least-developed Country Group

The LDC Group was able to secure, at a very early stage in the negotiations on the modalities for liberalisation of trade in both agricultural and non-agricultural products, acceptance that they should not be required to reduce tariffs in this Round. These countries would, however, be required to bind their tariffs in the non-agricultural sector against further increases. Their tariffs in the agricultural sector have been already bound against further increases in the Uruguay Round. It was also possible for them to secure acceptance of their demand that developed countries should provide duty- and quota-free access to "at least 97 percent of their tariff lines" by 2008[22] . In the area of trade in services, these countries have been able to secure acceptance of their demand that they should be exempted from making any commitments in the round for liberalisation of trade.

Small, Vulnerable Economies (SVEs)

Another important development in the Round is the emergence of the SVE group. It is necessary to note that the need to deal separately with the problems of SVEs was first raised in WTO discussions by some of the small island countries belonging to the Caribbean and the Pacific regions. Gradually, as a result of the work done on the criteria that could be adopted for identification of such countries, the coverage of the Group has been broadened to include, in addition to island countries, those that are small in size, are at a middle or lower stage of development and have an extremely small share in world trade. The coordinated position adopted by these countries has resulted in the provision in the modalities for negotiations on agriculture, that some 46 countries that have been identified as SVEs should in the agriculture sector reduce their tariffs by a percentage that is lower by 10 percentage points than the rates at which the developing countries would be reducing their tariffs. In the non-agricultural sector, these countries would not be reducing tariffs by using the formula, but would only reduce their tariffs in such a way that the average does not exceed a specified percentage. It is important to note that this categorisation has been adopted only for use in modalities in this Round and does not constitute (at least at present) a classification of countries that can be used for legal purposes under the WTO system.

Geneva Group of Commonwealth Developing Countries

While the four groups mentioned above are being used by their member countries for lobbying and building common positions, the role played by the Geneva Group of Commonwealth Developing Countries is largely confined to research and analytical work and to the preparation of background papers that are required by delegations in deciding on the approach that they might like to adopt on different issues under negotiations. One of the reasons for this is that the membership of the Group includes, apart from countries belonging to Africa and the Caribbean regions, those belonging to Asia, such as India, Malaysia and Pakistan, which are at a relatively higher stage of development. This makes it difficult for them to adopt a common approach on most of the issues, as the negotiating approach adopted by a country is often greatly influenced by its stage of economic development. The Group has, therefore, developed a practice that allows countries to make submissions by using papers prepared for discussions, in the names of member countries wishing to make submissions and not on behalf of the Group. Some of these countries have, after lobbying for support in the African and ACP Groups, resubmitted on behalf of the two Groups the proposals that they had submitted initially in their own names.

Thus, the work done by the Group on agricultural commodity issues provided a basis for submission by the ACP and African Group, which resulted in agreements being reached in the negotiations in the agriculture sector for modifications in the GATT rules to permit adoption of commodity agreements for stabilisation of prices by producing countries without inviting consuming countries to become their members, as is required by the present rules. In the area of trade facilitation, the Handbook on Trade Facilitation, which was prepared as a part of the work of the Group, has been found most useful by developing countries in their participation in the technical discussions that are taking place in the Negotiating Group on Trade Facilitation.[23]

Coordination and cooperation among the members of the groups discussed so far is greatly facilitated as their membership overlap. The groups have also developed the practice of holding joint meetings at the expert level for finalising the proposals to be tabled and for holding joint workshops at the level of Ambassadors and officials from the Mission for coordination of their positions at policy levels.

Issue-Based Alliances and Coalitions

While the regional and inter-regional groups mentioned above enable their member countries to formulate and take joint positions on some of the issues, a major effort to coordinate and evolve common positions of developing countries is being made by the issue-based coalitions in which countries belonging to different regions, having an interest in adopting a common approach on particular issues, participate.

Agricultural Products

Group of 20 and 33

The run up of the Cancún Ministerial meeting scheduled for September 2003 witnessed the formation of three new coalitions on specific issues. These included the coalition of the Group of 20 G-20 and the Group on Special Products and Special Safeguard Measures (later transformed into the G-33 and the coalition of cotton-producing countries.

Spearheaded by India and Brazil, the G-20 consisted of countries from Asia, Latin America and Africa that had an offensive interest in securing further liberalisation of trade in agricultural products by the developed countries by requiring them to make substantial reductions in tariffs and in the trade-distorting subsidies they granted to agricultural products and to discontinue the use of export subsidies. The getting together of these major agricultural exporting countries, particularly their first statement, challenging the approach adopted jointly by the EU and the US, was received with some concern by the developed countries. The US reacted aggressively to the establishment of the Group and put a lot of pressure on some of the members, especially smaller Central American and Latin American countries to disassociate them from the Group. This resulted in Colombia, Ecuador, El Salvador, Guatemala and Peru leaving the Group.

The G-20 has, by using the technical preparatory work it had undertaken, lobbied intensively for securing agreement that developed countries should eliminate their export subsidies by an agreed specified date and that they should agree to reduce significantly the overall level of other trade-distorting subsidies that they grant to agricultural producers. As the position taken by the Group conformed broadly to that taken by other developing countries, they generally rallied to support the proposals tabled by the G-20 in the Negotiating Group on Agriculture. This ultimately led to tentative agreement being reached on the export subsidies being eliminated by developed countries by 2013. As regards trade-distorting subsidies, as a result of the strong and unified position taken by the developing countries, some tentative agreement has been reached on the percentage by which they should be reduced by developed countries granting them. Similarly, the tentative agreements on the tiered formula on the basis of which the tariffs are to be reduced both by developed and developing countries are greatly influenced by the approach advocated by the Group.

More or less at the same time as the establishment of this Group, another Group, the G-33, came to be established. Its aims were defensive. First, it wanted to ensure that developing countries in which production is undertaken by poor farmers in small farms living at subsistence level should be allowed to exclude from the formula cuts the products for which they considered that the maintenance of the existing level of protection was necessary. Second it pressed for the establishment of a special safeguard mechanism (SSM) that would enable developing countries to levy additional duties, where they considered that imports of a particular agricultural product has increased beyond a specified trigger volume or its price has fallen below a particular trigger level.

It is interesting to note that from among the members of the G-20, countries where production is undertaken on small farms, such as Bolivia, India, Indonesia, Kenya Nigeria, Pakistan and Tanzania, have also become members of the G-33. The main objective of the Group is however not favoured by those members of the G-20, where production is undertaken on a large scale for exports, such as Argentina, Brazil and others. These countries, which have significant trade also with other developing countries in agricultural products, consider that exclusion by developing countries of special products from tariff reductions would reduce considerably the benefits they are expecting to secure from tariff reductions in the Round, particularly if they have significant trade in the tariff lines that are excluded. Some of them are also apprehensive that permitting developing countries to apply SSMs may also affect their exports, especially to countries where such exports are increasing.

However, in order to ensure that the broad approach that developing countries as a group were adopting in the negotiations on trade in agriculture is not affected by the differences on the two issues, they tacitly agreed to allow the members where production was being undertaken on small farms to join the G-33 and to press for the acceptance of the demand for exclusion of special products and adoption of rules for the application of SSMs. Such understanding and willingness on the part of members to allow other members to take differing positions when warranted by their differing trade interest, has enabled developing countries as a group to maintain unified positions on major issues under negotiation.

Cotton 4 Countries

Another coalition that came into existence in the Doha Round is the Group of 4 Cotton-Producing countries. The steep fall in the prices of cotton and the resulting decline in income of 10 million cotton producing farmers living at the poverty level made four highly cotton-dependent LDCs, Benin, Burkina Faso, Chad and Mali, form an alliance to press for the complete phase out of domestic trade-distorting subsidies and export subsidies which were granted by developed countries, particularly the US, for the production and export of cotton. In order to create greater awareness at the political level of the plight of farmers in cotton-producing countries, the President of Burkina Faso took an unusual step, in June 2003, of attending the meeting of the WTO General Council, which meets at the Ambassador level, to urge WTO member countries to ensure that positive measures were taken in the Round to address the problems faced by cotton-producing countries.

The initiative taken by the four cotton producing countries received general support from the ACP Group and most of the other developing countries. Formal support for the proposal from LDCs as a Group was, however, delayed as one of its members which had been able to develop their textile industry for exports to the US under the African Growth and Opportunity Act (AGOA) by using cotton imported from the US, considered that pursuing the cotton issue would not be in its interest. However, the country later withdrew its objection and the initiative came to be supported by the LDC Group as well.

The US however, in the initial period maintained that the low prices prevailing in international markets were not the result of subsidies granted by it and other countries, but were largely due to the competition posed to cotton by synthetic fibers that are being increasingly used in the production of textile products.

The long and protracted negotiations that followed led to adopting a two-pronged approach in addressing the cotton issue. First, member countries agreed to address the "trade issues" in the Doha Round. Second, it was agreed that in order to deal with the "development assistance aspects" the WTO should work with the Development Committee. The Director-General was also requested to consult with the World Bank, the IMF, the FAO, the International Trade Centre (ITC) and other international organisations on the assistance they could provide.

In the negotiations that have taken place on trade issues, the Cotton 4 countries with full support from other cotton-producing countries, have been able to secure recognition that cotton along with the subjects such as liberalisation of trade in agricultural and industrial products as well as development issues, form part of the core issues in the Doha Round negotiations. It has also been agreed that reductions in domestic distorting subsidies granted by countries on cotton be done at a rate that would be significantly higher than the rate at which US and other countries would be reducing the subsidies granted by them on other products. As regards export subsidies there is tentative agreement that the countries granting such subsidies should eliminate them by a date that will be much earlier than that agreed for the elimination of export subsidies on all other products (2013).

The discussions that have taken place on development assistance aspects have resulted in identification of areas in which assistance would have to be provided *inter alia* for improving efficiency and productivity in cotton production and for development of infrastructure for trade in cotton. Programmes have also been adopted by donor countries and by international organisations for providing assistance to cotton-producing countries. The US for instance has adopted the West African Cotton Improvement Programme, while the EU has established the EU-Africa Partnership on cotton as a part of its programme for assistance to ACP countries.

Industrial Products

NAMA Group of 11

This coalition to strengthen the bargaining position of the developing countries in the negotiations on industrial tariffs (non-agricultural products) was formed during the Hong Kong Ministerial meeting held in December 2005. Led by South Africa, it includes, in addition to India and Brazil, most of the countries from the developing world that are at relatively higher stage of development and as such were expected to apply the Swiss formula for making reductions in tariffs.

The reduction that results from the application of the formula, in a given rate of tariff, depends, as noted earlier, on the level of the coefficient. A lower coefficient results in higher reductions being made in a given rate of tariffs. A higher coefficient, on the other hand, results in lower reductions. The main thrust of the work of the Group was to ensure that the principle that developing countries be required to make a contribution that is "less than full reciprocity" was respected and hence there should be a minimum difference of 25 points between the coefficients to be used by developed countries and that used by developing countries. The complimentary aim was to ensure that the countries applying the formula had enough flexibilities, which took into account their need to maintain the existing level of tariffs for promoting economic development, by excluding certain tariff lines from tariff cuts or by making on them less than formula cuts.

By providing studied responses to the proposals made by the Chairman of the Negotiation Group from time to time, the Group has been able to secure agreement on modalities that would require developed countries to use the coefficient of eight, while the developing countries would be permitted to use coefficients of 20, 22 or 25. The flexibility that would be available for excluding tariff lines from tariff reductions would however depend on the coefficient used. The higher the coefficient used, the lesser the flexibility available.

Countries With Low Binding Coverage – Paragraph 6 Countries[24]

The main motivation for forming this coalition was the indication given by some of the developed countries that for developing countries with "low level of bindings in the industrial sector" they would be willing to agree to reductions being made on industrial products at rates lower than the rates at which they would have to reduce tariffs under the formula, if they agreed to bind all of their tariffs. As a result of the efforts made by the coalition led by Kenya and Sri Lanka, 13 developing countries would be reducing tariffs at less than the formula rate, on the understanding that they would bind all of their tariffs at a target average rate of 30 percent.

Measures taken to Ensure Transparency and Exchanges of Views among Groups and Coalitions

Both coalitions and regional groups recognised from the beginning that, in order to ensure that the approach adopted by developing countries as a whole remained mutually consistent and supportive, it was necessary to ensure transparency in their work by arranging meetings for exchanges of views among their members on the approach they were adopting. Toward this end they, particularly the three coalitions – the G-20, the G-33 and NAMA 11 – developed the practice of arranging meetings with the members of the ACP, Africa, LDC and SVE Groups, before making any important statements or presenting submissions to the Negotiating Groups. In such meetings, the members of the coalitions, either explicitly or implicitly gave their support to the efforts the LDCs, SVEs, ACP and African Groups were making to secure special and more favourable treatment, particularly on the extent to which they should be required to reduce their tariffs. In return, these groups supported the negotiating positions taken by the coalitions as they considered that the general approach adopted by them was broadly consistent with their negotiating positions.

The success of the coalitions in influencing the final outcome of the negotiations in the area of agriculture and non-agricultural products was also greatly influenced by the technical support the four countries – Brazil, India, Indonesia and South Africa – were able to provide by preparing research-oriented analytical papers. These countries also acted as spokesmen for the coalition in the meetings of the Negotiating Groups. The fact that throughout the negotiations, the members showed willingness to negotiate, by reviewing the position taken, in the light of the views expressed in the meetings of the negotiating groups, further helped the negotiating process.

Both the regional groups and coalitions have developed a practice of meeting on a regular basis. Such meetings are held first at the Ambassador level to decide on the approach that could be adopted on issues under negotiation, taking into account the views expressed in the discussions of the negotiating groups. The officials from the Missions then examine the issues at the expert level and prepare drafts of proposals to be tabled and of the statements to be made in the negotiating groups. These are further considered and final decisions taken in meetings that are again held at the level of Ambassadors.

The countries that were playing leading roles in the coalitions took special care to see in such meetings that the views of all countries, including those that were least developed or at a lower stage of development, were taken into account and they felt ownership for the views being expressed. The efforts the delegations from the countries that had the responsibility for leading the work of the coalition – Brazil, India, Indonesia and South Africa – took to ensure that in the preparatory work all member countries were able to participate and their views were fully taken into account in deciding the final approach gradually developed confidence on the part of the members that they could act as their spokesmen. This growing confidence in their leadership and the technical competence of their delegations also led the developing countries as a group to accept generally that India and Brazil could represent their interests in the meetings of the Groups of Four and Six, consisting of both developed and developing countries, that were held in the period when the formal negotiations in the WTO were suspended.

Ministerial Involvement in the Work of the Groups and Coalitions

Greater involvement of Ministers on a continuing basis in the negotiations is further improving the ability of developing countries to influence the course of the negotiations. The regional and cross-regional groups, as well as the issue-based coalitions, meet at the Ministerial level to bring out the political importance that their members attach to the negotiating approaches adopted by them. Further, to provide the opportunity for an exchange of views among members belonging to different groups or coalitions, joint meetings are arranged at the Ministerial level.

Thus, ACP and African countries and the LDC Group have been holding joint meetings under the umbrella Group of 90. The group gets its name from the numerical strength of the three groups. A recent development is to hold joint meetings to which, in addition to the Ministers and senior officials from the three groups mentioned above, those from countries belonging to the SVE Group and the issue-based coalitions, such as the G-20, the G-33 and NAMA 11 are invited to attend. This broader Group has come to be known as the Group of 110. The purpose of such meetings is to enhance coordination among developing countries and thus ensure the unity and solidarity of developing countries as a group. It is relevant to note that, to demonstrate their solidarity, separate supporting statements are often made simultaneously on behalf of the ACP, LDC and SVE Groups and issue-based coalitions, such as the G-20 and the G-33, when issues of negotiating interest and concern to developing countries are being discussed in the WTO negotiating bodies.

These groups, particularly the issue-based coalitions, are increasingly using the media to publicise and make known to the general public their negotiating positions. They also collaborate in making their positions known to non-governmental organisations working on trade and development problems.

Summing Up the Results of the Strategy Adopted by Developing Countries

To sum up, by consulting and coordinating their positions in the regional and interregional groups and later discussing the issues in groups with broader membership, such as Group of 90 and Group of 110, the developing countries were able to adopt common positions with respect to both their offensive and defensive interests in negotiations with developed countries. The coordinated approach they were able to adopt enabled them to secure in the agricultural sector *inter alia* commitments from developed countries for deeper cuts in trade-distorting subsidies, acceptance of the principle that they would be entitled to exclude from tariff reductions special products for which they considered the existing level of protection was necessary and the right to apply SSMs where imports increased beyond a specified volume trigger. In the industrial sector the common and unified position taken by the developing countries enabled them to ensure that in applying the Swiss formula, they could use the coefficients that would result in reductions in tariffs that take into account the fact that they are expected to make contributions that are less than full reciprocity. At the same time, the strategy adopted enabled the LDC, SVE and other groups to negotiate separately with developed countries for flexibilities in reducing their tariffs and for special and differential treatment taking into account their state of development or their special features.

Lessons for the Future

There could be seven lessons for the future from the experience of the efforts made by developing countries for consulting among themselves and building up common positions during the ongoing negotiations.

The first is that for evolving common positions, developing countries would have to continue to adopt a bottom-up approach under which an attempt is made to first discuss the issues at the level of regional or interregional groups and in coalitions. It is only after discussions have taken place in such fora that it would be desirable to bring the issues for discussions in a broader forum, by arranging joint meetings of groups and/or coalitions and later, meetings in which almost all of the members participate.

Second, while the aim of such consultations should be to find whether a coordinated approach is possible on the issues under discussion or negotiations in the WTO, it is necessary to recognise that, because of the wide differences in the level of economic development reached by member countries of the group, there could be a few areas in which adoption of such a common approach may not be possible. To maintain cohesion and solidarity of the group, members would have to make their best efforts to accommodate such differences in the overall policies they wish to pursue and where such accommodation is not possible, show tolerance and respect the different positions taken by some members.

Third, it is necessary to recognise that, while regional and inter-regional groups provide a permanent forum for consultations among their members, the issue-based coalitions may disintegrate or cease to exist after the objectives and purposes for which they had been created are achieved. It is, therefore, likely that some of the coalitions created in the Doha Round, such as the NAMA 11 and the G-33 may cease to exist as and when the Doha Round of Negotiations is completed. New ones may be established, taking into account the subjects or issues that are taken up for negotiations. For instance, if it is decided to take up the subject of trade-related aspects of climate change for negotiations, it is possible that some of the developing countries would form a coalition for discussions and exchange of views on the approach that could be adopted in the discussions in the WTO.

Fourth, the existing mechanism for consultations among inter-regional and regional groups and coalitions may need to be further strengthened in order to provide greater transparency to the work done by them to develop a common approach wherever possible. Greater responsibility for this would fall on the countries at higher stages of development – such as China, India, Brazil, Indonesia, South Africa and others – that may in the future take the initiative in establishing coalitions.

Fifth, the efforts that the countries that formed coalitions made to ensure transparency and get support for their approach were largely responsible to developing countries. These countries generally agreed that a few countries (China, India and Brazil) could represent them in small group consultations with developed countries that were arranged at the Ministerial level from time to time during the course of the negotiations in the Group of 4 or the Group of 6 to resolve the differences that were stalling the negotiations.

However, there were some whispers in small gatherings of developing country delegations that the three countries often failed to ensure prior consultations on the stand they were taking in such meetings. Against this background, it may be necessary to consider whether it may be desirable to institutionalise the informal arrangements that exist at present for consultations among the entire membership of developing countries, by holding on a more regular basis, (say once every two months) meetings of either the Informal Group of Developing Countries or the Group of 110 expanded to include all developing countries. It should be further agreed that such a group should meet at the Ministerial level before every Ministerial meeting and if necessary during the Ministerial meetings.

Sixth, there is an increasing view among political economists and policy makers in the developed countries that the division of countries between developed and developing is becoming increasingly anachronistic, particularly with the rapid progress that emerging countries are making in economic development. In their view, it is unrealistic to treat these countries as developing countries, as some studies forecast that in about two decades they would surpass the GDP of the developed countries. For instance, in a recent article, Susan Schwab, who was US Trade Representative from 2005 to 2008, has observed that the effort by emerging countries to maintain that they are developing countries is as unrealistic as "an elephant trying to hide behind mice."[25] Similar views were echoed by the EU Trade Commissioner, Karel De Gucht, who, at a recent seminar arranged by the OECD stated, "I would not call them – Brazil, India and China – now as developing countries."[26]

This issue related to the division of countries into two groups – developed and developing – is expected to become more controversial when Russia joins the WTO in a few months' time. The fact that the country considers that in the trade policy field, its interest are similar to those of developing countries is evident from its recent decision to become member of a Group, consisting of four emerging economies, Brazil, India, China and South Africa – the BRICS Group[27].

Seventh, as we have noted previously, while most of the coalitions that were formed in the Uruguay Round were mixed coalitions, in which both developed and developing countries participated (e.g. the Café au Lait Group and Cairns Group) most of the coalitions that were formed in this Round were those in which only developing countries were members. It is true that on certain specific issues in rule-based areas, a few joint proposals were tabled by delegations from both developed and developing countries, but on the whole such cooperation was limited. Part of the reason for this was the leadership provided by the emerging economies and their effectiveness in undertaking background research and analytical work that was necessary to get other developing country delegations to support them. In the post-Doha Round period, with the increasing trend of some of the developing countries to enter into free trade area arrangements with developed countries, it is possible that coalitions with mixed membership may emerge, particularly for developing common approaches in new subject areas that may be taken up for negotiations.

This said, it has to be recognised that the main bonds that hold developing countries together are mainly historical and political and not economic. If these bonds are to be further strengthened, it may be necessary to use the WTO also as a forum for promotion of greater cooperation among developing countries on a South-South basis. One of the ways this could be done is by ensuring that the technical assistance that developing countries like Brazil, China, India and others are providing to other developing countries – for *inter alia* building up the national-level institutional framework for the application of the WTO system and the removal of supply constraints they face owing to the inability of their exporters to comply with technical regulations or sanitary and phytosanitary measures – is made an integral part of the WTO programme of Aid for Trade to be developed in the Doha Round. For this purpose, it could be agreed that donor countries and international financial institutions, should upon request, make available to the developing countries that provide technical assistance to others, financial resources to strengthen and broaden the scope of their technical assistance programmes.

Part Five

Doha and Beyond: Possible Strategies for Conclusion of the Doha Round and Organising Further Negotiations

This brings us to the question of how the present deadlock that has paralysed the ongoing Doha Round can be resolved and the negotiations completed by the middle of the next year, if not by the end of this year. The Director-General, Pascal Lamy, stated in his progress report to the Trade Negotiation Committee at its April 2011 meeting that from "one to one meetings" (or "confessionals" as he calls them) he had had with key players, his assessment was that the differences in approach – particularly with respect to the "sectoral negotiations" in the industrial sector and in the agricultural sector – were not technical, which could be resolved in discussions at the ambassador level, but political, and thus would have to be addressed at the level of ministers and governments.

Therefore, the question that arises is how these differences can be resolved in the near future. The member countries have agreed to his suggestions to make their best efforts to see that these issues on which differences exist are discussed at the Ministerial meetings of ASEAN, the ACP, the OECD and other such groups. The general mood among Geneva-based delegations appears, however, to be one of pessimism. It is generally considered that election timings and the economic and political situations would make it difficult for major players to change their negotiating stances. In the case of the US, with the next presidential election due in the second half of the coming year, the approach the Administration could adopt in WTO negotiations is increasingly influenced by its assessment of how its negotiating position would likely be received by the party in opposition and by the general public. In India, the coalition government may not be inclined to change its position and show willingness to compromise, particularly if it believes to do so would create an impression among the general public that it is the result of pressures from outside, particularly the US. The government that has come in power in Brazil following the recent elections does not appear to be as open as the previous one to further liberalisation of trade in the industrial sector. And the new Chinese leadership, poised to take office in 2012, may not wish to start off by making what could be viewed as major unilateral concessions to the EU and the US.

Against this background, there increasingly appears to be a view among negotiators and policymakers that it may be desirable to be pragmatic and recognise that the Doha Round, particularly its component on liberalisation of trade, cannot be completed in the immediate future and the only way to solve the present deadlock would be to adopt a step-by-step approach and take up for negotiation subjects for which there are reasonable possibilities of completing the negotiations in the near future. Taking into account these considerations in the informal meeting of the Trade Negotiations Committee held on May, 31, 2011, the Director General suggested that it may be desirable to adopt the following three-pronged approach.[28]

First, negotiations on issues that would benefit the trade of LDCs should be held in a "fast lane" for completion as an "early harvest" before the forthcoming December 2011 WTO Ministerial meeting. These issues would include legally binding commitments by the developed countries to permit imports of all goods from these countries on a duty free and quota free basis. The developed countries should also agree on improvements in the applicable rules of origin and the acceptance of an LDC service waiver, which would provide preferential access for their service, products and suppliers. In addition, in view of the importance of cotton in the exports of some of the LDCs, the developed countries' commitment for deeper cuts in trade-distorting subsidies on cotton should be implemented in advance.

Second, the Director-General has suggested that the early harvest package would have to include some LDC-plus issues, with significant development components, on which negotiations could also be completed before the December Ministerial meeting. He has, however, refrained from making firm suggestions on the subjects that could be included for negotiations. He suggested that these would have to be identified by delegations through informal consultations.

A number of suggestions have been put forward informally by delegations on LDC plus subjects that could be taken up for negotiations on a priority basis. For instance, it may be desirable to include negotiations on the Agreement on Trade Facilitation, as its adoption would be a win-win situation for both developed and developing countries. Another possible subject could be the Agreement on Fisheries Subsidies, an area in which all participating countries appear to agree that international discipline is necessary to prevent over exploitation of fish stocks. If there is reluctance on the part of some countries to take up this subject for negotiations on a priority basis, consideration should be given to securing a commitment from developed countries to maintain a standstill on subsidies they grant to their fishing fleets in order to minimise overfishing.

The other subjects that could be taken up for negotiations include acceptance of the proposals for improvements in the rules relating to the extension of S&D treatment to developing countries on which agreement has been reached as well as those on which divergence still exists and the development of a viable package for Aid for Trade. Adoption of package on Aid for Trade would ensure that the financial resources required by developing countries for building technical capacities to apply the rules of the system and for removing supply constraints would be available to them on a systematic and regular basis.

It is important to note that even though the Director-General has indicated that negotiations on LDC issues and selected LDC-plus subjects should be completed before the forthcoming Ministerial meeting in December, further negotiations in at least some of these areas are not going to be without difficulties. For instance, on the extension of duty free and quota free access to LDCs, there is already an agreement that developed countries should allow at least 97 percent of these countries' imports on such a basis. The remaining three percent of exports was excluded mainly at the request of the US, which indicated that it may not be able to provide duty free access for textile products. Given the problems the textile industry in the US and other countries are facing, there could be doubts as to whether political pressures would permit the US to include textiles in its preferential schemes for LDCs. Likewise, on cotton, many analysts have serious doubts whether the US would be willing to agree to reductions in subsidies on cotton, in advance of an agreement on a total package on trade in agricultural and non-agricultural products. There are a number of issues, like trade facilitation and fisheries subsidies, on which it may be difficult to complete negotiations before the forthcoming December Ministerial meeting unless there is political will on the part of all countries to reach compromises.

Third, the Director-General has stated that it would be unrealistic to expect that negotiations in areas such as market access for industrial products, liberalisation of trade in agricultural products, trade in services and TRIPs issues, can be completed this year. The negotiations in these subject areas will have to be continued over the coming months, but in a "slow lane," and decisions will have to be taken at the forthcoming Ministerial meeting on a plan for completing them by an agreed target date.

The question that arises is what plan or strategy can be adopted for completing these negotiations. It is suggested that it may be possible to adopt one of the two following approaches.

The first approach is to continue negotiations in these areas with the expectation that it may be possible to find solutions on the basis of compromise solutions that have been suggested by the EU and others, which would permit developing countries certain flexibility in participating in sectoral negotiations. The second alternative would be to take a pragmatic but bold approach. If it appears that, as a result of the efforts made at the level of ambassadors and at the political level over the next few months, it is not possible to bridge the gap in views on sectorals and other issues, it would be desirable to take a decision at the forthcoming December 2011 Ministerial meeting to "pause" the negotiations for a period of 12 to 18 months, rather than pushing ahead with further repetitive discussions. There is a risk in continuing with discussions when there is no political will on the part of the participants to find compromise solutions that participants will focus only on developing new arguments to support their current views. As result, their positions will become more entrenched. This proposal for a pause or a suspension of the negotiations for an agreed period should not be taken to suggest that negotiations should be abandoned by throwing in the towel on what has been accomplished so far and rebooting to march ahead in other directions.[29] Rather, the purpose of the suspension would be to provide negotiators time to think, review their negotiating positions and engage in consultations with their negotiating partners both at a technical and political level outside the framework of the WTO. Thus, the hope is that they would then be able to come back to the negotiating table with fresh approaches to find compromise solutions at the end of the suspension period.

The Director-General had declared the suspension of negotiations on multilateral basis during certain periods and had decided to rely on Group of 4 - India, Brazil, the US and the EU to resolve them. He had later on expanded the membership to include Australia, Japan and China. These decisions were taken by him at the technical level, perhaps in consultation with the chairmen of the various negotiating groups and other ambassadors in order to provide time for key players to consult and find out if deadlocks could be resolved. The decision to suspend the negotiations for a year or so, under the above proposal, would be taken at a political level at a Ministerial meeting. In taking the decisions to suspend the negotiations, Ministers would be giving a political commitment to use the period of suspension to engage in negotiations outside the framework of the

WTO, to narrow differences and decide, taking into account developments in the economic and political situations in their respective countries, on the timing for the commencement of the negotiations in the WTO and a timeframe for their completion.

Two opposing views to this proposal are being expressed in public debate and informal discussions among negotiators. Those who are not in favour of a suspension, point out that this may tarnish the image of the WTO. Pascal Lamy has observed that since the GATT years, negotiations on reductions in tariffs have been the bread and butter of the organisation and further delay in completing negotiations may raise doubts about the effectiveness of the WTO. Others disagree. For instance, economist Martin Wolf points out that to hold that people will say the WTO has collapsed if the completion of the Doha Round is further postponed is simply absurd. There is increasing recognition that such negotiations are complex and that their pace is often influenced by a number of unforeseen economic and political factors. The same thought was expressed by the Ambassador of Brazil at the April 2011 meeting of the TNC when he stated that "Brazil rejects the notion that this organisation's credibility and legitimacy are in a death embrace with the Round."[30] Negotiation for the liberalisation of trade is only one of the functions of the organisation. Its other functions are to ensure that countries abide by the rules it lays down and to settle disputes that arise when the rules are not followed. These functions are as important as the role it plays in promoting the further liberalisation of trade through negotiations.

Post Doha Round: Would there be New Round After Doha?

What lessons for the future can be taken from the experience of the Doha Round? Would there be a willingness on the part of countries to engage in a new round of simultaneous negotiations on a wide range of subjects in the post-Doha Round period? Many analysts and observes are sceptical. It is argued that, with the increasing emphasis that is being placed on regional preferential trade arrangements, the world community is gradually losing its appetite for negotiations in the WTO for liberalisation of trade on a multilateral basis. Some negotiators from developed countries consider that the Doha Round could be the last Round of negotiations to be held under the auspices of the WTO, as with the further cuts countries would be making in their already low tariffs under the agreements reached in the Round, they would not be left with any leverage to bargain with developing countries to reduce their tariffs. That is why some have claimed the developed countries are pressing on emerging economies for further liberalisation of trade by participating in the sectoral negotiations in the present ongoing negotiations.[31]

There is also increasingly a view that the Doha Round has clearly highlighted the difficulties encountered in negotiating simultaneously on a wide range of highly technical and complex subjects among countries that are at various stages development and, thus, have widely differing trade interests. These difficulties will get more pronounced in the post-Doha Round period, when after a period of about five years or so the WTO membership will increase from 153 to about 180 or so countries when all countries that are at present negotiating for accession became its members. Many are also critical of the single undertaking rule, which requires that in order to ensure balanced progress in all areas of negotiations, the results should be implemented only after the entire negotiation is completed. The experience of Doha Round has shown that the single undertaking rule results in some countries stalling negotiations in areas where progress is being made on the ground that little or no progress has been in the subject areas in which they are interested. This adversely affects the progress of the overall negotiations and is one of the reasons why it has not been possible to complete the Round after nearly ten years. The rule also works to the disadvantage of developing countries, as it prevents implementation of the agreements and decisions of trade interest to them until such time as the negotiations in all subject areas are completed.

Alternative to holding periodic rounds: continuous negotiations

How then would negotiations take place in the WTO for further liberalisation of trade, if no new Rounds are launched? One possibility would be to develop procedures for "continuous or rolling" negotiations, in which subjects would be taken up for negotiations not simultaneously but sequentially. In this context, it is important to note that the desirability of not leaving further liberalisation of trade entirely to Rounds of negotiations has been recognised by the WTO legal framework. For instance, both the Agreements on Agriculture and GATS contain provisions requiring countries to engage in periodic negotiations for liberalisation of trade. Provisions for periodic reviews are also contained in the rule-based agreements, such as those on technical barriers to trade and sanitary and phytosanitary measures.

Against this background, it may be desirable to consider whether in the post-Doha Round period it could be agreed that negotiations should take place both for further liberalisation of trade and for improvements in the existing rules in accordance with the provisions of the WTO Agreements. It is relevant to note that both the agriculture and trade in services negotiations were started in January 2001, prior to the launching of the Doha Round in accordance with the provisions contained in relevant legal instruments. These negotiations were subsequently made a part of Doha Round when it was launched in November 2001.

If such an approach is adopted, it would be also desirable to ensure that subjects for negotiation are taken periodically in accordance with the provisions of the Agreements. In subject areas where legal instruments do not exist at present for holding negotiations on a periodic basis, such as industrial products, such instruments would have to be adopted. Decisions on which additional subjects should be taken up for negotiation should be taken every two years at the Ministerial meetings, taking into account the progress made. The objective should be to avoid simultaneous negotiations taking place, on more than four to five subject areas at any given time, including new subject areas.

The WTO multilateral trading system is at present facing serious new challenges as a result of the global financial crisis, which has resulted in slowing down economic activity, increasing unemployment, an inability of an increasing number of countries particularly in Europe to pay their sovereign debts and inappropriate exchange rate policies in some countries. There is also a growing view among some analysts that the difficulties encountered in the Doha Round negotiations among more than 150 countries at widely different stages of development will lead most countries in the coming years to rely on regional trade arrangements rather than the WTO to secure further reductions in tariffs and other barriers affecting trade in their main markets. As a result, in future WTO negotiations countries are likely to place greater emphasis on further strengthening the rules-based system in new trade-related subject areas.

In this context, it is important to note that, in his statement at the April 2011 meeting of the TNC, the Director-General pointed out that the delay in the completion of the Doha Round is preventing the organisation from taking up other subjects on which there is urgent need to develop new rules. These subjects include trade-related aspects of climate change and trade in energy products. Other issues that have been suggested for negotiations in the WTO include the implication of exchange rates for trade and the GATT rules governing the use of export restrictions and their implications for access to supplies and state capitalism. Also, there may be pressures from some delegations to take up the three so-called Singapore issues that were dropped from the agenda of the Doha Round owing to opposition from developing countries.

In the past, the differences on whether new subjects should be taken up for negotiations on rule making has been a matter of confrontation between developed and developing countries. The controversy over whether trade in services should be taken up resulted in open divisions even among developing countries in the pre-Uruguay Round period. In the light of this experience, it would be desirable for developing countries to undertake studies, if necessary with assistance from UNCTAD and other intergovernmental or non-governmental organisations, on some of the subjects that may be taken up for rule making and to begin as soon as possible consultations on the approach they could adopt, if necessary by forming subject or issue-based coalitions.

Annex I: Developing Country Coalitions in the WTO

Group/Coalition Name	Membership
African Group	Angola, Benin, Botswana, Burkina Faso, Burundi, Cameroon, Central African Rep., Chad, Congo, Congo (Democratic Rep.), Côte d'Ivoire, Djibouti, Egypt, Gabon, Gambia, Ghana, Guinea, Guinea Bissau, Kenya, Lesotho, Madagascar, Malawi, Mali, Mauritania, Mauritius, Morocco, Mozambique, Namibia, Niger, Nigeria, Rwanda, Senegal, Sierra Leone, South Africa, Swaziland, Tanzania, Togo, Tunisia, Uganda, Zambia, Zimbabwe
African, Caribbean, Pacific (ACP) Group	African Group members, plus Antigua and Barbuda, Barbados, Belize, Cuba, Dominica, Dominican Republic, Fiji, Ghana, Grenada, Guyana, Haiti, Jamaica, Papua New Guinea, St. Kitts and Nevis, St. Lucia, St. Vincent and the Grenadines, Solomon Islands, Suriname, Trinidad & Tobago
Least Developed Countries (LDCs)	Angola, Bangladesh, Benin, Burkina Faso, Burundi, Central African Rep., Chad, Congo (Democratic Rep.), Djibouti, Gambia, Guinea, Guinea Bissau, Haiti, Lesotho, Madagascar, Malawi, Mali, Mauritania, Mozambique, Myanmar, Nepal, Niger, Rwanda, Senegal, Sierra Leone, Solomon Islands, Tanzania, Togo, Uganda, Zambia
Small Vulnerable Economies (SVEs)[32]	Albania, Antigua & Barbuda, Armenia, Barbados, Belize, Bolivia, Botswana, Brunei Darussalam, Cameroon, Cuba, Dominica, Dominican Republic, Ecuador, El Salvador, Fiji, FYR Macedonia, Gabon, Georgia, Ghana, Grenada, Guatemala, Guyana, Honduras, Jamaica, Jordan, Kenya, Kyrgyzstan, Macao, Mauritius, Moldova, Mongolia, Namibia, Nicaragua, Panama, Paraguay, Papua New Guinea, Solomon Islands, St. Kitts and Nevis, St. Lucia, St. Vincent and the Grenadines, Sri Lanka, Suriname, Swaziland, Trinidad and Tobago, Uruguay and Zimbabwe
Geneva Group of Commonwealth Developing Countries	Bangladesh, Barbados, Botswana, Brunei Darussalam, Cameroon, Ghana, India, Jamaica, Kenya, Lesotho, Malaysia, Mauritius, Mozambique, Namibia, Nigeria, Pacific Islands, Pakistan, Singapore, South Africa, Sri Lanka, Swaziland, Tanzania, Trinidad and Tobago, Uganda, Zambia

Contd...

Group/Coalition Name	Membership
Informal Group of Latin American Countries	Antigua, Argentina, Barbados, Belize, Venezuela, Bolivia, Brazil, Chile, Colombia, Costa Rica, Cuba, Dominica, Dominican Republic, Ecuador, El Salvador, Guatemala, Haiti, Honduras, Jamaica, Mexico, Nicaragua, Panama, Paraguay, Peru, Saint Kitts and Nevis, Saint Lucia, Saint Vincent and Grenadines, Trinidad and Tobago, Uruguay, Venezuela
G-20	Argentina, Bolivia, Brazil, Chile, China, Cuba, Ecuador, Egypt, India, Indonesia, Kenya, Mexico, Nigeria, Pakistan, Paraguay, Philippines, South Africa, Tanzania, Thailand, Uruguay, Venezuela
G-33	Benin, Bolivia, Botswana, China, Congo, Côte d'Ivoire, Congo, Cuba, Dominica, Dominican Republic, El Salvador, Grenada, Guatemala, Guyana, Haiti, Honduras, India, Indonesia, Jamaica, Kenya, Rep. Korea, Madagascar, Mauritius, Mongolia, Mozambique, Nicaragua, Nigeria, Pakistan, Panama, Peru, the Philippines, St Kitts & Nevis, St. Lucia, St Vincent & the Grenadines, Senegal, Sri Lanka, Suriname, Tanzania, Trinidad & Tobago, Turkey, Uganda, Venezuela, Zambia, Zimbabwe
NAMA 11	Argentina, Brazil, Egypt, India, Indonesia, Namibia, Philippines, South Africa, Tunisia and Venezuela
Paragraph 6 Countries	Cameroon, Congo, Côte d'Ivoire, Cuba, Ghana, Kenya, Macao (China), Mauritius, Nigeria, Sri Lanka, Suriname, Zimbabwe
G-90	Composed of the members of the following groups: · African Group · ACP Group · LDC Group
G-110	The Group includes in addition to the members of the G-90, countries belonging to G-20, G-33 and NAMA 11 and SVE Group
Cairns Group	Australia, Argentina, Bolivia, Brazil, Canada, Chile, Colombia, Costa Rica, Guatemala, Indonesia, Malaysia, New Zealand, Paraguay, Peru, the Philippines, South Africa, Thailand and Uruguay

Endnotes

1 For more detailed explanation of the rules of the WTO Multilateral Trading System see WTO website www.wto.org.

2 Unlike the World Bank and the IMF, where management and senior staff members have the right to propose initiatives, the WTO Director-General and his senior staff have no such right. All such decisions have to be taken by the member countries. For instance, WTO management cannot prepare research papers providing broad policy advice without the specific authorisation of member countries. Secretariat officials generally refrain from expressing opinions on the issues under discussion if requested to do so in negotiation they provide only factual information on the differing views expressed by the participants.

3 Revised draft Modalities for Agricultural Products: WTO document TN/AG/W/4/Rev. 5.

4 Non-agricultural products (Market Access) Report of the chairman: WTO document TN/MA/W/103-Rev 3, Add. 1, April, 21, 2011 and 2008 Report on Draft Modalities TN/MA/W/103 Rev. 3.

5 Ibid. See Annex 7.

6 Ibid. note above: These countries are Oman, Singapore, Thailand, Chinese Taipei, United Arab Emirates and Lebanon.

7 Trade in Services, Report of the Chairman, TN/SA/36, April 21, 2011.

8 Trade Facilitation: Draft Consolidated Text, WTO document TN/TF/W/165/Rev. 8, April 21, 2011.

9 Rules: Communication from the Chairman: WTO document TN/RL/W/254, April 21, 2011.

10 Report of the Chairman, Negotiations on Subsidies and Countervailing Measures, WTO document, TN/RL/W/254, April 2011.

11 Report of the Chairman, Negotiations on Fisheries Subsidies, TN/RL/W/254.

12 Regional Trade Arrangements, Report of the Chairman, WTO document, TN/RL/251, April 21, 2011 and Note on Systemic Issues, TN/TP/21, April, 11, 2011.

13 Trade and Environment, Report of the Chairman, WTO document, TN/TE/20, August 21, 2011.

14 Report of the Chairman of the Special Session of the Council on TRIPs, TN/IP/21, April 21, 2011.

15 Dispute Settlement, Report of the Chairman, TN/DS/25/, April 21, 2011.

16 Development: Report of the Chairman, WTO document TN/CTD/26.

17 See para 44: Special and Differential Treatment, Doha Ministerial Declaration, WTO document: WT/MIN(01)Dec/W1, November 14, 2001.

18 Reports of the Chairman on Agricultural Products, Revised draft Modalities for Agriculture, TN/AG/26, December 8, 2008 and Report of the Chairman on Non-Agricultural Products (Market Access) TN/MA/W/103/Rev. 3 Add 1, April 21, 2011.

19 See Report of the Director General on his consultations on NAMA Sectoral negotiations, WTO document, TN/C/14, April 21, 2011 and cover note by the chair forwarding the reports of the various chairpersons on the development in the negotiations TN/C/13, April 21, 2011.

20 For more detailed analysis of the issue see Narlikar, A. 2005. International Trade and Developing Countries Bargaining Coalition in GATT and WTO. London: Rutledge, pp. 82-104·

21 Ibid. pp. 126-154.

22 This target date was accepted under the assumption that the Round would be completed by 2006. The LDCs are pressing that the obligation to provide duty free access should apply to all of their imports.

23 For more detailed description of the work done by the Group see Rege, V. 2011. Negotiating at the World Trade Organization, Lessons from the Commonwealth No. 2. London: Commonwealth Secretariat.

24 These countries are referred to often as Paragraph 6 countries as the provisions for extension of such treatment appeared for the first time in Paragraph 6 of the Cancun Declaration.

25 Schwab, S. C. 2011. 'After Doha – Why the Negotiations Are Doomed and What We Should Do About It', *Foreign Affairs*, Volume 90, No. 3. May/June 2011: 104-117.

26 See WTO Reporter, May, 26, 2011: Doha Round, EU Trade Chief cites Need to Review Developing Nation Flexibilities in Doha Talks.

27 It is relevant to note in this context that in the Generalised System of Preferences, the EU treats Russia as a developing country and provides to its imports preferential access. Proposals to exclude from the list of beneficiaries countries like Russia, Brazil and other developing countries that are at higher stages of development are being considered by the European Commission.

28 Chairman's Remarks, Informal Meeting of Heads of State, JOB/TNC/11, May, 31, 2011.

29 In his statement at the Informal TNC meeting held on April, 29, 2011, Pascal Lamy stated that his consultations indicate that proposals for abandoning the negotiations have not received support from any of the delegations.

30 Beattie, A. 2011. 'Time to Limit the Doha Damage'. *Financial Times*, May 2, 2011.

31 For a more detailed explanation of the assessment that has been made by different research institutions of the benefits that would accrue to developing countries from further liberalisation of trade, see Rege, *V. 2011. Negotiating at the World Trade Organization, Lessons from the Commonwealth No. 2. London: Commonwealth Secretariat*, pp. 115-121.

32 These countries would be treated as SVEs under the modalities that would apply for reductions in tariffs in the agricultural sector. The list of countries that would be treated as SVEs for reductions in tariffs on non agricultural products is slightly different.

Substantive Negotiating Issues

2

Agriculture – At the Centre of DDA Negotiations

Roberto Azevêdo
Ambassador of Brazil to the WTO

Braz Baracuhy
WTO agriculture negotiator & G-20 coordinator Mission of Brazil to the WTO

Introduction

Agriculture is the central component and the driving force of the Doha Development Agenda (DDA). Insufficiently regulated during the years when international trade was under the General Agreement on Tariffs and Trade (GATT), agriculture has effectively been brought into the multilateral trading system only very recently. Current rules accommodate decades of trade-distorting policies and practices by the developed world; thus, agriculture trade reform is the challenge and main objective of the Doha Round.

The Doha Round started in 2001 with the goal of reforming and strengthening the current international trading rules. Agriculture reform was the main reason for the launching of a new Round of trade negotiations. In 1995, members of the newly created World Trade Organisation (WTO) promptly recognised the unfinished business of agriculture reform. Article 20 of the Uruguay Round Agreement on Agriculture mandated the continuation of the reform process:

> Recognising that the long-term objective of substantial progressive reductions in support and protection resulting in fundamental reform is an ongoing process, Members agree that negotiations for continuing the process will be initiated one year before the end of the implementation period.

The origins of the Doha Round mandate lie in this single paragraph of the Agreement on Agriculture. Certain trading powers and, particularly, the European Union (EU) insisted that, in the absence of a new round – with a broad agenda, including industrial goods, services and rules on new topics such as investment, competition policy and trade and environment – it would not be possible to meaningfully liberalise its agricultural regime.

The Doha Round negotiations comprise a complex set of actors, interests and geometries that need to be balanced out under the negotiating principle known as "single undertaking." Therefore, the final level of ambition of the Round is supposed to reflect an overall balance of trade-offs. After ten years of negotiations, the current deadlock in the DDA reveals the impasse between established and new actors; between the unresolved past of trade rules and new challenges of the trade regime. Agriculture reform incorporates all these impasses and remains the key to the eventual conclusion of the Doha Round.

But why is agriculture – a sector that accounts for just 9.6 percent of total world trade according to WTO statistics – so important? First, agriculture rules are a symbol of protectionism and distortions in world trade. Developed countries normally protect their agricultural sectors with a mixture of subsidies and market access barriers. Despite the history of the GATT, agriculture was not brought into the multilateral trading system until 1995 as a result of the Uruguay Round. Second, agriculture is an essential component of the economies of a large number of developing countries, where the majority of the workforce is employed in the agriculture sector and thus livelihoods depend on it. Many of these countries face difficulties not only in selling to the developed country markets, but also they have to compete with subsidised products from advanced economies.

Thus, reforming agricultural trade disciplines to level the playing field of multilateral rules and to bring the development dimension into the WTO is at the heart of the Doha Round. A successful conclusion of the DDA in line with the Doha Mandate for Agriculture would be of significant importance to all developing countries.

Agriculture: From GATT to the WTO

Agriculture has traditionally enjoyed a distinct status in international trade negotiations. After World War II, the idea that agricultural products should not be treated as regular goods gained strength, and this was reflected in the GATT architecture.

After that, policies were driven by the notion that countries should be self-sufficient in food production. Food security was synonymous with self-sufficiency.[1] Overcoming natural comparative disadvantages in agriculture required not only massive governmental resources, but also protection of domestic markets from competition. That led to a further spurt in agricultural protectionism in developed countries. Given its status as a sector of economic activity that deserved special treatment, so went the idea, agriculture was not to be treated as a bargaining chip at the multilateral negotiating table.

This political decision came with mythology attached to it. Some of the rich countries managed to portray a canvas of an idealised rural life that had to be protected – for it would be linked to their "roots," or to the "natural way of life." Furthermore, the agricultural sector in developed countries is small, but very well organised and politically connected. Also, since the share of consumers' budgets allocated to food in rich countries is relatively small, non-farmers have little incentive to support reform, as the additional costs deriving from agricultural protectionism are relatively marginal. This is the logic of the collective action in political economy applied to agriculture.

As a consequence, developed country markets for agriculture were in practice exempt from implementing the GATT; thus, they became the wonderland of subsidies and market barriers. Layers of protectionism accumulated over decades with respect to agriculture, while trade liberalisation proceeded in industrial goods.

During the Uruguay Round (1986-1994), agriculture was brought to the negotiating table for the first time. The Uruguay Round Ministerial Declaration made an explicit reference to liberalisation in the three pillars of agricultural trade policy: market access, domestic support, and export subsidies.

The Uruguay Round was also the first to involve a significant number of negotiating areas. Negotiations were shaped as an integral package. This is the idea of a so-called single undertaking: nothing is agreed until everything is agreed. The principle allows for trade-offs in different sectors of the negotiation. Agricultural trade was brought into the system – a demand from developing countries – in exchange for the introduction of trade-related aspects of intellectual property rights (TRIPs) and trade-related investment measures (TRIMs) – a demand from developed countries. This was the "big bargain": to regulate what was perceived to be the trade of the future – intellectual property rights and investments – in a system that would finally deal with the most unregulated trade area of the past, agriculture.

The Uruguay Round bid farewell to a certain configuration of power in the world economy and a certain way of doing business in trade negotiations. The power configuration at the establishment of the GATT and throughout its rounds of negotiations was clear: the US and Europe were the trade powers and rule-setters of the multilateral trade regime. The *Quad* (the US, Europe, Japan and Canada) was the decision-making powerhouse of the Uruguay Round. Its conclusion came only after an agreement was struck between the US and Europe on agriculture (Blair House, 1992) and presented to the whole membership as a *fait-accompli*. The bargain accommodated their reciprocal interests. As a result, agriculture remained the most distorted part of international trade, with intricate layers of tariff barriers and subsidies, lagging behind other areas in terms of regulation and disciplines favouring liberalisation.

Agricultural tariffs were bound and reduced, quantitative restrictions were removed (although the "tariffication" process permitted countries to add their tariff equivalence to the existing tariffs, resulting in a substantial increase in protection levels) and disciplines were developed to constrain the use of domestic support and export subsidies. The Agreement on Agriculture was certainly a step in the right direction, but by no means a sufficient one.

After the Seattle debacle in 1999, when it was not possible to launch the Millennium Round, this reasoning gained increased acceptance, and the tragic events in New York in 2001 generated the necessary political impetus for the launching of a round at the WTO Ministerial in the capital of Qatar. The negotiating effort initiated in Doha represented a long overdue collective commitment to do away with protectionist barriers and trade distorting policies in an area of vital importance to competitive exporters from both the developed and the developing world, as well as to poor farmers in non-subsidizing countries.

Agriculture Negotiations in the Doha Round

The negotiations of the DDA were set in motion in 2002. The initial expectation was to complete the Round by 2005. The Doha Mandate in Agriculture was ambitious: substantial access to markets, substantial reduction of domestic support subsidies and the elimination of export subsidies. If development was the goal, agriculture had to be the driving force, or so the developing world believed and hoped.

It is possible to divide the negotiations into four phases, each of them with different actors, issues and configurations:

- from 2001 to the 2003 Cancún Ministerial, when "business as usual" confronted new forces;
- from 2004 to the 2005 Hong Kong Ministerial, with the definition of key concepts and landing zones for the agricultural negotiations;
- from 2006 to the July 2008 Mini-Ministerial in Geneva, with the definition of the general level of ambition; and
- from 2008 to this day, with the US attempt to redefine the level of ambition.

From 2001 to the 2003 Cancún Ministerial

Little progress was made in the early years of the Round in fulfilling the ambitious goals of the Doha Ministerial Declaration (November, 14, 2001), which pointed to agreement on modalities in agriculture by March, 31, 2003 and to concluding the Round by January 2005.

The initial solidarity and pledges of international cooperation in the Doha Ministerial Conference in the months following the 9/11 terrorist attacks did not translate into negotiated outcomes. The years 2002 and 2003 were mostly devoted to domestic discussions in the major trading partners aimed at defining their respective medium and long-term agricultural policy objectives, which would shape their negotiating mandates – the reform of the European Common Agriculture Policy (CAP) and the US Farm Bill. It was expected that, once concluded, these reforms would constitute the basis for a multilateral agreement on agriculture at the WTO. The US was divided between offensive and protectionist domestic interests. This situation offered the driving seat to Europe, which seized the opportunity to advance its view of the Round: modest new market access, preservation of the core features of its subsidy programmes with a continued shift towards the green box and the development dimension being met through the preservation of its system of preferences granted mostly to ex-colonies. This was perfectly consistent with the goals of the even more protectionist members, such as Japan, Norway and Switzerland.

The seeds of closer cooperation among developing countries, in particular, Brazil, China and India, were being planted. Early in 2002, India was defending an intermediary path in the agricultural negotiations, somewhere between the liberalising mantra of the Cairns

Group and the protectionist approach of the US and the EU. Both the need to protect its poor rural population and the emphasis on the development dimension appear in India's initial positions in the Round. Having just acceded to the WTO in 2001 and having paid dearly for that in terms of commitments in agriculture, China sympathised with the need for ensuring some policy space for its poor rural population. Despite being a member of the Cairns Group, which naturally favoured better market access conditions, Brazil understood the systemic value of the Doha Round and the priority accorded to also reforming the domestic support and export competition pillars of agriculture. The high level of ambition sought by the Cairns Group in market access did not adequately differentiate between developed and developing markets, which naturally posed problems for China and India, among other net-food importing developing countries. Thus, the potential of balancing offensive and defensive interests in market access to favour higher levels of ambition in subsidy reforms and to enhance the development dimension of the Round were taking shape. Here would lay the strength of the still unborn G-20.

The lack of progress naturally led to uncertainties about the tight deadlines set in Doha and anxieties about an understanding between developed countries – the EU and the US in particular – at the expense of developing countries' interests and concerns. The traumas of the Uruguay Round were very much alive. A credible result in agriculture was the *raison d'être* of the Doha Round. And yet, early signs seemed to augur a different outcome, one which would prioritise areas of interest for the rich nations – such as the so-called Singapore issues (investments, competition, trade facilitation and government procurement). The "development agenda" of the Round was quickly fading.

The first substantive negotiating proposals from the key delegations started to emerge in early 2002, while the Chairperson of the negotiating group for agriculture, Stuart Harbinson, circulated its "overview paper" on December 18, 2002. The first draft modalities for agriculture (TN/AG/W/1) were circulated on February 17, 2003. The stage was set for substantive negotiations to comply with the March 2003 deadline for modalities.

This was the first deadline to be missed, establishing a pattern that prevailed in the period since then. The CAP reform was delayed in light of complications arising from the EU enlargement, extinguishing all negotiating room for the Commission in Geneva. Since agriculture was the core and engine of the Round, other groups and countries were not prepared to move in parallel in other areas of the negotiations. In mid-2003, frustration was mounting to the point that the United States Trade Representative (USTR), Robert Zoellick, threatened members with a new Blair House: "If things don't move, I will decide everything with Pascal (Lamy, then EC Trade Commissioner) and whoever cares to join us." And indeed the Montreal Mini-Ministerial in late July witnessed renewed requests for the EU and the US to exercise leadership and to agree on a framework to move negotiations forward. The lack of movement in agricultural negotiations between the US and the EU continued to block advances in Geneva.

Calls for reviving a dying world order were becoming louder, as if a new Blair House agreement could replace the lack of negotiating will. The EU and the US tabled a joint framework paper on August, 13, 2003 (Job (03)/157) – four weeks ahead of the Cancún Ministerial. The framework agreement – a set of parameters for the elaboration of modalities – accommodated their interests in agriculture in terms of market access, domestic support and export subsidies. The self-serving character of this accommodation did not escape the membership. Moreover, the Doha mandate could hardly be considered as fulfilled under the terms of the EU-US proposal. Those bilaterally agreed parameters were duly reflected in the draft Ministerial Declaration for Cancún, elaborated by the Chairman of the General Council, Perez del Castillo (Job(03)/150/Rev.1). Given the experience of past negotiations, many thought that the joint proposal would be the "realistic" landing zone for an agreement.

Following the presentation of the joint EU-US proposal, conditions were set for the establishment of a new force in the negotiations: the G-20.[2] The first contribution by this new coalition of developing countries was a framework proposal tabled on August, 20, 2003 [Job (03)/162]. It resulted from discreet consultations between Brazil and a core group of developing countries that, with the onset of the negotiating crisis, quickly expanded to incorporate developing countries from Africa, Asia and Latin America. The G-20 proposal was ambitious in the reduction of subsidies and contained a market access formula differentiating developed and developing countries. The key elements were given: adherence to the Doha mandate in terms of ambition in the three pillars with special treatment provisions for developing countries.

The G-20 proposal created an immediate dilemma for developed countries: to keep the joint agreement and try to push for an outcome in Cancún based on the Perez del Castillo text or to engage with the G-20 and try to find a middle ground. After intense discussions in Geneva, the Chair's text arrived in Cancún with low credibility, despite the efforts of the US and the EU to bring onboard their traditional allies both in the developed and the developing world. What few people fully appreciated before Cancún was the fact that a third force, the G-20, now joined the US and the EU at the centre of the negotiating chessboard. The balance of necessary and sufficient conditions for an agreement had changed. Very few realised at the time that the "natural order" of the old GATT had expired.

Brazil's economic diplomacy in the WTO had been growing in activism in the previous years (the cotton case against the US and the sugar case against the EU, as well as the role played in the negotiation of the TRIPs and Public Heath Declaration). Those actions embodied key messages of the G-20: the need to reform agricultural rules and to boost the development dimension of trade.

In the Cancún Ministerial, a draft Ministerial Declaration known informally as the "Derbez text" was circulated on September 13, 2003 and incorporated, with few modifications, the Del Castillo text in agriculture. The G-20 not only blocked the agreement, displaying its political weight, but also proposed technically sound alternatives. In order to succeed, negotiations clearly had to go beyond the instructions the EU and the US negotiators had at that time. In other words, the mere overlap of their respective zones of comfort in agriculture would not suffice. All too late, both realised the strength, determination and operational capacity of the G-20. Contrary to past experiences with developing country coalitions, the G-20 resisted pressures and was able not only to counter the attempts to divide the group, but also to come forward with credible negotiating proposals. The G-20 and Cancún were what theory of negotiations calls a "critical moment": when a fundamental shift redefines the structure and the process of negotiations. The G-20 coordinated and organised the central demands of the developing world and offered a legitimate and operative channel for negotiations in agriculture.

The coalition's strength and consistency were tested in and after Cancún. The natural reaction from the developed world was to consider it just another old form of developing country coalition – temporarily effective to block agreements but unsustainable in the long run if appropriate divisive pressures were applied. The traditional lack of expertise of developing country coalitions, together with irreconcilable interests, would defeat the Group from within. However, the technical soundness of the Group and the new coherent and firmly determined forces it incorporated – Brazil, China, India and South Africa, among others – created a brand new political reality.

The G-20 is by any standard a significant group within the WTO. It encompasses almost 60 percent of the world's total population and 70 percent of the world's agricultural population. The group also accounts for more than 21 percent of the world's agricultural GDP. By bringing together developing countries, such as Argentina, Brazil, China, India and South Africa with different interests and from all regions of the developing world in a genuine desire to negotiate pragmatic solutions, the formation of the G-20 represents a first order political and symbolic change.

After the reality check of Cancun, the G-20 became an indispensable partner in the negotiations. It combined, in a single group, offensive and defensive agricultural interests, which strengthened its consensus-building vocation. Reflecting the internal balance of forces, the Group managed to develop common positions in technically solid and politically sound proposals. A comparison of the G-20 positions and the current draft modalities text in agriculture (TN/AG/W/4/Rev4) clearly shows the Group's success. In the three pillars of the negotiations, the positions of the G-20 are reflected both in terms of ambition – or very close to it – and architecture.

Observers were quick to point out the seeming paradox of the G-20: if major agricultural exporters, such as Argentina and Brazil seek more ambition, why should they construct an alliance with countries like China and India, both of which are net agricultural importers? Why did they not bet on a more cohesive and ambitious alliance of exporters?

However, what critics saw as a weakness of the G-20 (the conflicting interests of exporters and importers in a single coalition) was actually its strength: the group was able to build middle ground proposals that reflected almost perfectly the overall possible compromise among WTO members' positions. In brief, the G-20 is a good sample of the interests in agriculture of WTO developing members.

The G-20 sought in Cancún and continues to seek today a reform of the trade regime in agriculture to benefit developing countries, so that the multilateral trading system can redress the long historical imbalances created by the major subsidisers and act as an instrument of development.

An article by the USTR Robert Zoellick, "America will not wait for the Won't-do Countries," published in the *Financial Times* on September, 22, 2003, is a perfect example of how developments in Cancun were misperceived. After praising the virtues of del Castillo's text and the potential US reforms, he added:

> After the US pressed the EU to develop an agricultural framework that could achieve farm subsidy and tariff cuts far beyond those achieved in the last global trade negotiation, we asked Brazil and other agricultural powers to work with us. Brazil declined, turning instead to India, which has never supported opening markets, so as to emphasise north-south division not global agricultural reform.

Minister Celso Amorim put this in perspective in an article in the *Wall Street Journal*, "The Real Cancún," published on September, 25, 2003 – incidentally written before Zoellick's piece. Minister Amorim clearly defined the objectives of the G-20 and Brazil:

> We are not interested in North-South confrontation. To use an expression made popular by trade negotiators when combating protectionism under its many guises, our platform is about 'levelling the playing field', through the full integration of agriculture into the multilateral rules-based trading system. It is about addressing in a decisive manner the most important unfinished business of the Uruguay Round (should I say business that was never seriously taken up?). It is about honouring the terms of the Doha Development Agenda in an area unanimously viewed as its centrepiece.

Above all, Minister Amorim's message was one of change:

> The G-20 and other developing countries will not be reduced to the role of supporting actors in discussions that affect their development prospects. Consensus cannot be imposed through pre-cooked deals that disregard previous commitments and ignore the legitimate aspirations of the majority of the world's population.

A G-20 ministerial meeting held in Brasilia in December 2003 helped put negotiations back on track. The participation of the EU Trade Commissioner, Pascal Lamy, created the necessary platform of dialogue that was absent before and during Cancún.

From 2004 to the 2005 Hong Kong Ministerial

After Cancún negotiations resumed with the purpose of establishing a "framework" for agriculture – a midway frame of reference between the general mandate and the specific modalities. This was a clearly conceptual phase of the negotiations. The structure of the market access formula was central in the discussions during the first half of 2004 (the discussions on a "blended formula" finally shifting to a "tiered formula" with special and differential treatment). Tariff-rate quotas (TRQs) and some initial ideas were explored on market access flexibilities (sensitive products, special products and safeguards); the domestic support structure (overall cuts, product-specific disciplines and green box); and the elimination of export subsidies.

The G-20's sound technical contributions provided the basis for discussions. The negotiating process took different formats: the "Non-Group" of 5, also known as FIPs – "Five Interested Parties" (Australia, Brazil, the EU, India and the US), was a key forum for discussions. The presence of representatives of the G-20, the Cairns Group, and the G-33 gave it legitimacy and a means to keep the specific groupings and the membership engaged. On the political side, the G-20 often outreached for other developing-country groups. A particularly interesting development was the participation of Brazil, as coordinator of the G-20, in the G-90 ministerial meeting in Georgetown, on June 03, 2004. The commonality of concerns among developing countries on the centrality of agriculture and the development dimension was reinforced.

The Framework Agreement (WT/GC/W535) of August 01, 2004 (known as the "July Framework") represented an important substantive convergence of concepts and ambition. The G-20 positions and key issues of concern for developing countries were reflected in the draft framework for modalities in agriculture (Annex A): a cap for the overall trade-distorting domestic support (OTDS); cotton, the tiered formula, special products (SPs) and the SSM, among others. The document Job (04)/96, prepared by the Chairman of the agricultural negotiations, Tim Groser, was also an important element for reaching convergence. Groser and his successor, Crawford Falconer, both understood the moderating force of the G-20 and its capacity for engineering constructive and creative solutions.

The July Framework represented the end of the beginning of the agricultural negotiations. It vindicated the efforts of Brazil and the G-20 in Cancun. The FIPs and their outreach combined with the multilateral discussions created a new paradigm of decision, beyond the US-EU top-down format. Just one year after the tabling of the EU-US joint proposal, conversations were based on a text negotiated directly between developed and developing members. The July Framework marked the end of the duopoly in WTO decision-making.

The new target deadline for establishing modalities became the ministerial meeting scheduled for December 2005 in Hong Kong.

Once the negotiating structure was defined, the key issues moved to the level of ambition (cuts in subsidies, disciplines per product, formula cuts, TRQ expansion, etc).

A lot of effort in the multilateral process was dedicated to the somewhat Byzantine question of the *ad valorem* equivalents (AVEs) conversion – i.e., the methodology to convert non-*ad-valorem* duties into AVEs for the purpose of placing them in the tiered formula bands. But most of the substantive work was concentrated on the development of a "first approximation" paper that could establish some benchmarks in terms of ambition and trade-offs for Hong Kong. However, very marginal progress happened between July 2004 and the Hong Kong Ministerial. The G-20 tabled proposals in the three pillars of negotiations (domestic support cuts, green box, blue box, market access and export subsidies). Chairman Groser helped with two status reports of negotiations (Job (05)/126, June 27, 2005; and TN/AG/19, August 01, 2005) capturing the *acquis* of negotiations and recognising the G-20 contributions to the process.

But, the basic problem remained: the EU tried to minimise concessions in market access, while the US moved increasingly toward a defensive position in cuts and disciplines for domestic subsidies. In addition, further complicating the picture, the US refused to make any movement in domestic support until it had clarity on market access gains – a pattern that would be renewed in later stages of the negotiations.

The second semester of 2005 continued with meetings of the FIPs and the multilateral process in agriculture now conducted by Crawford Falconer. The lack of progress in agriculture hindered progress in other areas of the Doha Round, such as Non-agricultural market access (NAMA) and services. The notion of an equivalent horizontal level of ambition, having agriculture as its benchmark, was the position held by Brazil and the G-20. But on the road to Hong Kong, a series of movements determined what would be the basic dynamics of the Ministerial. The US presented a more ambitious proposal for the reduction of domestic support in the beginning of October; a few days later, the G-20 also tabled its own proposals on domestic support – correcting some bias of the US proposal – and on market access. That led to the isolation of the EU in market access.

By the end of October, the EU felt compelled to circulate its "proposal to move forward the DDA negotiations." But, technical analysis clearly showed the limits of the concessions in market access, despite Trade Commissioner, Peter Mandelson's best efforts in the media to prove otherwise. A letter by the EC, circulated on December, 01, 2005, tried to frame its views on possible outcomes for Hong Kong in all areas of the negotiation. Ideas for market access fell quite short of expectations. At the political level, Brazilian President Lula da Silva, US President Bush and UK Prime-Minister Blair became more involved with the Round and signalled commitment to its successful outcome.

The linkages between agriculture and industrial goods became increasingly evident. Pushing for market access in NAMA, particularly in developing country markets, was the way the EU found to counter the offensive it was under in agriculture. According to the EU, the demands from the G-20 and the US in agriculture had to find parallel efforts by developing countries in opening their markets for industrial goods and services. But the argument did not carry the day. The G-20 position – and indeed the position of the developing world as a whole – that agriculture should determine the level of ambition was politically well established and on solid ground. Agricultural reform in the developed world was the unfinished business of the Uruguay Round and of all previous rounds.

The Hong Kong Ministerial of December 2005 brought modest but far from insignificant outcomes. It was not possible to solve the market access conundrum in agriculture. The unity among developing countries was strengthened in Hong Kong and the historical declaration of the "G-110" (G-20, G-33, ACP, LDCs, NAMA-11, African Group and SVEs), recalled that agriculture was central to development. But important issues for the G-20 and other developing country groups were present in the Hong Kong Ministerial Declaration [WT/MIN (05)/DEC, December 18, 2005]:

- reiteration of key concepts in domestic support and market access;
- elimination of export subsidies by 2013;
- parallelism between agriculture market access and NAMA, with the former determining the level of ambition of the latter, established in Paragraph 24 of the Ministerial declaration;
- guidelines for DFQFMA for the LDCs; and
- specific provisions for cotton.

It should be recalled that, back in 2003, Benin, Burkina Faso, Chad and Mali formed the Cotton-4 and tabled a proposal concerning specific measures for cotton. These required substantive reforms in cotton subsidies in developed economies, whose effects on international prices had been demonstrated by the Brazil-US Cotton Panel. This specific initiative of the Cotton-4 would lead to the Hong Kong mandate in 2005, reiterating the 2004 framework, to address cotton "specifically, expeditiously and ambitiously."

As it became clear it would be difficult to establish modalities in Hong Kong, new deadlines were set: to conclude modalities by April 30, 2006 with a view to finish the Round by the end of 2006.

From 2006 to the July 2008 Mini-Ministerial in Geneva

After Hong Kong, negotiations resumed in Geneva until they were officially suspended by the Director-General, Pascal Lamy, in July 2006. The substantive conundrum remained. The EU felt strengthened by the support of its member states for not having made concessions during the 2005 Ministerial and tried again to change the focus to NAMA – thus shifting the basic idea that agriculture would determine the level of ambition. In order to divert its difficulties to conclude modalities, the EU sought bilateral discussions, in which developing countries should make better offers in NAMA. This prospect of bilaterals created opportunities for agricultural quota-based negotiations with the US and, by consequence, the possibility of a renewed *entente* on market access/domestic support to lower the level of ambition in Blair House style.

In the plurilateral formats, negotiations moved from the FIPs to the G-6 (Australia, Brazil, the EU, India, Japan and the US) and the G-4 (Brazil, the EU, India and the US) starting in Davos in January 2006. The absence of China in these critical geometries would only be remedied in 2008.

As discussions focused on agriculture and NAMA, the game moved to twisting the interpretation of paragraph 24 of the Hong Kong declaration: instead of agriculture determining the ambition in NAMA, the EU and Japan would argue that the declaration puts both at the same level and thus it would be inappropriate to declare agriculture the engine of negotiations.

The substantive shape of negotiations gradually evolved to form a negotiating triangle that had to be solved in order to unlock discussions: (i) cuts in subsidies by the US (OTDS and product-specific disciplines); (ii) agricultural market access in Europe (cuts, quota expansion and flexibilities); and (iii) industrial market access in developing countries (NAMA coefficient/flexibilities). The discussions on flexibilities for developed countries, in particular the sensitive products (SPs), began to gain importance as the overall level of cuts moved toward better defined landing zones.

The direct involvement of ministers and the mix of plurilateral and multilateral processes were not enough. Crawford Falconer issued a series of "reference papers" and finally his first draft modalities text (TN/AG/W/3, July 12, 2006). But the deadlines for the first half of 2006 were all missed. And Director-General Lamy suspended ministerial talks on July 24, 2006.

To further complicate this scenario, the imminent expiration of the US Trade Promotion Authority (TPA) increased the level of uncertainty in Geneva. Since its expiration in 2007, it has not yet been renewed. Furthermore, the G-33 raised its profile and put pressure on discussions over SPs and the SSM.

After the impulse given by a G-20 Ministerial Meeting together with the coordinators of developing country groups (African Group, ACP, Caricom, C4, LDCs and SVEs) in Rio de Janeiro (9-10 September 2006), an intensive multilateral process resumed in Geneva from late 2006 until the July 2008 Mini-Ministerial.

Agricultural negotiations intensified in Geneva under the leadership of Crawford Falconer. Meetings also continued in bilateral and plurilateral formats involving mostly Brazil, the EU, India and the US. The structure and level of ambition of the domestic support and market access pillars were central in those plurilateral discussions. The understanding of the negotiating triangle improved but there was no convergence in terms of landing zones. Brazil approached these bilateral and plurilateral meetings as a contribution – and not a pre-condition – to the multilateral progress in Geneva. Falconer's "challenge papers" from April to May 2007 pushed forward and tested the limits of negotiators. The G-20 positions continued to constitute the centre of gravity in the headline issues. But, while Falconer tried to accommodate all concerns in terms of the landing zones, discussions conducted in the NAMA negotiating group moved in a different direction. This would create a significant imbalance that still persists with respect to the reduction of the level of ambition in agriculture to accommodate sensitivities and allow for a conclusion on the one hand, and the lack of will to accommodate developing country concerns in NAMA on the other.

In parallel, the G-20 continued its effort to address the core issues of the unresolved negotiating triangle. The G-4 Ministerial in Potsdam, Germany, in July 2007 was yet another shot at a Blair House-like attempt by developed members, seeking to reverse the logic that agriculture determines the level of ambition and joining forces in NAMA. The failure of Potsdam was, in retrospect, a positive outcome. It empowered the multilateral process in Geneva and provided additional time to explore solutions on the complex issues of SPs – finally settled in the first half of 2008 after intensive months of plurilateral negotiations, involving Australia, Brazil, Canada, the EU and the US together with outreach members.

In the aftermath of the Potsdam failure, the multilateral process gained impetus in Geneva and legitimised the efforts of Falconer in searching for convergences. New draft modalities were circulated in mid-July – later to become TN/AG/W/4 (August, 01, 2007). Accommodating sensitivities of developed and developing countries in exchange for the sustainability of the package was the route chosen to advance negotiations. This was the case in the ranges for the OTDS cuts and for SPs. The result, of course, was the downgrading of ambition – but carefully done so as not to compromise the mandate. The exact opposite was sought in the new NAMA draft text. Thus, the two texts together reinforced the imbalance and the reversal of the logic of agriculture as the engine of the Round.

Nonetheless, based on the new text, a number of contributions from the G-20 and an intensive schedule of negotiations under different configurations and formats, the Agriculture Negotiating Group produced several working papers and three revisions of the modalities text: TN/AG/W/4/Rev.1, February 08, 2008, TN/AG/W/4/Rev.2, May 19, 2008 and TN/AG/W/4/Rev.3, July 10, 2008.

This last text was the basis for the July 2008 Mini-Ministerial. During nine days of negotiations in open-ended format and green rooms, Director-General Pascal Lamy attempted to extract a necessary – but not sufficient – agreement from the Ministers of the G-7 (Australia, Brazil, China, India, Japan and the US). Facing the near collapse of negotiations, Director-General Lamy tried his hand on a package that captured balances and trade-offs in the central issues of the agriculture and NAMA negotiations. But an insurmountable impasse involving the SSM precluded further progress and, ultimately, the conclusion of modalities at that time.

2008 to Today: New Ambition?

A few weeks after this failure to conclude modalities, the onset of the global financial crisis in September 2008 created a new and completely different scenario. The Group of Twenty Finance Ministers and Central Bank Governors (G-20) met in Washington in November 2008 and protectionism loomed in the horizon. The US became even more averse to trade liberalisation – except of course in areas in which it still felt competitive.

A last push was attempted from September to December 2008. The new negotiating triangle involved: (i) cuts in subsidies for US cotton; (ii) market access in developing countries in agriculture (SP/SSM); and (iii) industrial goods market access in developing countries (sectorals in NAMA).

Some progress was made on the understanding of the SSM among Australia, Brazil, China, the EU, India and the US. Falconer also addressed other areas of negotiation and, most importantly, reflected Director-General Lamy's July 2008 package of trade-offs to produce his TN/AG/W/4/Rev. 4 (December, 06, 2008). Plans for a new Ministerial in that month – the last one for the US Bush Administration – failed.

Under pressure from its private sector, the US resorted to demands for reopening selectively the July 2008 package and to push for bilaterals with the so called "advanced developing countries" (i.e. China, India and Brazil), seeking more market access in areas of its specific export interest. This approach effectively negated years of trade-offs in negotiations and upset the embedded equilibrium reflected in the December 2008 texts.

In the last WTO Ministerial Meetings in Geneva (December 2009), the vast majority of developed and developing countries sent an unequivocal message to preserve the package; still negotiations could not be concluded after more than two years since July 2008 and ten years of negotiations.

A new cycle of discussions in agriculture started in September 2009 under the leadership of a new Chairman for agriculture, David Walker, from New Zealand (as his two predecessors, Groser and Falconer). Discussions followed two different tracks: (i) substantive issues, which are bracketed/annotated in the December 2008 draft modalities for agriculture; and (ii) templates, i.e., an examination of data requirements to operationalise the modalities text and the scheduling of future commitments. More broadly, Director-General Lamy set up a "cocktail approach" – mixing different ingredients and different configurations in trying to reach convergences.

Two general principles have guided Brazil and the G-20's positions in the substantive discussions on agriculture:

- The December 2008 draft modalities are the basis for negotiations and represent the end-game in terms of the landing zones of ambition. Any marginal adjustments in the level of ambition of those texts may be assessed only in the context of the overall balance of trade-offs, bearing in mind that agriculture is the engine of the Round; and
- The draft modalities embody a delicate balance achieved after ten years of negotiations. This equilibrium cannot be ignored or upset, or we will need readjustments of the entire package with horizontal repercussions. Such readjustments cannot entail additional unilateral concessions from developing countries.

Most would agree that, over those many years of negotiations and trade-offs, it was certainly possible to craft a Doha package that is both balanced and ambitious across all areas of the negotiations. Nonetheless, the Doha Round remains deadlocked since July 2008, as the US continues to express its dissatisfaction with the package and to demand "more ambition" – i.e., more market access in sectors where it feels competitive in global trade, while disregarding flexibilities it secured as a result of trade-offs. Despite continuous efforts in Geneva, progress remains elusive.

Conclusion

The Doha Round is already the most ambitious in the history of the GATT/WTO system. The draft texts tabled in 2008 in agriculture and NAMA brought the Round very close to an agreement. The texts incorporate a decade of bargaining history. From the perspective of a developing country, like Brazil, attempts to reopen the package to extract further concessions from it would not be feasible without a major rebalancing of the trade-offs and the overall level of ambition achieved so far. This would send the negotiations back several years, if not condemn the Round to an insurmountable stalemate and final failure.

The credibility of the WTO to deal with the new challenges of this century relies considerably on the conclusion of the Doha Round in accordance with the mandate and taking into consideration the concerns of developing countries. Failure will have significant implications for the WTO as an institution and for the rules-based multilateral trading system. It will create incentives for more protectionism, more fragmentation of international trade and more instability.

The Doha Round will be concluded when balance and ambition are truly recognised as guiding principles. The contribution of developing countries in this Round is already unprecedented. The new multilateral trade regime in agriculture needs to complete the reform process that started in the Uruguay Round. It should redress historical imbalances and serve as an instrument for development. This is the only way to firmly set the course in the direction of a multilateral trading system that is credible, legitimate and development friendly.

Endnotes

1 This idea still finds echoes today. During the 2008 high prices in commodities, the UN rapporteur proposed this idea as a solution to the world's food security problems. He failed to consider the fact that food security is about the availability of food. It requires the generation of income and trade.

2 Current membership includes Argentina, Bolivia, Brazil, Chile, China, Cuba, Ecuador, Egypt, Guatemala, India, Indonesia, Mexico, Nigeria, Pakistan, Paraguay, Peru, Philippines, South Africa, Tanzania, Thailand, Uruguay, Venezuela and Zimbabwe.

3 Non-Agricultural Market Access (NAMA) – Balancing Development and Ambition

Shree B.C. Servansingh
Ambassador of Mauritius to the UN and other International Organisations including WTO

Introduction

Both agriculture and non-agricultural market access (NAMA) - or more commonly negotiations on industrial goods - attracted public attention in the Doha Development Agenda (DDA) negotiations, probably because market access gains through lowering of tariffs were more directly quantifiable. In the initial period of the DDA negotiations, agriculture monopolised most of the attention and engaged the energies of both negotiators and the media. Agriculture was considered by many to be the engine of the DDA in terms of sequencing and ambition.[1] Ironically, it now turns out that the potential complexity of NAMA was underestimated, as deep underlying differences in NAMA now cast a long shadow on the outcome of the DDA negotiations. Differences are proving to be more intractable in NAMA than in agriculture, and the DDA stalemate at present is primarily, though not exclusively, the consequence of huge divergences in NAMA among some of the major players. In fact, the WTO Director-General Pascal Lamy believes that NAMA sectorals are a gateway issue for the negotiations.[2]

It could be argued that the NAMA negotiations went through three phases. The initial phase can be said to be from the launch of the DDA in 2001 to the Hong Kong Ministerial Conference in December 2005. This phase could be characterised as one in which NAMA was still stymied in the shadow of agriculture and where the agenda of the NAMA negotiations was still being framed. A second phase began after Hong Kong and continued until the collapse of the July mini-Ministerial in 2008. It was a phase marked by polarisation, where the concept of enhanced market access and new trade flows clashed with the concept of less than full reciprocity and comparability of market access outcomes in NAMA and agriculture. The third phase could be said to have started in 2010, following instructions from G-20 world leaders and the resultant intensification of the process in Geneva. It was a phase marked by the debate over the issue of ambition in which NAMA issues exploded to the forefront of the DDA and led to the present impasse.

This chapter seeks to analyse the evolution of the negotiations in NAMA, more particularly from a developing country's perspective, and discuss the gains made by some developing countries and the gaps that remain for other developing countries, the different approaches/strategies used to negotiate outcomes and the political complexities that engulfed the NAMA negotiations after 2008 in the context of the global economic crisis and political constraints of different constituencies.

Industrial Tariffs and Trade Policy

The importance and weight of industrial goods in the global economy cannot be overemphasised. Industrial goods outside of agriculture constitute 94 percent of global merchandise trade, and this trade is concentrated not only in the developed countries, but also in more advanced developing countries. This is why developed countries insist on the concept of critical mass for participation in sectorals. Developing countries view the industrial goods sector in their countries in the context of their industrial development and the need to close their competitiveness gap with their developed counterparts, hence the need to avoid deep tariff cuts that could lead to deindustrialisation.

World Trade in Goods, by product category in the DDA Negotiations (1999-2005)[3]

Table 1: Share of the World (percentage)							
	1999	2000	2001	2002	2003	2004	2005
World Exports							
Agriculture products	7.1	6.1	6.7	6.8	6.7	6.2	5.9
Non-Agriculture products	92.9	93.9	93.3	93.2	93.3	93.8	94.1
TOTAL	100	100	100	100	100	100	100

It is beyond the scope of this chapter to analytically review the pros and cons of the role of tariffs as trade policy tools. Views differ enormously from one extreme, where proponents of unbridled trade liberalisation consider free trade as the vehicle for development, to another extreme, where others believe that some protectionism is necessary for domestic policy space and sovereign national development. These issues have not failed to permeate the NAMA discussions in the DDA. Generally, developed countries and other proponents of market opening have argued that trade opening facilitates development and the fact that South-South trade is increasing, tariff liberalisation in the South can only benefit developing countries. The developing countries on the other hand, emphasise the importance of tariffs as tools to promote industrial development domestically, protect infant industries, and create employment and revenue generation. Moreover, many developing countries do not have trade defence mechanisms (safeguards and anti-dumping) or find it too cumbersome to utilise them, so they rely mainly on tariffs as remedial measures. This is why the difference between applied and bound tariffs is important for developing countries in the WTO. Such differences in perceptions over tariffs as policy tools or obstacles and the asymmetry of competitiveness between developed and developing countries in the industrial goods sector have certainly informed the positions of negotiators in the NAMA discussions.

The DDA Mandate and Initial Phase of Negotiations

The specific mandate for industrial goods negotiations in the DDA is governed by paragraph 16 of the Doha Ministerial Declaration which states:

> We agree to negotiations which shall aim, by modalities to be agreed, to reduce or as appropriate eliminate tariffs, including the reduction or elimination of tariff peaks, high tariffs, and tariff escalation, as well as non-tariff barriers, in particular on products of export interest to developing countries. Product coverage shall be comprehensive and without *a priori* exclusions. The negotiations shall take fully into account the special needs and interests of developing and least—developed countries participants, including through less than full reciprocity in reduction commitments, in accordance with the relevant provisions of Article XXVIII bis of GATT 1994 and the provisions cited in paragraph 50 below. To this end, the modalities to be agreed will include appropriate studies and capacity-building measures to assist least-developed countries to participate effectively in the negotiations.[4]

Unwittingly, the scope of the mandate was broad and deep and already in its conception indicated the depth of ambition in NAMA by calling for tariff harmonisation through "reduction or elimination of tariff peaks, high tariffs and tariff escalation." It did not specifically contain restrictions on the extent and scope of applicability to developing countries except by stipulating that the negotiations will take into account interests of developing and least-developed countries (LDCs), including through less than full reciprocity.

It was understandable in this context that the initial elements of modalities of the first Chair of the NAMA Negotiating Group, Ambassador Girard, in May 2003 went more in the direction of accentuating ambition rather than special and differential (S&D) treatment or development concerns.[5] This was significantly borne out by an early pressure on the Chair to choose a Swiss-like formula, which is a non-linear approach known for its deep impact on cutting tariff peaks and high tariffs. The Girard proposals in fact contained a full cocktail that foreshadowed at that early stage an impending clash over ambition in NAMA. The Girard proposals comprised a modified Swiss formula for tariff reduction, a sectoral approach including zero for zero sectoral harmonisation, special and differential provisions, the special case of recently acceded members (RAMs) and non-tariff-barriers (NTBs.)

In the aftermath of the Girard proposals and prior to the Cancun Ministerial Conference of 2003, the debate in the NAMA negotiations started delving into the complexity of S&D issues, which was not clearly spelt out in the DDA mandate on NAMA. Many developing countries, more particularly the small and vulnerable economies (SVEs) of the African, Caribbean, and Pacific (ACP) and African Group, realised that they had made a mistake by not inscribing their development markers in the mandate regarding both their offensive interests (e.g. preferences) and their defensive interests, namely tariff-cutting concessions. In the same vein, another set of developing countries were concerned with the need for equity in their tariff concessions through less than full reciprocity (LTFR) and flexibilities to, *inter alia*, shelter vulnerable industrial sectors and protect employment in their countries. The depth and coverage of the tariff-cutting formula for developing countries became a thorny issue.

These differences could not be sorted out at the Cancun Ministerial Conference of November 2003, which ended in failure. The NAMA issues could not even be taken up in any depth in Cancun as other issues precipitated prematurely the collapse of the meeting. The Derbez Text of the Cancun Ministerial Conference only deferred the issue for the future by not making any specific recommendation on the formula, but advising that work continue on a non-linear formula.[6]

The Cancun Ministerial Conference ended in failure, but it was also a defining moment in the history of the WTO and multilateral trade negotiations, as it challenged the hegemonic influence of developed countries. It was Cancun that witnessed the birth of both the G-90 (an alliance of the ACP, the African Group and the LDCs, grouping some 90 small developing economies) and the G20 (a powerful group of mostly major developing country agricultural exporters). In the field of NAMA, the G-90 was mostly focussed on special and differential treatment in terms of the need to preserve their policy space as well as the need to address the important issue of preference erosion through a trade solution. The mandate has been so far silent on this issue or at best proposed non-trade solutions through greater capacity building.

Thus, in the period following the collapse of the Cancun WTO meeting and leading up to the 2004 July Framework Agreement, the complexity of the diversity of interests as well as the lines of conflict between the developed countries and the developing countries started to be drawn out more clearly and those differences were to determine the future agenda of the NAMA negotiating group. On the one hand, the developed countries (despite the earlier conciliatory moves of US Trade Representative Robert Zoellick and EU Trade Commissioner Pascal Lamy) hardened their position on NAMA and did not want to dilute the Derbez text at all, the more so as they were under pressure in agriculture to make real concessions. Developed countries were insisting on an ambitious formula. They could agree to an approach of formula with flexibilities, but insisted on a high level of ambition. The emphasis by the US negotiator was also on effective new trade flows to compensate pains in agriculture. The origin of this polarisation in favour of greater market access in the operationalisation of the Derbez text could be seen in the formation of a developed countries caucus called "Friends of Ambition" in 2004.[7]

On the other side of this polarising axe was a wide cross-section of developing countries now articulating a variety of positions, depending on the nature of their demands and levels of development. The ACP and African Groups became more vocal and were forcing the issue of preferences on the agenda while at the same time arguing for policy space and flexibility defensively. At the same time, the LDCs started to regroup more vigorously and began to develop the platform of duty-free-quota-free market access (DFQFMA). A number of other developing countries strongly opposed the Derbez text, and their battle-cry was built around the concept of LTFR and opposition to sectorals except if they were on the basis of voluntary participation.

It is from this perspective that one has to view the 2004 July mini-Ministerial meeting and the subsequent July Framework Agreement as well as the 2005 Hong Kong Fifth WTO Ministerial Conference. In these meetings, the different parts of the NAMA negotiations were just beginning to mature and crystallise into a negotiating agenda. There were no final breakthroughs, but the result was a better framing of the agenda in terms of the difficulty of defining ambition and balance through the formula and flexibilities and the supplementary modality on sectoral negotiations. At the same time, a number of other developing and non-developing country issues were gaining prominence as critical issues in NAMA, namely preference erosion, binding coverage, SVE flexibilities, Recently Acceded Members (RAMs), LDCs etc. The July Framework Agreement, therefore, could only gauge the extent of this lack of convergence and developing countries were successful in preventing the hermetic sealing of the Derbez text by forcing further negotiations on its elements:

> Additional negotiations are required to reach agreement on the specifics of some of these elements. These relate to the formula, the issues concerning the treatment of unbound tariffs in indent two of paragraph 5, the flexibilities for developing-country participants, the issue of participation in the sectoral tariff component and the preferences. In order to finalise the modalities, the Negotiating Group is instructed to address these issues expeditiously in a manner consistent with the mandate of paragraph 16 of the Doha Ministerial Declaration and the overall balance therein.[8]

There was no significant progress toward agreed NAMA modalities either in the lead up to or during the December 2005 WTO Ministerial Conference. One important development in the margins of the Hong Kong Ministerial Conference of 2005 was the creation of the NAMA-11[9] Group of countries that was already foreshadowed in the submission by some of these countries in the Committee on Trade and Development (CTD) on 1 December 2005.[10] The NAMA-11 was also critical in securing paragraph 24 of the Hong Kong WTO Ministerial Declaration, which introduced the notion of comparable ambition in NAMA and agriculture market access outcomes.[11]

In short, it could be argued that while the Hong Kong Ministerial Declaration was not able to agree on modalities in NAMA except for the LDC modality on DFQFMA, it was in the Hong Kong Ministerial Conference that the NAMA agenda was fully framed and the wide diversity of interest groups in contention for different outcomes manifested itself. In terms of the substance of the negotiations, the following issues were prioritised for NAMA modalities with ministers either indicating some new guidelines or reiterating past ones:

(i) definite choice of a Swiss formula with different coefficients and additional flexibilities for developing countries applying the formula;

(ii) the need to take into account LTFR but no common understanding of the concept was provided;
(iii) the pursuit of sectoral initiatives on a plurilateral non-mandatory basis;
(iv) guidelines for mark-up, conversion to ad-valorem duties, product coverage, NTBs and RAMs' flexibilities;
(v) the need to address the issue of preference erosion and pursuit of discussions in the direction of both trade and non-trade solutions;
(vi) the recognition of the concerns of SVEs and the need to provide flexibilities for them without creating a sub-category of WTO members; and
(vii) comparable balance between the level of ambition in market access for agriculture and NAMA.

In terms of the groupings of actors in the NAMA theatre, the landscape was getting crowded with traditional developed country players on the one hand and a multiplicity of developing country actors coming on the scene in organised groupings, namely NAMA-11, the ACP, the African Group, the LDCs, the SVEs and the RAMs on the other.

It should be noted that NAMA issues had not yet exploded in the DDA negotiations either in the vertical negotiating group or in the horizontal Green Room[12] discussions in Geneva prior to the Hong Kong Ministerial meeting or in the Ministerial Green Room in Hong Kong. It is safe to say that agriculture dominated the discussions in Hong Kong and that ministers postponed the difficult negotiations on NAMA with the result that only a better framing of the agenda was achieved. However, even in this light, the deep contradictions in positions could be sensed. The linkage of coefficients with paragraph 8[13] flexibilities by developed countries and the insistence by developing countries that paragraph 8 flexibilities was a standalone modality was not resolved, the wide difference over coefficients for developed as opposed to developing countries was glossed over and the concept of critical mass and its implication for non-mandatory participation in sectorals was not clarified, although there were heated debates and lively discussions in the NAMA group on many of those issues, such as critical mass, sectorals, LTFR, flexibilities and ambition, new trade flows, market access versus development, etc. Moreover, the issue of LTFR was not defined, and each party defined it in its own way as stated in paragraph 7 of Annex B of the report of the NAMA Chair.[14]

At the political level, during the Hong Kong Ministerial Conference, developing countries' solidarity was strengthened through the creation of a broad political alliance of developing country groupings that sought to unite and mutually defend developing countries' interests in the round. This alliance was loosely dubbed the G-110 and comprised of the G-20, NAMA-11, the ACP, the African Group, the G-33, the LDCs and the SVEs. The challenge for such a large grouping was, however, the manner in which it could transcend political rhetoric to demonstrate real solidarity on the ground given the varied interests of its constituents, which at times, if not conflictual are not necessarily complementary.

The Build-up to the 2008 July Mini-Ministerial

Ministers in Hong Kong set the deadline for modalities in agriculture and NAMA for April, 30, 2006. This set the scene for real negotiations on agriculture and NAMA to take place in early 2006. Real negotiations started in different configurations, namely at one level to address the mainstream issues of formula, flexibilities and sectoral modalities, although the developing countries disputed sectorals as a mainstream issue. On a different level, a number of separate meetings began addressing specific concerns of countries or groupings like SVE flexibilities, paragraph 6 binding coverage and ACP/African Group preference erosion issues.

The format was through Green Room meetings and restricted issue-specific meetings with participation calibrated for those with an interest in a specific issue either as opponents or proponents. This approach in the Geneva multilateral process was to be sustained up until the 2008 mini-Ministerial Meeting.

However, progress was not forthcoming, although a set of more focussed discussions took place in parallel with the Geneva multilateral process at the level of the G-6 (Australia, Brazil, the EU, India, Japan, and the US). The parameters that governed the developing countries' participation in the NAMA negotiations were the need to respect LTFR and comparative levels of ambition in market access between agriculture and industrial products as defined by paragraph 24 of the Hong Kong Declaration. The EU and the US argued for real and effective market access through "*new enhanced trade flows*." The major developed countries were pressing for a Swiss coefficient of 10 for developed countries and 15 for developing countries. Developed countries were also unhappy with paragraph 8 flexibilities and wanted to curtail its scope. On the other hand, the NAMA-11 proposed a spread of 25 points between the coefficients to be in keeping with LTFR.[15] Concurrently some work was started by the different proponents of sectorals, who started plurilateral meetings to develop broad outlines of their requests. Another development came through a group of so-called middle-grounders, which proposed a coefficient of 8-9 for developed countries as opposed to 19-23 for developing countries applying the formula.

Positions became increasingly polarised, and Pascal Lamy, Director-General of the WTO framed the problem as a triangle of issues with each side representing market access in agriculture, domestic support and NAMA, respectively. The mini-Ministerial meeting called by Pascal Lamy in June 2006 could not make any progress, and that prompted him, as Chair of the Trade Negotiations Committee (TNC) in the meeting of June 24, to suspend the DDA negotiations across the board.

The main lessons to be drawn from the June 2006 failure was the realisation that NAMA negotiations were complex, and the once-held view that once agriculture was settled, NAMA would fall in place was too simplistic. The horizontal linkages between NAMA and agriculture outcomes were now explicitly on the table and the question of level of ambition in NAMA were becoming a major obstacle to overcome in the NAMA negotiations.

When discussions resumed in late 2006, once again in parallel with the multilateral process at the level of the negotiating groups in Geneva, a process between the G-4 and then the G-6[16] at the level of senior officials and Ministers were set in motion to bridge the gaps. Unfortunately, the G-6 Ministerial meeting in Potsdam failed to agree on a deal in June 2007. The EU and the US were asking for a coefficient of 18 from the developing countries, while Brazil and India were ready to settle for 30 in view of the low level of gains in agriculture for developing countries. But, after Potsdam 2007 and in the period leading up to the 2008 meeting, the negotiations took a new turn toward even greater polarisation. The developed countries, mainly the US and the EU, articulated a negotiating strategy around the concept of high ambition in NAMA and asking for real market openings that would create new trade flows and cunningly started targeting emerging countries as having to contribute more, thus exonerating the rest of smaller developing countries from making similar commitments. It also became clear that through this strategy, the developed countries wanted to put pressure on the major emerging economies and prepare the ground to define what they call critical mass in sectorals determining who should participate therein. In their way, the US and the EU were also referring to balance in the negotiations, which could only be met through greater market access in NAMA for the payment requested from them in agriculture. In a broader political sense, they were indicating that the geography of the global trading system and the geo-economic equilibrium of the world have changed and the emerging economies had to contribute to the cost of maintaining international public goods in exchange for the benefit of admission in the club of global players.

At the same time, the emerging economies articulated their strategy on the concept of development as opposed to mercantilist concerns of market access of developed countries, which was thwarting the objectives of a development round. They argued that the demands of developed countries did not respect the principle of LTFR and the extent of the burden that such onerous concessions demanded of them in industrial products through both an ambitious harmonising Swiss formula and participation in sectorals would compromise their industrial development.[17] Moreover, in contrast to such onerous demands in NAMA, the level of ambition in agriculture, which was not impressive, was being undermined more and more by multiple layers of flexibilities being carved out for developed countries, hence tilting the balance in the negotiations against development.

It is in the context of such entrenched positions on both sides that the Chair of NAMA issued his first draft modalities text on July, 17, 2007 concurrently with agriculture.[18] In the wake of the Potsdam failure and the bitter blame game between developed countries and emerging economies that ensued, the reactions to the first draft modalities text in NAMA were hardly surprising. But, beyond the deep divergences on substance referred to above which subsisted in the first draft, the developing countries, more particularly NAMA-11, had serious difficulties with the negotiating process itself. First, the role of the Chair was deeply criticised. The NAMA-11 Group accused the Chair of adopting a top-down approach in the sense that he ignored their views and closed his text by being too prescriptive, thus allowing no scope for negotiations. The Chair was heavily blamed for proposing an imbalanced text and proposing figures that prejudiced or narrowly constrained the outcome or direction of market access outcomes in industrial goods. Against the protest of the NAMA-11 and its counter-proposals, the US stated that this "could signal the end of the Doha Round."[19] These protests against the Chair assumed greater significance as they contrasted singularly with the approach in agriculture negotiations, where the Chair took a cautious bottom-up approach to the production of texts.

The issuance of the first draft modalities text, opened a period of high density in the negotiations that would be sustained until the collapse of the 2008 July mini-Ministerial

Meeting. In the interim, the draft text went through several iterations with an impressive track record of closing several gaps, but failing to find consensus on the overarching issue of ambition in the mainstream of the negotiations. It is important to review the implications of these texts for different groupings, the strategies adopted by each one to attain its objectives and with what success and the role of the Chair in facilitating or constraining the purview of negotiating options.

It should also be observed that despite the criticism against Ambassador Don Stevenson, the NAMA Chair, he must be given some credit for having closed a number of difficult issues. He was sensitive to the issue that there cannot be a one-size-fits-all approach in terms of S&D treatment and the world could not be seen through the lens of a classical developed/developing country divide. In this regard, he perhaps pioneered a new approach in S&D treatment that used tailor-made flexibilities for different groups of countries or even individual countries as shall be seen below.

Preference Erosion

The issue of preferences was of great concern mostly to the ACP countries, the African Group and the LDCs. Many of these countries were bound with their former colonial countries through a system of non-reciprocal trade preferences. The successive Lomé I-IV Conventions between the ACP and the EU are typical examples. However, later on, other such preferential trading arrangements also came into being under the generalised system of preferences (GSP), namely the EU's "Everything but Arms Initiative" (EBA) and the African Growth and Opportunity Act (AGOA) of the US. Preferences became a passionate issue in the DDA negotiations between the G-90 countries and some Latin American countries, mainly because of the long-standing conflict over bananas. However, the mandate was not clear on how to treat this issue and there was much reluctance to find a trade solution to preference erosion as opposed to capacity building assistance.

The G-90 was able to force the issue on the agenda of both agriculture and NAMA negotiations in the July Framework Agreement. In NAMA, preferences were added to the list of areas where "additional negotiations are required to reach agreement on the specifics of some of these elements."[20] The mandate was further elaborated in the Hong Kong Ministerial meeting where Ministers "instruct(ed) the Negotiating Group to intensify work on the assessment of the scope of the problem with a view to finding possible solutions."[21]

The ACP finally elaborated a strategy based on the following elements to address the issue in the DDA negotiations:

(i) a methodology through the development of a vulnerability index to identify the preference tariff lines and determine the scope of the problem;[22]
(ii) the proposal of a transitional period for the longer staging of tariff reductions in the market of the EU and the US for the identified tariff lines;
(iii) the need to provide adjustment assistance during the transition period through Aid for Trade to build competitiveness in the ACP countries.

Following lengthy negotiations, an architecture based on a list of tariff lines most prone to preference erosion on the EU and US markets was identified for longer staging of tariff reductions over 10 years in the EU and US markets. The lists are contained in Annex 2 and 3 of the NAMA text of December 2008.

Disproportionately Affected Countries

The modalities for preference erosion did not meet with total consensus in July 2008 because of the issue of disproportionately affected countries (DAC). Some developing countries, in particular Pakistan and Sri Lanka, had serious concerns about these modalities on preferences. Textile and garments exports were vital for their economies and stalling or longer staging of MFN tariff reductions would put them in disadvantageous positions, mainly *vis-à-vis* one of their major competitors, namely Bangladesh. Consequently, it was agreed to make some allowances for such disproportionately affected countries, like Pakistan and Sri Lanka. A limited number of tariff lines were selected in ANNEX 4 of the NAMA modalities text for tariff reduction in a shorter period, namely six years rather than ten years, so these countries could enjoy the benefits of tariff liberalisation for these limited products on both the US and EU markets. However, this dispensation for Pakistan and Sri Lanka provoked a reaction from Bangladesh, which was later joined by Nepal and Cambodia, which protested that they would be disadvantaged on the US market. Under the EBA initiative, they already enjoy DFQFMA in the EU market, but they did not have such access in the US market. Therefore, if Pakistan got a faster liberalisation on such lines on which Bangladesh did not get free access under the 97 percent DFQFMA Hong Kong decision, this would disadvantage the latter. Bangladesh argued that, as a matter of principle, it would be an act of gross inequity and injustice to give a developing country better access than an LDC. The Ambassador of Bangladesh, D. Bhattachariya, in successive Green Room meetings on this issue in June/July 2008, cunningly used the anti-concentration argument of the US on formula/flexibilities against it. He stated that he would forego the DAC status if the US agreed to an anti-concentration clause in its 3 percent exclusion of tariff lines from DFQFMA. If this was not possible, then Bangladesh insisted that it should get DAC status on the same lines as Pakistan.

However, a division ensued among the LDC Group itself. The African LDCs dreaded the competitive superiority of Bangladesh, which could displace their goods on the US market. They opposed any DAC provisions for Bangladesh. Thus, the LDCs could not have a common position on this issue and subsequently the African Group and ACP supported the African LDCs as they believed they would also be negatively impacted by Bangladesh on the US market. The opposition to Bangladesh thus enlarged and many other non G-90 developing countries did not want to reopen the annexes as they feared this could unravel the whole preference package and disturb the balance reached on this issue. Unfortunately, this issue remains unresolved to date.

Paragraph 6 Countries: Binding Coverage

The flexibility for a group of developing countries referred to as paragraph 6 countries with an existing low binding coverage (less than 35 percent of tariff lines) was initiated in the Girard text where those countries were requested to bind 100 percent of their tariffs at 28.5 percent.[23] In return, they would not be applying the Swiss formula. The main bone of contention for these countries was the figure of 100 percent of tariff lines, which they protested curtailed their policy space domestically. The July Framework introduced brackets around the 100 percent figure in paragraph 6 of Annex B of this modality as agreement could not be found on the figure of 70 percent put forward by paragraph 6 proponents. It was surprising how much negotiating energy was spent on such a simple flexibility requested by a group of developing countries. The ACP and AU Coordinator, which was Mauritius and Kenya respectively, participated in a number of restricted meetings with the EU and the US as the main opponents to sort out this issue.[24]

The strategy used by the paragraph 6 countries was not to concede up to the last minute and to canvass the support of other advanced developing countries, like Brazil, China, India and South Africa, mainly after the G-110 alliance in Hong Kong to support their case. It was pointed out that binding was in itself an important concession in the WTO and binding 70 percent of tariff lines from a low baseline of 15 percent was a huge concession. The paragraph 6 countries also argued that such flexibility was needed to maintain policy space in their trade policy at the domestic level and also to make allowances for impending regional free trade and customs union agreements. The developed countries were keen to get rid of this issue, as it accentuated the impression of a North - South divide in NAMA negotiations with similar entrenched positions elsewhere on the formula and sectorals. The paragraph 6 countries finally proposed a three-band approach with those which have the lowest share of bound tariffs to bind in the lowest band with the lowest target of tariff lines that would need to be bound.[25] Ultimately, just before the Chair issued his third revised text in July, this issue was closed when agreement was reached to adopt a two-band approach. Those members with less than 15 percent of bindings would increase their coverage to 75 percent while those with bindings between 15-35 percent would bind 80 percent of their tariff lines, both groups of countries to bind at a target average of 30 percent.

The objective of the developing countries represented in paragraph 6 was to preserve policy space and to ensure that they do not put themselves in a position where if there is a new round of negotiations in the future, they are compelled to apply the Swiss formula. They have kept their negotiating space for the future and could offer 100 percent bindings and at a new target average in the future.

Small, Vulnerable Economies (SVEs)

Fundamental changes in the global economy with its consequent geo-economic impact brought about important mutations in the balance of power among countries in the WTO. The emerging economies of the developing world were becoming key players mainly in global trade while a number of other smaller developing countries were being marginalised or faced inherent structural constraints, as their small size did not enable them to take advantage of booming global trade. The need to "examine issues relating to the trade of small economies" and to frame responses to the trade-related issues of SVEs for their fuller integration in the multilateral trading system was part of the Doha mandate.[26] The special circumstances affecting this category of countries as well as the need to devise flexibilities to address their concerns in the DDA negotiations were recognised at the Hong Kong Ministerial Conference while at the same time members insisted on not creating another sub-category of WTO Members.[27]

A major challenge for the SVEs was to establish criteria to identify who they are and to make concrete proposals on treatment of SVEs in the negotiations. Both challenges proved quite difficult from the start. Much of the post-July Framework exercise for the SVEs was to devise vulnerability indices to define an SVE. This proved difficult internally among SVEs and met with opposition by some other members, who saw in such a demarche an attempt to create another sub-category of members. The search for defining criteria that would be applicable horizontally was finally dropped and the use of contextual criteria in the specific circumstances of each negotiating group was adopted. The criteria used in NAMA to identify SVEs were members with a share of less than 0.1 percent of NAMA trade for the reference period 1999 to 2001.

The question of treatment for SVEs in the NAMA modalities for tariff cutting was more controversial and took a longer time to settle. The proponents were requesting a "para-6-like" treatment with different target averages. Eventually the NAMA Chair in his July 2007 text proposed architecture with the agreed eligibility criteria and a banded approach with three target averages (22/18/14) and a minimum cut of 10 percent on 95 percent of tariff lines. While the SVE Group basically agreed with the architecture proposed, they were vehemently opposed to the Chair's figures. The Chair's text on SVEs went through several iterations until the final architecture was stabilized with a four-band approach.[28]

The important conclusion to draw from the SVEs' flexibility is that despite protests not to create another sub-category of members, a differential treatment for SVEs across different areas of the DDA negotiations cannot but portend to fundamental changes in the approach to S&D treatment for the future in the WTO. By virtue of their smallness and their inherent vulnerabilities, SVEs have a morally compelling case for differentiation in treatment in the WTO and it is politically difficult for either wealthy developed countries or growing advanced developing countries to oppose such dedicated flexibilities for them. The acceptance of the very concept of SVEs in the WTO's work methods and policy decisions signals a novel approach toward special and differential treatment in international trade policy.

Recently Acceded Members (RAMs)

In 2006, there was an informal consensus in Council that those members who joined the WTO after the Uruguay Round could be considered RAMs. The problem was recognised as early as in the Girard text of 2003, which made some proposals regarding higher coefficients or longer staging or "grace periods" for RAMs. These proposals could not garner consensus then, and the 2003 Derbez text and subsequently the 2004 July Framework Agreement and the 2005 Hong Kong Ministerial Declaration all agreed only on the principle of greater flexibility.

> We recognise that newly acceded Members shall have recourse to special provisions for tariff reductions in order to take into account their extensive market access commitments undertaken as part of their accession and that staged tariff reductions are still being implemented in many cases. We instruct the Negotiating Group to further elaborate on such provisions.[29]

It should be noted that SVE RAMs have access to the SVE modality, in particular the fourth band that was added where members whose bound average tariff of NAMA lines below 20 percent will apply a minimum 5 percent line-by-line cut on 95 percent of their tariff lines or bind at the resulting average of such a line-by-line cut.[30] Most of the other RAMs, except China, Croatia, Oman and Chinese Taipei, are exempted for any tariff reduction beyond their accession agreements.

Finally the modality that was retained for the few RAMs applying the formula was an extended implementation period of three years.

Formula and Flexibilities

Together with the sectorals, it is formula and flexibilities that constitute the main core of the NAMA negotiations. When the exempted countries not applying the formula are discounted, only about 45 countries will be applying the formula. However, they account for 90 percent of NAMA trade.[31] In contrast to previous GATT practice, a singular feature of the approach to industrial tariffs in the DDA negotiations is its overwhelmingly ambitious objective. For the first time, a combination of two highly ambitious tariff-cutting methodologies are being used concurrently, namely a harmonising Swiss formula plus an even more ambitious harmonisation approach through sectorals, a variant of the request and offer approach. The downside of such an approach is its offensive character, which pushes members either to very high trade opening or to significantly reduce their tariffs on targeted products through sectorals or to reduce high tariffs or peaks. Such an approach focuses mainly on export interests and can quickly mobilise exporting or protectionist lobbies in domestic constituencies vehemently in favour or against the round.

In his first draft NAMA modalities text of July 2007, the Chair produced coefficients of 8/9 v/s 19-23 for developed and developing countries, respectively, and unbracketed figures for flexibilities to formula-applying countries that reproduced the figures of paragraph 8 of the July Framework Agreement.

He thus froze the figures on flexibilities and reduced the negotiations only to a narrow range on the coefficients, which produced a bitter response from developing countries, more particularly the NAMA–11. After July 2007, an intensive process of negotiations started among the members, and the draft text went through various iterations namely, the first revised draft text on February, 08, 2008, the second revised draft text in May 2008, the third revised draft text in July 2008 and the fourth revised draft text in December 2008.

Each successive text recoiled back from the extreme initial draft and gained in sophistication by "flexibilising the flexibilities" in favour of developing countries. However, disagreement over the broad parameters within which the NAMA negotiations were conducted remained, namely the concept of development and LTFR v/s real market access and new trade flows. This was borne out by a new controversial element introduced by developed countries that further vitiated the negotiations, namely the anti-concentration clause. The major issues that dominated the negotiations on formula and flexibilities in the build-up to the July mini-Ministerial meeting were:

(a) The linkages between coefficients and flexibilities

Initially, the flexibilities were for developing countries a standalone modality. Essentially, it was argued that the flexibilities were an important component of special and differential treatment while the coefficients were to be judged from the LTFR perspective and were the anchor points for ambition and comparability with agricultural market access outcomes. Eventually, developing countries conceded that both variables must be considered together in order to secure compromises on the coefficients. It was thus that "a sliding scale" was explored where a direct linkage was introduced between the coefficients and the flexibilities. In other words, the lower the coefficient, the greater the flexibility for the percentage of "no cut" or "half cut" for sensitive tariff lines that developing country members can shelter and *vice versa*. This gave developing countries a wider choice to adopt modalities more in keeping with their specific tariff profiles. At the same time, developed countries tried to balance the extent of flexibilities granted with differential coefficients and the new concept of anti-concentration clauses.

While the linkages between formula and flexibilities seemed to be an approach acceptable to both developed and developing members at that stage, there was considerable disagreement up until the July Ministerial meeting on the figures in both modalities. Developing countries were still asking for coefficients nearer to 30 while developed countries wanted coefficients below 20. The Chairman in his May text tried to frame a range, namely 19 to 26, which in fact represented the highest the developed countries could accept subject to the specifics of the flexibilities and an appropriate anti-concentration clause. For the developing countries, it represented the lowest they could accept provided the flexibilities were not constrained beyond a certain limit. At that stage, while the parameters of LTFR and paragraph 24 comparability with agriculture remained overarching considerations in the public face of the negotiations, in actual fact it was numbers crunching in the restricted meetings along the ranges proposed by the Chair that were driving the members. The innovation in the architecture of the May text is that there are three ranges of figures (19-21, 21-23 and 23-26) corresponding to three sets of flexibilities with bracketed ranges there also.[32]

The same architecture with bracketed figures was reproduced in the July 2008 Chair's draft text as no further compromise could be reached. It was felt that it was now a ministers' call through a horizontal process in the negotiations, which will consider trade-offs in other sectors of the negotiations. The Ministerial meeting of July 2008, which collapsed apparently on its inability to find consensus in agriculture, could not adequately discuss the figures of the NAMA package put forward in the Lamy one-page text. However, it would seem that at least the members of the G-7[33] could live with the Lamy package. Some countries, namely Argentina and Venezuela, explicitly rejected the compromise. Others argued that it was not multilaterally discussed and could not be a consensus document. The Chair published a report on August, 10 explaining the state of play and the messy process of the July mini-Ministerial meetings. Finally, the Lamy compromise was reproduced in the Chair's December 2008 draft text without brackets and the situation in NAMA formula and flexibilities stands as is today, namely:

- For developed countries, a coefficient of 8 with no recourse to flexibilities.
- For developing countries, coefficients of 20,22 and 25 to be used as follows:

Countries using a coefficient 20 have the choice of either

- (i) less than formula cuts for up to 14 percent (the 10 July draft said [12-14] of non-agricultural national tariff lines provided that the cuts are no less than half the formula cuts and that these tariff lines do not exceed 16 percent (the 10 July draft said [12-19]) of the total value of a member's non-agricultural imports; or
- (ii) keeping tariff lines unbound, or not applying formula cuts for up to 6.5 percent (the 10 July text said [6-7] of non-agricultural national tariff lines provided that they do not exceed 7.5 percent (the 10 July text said [6-9]) of the total value of member's non-agricultural imports

Countries using a coefficient of 22 could have either

- (i) less than formula cuts for up to 10 percent of NAMA tariff lines, provided that the cuts are no less than half the formula cuts and that these lines do not exceed 10 percent of the total value of the member's non-agricultural imports; or
- (ii) keep tariff lines unbound, or not applying formula cuts for up to 5 percent of NAMA tariff lines provided they do not exceed 5 percent of the total value of a member's non-agricultural imports.

Countries applying a coefficient of 25 (paragraph 7c) did not have recourse to any flexibilities (paragraph 111 to 113 of South Centre Oct.2008).

As seen below, there were further accommodations within this general rule with country-specific flexibilities but they were not settled conclusively in terms of closure on the figures for such flexibilities.

(b) Country-Specific Flexibilities

While general consensus was building on the sliding scale of coefficient plus flexibilities as the general rule to determine developing countries' contributions in tariff reduction in NAMA, a number of countries could still not reconcile the specific circumstances of their countries with the general rule and argued for additional flexibilities.

(i) South Africa consistently argued and demonstrated empirically that the modalities as they are would have an imbalanced impact on it in that it will be contributing more proportionately than developed countries in tariff cuts. At the same time, with a coefficient of 22, 23 percent of tariffs will be taking a cut of more than 30 percent on applied rates. South Africa will thus assume a disproportionate share of the burden, the more so as it will not get comparable benefits in agriculture or services. Moreover, South Africa argued that there was a morally compelling reason to extend greater flexibilities as at its accession South Africa was deemed a developed country and assumed obligations accordingly. It also drew attention to the fact that it formed part of the Southern African Customs Union (SACU), which comprised an LDC and other SVEs which would have to assume the same burden of tariff cuts. South Africa was requesting that it should be compared with other comparable developing economies and its contribution be assessed accordingly.

There was generally sympathetic understanding for the situation of South Africa, and the revised text of May 2008 provided for additional [1-6] points in the flexibility under paragraph 7 b (i).[34] However South Africa was demanding a higher figure, which explains the square brackets. Consultations pursued and although the issue is not yet resolved, some progress has been made and the situation stands as follows today:

1. As an exception, Botswana, Lesotho, Namibia, South Africa and Swaziland shall include a common list of flexibilities in their schedules and shall have recourse to [6][8][35] additional percentage points in the flexibility provided under paragraph 7(b)(i)[36]. In addition, three of these percentage points, which shall be used only in respect of tariff lines falling within the clothing [and footwear] sectors (HS chapters 61-62 [and 64]), shall benefit from a grace period of [3][5][37] years, which shall be implemented as follows: the first reduction on these lines shall be implemented three years after the first reduction required under paragraph 6(f) and each successive reduction shall be made effective on 1 January of each of the following years.
2. South Africa commits to negotiate, at the time of establishment of modalities,[38] the terms of two sectoral initiatives of its choosing, without prejudice to its final decision to participate in those outcomes.[39]

(ii) Both Argentina and Venezuela made similar representation, arguing that the standard paragraph 8 flexibilities would not be adequate to address their situations. The Chair conducted specific consultations on these cases and requested data from these countries to support their cases. There was less empathy among the developed countries for these two countries. For Venezuela initial attempts went in the direction of allowing it access to the SVE's modality or some additional points of flexibilities.[40] But, this did not garner consensus. In the last texts of December 2008, both cases were left pending although they not removed from the modalities text implying on-going negotiations.

(iii) The situation of Mercosur as a customs union was brought to the negotiating table by Brazil. The scope of the flexibility for "no cuts" or "half cuts" did not favour countries in a customs union as the sensitivities of one could engulf the entire (12-14 percent) of tariff lines. Thus, Brazil was requesting a higher percentage of sensitive exclusion from the formula. Several formulae / proposals were explored while the very principle of flexibilities to be granted because of customs union was questioned by some. Ultimately, the compromise was to allow members of Mercosur to use the value of trade limitation in paragraph 7 calculated on the total value of Brazil's non-agricultural imports.

(c) Anti-concentration

As the linkages between coefficients and flexibilities grew together with demands for additional flexibilities for country-specific situations and customs unions, the developed countries raised concerns about the lowering of ambition in NAMA. They insisted on the need for real market access and new trade flows[41] and called for an "anti-concentration clause" that would limit the use of flexibilities to shelter a large percentage of sensitive tariff lines in a chapter and also urged for a "top-up" of market access by participation in sectoral negotiations. This issue became a major bone of contention in the negotiations as the developing countries argued that this restriction was not in the mandate, which only states that flexibilities should not be used to exclude entire HS (Harmonised Commodity Description and Coding System) chapters. When a compromise not to exclude an entire HS chapter made its way into the architecture of modalities in the July 2008 draft, there was no consensus on the figures either the minimum number of tariff lines or the cap on the percentage value of trade of the member in each HS chapter. These were left blank for Ministers to decide. But, the developing countries wanted to keep the restriction as low as possible and proposed 10 percent of lines while the developed countries proposed 40 percent of lines. The Ministers in the July meeting finally agreed on at least 20 percent of lines to be subject to formula cuts corresponding to at least 9 percent of the value of trade in that chapter.

The aggressive stand of developed countries on anti-concentration demonstrated their offensive stand in NAMA for real and new market access, mainly in the markets of emerging developing economies. It demonstrated a contrast also on how flexibilities for developed countries in agriculture (sensitive products) were increasing while corresponding flexibilities for developing countries in NAMA were contracting.

Sectorals

The Chair's draft modalities texts only articulated a general section on the issue of sectorals as the sectorals negotiations before the July 2008 mini-Ministerial meeting followed a plurilateral track rather than the multilateral one. This was mainly because it was assumed on the basis of the Doha mandate and the subsequent Hong Kong Ministerial Declaration that participation in sectorals was on a non-mandatory basis. This was interpreted as meaning on a voluntary basis by developing countries, while developed countries insisted that sectorals were an integral part of the NAMA negotiations and the modalities should define non-mandatory participation. One of the elements of these modalities was the concept of critical mass, which the developed countries defined as embracing substantially all trade in that sector. The target of developed countries was to ensure that the emerging developing countries did participate in certain key sectorals to ensure effective market access openings and new trade flows. As for non-formula applying countries, there was no compulsion for them to join sectorals.

The issue of sectorals, in fact, became a very controversial one in the July mini-Ministerial. While the Swiss formula itself is one that delivers the highest ambition of all the GATT tariff-cutting instruments, a sectorals component adds depth in tariff cutting in selected sectors by going below the formula, including tariff elimination. The developed countries have always insisted on the inclusion of sectorals as a necessary component in NAMA to deliver real market access. This is why emerging developing countries' participation could not be an option but a requirement. At the July mini-Ministerial meeting the US insisted on language that would compel the emerging developing countries to participate in at least two sectorals of export interest to the US. This was an important condition for the US to convince its reluctant domestic constituencies to accept the Doha package.

It became a very divisive issue in the July 2008 mini-Ministerial meeting. The conundrum over sectorals was difficult to resolve. The developing countries sat tight on their understanding of the mandate that participation in sectorals was voluntary and would sequentially follow after modalities at the time of scheduling. The developed countries needed a more definite commitment by the emerging economies, but they could not press for mandatory language as the legal constraints of the mandate played in favour of developing countries. This dilemma is reflected in the drafting difficulty in the Lamy package that was finally concocted at the last minute on the part relating to sectorals and the obvious difficulty of securing a clear mandate. It became one of those clever drafting ambiguities where each side could emphasise its own interpretation:

> Recognising the non-mandatory nature of sectoral initiatives, at the time of establishment of modalities, the Members listed in Annex Z have committed to participate in negotiating the terms of at least two sectoral tariff initiatives likely to achieve critical mass. Other Members are encouraged to participate in order to assist in reaching critical mass. Any developing country Member participating in final sectoral initiatives will be permitted to increase its coefficient (in such increment as will be determined by no later than two months from the date of establishment of these modalities) commensurate with its level of participation in sectoral initiatives.

While the non-mandatory nature of participation is recognised, one does not know the mystery behind the list at Annex Z and whether commitment has been obtained for a critical mass in that list in the discussions of the G-7 in July 2008. The developed countries see in Annex Z an indispensable ingredient to complete modalities in NAMA. One should also note another linkage with the coefficient, which stipulates that participation in sectorals will enable a participant to increase its coefficient although the details of the linkage were not yet worked out.

Whatever was the tacit agreement in July among the G-7, it melted like snow in the following months with positions back to the starting block, namely voluntary participation versus a necessary component of market access opening. The difficulties were clearly obvious in the ensuing December 2008 draft text of the Chair where the whole of paragraph 9 remains in square brackets and Annex 7 regarding the list of participants proposes two options, one by the proponents committing members to participate by name in each sector and the other leaving it open by the non-proponents.[42] Susan Schwab, the USTR and Chief US trade negotiator, dissociated herself from the December text and expressed her disagreement on the section dealing with sectorals.[43] In such circumstances, it was clear that sectorals remained a deeply divisive issue and the further polarisation of positions on that issue was part of the reason the scheduled meeting of ministers that Pascal Lamy initially planned for December had to be called off. This new failure opened a long period of inertia in the NAMA negotiations, where market access issues were practically frozen and the Chair filled in the time by addressing almost uniquely non-tariff barriers (NTBs).

Failure of July Mini-Ministerial Meeting

The July Mini-Ministerial meeting failed apparently over the inability to agree on the parameters of a special safeguard mechanism (SSM) among the G-7. However, the SSM was only the immediate trigger that precipitated the failure. The real causes were more fundamental and not exclusively the SSM. The underlying reason was the growing development deficit that slowly crept into the negotiations and emptied the development ambition of the DDA mandate. There was a clear feeling among the developing countries that the imbalances that the DDA was meant to correct were not being addressed and the outcome was being skewed more in their disfavour. While in agriculture, higher ambition, which served a developmental objective, was being consistently diluted through multiple flexibilities for developed countries, in NAMA the developmental concerns of protecting industrial development and employment in developing countries were being denied by a predatory mercantilist approach of seeking higher market access in developing countries.

In NAMA specifically, the frustration of the developing countries was clearly communicated in the several statements of NAMA-11 in the TNC.[44] The contradictions between development and mercantilism in NAMA led to a skewed negotiating process, which successively produced texts that were imbalanced and placed the developing countries in the uncomfortable position of having to criticise the approach and content of the Chair's texts. Moreover, the non-inclusive approach of Pascal Lamy in negotiating an outcome through a restricted G-7 ministerial grouping was also to blame as it marginalised the rest of the membership and turned even the somewhat larger Green Room membership into a mere *façade*. Most of the ministers sat idly for most of the July meeting waiting for the deliberations of the G-7. Even within the G-7 meetings, the developing countries were uncomfortable as traditional divide-and-pressure tactics were being used. It is rumoured that Indian Minister Kamal Nath walked out in protest at one moment and refused to attend part of the G-7 meeting so as not to be associated with its outcome.

Non-Tariff Barriers (NTBs)

The NAMA mandate also includes negotiations on NTBs. This was a demand primarily of developing countries to address the perception that low tariffs in the developed countries were effectively countered by the incidence of NTBs.

In Hong Kong, Ministers recognised that progress had been made in the identification, categorisation and examination of notified NTBs. They also took note that members were developing bilateral, vertical and horizontal approaches to the NTB negotiations and that some NTBs were being addressed in other fora, including other negotiating groups. Most important, they recognised the need for specific negotiating proposals and encouraged participants to make such submissions as quickly as possible. In other words, it would be for the member facing a particular barrier to propose how to solve it.

These proposals started being submitted in 2006. The most recent versions of these proposals were complied in Annex 5 of the December 2008 text. Besides the ten bilateral requests that have been circulated in the TN/MA/NTR series, 13 specific negotiating proposals were submitted in several areas, including on horizontal issues such as procedures for the facilitation of solutions to NTBs, remanufactured goods, export taxes and export restrictions as well as on vertical initiatives on automotive products, electronics products and textiles, clothing and footwear.

Since some proposals received wider support than others, while a few were strongly rejected, it was envisaged in the December 2008 text that a decision would be taken on which of these horizontal and vertical proposals would subsequently move toward final, text-based negotiations. This would not mean, however, that the other proposals would be abandoned or that new proposals could not be submitted.

In this context, the Chairman noted that seven of these proposals merited "particular attention" (see paragraph 24) of the December 2008 text:

1) Ministerial Decision on Procedures for the Facilitation of Solutions to NTBs;
2) Ministerial Decision on Trade in Remanufactured Goods;
3) Negotiating Proposal on NTBs in the Chemical Products and Substances Sector;
4) Understanding on the Interpretation of the Agreement on Technical Barriers to Trade as Applied to Trade in Electronics;
5) Agreement on NTBs Pertaining to the Electrical Safety and Electromagnetic Compatibility (EMC) of Electronic Goods;
6) Understanding on the Interpretation of the Agreement on Technical Barriers to Trade with Respect to the Labelling of pertaining to Textiles, Clothing, Footwear and Travel goods.
7) Agreement on Non-Tariff Barriers pertaining to Standards, Technical Regulations and Conformity Assessment Procedures for Automotive Products.

As the work on market access came to a standstill after 2008 in NAMA, the Chair devoted most of his attention to NTBs proposals. Some intensive work was undertaken in 2009/2010 through several dedicated sessions on NTBs. These sessions provided an opportunity for an exchange of questions and answers on the various NTB proposals. Toward the end of the year, these question and answer sessions were replaced by more text-based negotiations in smaller groups. The focus has been on the seven proposals that have been identified in the draft modalities text as meriting special attention as well as an additional TBT-related vertical proposal submitted in 2009. This set of proposals has been referred by the NAMA Chair as "Wagon 1"proposals. All other NTB proposals (classified as "Wagon 2" proposals), remain on the negotiating table and the Chair is consulting members as to the best time and manner to discuss them.

Although it was envisaged in the December 2008 text that the text-based negotiations on NTBs would continue after the adoption of the modalities, members have not remained idle in 2009/2010 and have been working intensively on the NTBs front, including detailed discussions on many of the proposals. However, in 2008/9, the G-90 countries remained basically idle in these negotiations as most of the discussions were focussed between larger developing and the developed countries. When in 2010 the ACP Group started engaging in the negotiations, most of their proposals were limited to S&D treatment in terms of technical assistance, capacity building and financial help to participate in standards-setting bodies.

Such a state of affairs is perfectly understandable as NTBs are very complex issues. Although some advanced developing countries are now able to have a greater understanding of these issues and undertake more studies to shed light on their obnoxious effects on exports, it is still technically difficult to assess these extra costs for exporters. The SVE's lack of capacity prevents them even more from having any hold on the NTBs negotiations. It remains an area of opacity for most developing countries, although it is generally accepted that these are the next generation issues for trade negotiations. Thus, developing countries will have to build capacity in this area and prepare themselves more adequately to engage in such negotiations. There is no agreed list of non-tariff measures (NTMs) so far, but they permeate all measures affecting trade and they are non-exhaustive as governments keep legislating new measures continuously. Many NTBs are WTO compatible and even necessary to protect human and animal welfare. But, there is a host of measures that are non-transparent and that unnecessarily adds to the costs of exports and hence has a distortive effect on trade.

The Stalemate: From End-Game to the End of the Game

After a long period of paralysis in the market access areas of both NAMA and agriculture, the G-20 leaders tried to instil a new impetus in the negotiations by instructing the negotiators to intensify their efforts and use the window of opportunity in 2011 to conclude the round.[45] There were also signs in the US that President Obama was showing some readiness to give some attention to trade.

In Geneva, this attempt to revive the process of the negotiations started first with the mini-Ministerial in New Delhi in August 2009, which encouraged the re-involvement of senior officials from the capitals in the negotiating process in a structured manner and on a regular basis. The unproductive outcome of such regular senior officials meetings gave way to new attempts at forming new groups, such as the G-19/ G-23 co-chaired by the EU and India. The latter meetings suggested the re-appropriation of the process by ambassadors who started exploring possible solutions to the persisting gaps in an informal horizontal process but not necessarily involving negotiations. Thus, a number of small Ambassadorial Group Meetings (AGMs) started brainstorming in all areas of the negotiations which helped tremendously in obtaining greater clarity on the gaps among the members and what was required to enter into an end game.

The AGMs provided useful lessons on both the substantive gaps in the negotiations and on the process to resolve them. Among others, three things became clear:

(i) the issue of ambition in the DDA, mainly in NAMA was the big elephant in the room and had to be addressed;
(ii) the market access areas in agriculture, NAMA and services had to be prioritised for an end game scenario;
(iii) these issues could be addressed only in a horizontal negotiating process and in a restricted group through a real give and take.

It was in this context that the G-11[46] came into existence and marked a real break in the history of the negotiations so far by adding a horizontal dimension in the process and structure of the negotiations. Obviously, the multilateral process in Geneva in the meantime continued and meetings were held to address mostly technical issues in agriculture and NTBs in NAMA. The expectations were that the G-11 would provide inputs or compromises on the three market access areas to draft new texts for a real end game.

In the deliberations of the G-11[47] the clash over how to define the ambition level of the round was revealed over deep disagreements in NAMA sectorals. From a conceptual difference initially on how to understand and arrive at an acceptable level of ambition in market access, the difference became a fundamental one, touching at the very principle of GATT/WTO balance of rights and obligations. For a large number of developing countries, including the emerging economies, the level of ambition is already benchmarked in the December 2008 texts and any deviation too wide or too deep from that landing zone would lead to an unravelling of the texts and to a new negotiation altogether. The so-called stabilised parts in agriculture could not be considered so any more if the rules of the game were to change in NAMA and services.

Thus, for many developing countries sectorals could not be used to determine the ambition level in NAMA, which was already provided for by the Swiss formula. Sectorals serve only as a top-up to deliver some more market access in industrial goods. Moreover, any top up must be matched by equivalent market access trade-offs in agriculture or services for developing countries and not by token contributions in other pillars like domestic support. The developing countries in the G-11 therefore wanted to fix the parameters of ambition holistically first and within the landing zones of the December 2008 texts before proceeding to the specifics of the negotiations at the micro level in the respective market access areas or any proposal in NAMA. Moreover, countries like Brazil made clear that raising the level of ambition beyond a certain point in NAMA through sectorals would be unsustainable for the Brazilian economy and would not be acceptable even with any generous counter payment in agriculture.

At the same time, however, the US approach and understanding was totally different. While not discounting horizontal linkages and trade-offs with other market access areas, its view on NAMA's level of ambition delivered only through the Swiss formula was inadequate for the US to conclude a deal. A sizable increase would be necessary through sectorals in the important sectors of chemicals and industrial machinery. Its approach was not from the holistic to the specific, but started with specific negotiations on specific sectorals on a bilateral basis with the emerging economies and gradually built up the level of ambition through such negotiations. In that respect, the US agreed to use the "product basket approach" as a new architecture for sectoral tariff cuts. The US sold this as a compromise because it signals a lowering of ambition from its earlier zero-for-zero tariff cut in sectorals.

The US also wanted to concentrate on bilaterals to seek out more market access for two reasons. First, it did not and could not pay more in agriculture and a horizontal process would and did force it in that uncomfortable position. In fact Brazil asked for symmetry in market access efforts between agriculture and NAMA. Second, the US believed that the coefficient of 8 could not be pocketed by emerging countries without any bigger effort on their part, implying that the US already believed it was making a big payment by accepting coefficient 8 and therefore that its demands on sectorals should not be expected to be matched by spectacular efforts in agriculture.

The emerging economies had so far resisted a one-to-one bilateral negotiation with the US as it would focus mainly on NAMA and it would isolate them as emerging economies, which was the strategy of the US. Nonetheless, and in view of the fact that the bilaterals would be carried in the context of the G-11 horizontal meeting, the emerging economies agreed to have bilaterals with the US. The bilateral negotiations mainly with China provided an opportunity to test the "product-basket approach" to sectorals. Unfortunately, it turned out that each member had its own conception of the product basket approach. Before the major members could engage in a detailed line-by-line negotiation over the product-basket approach, the bilaterals were stopped over irreconcilable differences on the elements of the product-basket architecture. The US was looking for sweeping harmonisation in sectors like chemicals and industrial machinery through a majority of lines in the first zero-for-zero basket. China was proposing a first basket of zero for zero, in which only developed countries would contribute and a zero for χ basket in which developing countries would self-designate tariff lines.

While there were other issues discussed in the bilaterals, it was mostly the differences on NAMA sectorals that led to its failure and its abrupt end. The G-11 in the same breath could not subsist any further and had to acknowledge that differences over ambition mainly in the NAMA sectorals were unbridgeable. This is what led to the crisis and the impasse that now threatens the failure and perhaps abandonment of the DDA single undertaking.

The impact of the formula cut combined with demands for sectoral harmonisation, were far-reaching for the emerging economies. For example Brazil under a formula cut with coefficient of 20 with flexibilities would be making an average cut of 54 percent on bound rates and an average applied cut of 10 percent (new average applied 9.7 percent) with cuts on 51 percent of all applied tariffs in NAMA. Apart from almost eliminating its policy space completely, this would lead to substantial reductions in applied rates in key manufacturing sectors, like autos and auto-parts, footwear, textiles and clothing and toys.[48] With sectorals, the Peterson Institute[49] indicates that Brazil, China and India would have trade deficits for the product coverage of the sectorals. For China, the three sectors of chemicals, industrial machinery and electronic and electrical products involve 43 percent of China's total NAMA tariff lines and more than 55 percent of its total NAMA imports.[50] This is the universe of its trade that will be directly impacted as its applied rate is almost the same as its bound rate. India's trade deficit in 2010 was 11 percent of its GDP and it has about 12 million people who join the employment market every year.[51] Under these circumstances, the huge adverse impact of sectorals on the economy of the emerging economies are evident. The emerging economies believe that the deal on sectorals is basically non-reciprocal as they would provide market access to developed countries without any returns in NAMA which would seriously undermine their development prospects in the industrial sector.

When the G-11 reported its inability to bridge differences among the major players with some even suggesting that the differences are not bridgeable, there was at first consternation and anger among the rest of the membership. Mostly the loose group of "Friends of the System" refused to be put in front of a *fait accompli* and Pascal Lamy also believed that he should hear first hand from the protagonists to draw his own conclusions. He therefore started a series of confessionals with the major players.

Unfortunately, his consultations only confirmed the stalemate and his conclusions were even more disturbing for the round. He argued that there is a fundamental gap in expectations in sectorals that is not amenable to a technical resolution. One side was calling for harmonisation of tariffs with emerging economies through near tariff elimination in major sectors. This was a change in the traditional balance of rights and obligations that has characterised GATT/WTO based on differential treatment between developed and developing countries and as legally ordained by the DDA mandate. The concluding paragraph of his report on his consultations is revealing:

> In sum, there are fundamentally different views on the ambition provided by the Swiss formula as it currently stands, on whether the contributions between the different members are proportionate and balanced as well as on what is the contribution of sectorals. I believe we are confronted with a clear political gap which, as things stand, under the NAMA framework currently on the table, and from what I have heard in my consultations, in not bridgeable today.[52]

Conclusion

It could be said that the NAMA negotiations ultimately floundered on the conflict between market access mercantilism on the one hand and development concerns on the other. But, this failure in large measure also shows the complexity of finding a new balance in global economic governance in today's globalised world. The dominant role of developed countries in determining the contours of a deal for the rest is no longer on the cards. However, the relative role and weight of the emerging economies in defining this new equilibrium has yet to crystallise. At the same time, smaller developing countries argue that a "one-size-fits-all' approach cannot accommodate the diversity of interests in the developing world. The WTO will have to reckon with this reality in the future.

It is very difficult to chart a way forward out of the difficult impasse that the DDA finds itself in at the moment. The problem is essentially a political one, in which the political will to engage constructively to find a solution is not present among some of the major players, more particularly some developed countries that want to change the rules of the game drastically. It is now an accepted fact that it will be difficult to conclude the round in 2011. There is an attempt to try to deliver an early harvest, which will have an LDC package at its core in December while maintaining the single undertaking. This would imply that the other elements of the DDA mandate will have to be negotiated post-2011 and Ministers in December will have to agree on a work programme to achieve this. Under any circumstances, developing countries would have to insist on the development mandate and prevent the progress obtained so far from being unravelled.

However, for the sake of posterity it is important to draw some lessons from the NAMA negotiations for developing countries. The role of chairs is very important and the need for them to respect certain guidelines is very important. In NAMA one of the Chair's prejudiced the outcomes in his successive texts by imposing his subjective views of what the general consensus is or should be instead of adopting a genuine member-driven bottom-up approach. This complicated the negotiations for developing countries as they had an uphill task to deconstruct a prescriptive approach that sought to foreclose the negotiations or limit them within a predetermined scope. In rejecting or criticising the chair's text every time, the developing countries were made to appear as negative players all the time. It is also important in a negotiation to get as much clarity on the mandate as possible. This has to be done at the outset of the mandate or at the start of the negotiations. The lack of a proper definition of LTFR and the anti-concentration clause are such examples. Moreover, important issues (like preferences) of concern to some developing countries were completely absent from the mandate and it became an uphill task to get them on the agenda of the negotiations.

Another important lesson is to recognise and manage the diversity in interests and groupings among the developing countries. It is counter-productive to gloss over such differences or to have a reductionist view of development by privileging one grouping. Divisions (not diversity) generate weaknesses that adversely affect outcomes and the negotiating process. In the early stages, the developing countries were either not organised at all or lacked coherence. At Hong Kong when developing countries got their act together and realised the need for political solidarity, their participation in the negotiations was from then on more incisive and coherent. Some of the gains made in the developing country issues owe as much to intra-developing country cooperation as to developing country solidarity. For example, much of the preference erosion dossier was stuck because of developing country divisions. The ACP coordinator was able to unlock the stalemate following bilateral consultations with India and Thailand where he accommodated their concerns on tuna and gems and jewellery lines in exchange for their acceptance of the package. Similarly, the ACP and the African Group supported the NAMA-11 and the request for country-specific flexibilities for South-Africa.

Endnotes

1 Several statements by the G-20 and the African Group in the Trade Negotiations Committee (TNC) bear witness to this.

2 Statement by Pascal Lamy at the TNC meeting, March 29, 2011. Many developing countries did not agree that NAMA sectorals were a gateway issue and they argued that many unresolved issues in agriculture negotiations like SSM, new TRQ creation, Sensitive Products, etc. are more vital issues for developing countries and they are more important than sectorals in NAMA in keeping with the development DDA mandate.

3 Reproduced from Low, P., and Santana, R. 2009. 'Trade Liberalisation in Manufacturers: What is left after the Doha Round?', Journal of International Trade and Diplomacy 3(i) (Spring 2009).

4 Ministerial Declaration adopted at the Fourth Session of WTO Ministerial Conference on November 14, 2001.

5 Draft Elements of Modalities for Negotiations on Non-Agricultural Products, WTO document TN/MA/W/35, May 16, 2003.

6 Draft Cancun Ministerial Declaration, WTO document Job (03)150/Rev.3, September 13, 2003.

7 Members were: Australia, Canada, EU, Japan, New Zealand, Norway, Switzerland and US. The aim of the Group was to maximise tariff reductions and achieve real market access. See WTO website: Groups in the WTO.

8 The July 2004 Framework Decision of WTO General Council, Paragraph 1 of Annex B, WTO document WT/L/579, August 02, 2004.

9 The NAMA-11 consists of Brazil, India, South Africa, Argentina, Namibia, Egypt, Indonesia, Philippines, Tunisia and Venezuela.

10 Reclaiming Development in the WTO Doha Development Round, WTO document WT/COMTD/W/145, December 01, 2005.

11 Hong Kong Ministerial Declaration, WTO document WT/MIN(05)DEC, December 22, 2005.

12 Horizontal discussions are meetings held to discuss issues horizontally and not exclusively in the vertical negotiating groups. It allows for linkages and trade-offs between issues across the negotiating areas in the search for balance in the overall outcome.

13 Paragraph 8 refers to flexibilities available to developing countries applying the formula at paragraph 8 of the July Framework Agreement, hence the appellation paragraph 8 flexibilities.

14 Paragraph 7 of Annex B, WTO document WT/MIN(05)/DEC, December 22, 2005.

15 WTO document TN/MA/W/86, June 08, 2007.

16 G-6 consists of US, EU, Brazil, India, China and Australia.

17 Statement by the Ambassador of Brazil at the TNC meeting in June 2007.

18 Draft NAMA Modalities, WTO document Job(07)/126, July 17, 2007.

19 'Developing Countries reject Doha Round plans for tariff cuts', Financial Times, October 10, 2007.

20 July Framework Agreement, Annex B, WTO document WT/L/579, August 02, 2004.

21 Paragraph 20 of WTO document WT/MIN(05)/Dec, December 22, 2005.

22 WTO document TN/MA/W/53, 11 March 2005, and WTO document Job (05)/301, November 18, 2005.

23 The figure of 28.5% represents the overall average of bound tariffs for all developing countries after full implementation of their Uruguay Round concessions.

24 The author is speaking from direct experience as he was the Chief Negotiator of the ACP Group and together with Kenya, negotiated for Paragraph 6 countries.

25 WTO document Job (08)/11/Rev.1, March 13, 2008.

26 Paragraph 35 of the Doha Ministerial Declaration of November 14, 2001.

27 WTO document WT/Min(05)/DEC, December 22, 2005.

28 Paragraph 13 of Fourth revision of draft NAMA Modalities text, WTO document TN/MA/W/103/Rev.3, December 06, 2008.

29 Paragraph 11 of Annex B of the 2004 July Framework Agreement, WTO document WT/L/579, August 02, 2004.

30 WTO document TN/MA/W/103, February 2008.

31 Low, P., and Santana, R., Supra. Fn. 3.

32 Paragraph 7 of WTO document TN/MA/W/103/Rev.1, May 20, 2008.

33 G-7 comprised of EU, US, China, Brazil, India, Australia and Japan.

34 WTO document TN/MA/W/103/Rev.1, May 20, 2008.

35 6 if the coefficient is 22, and 8 if the coefficient is 20.

36 The attention of Members is called to the loss of tariff revenue by Lesotho, Botswana, Namibia and Swaziland resulting from these tariff reductions, and in particular the LDC status of Lesotho. This loss of revenue may warrant a priority for targeted Aid-for-Trade assistance.

37 3 if the coefficient is 22, and 5 if the coefficient is 20.

38 Provided this is the common understanding among all participants.

39 Paragraph 2 (ii) of Textual Report of NAMA Chair in WTO document TN/MA/W/103/Rev.3 /Add1, April 21, 2011.

40 WTO document TN/MA/W/103/Rev.2, July 10, 2008.

41 Statement by Susan Schwab and Peter Mandelson at the OECD meeting in Paris on June 05, 2008.

42 WTO document TN/W/MA/103/Rev.3, December 06, 2008.

43 Trade Report International Groups, Washington Trade Daily. December 2008.

44 See statement by South Africa at the TNC on July 22, 2008.

45 G-20 Declaration, November 2010, Seoul, South Korea.

46 G-11 comprises EU, US, China, India, Brazil, Argentina, South Africa, Japan, Australia, Canada and Mauritius.

47 The author was a participant in the Ambassadorial small group meetings and the G-11 and is writing from this vantage point.

48 Statement by Brazil at the TNC meeting on March 08, 2011.

49 Adler, M., Brunel, C., Hufbauer G. C. and Schott J. J. 2009. 'What's on the Table? The Doha Round as of August 2009'. Peterson Institute for International Economics Working Paper Series, Working Paper 09-6.

50 Statement by China at the TNC meeting on March 29, 2011.

51 Permanent Mission of India to the UN in Geneva.

52 Paragraph 14 of the Report by Director General on his consultations on NAMA sectoral Negotiations, WTO document TN/C/14, April 21, 2011.

4 Trade in Services – Safeguarding Developing Country Interests

Guillermo Malpica Soto
Director General of Services Negotiations
Ministry of Economy, Mexico &
Former Economic Counsellor Permanent Mission of Mexico to WTO

Introduction and Background

This chapter will present the most important concepts and developments related to trade in services negotiations at the multilateral level, with an emphasis on the role played by developing countries in the negotiations, the opportunities from their involvement and some recommendations for them to better participate in the multilateral arena. The ideas and concepts presented are taken not only from the existing literature on this topic, but also from the experience of the author's country in trade in services negotiations as one of the pioneer developing countries negotiating trade in services disciplines in international agreements.

Services development is fundamental in the growth and development strategies of both developed and developing countries. That is because services are an important component of countries' GDP and employment (they represent about 60 percent of both production and employment). It is also because of the role of several services sectors as drivers for the efficient production of other services and manufactures.

However, in contrast with the importance of services within national economies, the portion of international trade in services in total trade is still small, at about 20 percent on a balance of payments (BOP) basis. Although most trade in services is still from developed countries, many developing countries are successful services exporters. For example, Brazil, Costa Rica and Uruguay export professional services and services related to information technologies, and Mexico exports communication and distribution services.[1]

Besides the structural challenges that every developing country faces and that should be studied in depth in a separate project, one of the reasons the proportion of trade in services seems small is the lack of accurate and sufficiently disaggregated statistics on trade in services in many developing countries, which underestimates the value of trade in services as compared with trade in goods. Other reasons could be the relative lack of national studies to explore developing countries' opportunities from international trade negotiations. According to Geza Feketekuty, empirical evidence from trade agreements, such as the General Agreement on Tariffs and Trade (GATT) and the European experience of integration suggests that the maturity period of such agreements goes from one to two decades.[2] The GATS, which was the result of the first multilateral negations on trade in services, and the North American Free Trade Agreement (NAFTA), which was the first regional trade agreement involving developed and developing countries that included trade in services obligations, are still within this maturity period. Therefore, assessment of their use and effectiveness should take this into consideration.

Trade in services was introduced for the first time in multilateral trade negotiations during the Uruguay Round of the GATT launched in 1986. According to Rashmi Banga,[3] the inclusion of services trade in multilateral negotiations was the result of the compromise of four groups of countries at that time: the US and some members of the Organisation for Economic Co-operation and Development (OECD), which were proponents of including services disciplines and commitments in the Uruguay Round;[4] the European Community and some other OECD members, which were working towards an overall compromise; a group of ten developing countries (G-10), led by Brazil and India, which strongly opposed the US initiative; and a group of 20 developing countries (G-20), which were prepared to accept the US proposal depending on the terms. The compromise materialised in 1987, when a Group on Negotiations on Services (GNS) was established and the discussion centred in the creation of a set of rules for trade in services, borrowing some concepts from the GATT and taking into consideration the scarce studies on this field, mainly by developed countries under the OECD during the 1980s and studies by the United Nations Conference on Trade and Development (UNCTAD) under its work programme on services, established as a result of the mandates from Decisions 309 (XXX), 380 (XXXVI) of the Board of Trade and Development and the Final Act of UNCTAD VII.[5]

During the first two years the discussion of the disciplines and obligations for multilateral trade in services were driven by the North-South debate. Developing countries, led by India, were afraid of the inclusion of services disciplines because that could be a first step towards the inclusion of an investment agreement in the GATT.[6] Investment-related disciplines were of interest for developed countries because at that time trade in services was mainly supplied through the commercial presence of the services provider in the services consumer country. At the mid-term Ministerial Conference of Montreal, held in December 1988, the draft text on services had more than a hundred brackets. During that ministerial conference, the main differences were solved when developing countries could get an equal treatment for movement of natural persons (as one of the modes of supply of services) as that provided to the commercial presence, besides the flexibility provided by the text on progressive liberalisation through successive rounds of negotiation and the possibility of a slower pace for developing countries in the liberalisation process (contained in GATS Article XIX).

The text negotiation moved more smoothly from that point, allowing for the conclusion of what would be the GATS, which entered into force in January 1995 as part of the results of the Uruguay Round. Although development provisions permeate the GATS, the main ones are contained in GATS Articles IV and XIX, which will be explained in detail in the next section, together with other relevant provisions of this Agreement. It is interesting to mention that the chair of the services group during the Ministerial Conference in Brussels in 1990 was a developing country, Mexico.

Unlike trade in goods, the main barriers to trade in services rely on domestic regulations, which, together with the very unique nature and diversity of services, made it necessary to create a very specific conceptual and legal framework for trade in services negotiations, starting with the difficulty involved in defining a service.

Another specific complexity of services negotiations comes from the negotiation method. The main negotiation method in services is the request-and-offer approach performed mainly at the bilateral level. This approach is well known, but it is useful to mention that in the context of services negotiations it is resource-intensive and requires a great deal of internal coordination (inter-agency and with the relevant stakeholders from the private sector) which sometimes puts developing countries at some disadvantage. Before engaging in negotiations, countries need to have a clear idea of their offensive interests (those sectors where they would like to see commitments made by other members), as well as their defensive interests (which sectors are the most sensitive to international competition and therefore should be very carefully analysed before making a commitment). This may seem to not be very difficult at a first glance, but can be complicated when the country does not have reliable data to study its strengths and weaknesses and when the national private sector is not organised, aware or participative enough to provide inputs for the negotiators.

In addition, the preparation of requests and offers requires a team of trade in services experts, which in many developing countries is very small and sometimes not enough to cover all the topics involved in the multilateral negotiations. At the end of this chapter we will provide some recommendations for better participation in multilateral trade in services negotiations, drawing from some literature on the matter and adapting it to the reality and experience of developing countries.

A final fact to be considered in the current negotiations regarding the negotiating method in services is that the increasing number of members at the WTO makes negotiations extremely slow. It is not the intention of this chapter to discuss a reform of the WTO, but it may be time to start analysing this fact under a more systemic approach in order to propose more efficient alternatives.

Key Issues in Services Negotiations

We will start this section with a brief description of the main disciplines contained in the GATS, how they have been applied through the first years of this agreement and how they are relevant for developing countries. Although they are very well known to the people involved in services issues, it is worthwhile to give them a quick review to discuss their relevance for developing countries.

The GATS is a set of multilateral rules and principles related to trade in services that aim at expanding trade under conditions of transparency and progressive liberalisation, and as means of achieving economic growth for all members and economic development for developing countries. In addition, each member has a list of specific commitments with a flexible structure and a list of most favoured nation (MFN) exemptions, both of which are integral part of the agreement.

In principle, GATS applies to all services sectors with the exception of services supplied in the exercise of governmental authority (GATS Article I:3(b)) and measures affecting air traffic rights and services directly related to the exercise of such rights. The first exception is important to understand because sometimes the GATS is feared as an agreement that will oblige members to liberalise services, such as public education and health, and that is not the case. In fact, the right to regulate to meet national policy objectives is captured in the GATS preamble, which stresses the particular need of developing countries to exercise that right.

Among the GATS obligations, there are general or unconditional provisions that apply to all sectors independently of the commitments taken by each individual member, and specific or conditional obligations that only apply to those sectors included in the members' lists of commitments.

One unconditional obligation is the MFN obligation, which constitutes the pillar of the multilateral system. There are exemptions to this principle, which are listed by each member only when they accede to the WTO or during the Uruguay Round. There is, however, a sector in which members are allowed to introduce exemptions to MFN in this round: the maritime transport services sector.[7]

This is relevant particularly when countries prepare legislative initiatives to regulate a specific sector to include reciprocity requirements. Under GATS rules, reciprocity requirements are in violation of the MFN principle and therefore, they cannot be introduced in new legislation. When designing the new regulation to cover those gaps, developing countries need to bear in mind that, although their right to regulate is preserved by the GATS, they have to be respectful of their international commitments, including of course the GATS MFN obligation. In some sectors, especially those where an incumbent operator still has substantial market power, there is sometimes the temptation or the political pressure to preserve this power through the argument that national operators should get reciprocal treatment when trying to operate in a foreign country.

Besides each member's list of MFN exemptions, there are other cases where a deviation of MFN is permitted: when countries sign economic integration agreements providing each other preferential treatment (Article V), and when they mutually recognise regulatory standards or certificates for the supply of a service (Article VII). Under Article V provisions, members have to comply with certain coverage and impact criteria and go through a process of examination by the other WTO members, but this process needs to be strengthened in order to be properly operationalised.[8] However, the possibility of concluding mutual recognition agreements for professional services is one feature of the GATS that can be exploited by developing countries, recognising that the greatest export potential in trade in services for them is probably in the temporary movement of natural people and that a mutual recognition agreement tends to facilitate the procedures for the granting of licenses for the professional practice.

Another general obligation is transparency, captured in GATS Article III. Under this obligation, members are required to publish all measures of general application and to provide national enquiry points to respond to other members' requests of information. This obligation, which might have been more burdensome in the past for developing countries, now is not, thanks to the availability of electronic means of publication. Transparency is, however, one of the obligations that need to be strengthened in order to make it fulfill its original purpose.

Two of the most important conditional obligations are those related to national treatment (NT) and market access (MA); their importance also derives from the fact that those two principles are used to schedule each country's specific commitments under the listing approach used in GATS and known as a positive listing.[9] But, they are also important because when commitments are scheduled, countries are able to know better the state of openness of a specific sector and they can decide the margin of negotiation they want to provide themselves.[10]

The MA principle established six types of limitations that a country should eliminate to allow complete access to a specific sector (GATS Article XVI). It is not very difficult to identify and schedule those limitations when they are expressed in the form of a numerical limitation (e.g. the number of services providers for cinema projection services shall not be more than five in each city below 1000 people). The main problem of identification comes when those limitations are expressed in current legislation as economic need tests (ENTs), because often they are not very clear or the criteria for their application are not well defined, which adds uncertainty for the consumer and accords discretion to the regulator. When scheduling specific commitments, developing countries must be extremely careful with MA limitations related to ENTs, because they might end up making a commitment beyond their intention owing to a lack of clarity in the scheduling technique.

The NT obligation is another principle taken from GATT. Under this obligation, a country shall grant to services and services providers from another country the same treatment that is accorded to its own services and services providers (GATS Article XVII). This non-discrimination obligation covers *de facto* and *de jure* cases for the specific sectors listed in the schedules.

GATS Part IV is essential to understand the flexibility granted under this structure to developing countries, because it refers to the lists of commitments and the progressive liberalisation. Article XIX states that, the difference in level of development must be taken into account in the process of progressive liberalisation. Developing countries are allowed to have flexibility for opening fewer sectors, liberalising fewer types of transactions, progressively extending market access in line with their development situation and, when making access to their markets available to foreign service suppliers, attaching to such access certain conditions (GATS Article XIX:2).

Article XX explains the creation of the lists of specific commitments for each member and the process of scheduling is further detailed through guidelines that were updated in March 2001.[11] The architecture of the lists comes from a positively listed sector and subsector indicated in the first column, followed by a column for MA limitations and a column for NT limitations listed in a negative way, plus a fourth column for additional commitments. Under this particular architecture, developing countries have the flexibility of taking commitments only in those sectors and subsectors they want, with the particular limitations they decide on MA and NT and only in the modes of supply they choose.[12]

That flexibility has to be perfectly understood by developing countries in order to take advantage of it in the best manner. A mistake in scheduling the precise sector countries want to commit or the specific mode of supply can lead to an international dispute. Although there are several goods cases that have made reference to services disciplines, there have been only three cases related completely to trade services in the history of the dispute settlement mechanism provided by the WTO that have reached the panel instance. In all three of them a developing country was involved, twice as respondent (US v. Mexico, telecommunications services, 2000; and US v. China, distribution services, 2007) and once as a complainant (Antigua and Barbuda v. US, gambling services, 2003).[13] The gambling case is very interesting because it involved a small developing country challenging the US for a violation of its commitments and because of the controversial use the US made of GATS Article XXI to bring its measures into conformity. The three cases included a discussion of the scope of a specific commitment through the sector and subsector column or through the modal limitations that were scheduled. That is why scheduling clarity is essential when making a commitment.

GATS Article XXI, the last one in Part IV, provides another proof of the flexibility that the GATS architecture provides to developing countries when making specific commitments. Article XXI provides the right to modify the schedules of any country after they are in force. Of course, that possibility is subject to compensation for all affected members, but it is still a tool that can be used by members if a specific problem arises as a result of a changing situation that makes it difficult to comply with an agreed commitment under the GATS framework. That flexibility is not present in other bilateral or regional agreements related to services commitments. Unfortunately, this provision was used by the US to avoid complying with the panel recommendations in the case against Antigua and Barbuda, a move that resulted in a debate on the need to better regulate its use.

Besides the general and specific obligations mentioned above, there are several other disciplines of particular relevance for developing countries. The desire to increase the participation of developing countries in international trade in services is captured in the GATS Preamble and further detailed in Article IV. Article IV provides for cooperation between developed and developing countries to increase developing countries' participation in trade, through access to technology, access to distribution channels for their products and information networks and through commitments by developed countries on sectors and modes of developing countries' export interest. Many countries have criticised the difficulty - or lack of commitment by developed countries - to make provisions contained in GATS Article IV operational. This is also one of the provisions that require further analysis to go beyond an aspiration. The creation of an agreed set of criteria to assess the fulfilment of Article IV provisions, according to Article XIX:3, is an idea to be explored as a systemic issue in GATS future discussions.

Special consideration for developing countries is also found in GATS Article V, related to flexibility when assessing the level of liberalisation agreed under a regional trade agreement (RTA) to which developing countries are parties. On the other hand, Article XXV refers to technical assistance needs of developing countries that can be provided multilaterally by the WTO Secretariat and decided by the Council for Trade in Services (CTS).

GATS Article XV, on subsidies, refers to one of the issues that are still to be developed in the GATS framework and that is discussed in one of the CTS subsidiary bodies, the Working Group on GATS Rules. Article XV provisions recognise the role that subsidies play in certain development programmes of developing countries and mention that role has to be taken into consideration when creating the multilateral disciplines. Work under these provisions is still in a very initial phase, but developing countries have to take this flexibility into the discussion to make sure it is reflected in the final outcome.

Finally, the Annex on Telecommunications provides flexibility to developing countries when complying with the provisions related to access to and use of public telecommunication services. It also states the obligation to provide technical cooperation for developing countries at international, regional and sub-regional levels.

> Although GATS Article VI, on domestic regulation, does not contain specific wording to provide flexibility to developing countries, this is a very relevant set of provisions for them since the many barriers to trade in services are contained in non-discriminatory regulatory measures, which sometimes are disguised restrictions under the argument that they are designed to pursue a legitimate policy objective. The distinction between a measure taken to pursue a legitimate policy objective and a measure taken for protectionist purposes is not always easy and clear. Developing countries should therefore participate in an active manner in the pending creation of domestic regulation disciplines related to qualification requirements and procedures, requirements for licenses and technical standards mandated by GATS Article VI:4. They should do this with a view to ensuring that those measures do not constitute unnecessary barriers to trade.

We cannot finish this section without making a particular review of provisions related to LDCs in GATS. LDCs are mentioned in four places in GATS: the Preamble, Article IV, Article XIX and the Annex on Telecommunications. The Preamble recognises the LDCs' serious difficulty in view of their special economic situations and their trade, finance and development needs. Article IV repeats the same formulation to ask WTO members to comply with the provisions related to the need to increase the participation of developing countries in international trade, prioritising the needs of the LDCs. Again, operationalisation of GATS Article IV is still a pending issue, even in the current round, when a document with modalities for LDCs was approved in September 2003 and their implementation is being discussed at the CTS meetings. Article XIX calls for the creation of the modalities mentioned above during the successive rounds of negotiations and the Annex on Telecommunications asks for special consideration for LDCs in the transfer of technology and training with the aim of enhancing their telecommunications infrastructure and expanding their telecommunications services trade.

According to Aaditya Mattoo and Lucy Payton,[14] LDCs have pursued three objectives during services negotiations at the WTO: retaining flexibility in making commitments, getting commitments from developed countries in sectors of export interest to them and obtaining capacity building assistance for their services sectors. They mention that LDCs have only succeeded in the first objective, and we would add, it is still under discussion if that strategy taken to an extreme is the best possible option given the need for infrastructure development and technology transfer in services sectors in those countries.

Mattoo and Payton explain that LDCs have retained the flexibility provided by GATS Article IV in LDC modalities of 2003 and they went even further during the Hong Kong Ministerial Conference held in December 2005, where they got the possibility of not giving any new commitment in the current round. In our opinion, giving LDC members the opportunity of participating in the current Round only as receivers of commitments from other countries in some cases can make them to miss the opportunity of receiving foreign investment with its associated component of technology transfer in sectors that are essential for their development. The issue here is not whether LDCs have to make new commitments, but the need for an internal analysis to determine which liberalisation commitments help the broader economic development policies and in which sequence with respect to the internal reforms for each sector.

With respect to the other two objectives of LDCs' positions at the WTO negotiations, Mattoo and Payton explain that countries have not complied with the exhortations to make commitments in those sectors of export interest for LDCs and there are some improvements in the current round in terms of capacity building assistance to LDCs, which as we mention is fundamental for LDCs to help them to carry out national assessments of trade in services and to define their offensive and defensive interests.

Participation of Developing Countries in the Services Negotiations: An Evaluation

The current round of multilateral negotiations, the Doha Round, has been named the "development round." Under the Doha Development Agenda (DDA), trade in services enters its second round of commitments after the Uruguay Round, and the participation of developing countries in this process has evolved significantly. In this section we will describe the main results of the Uruguay Round commitments, the most relevant events for services in the Doha Round and the participation of developing countries in both processes.

As a result of the Uruguay Round and the "extended negotiations" on Mode 4, telecommunications services and financial services, one third of WTO members committed on 20 services sectors from a total of 160, one third committed between 21 and 80 sectors, and the remaining group committed more than 80 and up to 148 services sectors.[15] Among the 25 countries in the upper group (more than 121 sectors committed) there are several developing countries, such as Colombia, Republic of Korea, Malaysia and Mexico. If we extend the group to include the countries that committed between 80 and 120 sectors, we find Argentina, Chile, the Dominican Republic, Indonesia, Lesotho, Panama, South Africa, the Philippines and Thailand, among others.

On a sectoral basis, the most committed sectors were tourism and business services, followed by financial, communications and transport services, while the least committed sectors were health and education. By Mode of supply, the best commitments are in Mode 2, followed by Modes 1 and 3. Full Mode 4 commitments, which were of particular relevance for developing countries, were rare, coming mainly from a few LDCs such as Haiti and Angola.

Measured by volume of trade, the most important Mode of supply is Mode 1, followed by Mode 3, Mode 2 and Mode 4. Roughly speaking, Modes 1 and 3 together represent about four-fifths of total services trade, while Mode 2 represents almost one-fifth, leaving Mode 4 with approximately 1 percent of total services trade.[16]

Just by looking at the level of commitments taken during the past round one could say that the level of participation of developing countries was important. However, it is our sense that it was not until the current round that developing countries really played an important role in services negotiations, although bargaining power differs between one developing country and another, depending mainly on their market size and ability to organise to table common interests in a collective manner.

As a result of the architecture of the GATS, services negotiations did not require a formal launching through a new round to start. GATS Article XIX:1 provides that a new round as in the case of negotiations of agricultural commodities, should be held not later than five years after the entry into force of the agreement. This provision, which is known as the built-in agenda, allowed members to start discussions on services earlier than for the other multilateral issues, which needed a formal start through a Ministerial Conference, which happened in November 2001 in Doha, Qatar.

Actually, the first outcome of services negotiations, the negotiating guidelines and procedures, were agreed before the Doha Ministerial, in March 2001.[17] This negotiation of the negotiating guidelines and in general, the first two years of services negotiations (2000-2001) provided an opportunity for developing countries to table in an organised manner their interests and sensitivities. More than 100 proposals presented in that period related to the structure and the content of the negotiations. Many sectoral papers were also submitted by developing countries, individually or in groups. For example, in January 2001 Argentina submitted a communication on the assessment of trade in services (envisaged in GATS Article XIX:3) and the participation of developing countries;[18] a group of countries also presented their views on the same topic in October 2001;[19] a group of countries presented a communication on the increasing participation of developing countries in services trade and the effective implementation of Article IV in December 2001;[20] and many sectoral papers were presented by Costa Rica, Colombia, Mercosur, Mexico, and India in sectors, such as tourism, computer and related services, telecommunications, distribution, environment, maritime and air transport and temporary movement of professionals.

For the negotiation of the negotiating guidelines, developing countries participated in a very active manner, presenting position papers as a group of countries, which provided them greater bargaining power.[21] The results were guidelines with several references to the special situation of developing countries and their particular interests: a reaffirmation of flexibilities provided by Articles IV, XIX, and XXV; the obligation to take into account the level of development and size of economies; flexibility to developing countries in the review of MFN treatment exemptions; modalities to give credit to autonomous liberalisation; and the obligation to take into consideration the needs of small delegations when scheduling meetings.

The Doha Declaration in November 2001, which endorsed the work done in the almost two previous years, reaffirms the negotiating guidelines and procedures and established a roadmap for the conclusion of services negotiations as part of the single undertaking of the round: presentation of initial requests by June, 30, 2002, presentation of initial offers by March, 31, 2003 and the conclusion of the round no later than January, 01, 2005, with a stock- taking ministerial conference in 2003. After the failure of the Cancun Ministerial in 2003, the efforts to resuscitate the round resulted in the July Package of 2004, when a deadline to submit revised offers was agreed in trade in services negotiations.

As of the end of June 2008, 71 initial offers and 31 revised offers had been submitted by WTO members. Some of them are not publicly available, but initial and revised offers were submitted by several developing countries, including Brazil, Chile, Colombia, Egypt, India, Malaysia, Mexico, Thailand and Uruguay.

In December 2005, during the Ministerial Conference in Hong Kong, the important participation of developing countries resulted in new directions for services negotiations in Annex C of the Ministerial Declaration: new suggested parameters by mode of supply; a reduction of the number or scope of MFN exemptions; full and effective implementation of LDC modalities; intensification of efforts to conclude the mandates for GATS rules (which were a pending issue from the Uruguay Round[22]); the development of domestic regulation disciplines according to GATS Article VI:4; the creation of plurilateral requests as a complementary modality, to be submitted by February 28, 2006; special consideration to the trade-related concerns of small economies; and new deadlines for the submission of second revised offers and final lists of commitments, following a sequence after agriculture and non-agricultural market access (NAMA) modalities.

Developing countries' activity in trade in services negotiations has been very important to balance the demands of developed countries. Some important proposals have been presented in domestic regulations, where developing countries such as India and Mexico have tabled text proposals related to qualification procedures and requirements and technical standards, to mention an example. In GATS rules, some Association of Southeast Asian Nations (ASEAN) countries have been pushing for the creation of an emergency safeguard mechanism (ESM), and several plurilateral requests are led by developing countries (Chile leads the computer and related services plurilateral; Mexico leads the audiovisual plurilateral; Colombia, the plurilateral on Tourism services and India, the plurilaterals on Modes 1 and 2 as well as the one on Mode 4).

After the suspension of negotiations in July 2006 and the resumption in January 2007, developing countries also played an important role in the final balance of two other important initiatives in services: the chair's text presented in May 2008 and the Ministerial Signaling Conference in July 2008.

In 2008, the chair of the Special Session of the Council for Trade in Services issued a report providing for elements for the completion of services negotiations.[23] Although the text could not be agreed because of four members' (Bolivia, Cuba, Nicaragua and Venezuela) objections, the text provides some guidelines for the conclusion of negotiations and makes special mention of several developing country demands: reaffirmation of flexibilities to developing countries provided by GATS provisions, negotiating modalities, LDC modalities and Hong Kong Ministerial; special mention of Modes 1 and 4 as those of export interest for developing countries; commitments shall be commensurate with the levels of development, regulatory capacity and national policy objectives of individual countries; consideration to proposals from small economies; consideration to proposals related to special and differential treatment; and special priority to sectors and modes of supply of export interest for LDCs.

Finally, the Signaling Conference was a meeting, held at the ministerial level, with the objective of letting the most ambitious members in services sectors have an indication of the level of commitment that the invited members proposed to bind after complying with the sequencing mandated by the Hong Kong Ministerial. More than half of the 30 countries participated in this meeting were developing countries. During their participation, some members called for a balanced and ambitious result in negotiations, mentioning that an ambitious result in services should necessarily include positive results in domestic regulation and GATS rules. The indications given by the members had no legal value but provided an idea of the potential commitments. Taking a backward look at the participation of developing countries through the two rounds with services negotiations, we can perceive a radical change in position, with many developing countries now on the side of those countries pushing for an ambitious outcome in services.

Although the domestic importance of services has already been stated, it is true that trade in services negotiations do not attract the same level of importance in comparison with other negotiating issues. They are usually regarded as one of the three pillars in multilateral negotiations, together with agriculture and NAMA negotiations and as such, they are mentioned in ministerial declarations. But the time devoted at the highest level to this pillar is never equivalent to the time devoted to the other two pillars. Some people consider that the absence of negotiating frictions might have been attributable to an almost complete lack of commercially meaningful substance. It could also be that services negotiations are a relatively new matter in international negotiations and the flexibility provided by the GATS structure allows a margin of negotiation before countries start making commitments beyond their current legal framework. Another possible explanation is that not many countries have realised the potential gains of services liberalisation and they have not engaged in that issue with the same sense of ambition as with the other two pillars.

Lessons for Developing Country Negotiators from the Experience of Services Negotiations

There are several lessons to be taken from this summary of developing countries' participation in services negotiations. The first is that an increasing number of developing countries are realising that services negotiations can bring benefits. Benefits coming from the technology transfer that some modes of supply and an adequate domestic policy can bring, as well as benefits from access to more services markets are undeniable. But before making commitments a clear picture of the domestic regulatory and legal framework needs to be in place. It is a mistake to sacrifice the potential benefit of liberalisation under the excuse that it is for the preservation of policy space, as if these two objectives were mutually exclusive, but it is also a mistake to fully engage in trade in services negotiations without having a good idea of offensive and defensive interests.

A second lesson is that, in order to better participate in international trade negotiations, developing countries should do the internal homework first in terms of inter-agency coordination: independent of its individual bargaining power, a country will face difficulties during the negotiation if it does not have a clear picture of its offensive and defensive interests. This is especially relevant when scarce human and financial resources suggest a very rational and targeted participation in multilateral meetings and bilateral, plurilateral and multilateral negotiations. The need for undertaking a national study to identify strengths and weaknesses at the sectoral and modal level is evident and in this regard, the participation of the relevant governmental agencies is fundamental. There are two challenges for developing countries when preparing for a successful participation in multilateral negotiations. One is the creation of an interlocution mechanism with the services industries to have proper inputs before, during and after each negotiation. The national coalitions of services industries are a very useful tool to focus the participation of developing countries in services negotiations. Two is the improvement of trade in services statistics. Complete, accurate and sufficiently disaggregated trade in services statistics provide developing countries with an analytical tool to assess trade liberalisation and to identify opportunities and threats.

A final lesson comes from the ability to use a coalition of countries as a tool for expanding bargaining power. This chapter provides examples of developing countries presenting proposals in groups in order to provide more support for their preparation and defence. There will be a complete section in this book that will go into detail on this topic, but it is worthwhile to acknowledge the importance of appropriate grouping to place in a better manner a specific interest of developing countries in the negotiating agenda. In services negotiations, informal and *ad hoc* coalitions of countries are perhaps more used for specific topics of the negotiation than formal or rigid coalitions.

Endnotes

1 Sáez, S. (ed.) 2009. Trade in services negotiations: A guide for developing countries. The World Bank, p. 2.

2 Feketekuty, G. 2000. 'Improving the Architecture of the General Agreement on Trade in Services', in Stephenson, S. (ed.), Services Trade in the Western Hemisphere: Liberalization, Integration and Reform. p. 20.

3 Presentation during an interactive session with the regional media, UNCTAD-India, December 14, 2005. Available at: http://www.unctadindia.org/uploadFile.asp?upFile=InteractiveSessionWithTheRegionalMediaRepresentatives-14December2005_RashmiBanga.pps.

4 The US had made a first attempt to include trade in services during the GATT Ministerial meeting of November 1982, but it failed because the EU and developing countries did not support that initiative.

5 UNCTAD/PNUD/SECOFI. Mexico: Una economía de servicios. 1991. p. xxvii.

6 Mattoo, A., Stern R. M., and Zanini G. (eds.) 2007. A Handbook of International Trade in Services. Oxford University Press. p. 589.

7 This is because at the end of the Uruguay Round there were four sectors where members decided to continue negotiating in order to achieve a higher level of commitments. The "extended negotiations" covered the movement of natural persons, maritime transport services, telecommunications services and financial services. For all, except for maritime transport services, new commitments were taken, incorporated through addenda to the final Uruguay Round lists and formalised through protocols. For maritime transport services, negotiations were suspended until the next round, so they never formally concluded, providing members the chance of introducing exemptions to MFN treatment only in this sector during the current round of negotiations.

8 It is interesting to note that a similar procedure for economic integration agreements is permitted under GATT Article XXIV. However, in the services case developing country members do not have the flexibility provided under GATT by the so-called enabling clause. Such an enabling clause for services was one of the proposals presented by India that was dropped during the Montreal Ministerial meeting in order to come to an agreement in the GATS draft.

9 Debate between positive and negative lists for services negotiations is an old and, in our opinion, an exhausted debate. In more recent negotiations there is a variety of mixed approaches and in terms of level of ambition what is important in a list of commitments or reservations with the clarity to know exactly what the country is willing to commit, instead of the listing approach.

10 One of the flexibilities that GATS provides to its members, but can be especially used by developing countries, is the possibility to bind a level of commitment that not necessarily reflects the level of openness granted by the current legislation. That is, the negotiator has the possibility to establish a level of commitment that allows him or her a margin of negotiation even without the need of a legislative change.

11 GATS document S/L/92, March 28, 2001.

12 During the negotiation of GATS text there was a discussion on how to define a service. The pragmatic solution to this complexity came through the definition of the way or mode in which a service can be provided, depending on whether the supplier or the consumer of a

service moves to provide the service and how is this movement. So it was agreed on four modes of supply of a service: cross- border supply (Mode1), consumption abroad (Mode 2), commercial presence (Mode 3), and presence of natural persons (Mode 4).

13 For a detailed description of each case, see: http://www.wto.org/english/tratop_e/dispu_e/dispu_agreements_index_e.htm?id=A8#selected_agreement.

14 Mattoo, A., and Payton., L. (eds.) 2007. Services Trade and Development: The experience of Zambia. The World Bank. p. 4.

15 Adlung, R. 2000. 'Services Trade Liberalisation from Developed and Developing Country Perspectives', in Sauvé, P. and Stern, R., (eds.), GATS 2000: New directions in services trade liberalisation. Brookings Institution Press, p. 112.

16 Karsenty, G. 2000. 'Assessing Trade in Services by mode of supply', in Sauvé P. and Stern, R. (eds.) GATS 2000: New directions in services trade liberalisation". Brookings Institution Press, p. 33.

17 GATS document S/L/93, March 29, 2001.

18 GATS document S/CSS/W/44, January 29, 2001.

19 GATS document S/CSS/W/114, October 09, 2001, presented by Cuba, Dominican Republic, Haiti, India, Kenya, Pakistan, Peru, Uganda, Venezuela and Zimbabwe.

20 GATS document S/CSS/W/131, December 06, 2001, presented by Cuba, Pakistan, Senegal, Sri Lanka, Tanzania, Uganda, Zambia and Zimbabwe.

21 See GATS S/CSS/W/7, October 04, 2000, from Mauritius on behalf of the African Group; and S/CSS/W/13, November 24, 2000, from Argentina, Brazil, Cuba; Dominican Republic, El Salvador, Honduras, India, Indonesia, Malaysia, Mexico, Nicaragua, Pakistan, Panama, Paraguay, Philippines, Sri Lanka, Thailand, Uruguay, Bolivia, Colombia, Ecuador, Peru and Venezuela.

22 GATS Rules mandates refer to emergency safeguard measures (ESM), contained in GATS Article X, public procurement, (GATS Article XIII) and subsidies (Article XV).

23 GATS document TN/S/34, July 28, 2008.

5 Trade Facilitation – Negotiations towards a Win-Win Outcome

Manzoor Ahmad
Former Ambassador of Pakistan to the WTO

Introduction and Background

Trade Facilitation is the only surviving issue of the four "Singapore issues" (the other three being competition policy, investment and transparency in government procurement) taken up for future work in the first Ministerial Conference of the WTO at Singapore in 1996. The account of the evolving negotiations, groupings and alliances among countries, their initial positions and the compromises they make results in an interesting case study.

Though the Singapore Conference is considered the starting point for negotiations on a new agreement, the WTO is no stranger to trade facilitation. As far back as 1947, the WTO's predecessor, the General Agreement on Tariffs and Trade (GATT), included various articles covering transparency and harmonisation of international trade standards and procedures; these formed the bases for GATT 1994. Besides GATT Articles V, VIII and X (which are discussed below), some other examples are the WTO agreements on technical barriers to trade (TBT), import licensing, and customs valuation.

Following the Singapore Conference, an exploratory process was initiated. This mainly consisted of gathering relevant information from concerned international and regional organisations. During this initial phase, developed countries played a more active role by sharing their experiences and providing resource persons for seminars and workshops to clarify the concepts and explain why these issues needed to form part of the WTO work plan. Developing countries were not then convinced of a need to start negotiating new issues while they were still struggling with implementation of the Uruguay Round commitments.

When the Agenda and work plan for the 1999 Seattle WTO Ministerial was being finalised, trade facilitation and the other Singapore issues became mostly a North-South question. While developed countries felt that the exploratory work had justified the launch of negotiations on all these issues as part of the new WTO Round, most developing countries were not convinced and felt that more work was needed.

Since no agreement on launching a new Round could be agreed at Seattle, no decision was taken on launching negotiations on Singapore issues, including trade facilitation. There was, however, one notable development. While the discussions during the exploratory phase had focussed on a laundry list of trade facilitation issues, an understanding was reached at the conference regarding (the reduced) scope of trade facilitation negotiations. The draft declaration specifically stated:

> Negotiations shall be aimed at maximising transparency, expediting the release of goods and reducing, simplifying, and as appropriate, modernising and harmonising border-crossing requirements, procedures and formalities. In this context, the negotiations shall also consider specific measures to enhance the implementation of GATT 1994 Articles V, VIII, and X, and where appropriate, complement and expand the applications of provisions in other relevant WTO agreements.

Despite this draft agreement as well as the understandings not being formally approved, the discussions since 1999 have focussed on the three articles mentioned above.

Over the following two years, including in the run up to the Fourth WTO Ministerial Conference in Doha, Qatar, in 2001, repeated attempts were made by the proponents to place the four Singapore issues, including trade facilitation, on the agenda of the proposed new Round of multilateral trade negotiations. However, no consensus could be reached. A compromise was worked out, saying:

> Negotiations will take place after the Fifth Session of the Ministerial Conference on the basis of a decision to be taken, by explicit consensus, at that session on modalities of negotiations. In the period until the Fifth Session, the Council for Trade in Goods (CTG) shall review and as appropriate, clarify and improve relevant aspects of Articles V, VIII and X of the GATT 1994 and identify the Trade Facilitation needs and priorities of members, in particular developing and least-developed countries. We commit ourselves to ensuring adequate technical assistance and support for capacity building in this area.[1]

During the period between the Doha (2001) and Cancun (2003) Ministerial Conferences, there were two tracks of discussions in the Council for Trade in Goods (CTG). On the one hand, members continued to discuss the substance of a possible framework or modalities while on the other they continued to deliberate on the political aspects of what decisions should be taken at the Fifth Ministerial.

Discussions on substance continued to focus on how to improve and clarify GATT Articles V, VIII and X; trade facilitation needs and priorities and the efforts that were being made by donor members, the WTO and other international organisations.

On the political aspect, there were two views. While many developing countries argued that, in terms of the Doha Declaration, negotiation could not begin until the WTO members explicitly agreed on the modalities of negotiations, developed countries were of the view that consensus was needed only for modalities of negotiations and not for starting negotiations.

During the rather hot summer of 2003, negotiators were crammed in various rooms trying to make some progress. But positions remained far apart. The Chair of the General Council prepared draft texts for the forthcoming Ministerial Conference at Cancun under his responsibility. The Singapore issues assumed a "make or break" role with the proponents, notably the EU, insisting that all the Singapore issues were a part of one package. This "all or nothing" approach meant that many developing countries refused to budge on inclusion of even relatively easier issues, such as trade facilitation, as a part of the Doha Agenda. Although in the final hours of the Conference (on September, 14), the EU finally indicated that it could drop investment and competition from the agenda, this concession came too late. Furthermore, at that time it was not clear what was on the table on other issues; so developing countries refused to accept this last-minute concession. Many felt that had the conference not been adjourned so suddenly, consensus could have emerged on including trade facilitation as a part of the Doha Development Agenda (DDA).

The recrimination and blame game following the failure of the Cancun Ministerial proved to be short lived. To break the deadlock, in December 2003, Bangladesh, on behalf of least-developed countries (LDCs) and supported by 15 developing countries including China and India, submitted a document[2] showing willingness to discuss trade facilitation provided the other three Singapore issues were dropped. The document also pointed out the future direction of negotiations in this area. Since almost a third of the WTO members, including almost all the developing countries that had so far expressed serious reservations about the Singapore issues, were willing to discuss trade facilitation, achieving consensus on negotiations became easier.

Once it became apparent that the inclusion of trade facilitation in the DDA was imminent, the negotiating tactics had to change. This new phase required pooling negotiating expertise and building alliances. One of the first steps several countries took was to form a coalition of the like-minded. In early 2004, 19 countries, consisting of Bangladesh, Botswana, China, Cuba, Egypt, India, Indonesia, Jamaica, Kenya, Malaysia, Mauritius, Nigeria, the Philippines, Tanzania, Trinidad and Tobago, Uganda, Venezuela, Zambia and Zimbabwe, got together to set up an alliance known as the "Core Group." The African Group and the LDC Group also often aligned themselves with this Group and often took similar positions. In any event, many of their members were also part of this coalition. A significant number of other developing countries that did not formally become a part of this alliance also often supported this coalition on many key issues. Prominent among these countries were several Latin American countries, including Argentina, Brazil, El Salvador, Mexico, Nicaragua, Peru and Uruguay, and some Asian countries, such as Pakistan and Sri Lanka.

This coalition played a very significant role in shaping the agenda of the trade facilitation negotiations since its inception. It successfully made counter arguments to the alliance of developed countries (but also including some developing countries) known as the Colorado Group, which had been active since 1999. This Group (also called as the "Friends of Trade Facilitation") included Australia, Canada, Chile, Colombia, Costa

Rica, the EU, Hong Kong, China, Hungary, Japan, Korea, Morocco, New Zealand, Norway, Paraguay, Singapore, Switzerland and the US.

When negotiations on formulating modalities got under way in 2004, developing countries and in particular the LDCs sought clear provisions about the scope of the negotiations; the nature of the new commitments; the extent of special and differential (S&D) treatment and the availability of technical assistance and capacity building, including financial assistance for implementing any new commitments. They insisted that the scope of negotiations should be limited to clarification and improvement of relevant aspects of Articles V (Freedom of Transit), VIII (Fees and Formalities Connected with Importation and Exportation) and X (Publication and Administration of Trade Regulations) of the GATT 1994. Moreover, they demanded that any new regulations related to trade facilitation be accompanied by generous technical and financial support. Similarly, and based on developing countries' past experience with S&D provisions in some Uruguay Round agreements, they insisted that the S&D provisions in the trade facilitation area should be linked to their implementation capacities and should not consist of merely longer transition periods. In fact, developing countries should not be asked to undertake new commitments without providing them assistance to implement the commitments.

Developed countries were hesitant to give in to most of these demands, but developing countries, in particular the African Group and LDCs, refused to compromise and eventually were able to get all their key demands accepted in the draft modalities. These modalities were contained in Annex D[3] of the draft package on the Doha Round adopted by the WTO General Council on 01 August 2004. The modalities comprised 10 paragraphs, but broadly speaking they can be grouped into the following three categories:

Scope of negotiations: It is defined in terms of Paragraph 1, which limits the scope to clarification and improvement of relevant aspects of Articles V, VIII and X of the GATT 1994.

S&D treatment: It is covered by paragraphs 2 and 3 of the modalities. Under these provisions, S&D principle is not limited to longer transition periods and in fact is linked to the implementation capacities of developing countries and LDCs.

Technical assistance and capacity building: These provisions are included in paragraphs 4 to 8 and relate to identifying trade facilitation needs and priorities, support and assistance for developing countries during negotiations and for implementing any agreed commitments. In order to make technical assistance and capacity building more effective, relevant international organisations, including the IMF, the OECD, UNCTAD, the World Customs Organisation (WCO) and the World Bank have been asked to undertake a collaborative effort in this regard.

While the modalities gave a clear road map for how negotiations should proceed, there were different interpretations of various clauses of Annex D. In the initial stages, the foremost was about the scope of negotiations: whether there should be a new elaborate agreement or whether the negotiations should focus on clarification of GATT Articles V, VIII and X. Other important issues that continued to be discussed were how specific the

S&D treatment should be for developing countries and whether technical assistance also implied binding financial commitments.

In addition to what was being done at the WTO, parallel work was carried out by international organisations, think tanks and academic institutions. Their focus was on explaining various aspects of the negotiations and finding the best way forward for narrowing the gaps and laying the foundation for updated rules so that they are easily implementable and do not impose an undue burden on developing countries.

As a follow-up decision of the General Council of July 2004, the Trade Negotiations Committee established a new Negotiating Group on Trade Facilitation (NGTF) on 12 October 2004. There were intensive consultations as to who should chair this new negotiating group. The Core Group nominated its coordinator, Ambassador Mr. Yacob Muhamad Noor of Malaysia. However, the "Friends of Trade Facilitation" were of the view that the chair should not be the coordinator of a specific group. Nevertheless, the Core Group persisted and their firmness prevailed. Ambassador Noor was eventually elected as the first Chair of the Group. The level of influence of developing countries, in particular the Core Group, became apparent from this election.

The Negotiating Group held its first session on 15 November 2004 and started its work in earnest. During its first year, it discussed about 60 written submissions tabled by members representing the full spectrum of the WTO membership.

Main Proposals Submitted by Developing Countries

The submissions and their evolution are grouped in the following three phases or generations:

- First generation proposals: These were submitted during 2005 and were mostly about seeking clarifications in general terms.
- Second generation proposals: These were submitted during the first half of 2006 and were either refined versions of earlier submissions or were proposals consolidated in single documents or sponsored by wider groups of WTO members.
- Third generation proposals are those issued after June 2006. These are proposals in legal text format and are currently on the table.

The first generation proposals initially came from developed and newly advanced economies. In response, developing countries sought clarifications and asked questions on the various aspects of those proposals. For example, in Job 05/64 and Job 05/84 circulated in April and July 2005 respectively, India, Kenya and the Philippines on behalf of the Core Group sought a large number of clarifications on the proposals submitted prior to that period. Similarly, in its submission on 20 May 2005, Egypt asked 28 probing questions of various developed countries regarding their proposals on Articles VIII and X. As the negotiations started to make progress, the role of developing countries also evolved. They not only sought clarifications, but also started making their own proposals.

An unusual development in these negotiations was that very early on differences from the perspectives of developing and developed countries started getting blurred on many issues. The submission by Uganda and the US on March 21, 2005 about the abolition of consular fees was one of the first such joint proposals.[4] This was followed by two proposals by developed and developing countries on transit procedures: one by Bolivia, the Kyrgyz Republic, Mongolia, Paraguay, and Moldova with Japan and the other by Paraguay and Rwanda with Switzerland.

The joint proposal by India and the US submitted on July 22, 2005[5] on the establishment of a practical and forward looking multilateral mechanism for the exchange and handling of information between members was also a significant event. It was the first time in the history of the WTO/GATT that India and the US had co-sponsored a negotiating document. Since then, joint communications from developed and developing countries have become a norm rather than an exception.

As the negotiations gained momentum, so did the submissions from developing countries. In the Negotiating Group meeting on May 02-04, 2005, they made several written submissions, which included those from China and Pakistan;[6] Peru;[7] and Rwanda (on behalf of the African Group).[8] Through these submissions, they attempted to identify specific problems and the suggestion of practical ways to improve the relevant elements of Articles V, VIII and X of the GATT 1994 and enhance their effectiveness. They emphasised the central importance of the identification of national needs and priorities and their linkages to technical assistance, capacity-building and S&D treatment. They also suggested the need for a more in-depth analysis of how those elements should interact and interrelate in future disciplines.

A group of Latin American countries, including Argentina, Bolivia, Brazil, Chile, Colombia, Ecuador, El Salvador, Guatemala, Honduras, Mexico, Paraguay, Peru and Uruguay took up this challenge. Through document TN/TF/W/41 circulated on June 02, 2005, they attempted to address the issue of the interrelationship between the elements of Annex D, and also developed some preliminary ideas on a possible approach to ensure that the developing countries and LDCs take full advantage of the benefits of trade facilitation and lessen any attendant costs. Similarly, Pakistan and Switzerland on September 16, 2005 proposed specific measures.[9] They suggested that each member undertake a thorough self-assessment of its existing systems and identify which technical measures under negotiation it could implement and in what time frame; that there should be a pledging mechanism for technical assistance and capacity building (TA&CB) and funding through multiple channels; that the WTO Trade Facilitation Committee (TFC) should endorse members' obligations (TF measures) and commitments (TA&CB and funding); and that there should be multilateral endorsement of implementation capacities.

Mauritius on behalf of the African, Caribbean and Pacific (ACP) Group made an important submission on November 09, 2005.[10] This document was circulated at a time when many developed countries were showing a lack of commitment for financial assistance and opposing any link between acceptance of obligations and the capacity to fulfil them. In this document, the sponsors asked for assurance that development would be the main objective and focus of these negotiations. It further demanded that S&D treatment in favour of developing countries and LDCs be made fully effective and operational. Other key points of the document were that international cooperation should be enhanced through the provision of sufficient and effective TA&CB and that the outcomes of the negotiations should reflect the needs of these countries for development policy space and flexibility. The document also sought assurance that developing countries would not be obliged "to undertake investments in infrastructure projects beyond their means." Another proposal contained in the document was to ask the WTO Secretariat to prepare a study on various trade facilitation tools, the physical and policy infrastructure required for implementing such tools, and the time frame required for adopting such regulatory changes.

When the time came to present the Negotiating Group's report to the Hong Kong Ministerial meeting in December 2005, serious rifts appeared between the overall approach of developing and developed countries. The main issues were about sequencing: should needs assessment be tackled first followed by WTO commitments or should it be the other way round. Developed countries pushed for moving into text-based negotiations, while African countries and the LDC Group wanted more clarity about TA&CB commitments (including secure funding) before starting text-based negotiations. Eventually a compromise was reached about the future work programme, recommending that negotiations be intensified to identify the trade facilitation needs and priorities of individual members; identify the cost implications of measures and make the provisions of TA&CB during the negotiations fully operational in a timely manner. It was also agreed that technical assistance would be "backed by secure funding" and that the NGTF – to fulfil all aspects of its negotiating mandate – should move into focused drafting mode as this would facilitate the timely conclusion of the negotiations. These recommendations were agreed on by the negotiating group before the start of the Conference and were adopted by the Ministers as Annex E. Adoption of these recommendations brought momentum back into the negotiations.

During the first six months of the post Hong Kong Ministerial period, the concepts contained in previous submissions were refined and several similar or convergent proposals were consolidated into single documents or sponsored by wider groups of WTO members. As was agreed at the Hong Kong Ministerial, the operationalisation of S&D and TA&CB concepts received deeper examination. Building on the earlier work, two very significant written submissions were made at the April 05-07, 2006 meeting of the Trade Negotiations Committee (TNC). These included one by a group of Latin American countries (Chile, Dominican Republic, Ecuador, Guatemala, Honduras, Mexico, Nicaragua, Paraguay and Uruguay - W81) and the other by a group of Asian countries (China, India, Pakistan and Sri Lanka - W82). These proposals received a lot of support from other members that asked the proponents to join hands to move the process further. Several developed members, including Canada, the EU, Japan and Norway, also offered assistance. This was another landmark event in the negotiations, as it brought at one platform developed and developing countries. This led to the genesis of proposal (W137) that forms the basis of what we see today. This proposal by developed and developing countries together also encouraged the Core Group of developing countries to submit their own proposal (W142 and 147). These two proposals laid down the contour of S&D and TA&CB. This also encouraged developing countries to move to text-based negotiations or enter the third generation proposals.

The African Group also fully participated in this process by making submissions. On May, 09, 2006, the Delegation of Benin, on behalf of the African Group, circulated a detailed but focused submission[11] entitled "Implementing the Technical Assistance and Capacity Building and Special and Differential Treatment Mandates of Annex D of the July 2004 Framework." African Group provided a comprehensive list of TA&CB and S&D elements to be included in the trade facilitation agreement. This list included: the establishment of a clear and precise diagnosis of the situation in hand in each concerned country; designing well-targeted TA&CB programmes; ensuring that their different components are mutually supportive; setting benchmarks verifying that all necessary steps are taken for achieving the expected benefits; and support and assistance during the trade facilitation negotiations. The document also specified the elements that should be included as S&D treatment and how flexibility should be maintained.

The summer of 2006 was a gloomy period for the Doha Round negotiations as a whole. It seemed that the negotiations that had been on life support for some months, were finally collapsing when the trade ministers of the G-6 – Australia, Brazil, the EU, India, Japan and the US – failed to make any progress, and Pascal Lamy, Director General of WTO, decided to suspend any further negotiations and called for a time out. Many ministers and other commentators called it the end of the Round and announced that they would look for regional or bilateral trade negotiations. During those days, Mr. Kamal Nath (Indian Commerce Minister) and Peter Mandelson (the EU Trade Commissioner) jointly wrote an op-ed in the *International Herald Tribune* of July,05, 2006, entitled "Doha Round: It's not only What we Trade, but How." This article showed that the Doha Round was about more than market access and highlighted the benefits of a new agreement on trade facilitation. It noted "efforts to update the multilateral rulebook are making good progress and must be a centrepiece of a final Doha agreement. If the multilateral trading system is the engine room of the global economy, trade-facilitation rules are the oil in the machine." No doubt this op-ed brought further enthusiasm in the trade facilitation negotiations at a time when negotiations in other areas were not making much progress.

Noting the progress in trade facilitation during the years 2007 to 2009 and the fact that there were serious differences in other areas of negotiations, there were suggestions in some quarters that as an early harvest an agreement on trade facilitation could be worked out in isolation from other areas, such as agriculture and NAMA. No doubt this progress owed a lot to the fact that developing country delegations, despite their limited human resources, never showed any sign of fatigue or lack of interest in the trade facilitation negotiations. Also generous funding support from developed countries, like Norway and others ensured that the capital-based delegates from the LDCs continued to attend the meetings.

The progress achieved during this period encouraged many delegations to suggest a Chairman's text where different textual proposals could be consolidated. This proposal received wide support, but the US remained sceptical for a while and this work was held up. Eventually the US showed some flexibility in its position, and in December 2009 a Draft Consolidated Negotiating Text (DCNT) was circulated in document TN/TF/W/165. This was as an important step in the direction of a new trade facilitation agreement.

It took the entire year 2010 to refine the language of the Draft Text and bring it as close as possible to the legal language. This text from the very beginning was considered user-friendly but not necessarily reader-friendly. If the number of square brackets (indicating texts where there were some disagreements) can be seen as a useful indicator, one could easily say that no progress was made during 2010. If in a given meeting, certain square brackets were cleared, an equal number, if not more, were added to the text. After each meeting, the WTO Secretariat issued a revised Draft Consolidated Negotiating Text (DCNT) and by end 2010, there were six such revisions.

The phase leading up to circulation of the DCNT and its subsequent revision made two aspects pronounced. First it showed that negotiations in the plenary setting (full group meetings) was not an efficient way of working on refining the texts. Whenever there was some suggestion to amend or replace a certain phrase, the delegates would start discussing the concepts and the national positions. That was precisely the reason that, despite a large number of meetings in 2010, no progress could be made.

A second factor that had slowed the progress or rather contributed to 'slippage' of negotiations was the provision of financial assistance in the area of S&D treatment by the developed countries. The developing countries and LDCs were looking for some language in the text that would ensure an 'enforceable' obligation on the part of developed countries for provision of technical assistance 'backed by secure funding' as had been agreed in Hong Kong. Developing and LDC members were cognisant of the fact that international financial institutions (IFIs), not being members of the WTO, could not be made a party to enforceable obligations, even though they were mentioned in Appendix-D. The contribution from IFIs would remain optional or result from some bilateral funding arrangements.

A proposal from the US specially came under sharp criticism from many members, as the position appeared to be a 'back tracking' from the explicit commitment made at Hong Kong. Also, this seriously impacted the momentum of negotiations. Many developing countries, presumably as a reaction, made suggestions to change obligatory language (shall) to the best endeavours expression (may) without even realising that it might not be in their own interest.

Toward the end of 2010, the situation improved and the membership realised that to refine the text in an efficient manner, there was a need to develop some mechanism to work in small groups dedicated to specific topics. This led to giving the responsibility to 12 facilitators who convened informal meetings to 'clean' the text for respective areas (articles of DCNT). This seems to be producing results. It is widely anticipated that a consensual Chair's text can be agreed in the next few months.

There are, however, several contentious issues on which the positions of various members remain far apart. One such issue relates to the scope of customs cooperation between customs and other authorities on trade facilitation and customs compliance. Since it is consuming a lot of time in the negotiations and has a very strong North-South dimension, a summary of the issue and the related current proposals in the NGTF are given below.

Customs Cooperation

The basic issue with respect to customs cooperation is about how much data exchange to combat fraud should be part of any eventual agreement. Most developing countries would like to see a mechanism where customs administrations should be able to seek assistance on all the data elements contained in the import or export declaration. Those who support this proposal argue that having such a mechanism would facilitate customs administrations to cope with problems of being systematically defrauded of their customs and other revenues.

At the same time, most developed countries prefer that exporting administrations should have total discretion in refusing to exchange data if they do not want to, or if their current laws prohibit it. They argue that routine exchange of data on individual transactions would be administratively burdensome.

There are currently two major proposals under consideration in the NGTF: one by India[12] and a second by Canada[13]. The Indian proposal (strongly supported by Brazil, Sri Lanka and South Africa) seeks to establish a mechanism for exchanging specific information upon request in cases where there is reason to doubt the truth or accuracy of the declaration filed by the importer or exporter. This specific information will be related to matters such as customs valuation, HS (Harmonised Commodity Description and Coding System) classification, full and accurate description, quantity and origin of goods.

The Canadian proposal meets some of these concerns (e.g. relating to customs valuation) by proposing that if a member has reasonable grounds to doubt the truth or accuracy of the supporting documentation, it may request assistance from the exporting member on mutually agreed terms. This would, however, be contingent on several stringent conditions. For example, this proposal seeks to ensure that before making a request the requesting member would fully justify it by giving a summary of the reasons for the request; that the member being asked to provide the information would do so only if such cooperation and assistance was consistent with its domestic law and procedures; and that the number of such requests would be limited to a certain agreed number per year.

Another important aspect of the negotiations is the work on the needs assessment of developing countries and LDCs for eventual implementation of the agreement. Given that the proposed Agreement on Trade Facilitation would be unique in many of its features and that it would not be "one size fits all," so has been the search for a framework for its implementation. The commitments would be designed in a way that would enable developing countries and LDCs to have the flexibility to schedule their trade facilitation reforms into the following three categories:

a) first, reforms that they can agree to implement immediately once the agreement is finalised;
b) second, where the national needs assessment exercise has shown they would require time to carry out; and
c) third, where they require not only time but also TA&CB to complete satisfactorily.

For this purpose, the WTO in close collaboration with other international organisations, particularly the WCO and the World Bank started working on national needs assessment. In the initial stages of this exercise, questionnaires were circulated to developing countries and LDCs. But, this did not produce any worthwhile results. Developing countries were sceptical about the intention of this exercise. There was a perception that this exercise could eventually be used to determine what kind of binding commitments they would be expected to undertake. Therefore, it was decided to develop a self-assessment manual.[14] It consists of standards and guidelines for the needs assessment and sets out the format used in the negotiations. This approach of self-assessment with the help of international and local experts was much more successful. Almost 100 countries have so far volunteered for it and have been assessed.

Role of Developing Countries in Shaping this Agenda

This may have been the first time in the history of the GATT and the WTO that developing countries played a central and very assertive role. First, they refused to accept the view of developed countries that negotiations could start without having a consensus to that effect. They sought several assurances about the nature of negotiations and the commitments that may result from those negotiations before agreeing to negotiate. They also made sure that the modalities clearly spelled out that any new commitments would be accompanied by technical and financial support; they would be assisted not only in participating in the negotiations, but also during the implementation stage and that they would not have to take on any new commitments until they had been provided with the assistance they needed to fulfil them.

While they were firm in safeguarding their interests, they were at the same time constructive. They made a large number of well-argued submissions either individually or with other developing or developed countries.

Developing countries have had unprecedented success in the negotiations so far. Their prudent and cautious step-by-step approach meant that adequate safeguards for negotiating S&D and technical and financial assistance were built in the modalities for negotiations. As the negotiations progressed, they ensured that whatever was agreed on would be put into practice while the negotiations were still making progress.

In this connection, two of the demands are being already met to the satisfaction of developing countries. First, low-income-countries that are unable to participate effectively as they find it difficult to bring their experts to visit Geneva are being provided the means to do so. Second, they have been given expert support to review their existing trade facilitation practices and to assess their needs for meeting new commitments.

Major Differences in the Negotiating Positions of Developing Countries

Developing countries have very diverse economies, levels of development and geographies. It is therefore natural that they would have different needs and different approaches to any new international rules. The following is a sample of the issues on which differences exist among developing countries.

Transit goods: While land-locked and several other countries support national treatment and freedom of route for transit goods, others do not want to go that far.

Advanced ruling: There is a consensus on the concept but not on the scope. Considering the human resource capacity needed to give advanced rulings on customs valuation, duty drawback, quotas, etc., many developing countries prefer a limited scope, such as that relating to customs classification or rate of taxes applicable.

Publication of trade regulations: Current practice in several countries is that regulations, particularly those involving changes in taxation rates, enter into force immediately. Therefore, they find it difficult to accept changes that would make it mandatory to provide sufficient time for comments between the publication and entry into force of the new regulations.

Levy of fees and charges: Different practices are prevalent in different countries. Hence it is difficult for many countries to accept the provision that "fees and charges shall not be calculated on an *ad valorem* basis."

Elimination of Consular fee: Many countries feel that they need to keep charging a consular fee as it is a revenue measure. Others feel that this is a non-tariff barrier and needs to be abolished.

Elimination of Pre-Shipment Inspection Companies (PSIs): Many question the role of PSIs, which they consider as creating delays and hurdles to international trade, while others are strongly in favour of retaining them.

Concluding Comments

Negotiating dynamics during trade facilitation negotiations were unique in many ways compared with those followed for any previous WTO/GATT agreements or even for the ones being negotiated in the on-going DDA. It was for the first time that before agreeing to negotiate an agreement, developing countries and in particular the LDCs made sure they were aware of the parameters of what was being negotiated.

Since the WTO/GATT negotiations take years to complete, in the past, the final outcome was often substantially different from what developing countries had envisaged it would be when they agreed to start the negotiations. For example, at the end of the Uruguay Round, many developing countries were bitter about the eventual agreements on TRIPs or TRIMs whose scope went far beyond what was originally envisaged.

While negotiating the Agreement on Trade Facilitation, they were mindful of those pitfalls. They made sure that they continued to engage and undertook only those commitments that they would be able to meet or took on only such additional commitments for which they would be given technical assistance or even financial assistance.

The LDCs exercised due vigilance whether it was during the July 2004 Framework Agreement or the Hong Kong Ministerial Declaration in 2005 or whenever the draft

Chair's text or compilation of proposals were circulated. Even the resource-constrained countries that do not have adequate representation in Geneva and are unable to be present in many negotiating groups made sure that they were provided with resources to get their capital-based experts in Geneva for participation in negotiations. Also, for the first time, a mechanism was provided for Geneva-based negotiators to visit their major ports or capitals along with international experts to familiarise themselves with their countries' trade facilitation needs and priorities and to have an idea about the cost implications of proposed measures.

During the previous WTO negotiations, the involvement of other donor agencies and international organisations was minimal. These donor organisations, nevertheless, later insisted that certain measures be implemented in recipient countries as part of structural adjustment. In the case of the Trade Facilitation Agreement, such organisations had been specifically made a part of the whole exercise; therefore they assumed ownership of many capacity building and financial assistance schemes. Even the WTO Secretariat was far more involved in TA&CB contrary to the usual argument that the WTO is not a development organisation.

The proposed Agreement on Trade Facilitation clearly shows that with the right approach, developing countries can pursue their interests effectively and successfully.

While negotiating the Trade Facilitation Agreement, developing countries were pragmatic and based their positions on the interests of their countries. Often their negotiating positions differed from one another. When their interests called for it, they collaborated with developed countries. In the past, such collaboration seemed to be more a result of the divide-and-rule policies of developed countries rather than a genuine pursuit of self-interest. In the long run, this will pave the way for a true multilateral approach to international trade issues.

All in all, when the negotiations are finally concluded successfully, it will be the first case in the history of the GATT/WTO where an agreement was achieved based wholly on cooperation and not as a result of pressure.

Endnotes

1 The Doha Ministerial Declaration, WTO document WT/MIN(01)/DEC/1, November 14, 2001.

2 WTO document WT/GC/W/522, December 12, 2003.

3 Annex D of WTO document WT/L/579, August 02, 2004.

4 WTO document TN/TF/W/22, March 21, 2005.

5 WTO document TN/TF/W/57, July 22, 2005.

6 WTO document TN/TF/W/29, April 28, 2005.

7 WTO documents TN/TF/W/30, April 27, 2005.

8 WTO document TN/TF/W/33, April 28, 2005.

9 WTO document TN/TF/W/63, September 19, 2005.

10 WTO document TN/TF/W/73, November 10, 2005.

11 WTO document TN/TF/W/95, May 09, 2006.

12 WTO document TN/TF/W/103, May 10, 2006.

13 WTO document TN/TF/W/154, March 10, 2008.

14 WTO document TN/TF/W/143 and revisions, April 12, 2007. "WTO Negotiations on Trade Facilitation – Self Assessment Guide – Prepared by the World Bank in Cooperation with the WTO Secretariat and other Annex D Organizations".

6 TRIPs in DDA – Personal Perspective of a Developing Country Negotiator

Guilherme Patriota
Special Advisor to the President on International Affairs
Former Minister at Brazil Mission to the WTO

A Big Stake Business

Representatives of developing countries, whether diplomats, lawyers or officials from ministries of trade, will find it particularly difficult to handle negotiations on intellectual property rights (IPRs) that take place in Geneva. They must be aware of the pitfalls when dealing with one of the most challenging and arguably one of the most important of the negotiating dossiers.

The Agreement on Trade-related Aspects of Intellectual Property Rights (TRIPs) provided enough critical mass for the Uruguay Round to follow its course to a final conclusion. It made the Uruguay Round's "single undertaking" appealing enough for the big IPR-reliant corporations of the developed world to support its adoption as a package in 1994.

Some would claim that the absence of substantive potential outputs for IPRs, apart from geographical indications (GIs) of interest to Europe and a TRIPs disclosure of origin requirement (of interest to many developing countries), explains the protracted nature of the Doha Round process. According to this view, there would be a lack of interest in a final deal from the more powerful intellectual property (IP) constituencies.

Many IP-dependent corporations strongly influence policy formulation within their home governments. Because of this, one could consider that a multilateral round will probably not be brought to a close without their agreement or consent.

Big Pharma has its own Permanent Mission in Geneva, at the Place des Nations. It is many times bigger than most Missions from developing countries, and its role is simply to monitor all that goes on in the Swiss town that can remotely affect their unlimited drive for legally enforceable proprietary rights.

It has come to light on different occasions that members of that Mission have privileged access to information.

A confidential draft final report of the World Health Organisation (WHO) Commission on Intellectual Property Rights, Innovation and Public Health (CIPIH) was circulated among commission members with substantive amendments and editorial changes authored (in still visible "track-changes") by an International Federation of Pharmaceutical Manufacturers & Associations (IFPMA) official who evidently benefited from prior knowledge of the document's content. The fact that a former Head of State chaired the CIPIH did not prevent the leak from happening. And yet another leak occurred with respect to confidential documents of the WHO Expert Working Group on innovative financing for research and development. Incidents such as these tend to be dismissed as anecdotal. Nevertheless, they have been exposed in the specialised media and illustrate the non-level playing field delegates from developing countries have to operate in.

IPR negotiations are a big stake business, with money at the core. Royalties have flowed at higher rates from the LDCs of the South to the richer countries of the North, thanks to the global extension of proprietary rights facilitated by TRIPs.

Lowering the cost of critical medicines and health treatment in the South, as well as expediting marketing of alternative less-expensive generics became a bigger challenge for health ministries in needy nations thanks to the tighter standards of protection afforded to patent holders in developing markets.

TRIPs broadened patent coverage for the subject matter (making process and product pharmaceutical patents mandatory for all, rich and poor, developed and developing), and extended the duration of the corresponding economic monopoly associated with it to a minimum of 20 years. In addition, more patent prolonging devices and gimmicks were adopted at a practical level. Some immediately come to mind, and have been widely written about, such as evergreening, test data protection, patent linkages, second-use patents, polymorphs, protection for products lacking in inventive step, recounting of patent term in third countries through pipeline patents, outlawing of parallel imports, and so forth.

Parallel Tracks, Forum Shopping and the Path of Least Resistance

In other words, IPRs are very important for the big holders, and the push for more protection and stronger rights will continue. To further their agenda, big holders will opportunistically exploit the path of least resistance to treaty making, overstepping the boundaries set out by negotiating mandates agreed to by developing countries, and ignoring the specific nature of different negotiating fora, if necessary.

Even general principles of diplomatic ethics, gentlemanliness and transparency can be set-aside for the greater cause of stronger and more enforceable global monopolies, as can attest delegates from developing countries who have wandered off the beaten track with respect to the "conventional wisdom" at the WTO, World Intellectual Property Organisation (WIPO), the WCO or the WHO.

If tasked to represent their country's interest in the TRIPs Council or if drawn into the protracted Doha Round, under an IPR-related mandate, developing country delegates must be aware that theirs is not a single-track affair.

As one confronts an attempt by members of the EU and the US to impose IP-enforcement in the agenda of the TRIPs Council, one must be aware that a group of EU-US like-minded countries are secretly making strides outside the formal multilateral framework on an Anti-Counterfeiting Trade Agreement (ACTA), much of it (or of what has been leaked of it) of dubious TRIPs consistency, and no part of it falling within the Doha Work Programme. In April 2010, participating countries disclosed the negotiating text under great pressure from civil society groups in Australia, Canada, the EU and the US. In October, a final text with few brackets was made public. In December 2010, participants announced the conclusion of negotiations and stated that the signing of the treaty was imminent. On the question of ACTA´s compatibility with the TRIPs Agreement, interesting information can be found on Canadian Professor Michael Geist´s Internet blog.

The International Medical Products Anti-Counterfeiting Taskforce (IMPACT) is another initiative to be mindful of at the WHO. Launched in 2006 by a coalition of Big Pharma companies, its stated goal was to combat all forms of production and trade in fake or substandard medicines. In practice, however, this group has paved the way for Big Pharma representatives to directly steer discussions within the WHO (though it is claimed that IMPACT is not a WHO forum as such, but an industry established group meeting within the WHO structure). Meetings are held on issues of IP enforcement that are extraneous to the UN specialised agency. For instance, there is a push for interpretations of the term "counterfeiting" (of drugs and medicines) that go beyond the TRIPs Agreement, which defines it as a trademark violation only – not a patent violation. The group also has shown a tendency to associate more affordable generic drugs with substandard medicines, thereby promoting the idea that more expensive proprietary drugs are "safe" while generic versions are "risky."

The experience of a developing country delegate indicates that one should always be mindful of parallel negotiations on the IPR agenda, which could have the effect of circumventing developing country's greater unity and knowledge of the issues in Geneva[1].

Dealing with multiple negotiating fronts at the same time is a real challenge for the less resourceful developing country negotiators, Missions and governments.

Developed countries, along with their supporting corporate constituencies, know it, and that is one reason they resort to such tactics.

The IPR agenda, thus, moves along, simultaneously at the WTO, WIPO, WHO and WCO; within bilateral free trade agreements (FTAs) negotiated with developing countries by the US or the EU (Economic Partnership Agreements - EPAs); nationally, through bilateral cooperation or lobbying of domestic political forces; or even outside the formal multilateral framework, as a moving target convened in different cities world over, which was the strategy adopted for the secret ACTA negotiations.

Therefore, developing country delegates need to follow the full IPR agenda and not just the specific issues or committees to which they are assigned. Their political Missions in Geneva, often in charge of WIPO and WHO, must coordinate with their trade Missions in Geneva, in charge of the WTO; as well as with their home-based IPR desks. It is also useful for the Geneva Missions to consult different national constituencies, both governmental and non-governmental, and across different postings within their foreign affairs network that can inform them of bilateral IPR negotiations involving the respective host countries.

Often, it will come as a surprise to a delegate from a developing country that an entrenched position sustained in Geneva with great effort has fallen prey to a bilateral free trade agreement involving another developing country. There are a number of examples, but the objective of this paper is to alert delegates to real-life negotiation strategies, not to point fingers at particular countries that have fallen prey to them. These tactics are meant to advance the global corporate IPR agenda. Those who promote it are aware that it undermines the potential for stronger convergence among developing countries in Geneva.

IPRs might even seep into apparently unrelated areas of negotiation, such as bilateral investment protection agreements. A study by the Organization for Economic Co-operation and Development (OECD) "to clarify the extent to which and how international investment agreements (IIAs), including regional trade agreements (RTAs) with an investment chapter, increase the scope of IPR protection beyond TRIPs minimum standards"[2]can provide sufficient evidence of this practice.

The Lack of a Shared Conceptual Framework

Another big challenge in IPR negotiations for a developing country delegate is the lack of a widely shared conceptual framework from which to draw one's argument for or against different positions. One wishes there were intellectually sound and evidence-based analyses accommodating the diverse specific realities of developed and developing countries; differentiating net technology producers and innovators from the net technology importers and laggards; and the IPR haves and IPR have-nots.

In real negotiating scenarios, submissions and statements are not necessarily consistent from the legal or economic point of view. There can be some degree of manipulation of the WTO jargon at the service of unstated corporate interests from nations at the forefront of technology production and innovation.

These nations negotiate higher standards of IPR protection from the standpoint of economies detaining the better half of protected assets traded globally. They will spare no effort to convince developing countries that accepting longer and stronger monopolies for holders from a few countries in the North is good for their own economic development, however weak or unconvincing the arguments used.

Big Pharma and the Business Software Alliance (BSA), among other similar entities, have refined the art of dogmatic argument and propaganda designed to influence thinking on IPRs.

The local press, academics and other opinion formers will be recruited to shape public debate within developing countries in order to move the domestic agenda in a certain direction. These initiatives may undermine support for official positions being expressed in Geneva. Heads of IP offices may suffer great pressure from lobby groups, sometimes having to uphold institutional integrity under unfavourable conditions of resource scarcity and international cooperation dependence. If they capitulate, these institutions may start to develop agendas of their own, possibly contradicting broader foreign policy goals pursued at higher levels of government.

The negotiating jargon and logic one has to work with at the WTO has the additional burden for developing country negotiators of not being transparent to those outside immediate WTO circles, including members of the broader public that could have a stake in final outcomes. These stakeholders include the national private sector, academics, or non-governmental organisations (NGOs) and, especially, the common citizen back home who will end up bearing the consequences of less-affordable trademark medicines and delayed generics, among many other possible negative outcomes.

The WTO Microcosm: A World All its Own

More experienced, specialised or long-serving negotiators tend to better manipulate the Byzantine jargon and practice of the WTO.

Special courses for aspiring delegates from developing countries coordinated by the WTO can be ground for particular views to be expressed on what is permissible in terms of treaty interpretation, application or negotiation. During actual negotiations, members of the Secretariat are regularly called to provide their "technical" inputs or expertise. It is difficult for a delegate from a developing country to oppose these views when they are not supportive of their national negotiating positions, and I would not venture to comment on the number of times they are not.

WIPO has similar programmes, starting at even younger ages, bringing into Geneva for IP learning tours carefully selected relatives or young individuals of the national policy establishment from different developing countries. During their stay WIPO will showcase the importance of IP under very specific perspectives, probably not the ones more aligned with what the delegate of their own nationality would defend in a real negotiation scenario at the organisation.

Not unlike practices in other multilateral organisations, power is exerted by Member States with greater leverage. Higher positions in the Secretariat will tend to be occupied by nationals from developed Member States or by officials who will have ascended to those positions with a degree of consent from countries exerting greater influence. These senior members of the Secretariat may be predisposed to some form of spontaneous like-mindedness with fellow countrymen delegates or with the Missions perceived as carrying more weight in the day-to-day business of the institution, including decisions on jobs and promotions.

In the course of real negotiations one should maintain a healthy degree of critical assessment with respect to expertise coming from members of the Secretariat, however independent they may seem or be. In the case of TRIPs, never did the mandated informal consultation process on the outstanding implementation issues, based on someone acting as "friend of the Director-General," leave the purview of a very senior US member of the Secretariat with former ties to a large biotech firm and to the pharmaceutical multinationals. It was up to him to seek progress on the TRIPs disclosure of origin requirement and on GIs. As a delegate of Brazil, I underwent one-on-one "confessionals" on these issues, and faced some very sceptical comments from this official on the viability of my government's proposals ever making it in light of staunch opposition from US and European biotech and pharmaceutical industries.

Developing country delegates will often need to resort to some degree of creative reasoning with respect to the nature and scope of mandates and treaty provisions in order to push through their interests when these are unaccounted for in the negotiating process. Defending your positions and reasoning, however *sui generis* they may seem, is a must, even for a newcomer; doing it with self-confidence and a certain gusto will make it all the more effective.

One cannot afford to wait for full mastery of issues to become outspoken or resourceful when your country's national interest is at stake. NGOs and the press (which are unfortunately denied greater access to the negotiating process and to key documentation at the WTO), along with the South Centre and other organisations better equipped to think from the standpoint of less developed countries and more vulnerable societies, can be a great source of support for a developing country negotiator.

The Demise of Neo-liberalism, and the Discontinued Body of Independent Theoretical Work in Support of the South

Turning back to the issue of a conceptual framework, it is regrettable that for a number of years from the 1980s up to the international financial crisis of 2008 much of the accumulated corpus of independent thinking on economic development and trade produced by such agencies as UNCTAD and the Economic Commissions of the UN was discontinued, deliberately discredited or simply faded. This happened during the prime years of the "Washington Consensus," which left little room for thinking outside the neoliberal box.

The potential for self-destruction in the wake of neo-liberalism was more widely acknowledged when systemic failure struck at the core of the international system, hitting the financial markets of the major economies.

Responses to the crisis by the neoliberal formulators themselves have been an ABC of anti-Washington consensus policies, including fiscal stimulus packages, expansion of the monetary base, state-funded support for market-failed private banks and financial institutions, induced competitive monetary devaluations and so forth. Changing the rules of the game when it is your turn to comply is a privilege only the masters of the playing field can afford.

The recent trend of competitive exchange rate devaluations to which some of the key major economies have resorted in their reactions to the crisis has had the effect of eroding significant margins of market access that were painstakingly negotiated during years of multilateral trade rounds under the GATT 47 and the WTO.

Calculations for Brazil indicate that tariffs for certain sensitive sectors would now have to be raised to 180 percent *ad valorem* simply to compensate for devaluation of international reserve currencies *vis-à-vis* the Real, thereby re-establishing pre-2008 margins of effective protection. This is hugely detrimental to industry in developing countries that have struggled to achieve a reasonable degree of macroeconomic stability, and thereby managed to uphold with sacrifice the value of their national currencies in previous recessions and throughout the 2008 international financial meltdown.

While the impact of currency manipulation on market access can be many times superior to those of tariff reduction commitments, IPRs are essentially unaffected by them. After the 2008 debacle, the value of royalty remittances from the more stable economies of the South to the devalued economies of the North will in fact increase along with the changing exchange rate differentials, thereby raising returns on marketing of IPR assets in developing and emerging economies.

This will come as yet another unexpected windfall for the big IPR holders of the North: TRIPs will have extended the strength and duration of their IPRs "South of the border"; while the 2008 crises will have raised the value of their royalty remittances thanks to competitive exchange rate devaluations of the international reserve currencies.

WTO courses for developing country officials, however useful to provide needed introduction to the technicalities of negotiations, are no substitute for a reflection from the South on the big issues of development and the trade-offs of complex multilateral IPR rounds.

Developing country TRIPs negotiators should revisit older material from the Economic Commission for Latin America and the Caribbean (ECLAC), in particular the writings of Argentinean Raúl Prebish and Brazilian Celso Furtado, founders of an autonomous branch of development economics. Much of their output is currently being revisited in light of challenges posed to developing countries in their renewed quest for technology absorption, production and specialisation.

Prebish expressed in clear terms the dangers of developing countries settling into the role of global producers of low value-added raw materials or specialising in low-yield low-technology agricultural production systems.

Criticising the conceptual base on which the international rules-based trading system evolved as per the GATT 47, Furtado emphasised that developing countries needed to guide their international positions on the basis of "dynamic comparative advantages," not static ones.

This meant questioning all national and international norms that impose *ex-ante* restrictions on options available to less advanced countries in their policies for economic and industrial development.

Obviously, accepting changes to the TRIPs Agreement that unduly strengthen IPRs concentrated in the hands of a few "haves" while offering no technological trade-off to the IPR "have-nots" (developing nations) would be a non-starter from the traditional UN ECLAC point of view.

Some of the reasoning behind early ECLAC thinking has been recaptured, more recently, by the "policy space" concept at the center of the United Nations Conference on Trade and Development (UNCTAD) XI São Paulo Consensus adopted in 2004 - an opportune tribute to Furtado and Prebish.

Writings from the 1970s by authors such as Carlos Correa, published under an UNCTAD series on IP and transfer of technology, should be re-edited and made more accessible. Correa knew that contrary to what big business may hold, IPR protection is not a moral issue, and does not promote technological development where conditions for it do not exist; it is a negotiated term for access to and development of technology.

Depending on the particular situation, one can argue that IPRs actually hamper competition and artificially dictate return on investment and profit margins without necessarily expressing any particular correlation to cost or conditions of production and trade. A non-disclosed amount of resources invested in research and development (R&D) (pharmaceutical companies tend to assert very high investment numbers in R&D, but never allow their accounting books to be publicly scrutinised) is supposed to be legitimately recovered by the innovative entrepreneur thanks to the IP system, but in today's world of global corporate dominance and asymmetric markets, such claims fall outside the realm of the verifiable truth.

It must be said that the most successful Brazilian technology based industries emerged from a benign combination of national political consensus and state activism. The Brazilian IPR system (in fact still of little significance for the domestic industry) had little to do with their creation and subsequent evolution.

This is true for small giants, such as Petrobras, one of the world's largest deep-sea oil drilling companies; EMBRAER, producer of business jets, military training planes and regional aircrafts and Embrapa, the agricultural research institute responsible for Brazil becoming one of the world's largest producers of grain and livestock. All of them put together will hold no more than a handful of patents, though presumably now that they are big and have consolidated in their respective fields, patent numbers may start to become a matter of interest or concern.

Making a quick jump of over some 50 years since ECLAC started with Prebish and Furtado, we can find in Nobel Laureate Joseph Stiglitz (among other similar analysts and policy formulators) a welcome renewal in independent economic theorists.

In a presentation in 2005, Stiglitz underlined the non-temporary nature of exclusive rights conferred to IP holders by a patent. Although TRIPS establishes 20 years as the minimum duration, the power of market domination conferred to the holder by a patent monopoly can last much longer, due to a combination of first entrant advantages and an acquired capacity to influence the conditions and pace for the marketing of further innovations on competing products.

Stiglitz's "Initiative for Policy Dialogue," launched in July 2000, provides great insights for developing country delegates wishing to unveil the intricacies of IPRs from a less self-interested corporate perspective. One of the task forces created under the initiative focuses on intellectual property and can be accessed at http://policydialogue.org.

Changing TRIPs from Outside the WTO

Corporate IPR agendas pushed by the captured governments of the developed countries will move forward relentlessly in several fronts and fora simultaneously. This requires developing country delegates to be informed and aware of different negotiating processes and their interrelationships, lest they end up focusing only on a Doha Round IPR debate while deep action is going on elsewhere.

It is therefore difficult to focus this particular article on TRIPs alone, when much of what is advancing with respect to IPRs that is substantive, currently falls outside of the Doha framework.

These processes include the ACTA – the shadowy parallel rewriting of TRIPs Part-III, mentioned above, that may hamper international trade in legitimate goods from developing countries through extraterritorial extensions of IPRs imposed as border measures.[3]

There is constant pressure at the WIPO in favour of the transnational corporate dream of a global patent. Actually, it would be more precise to describe it as a patent better to enforce in less-safeguarded foreign developing countries and emerging economies than in the more IP-savvy markets of developed countries.

Differences of substance among the OECD members – first-to-file versus first-to-invent, different benchmarks for assessing patentability, different local working requirements applied to publicly funded inventions, different litigation and judicial practices and culture – provide them ample "policy space" to tweak their industrial policies. This means developed countries usually retain room to manoeuvre their way out of a prospective global patent "straight jacket"; not so developing countries, whose national patent systems are usually not as sophisticated or complex.

There is the WIPO "digital agenda," started right after the adoption of the Uruguay Round package, which led to two agreements that provide stronger exclusive rights to copyright holders than those previously protected under the more balanced Bern Convention of 1886 (revised several times thereafter).

It was alleged that new developments in digital technology required updating the Bern standards to safeguard holders' rights (not necessarily those of authors or artists; but those of the transnational entertainment and sports industries) against unauthorised copies of their products in the digital format.

In this apparently innocent updating of older legal instruments, there was much to be gained by big business and much to be lost by common citizens, especially those in developing countries where the public domain and exceptions and limitations to rights are less safeguarded.

As an example, one can point to the legal endorsement by the WIPO 1996 digital treaties[4] of the so-called technological protection measures (TPMs). Such "updated" provisions had the effect of reducing citizens' access to private copies of music, books, teaching materials, video excerpts and a plethora of other information sources.

Circumventing TPMs (technology embedded in digital products to prevent copies), whether the product is actually protected or not in a particular national jurisdiction, was essentially criminalised by the WIPO 1996 treaties, in a move that runs counter to the expected "democratisation" of information in the age of knowledge societies.

Copyrights are being pushed, universally, from an already lavish "author's life plus 50 years" of the Bern Convention, to "author's life plus 70 years"[5]. Exceptions and limitations to rights, several of them found in domestic laws of developed countries, such as the US fair use exception, were not included in the new WIPO treaties. Had those exceptions and limitations been made universal or mandatory for all WIPO members their widespread adoption would have protected individual rights and social welfare in developing countries against encroachment from the higher levels of IPR protection afforded to holders.

The critically important 45 recommendations adopted by the WIPO General Assembly in 2007, which make up the "WIPO Development agenda," can provide a platform for rebalancing IPRs from the perspective of developing countries' needs and priorities. They set negotiating principles and benchmarks that are relevant for any future IPR substantive treaty-making exercise, whether at WIPO or in the WTO.

What to Expect at the WTO/Doha Negotiating Table

TRIPs is the only Uruguay Round Agreement amended thus far. This process was finalised by a decision of the General Council (functioning as Ministerial Conference) in December 2005. The goal was to make permanent in the TRIPs Agreement the "temporary" waiver to Article 31 (f) adopted as a result of the Ministerial Declaration on TRIPs and Public Health of 2001.[6]

The main purpose of the waiver was to modify the rules of Article 31 in the Agreement, which authorised countries to issue a compulsory license for the manufacturing of patented products, if they considered that the patent-holding company was charging unreasonably high prices for them. The Article however provided that such licenses should be given predominantly for supplying the domestic market. The rules therefore prevented production of generic drugs under a compulsory license for export to third markets. The temporary waiver from those rules adopted in 2003, which subsequently became a permanent amendment to the TRIPs Agreement, provided that countries that had manufacturing capacities to produce generic versions could grant compulsory licenses to their pharmaceutical companies to produce cheaper generic versions for supply to developing countries that did not have manufacturing capacities to produce them. The waiver, however, laid down strict conditions with a view to ensuring such generic versions were not diverted for sale in other markets.

It is interesting to note in this context that when the strenuous negotiations on the text of the waiver were nearing completion, some of the developed countries that were pressing for additional stricter conditions (Pharma inspired) insisted that these tougher conditions should at least be read out by the Chairman. The waiver was adopted and the Chairman read out his statement. But there was no formal link between one action and the other. This detail is very important. Later on, after these decisions were taken and the official documentation was issued, delegates who tried to obtain the decision document from the WTO website found out, to their astonishment, that the Secretariat, on its own initiative, had inserted an "asterisk" into document WT/L/540 and Corr. 1 to indicate that the waiver was subject to the statement read out by the Chairman[7]. This constituted serious manipulation of a formal agreement by Member States, and a heavy handed attempt to distort WTO law and practice, as from the legal point of view a waiver is considered to be a legally binding stand-alone document.

On the negotiation of TRIPs issues in the Doha "development" Round, one must demystify what many in Geneva would describe as the extremely complex and technical nature of the IPR mandates. This view is often raised as a barrier to the non-partisan observer giving his or her objective opinion against the types of bargains one could actually strike within the given TRIPs/WTO framework as a matter of fact.

It is true in many respects that the devil is in the details. But it has become strikingly clear as the Doha Round progresses towards prolonged stagnation that it is the political will and the capacity to muscle in economic and political pressure that pushes the process forward. Therefore, the knowledge of treaty intricacies we are often led to invest in may not be enough, on its own, to define the outcomes of negotiations.

Self-referential specialisation in the WTO tends to legitimise the broader, highly prescriptive, highly managed framework for global trade. One can easily get lost in the forest for gazing too vigorously at the particulars of specific trees.

TRIPs itself was not considered a pro-development or pro-developing country outcome. Its conclusion came at the end of the Uruguay Round's single undertaking and worked as an inducement for the adoption in Marrakech, in April 1994, of the full package of treaties, including the Agreement establishing the WTO.

When documents of such legal intrusiveness are in order one can never be careful enough in submitting them for prior in-depth analysis by specialised national institutions or socially representative bodies.

Countries should not join in a leap of faith, however enthusiastic they may have been at the time with the neoliberal wave (those were the heydays of the Washington Consensus). For some developing countries, however, it might have been difficult to resist pressure from the national business constituencies' narrower, short-term trade interests, which could be caricatured as follows – tariff reductions for a couple of low-value raw products sold abroad by the business elite of some developing country against critical extensions of market monopolies for high-value IPR-embedded products for the globalised corporations of the developed ones.

IP is not a short-term issue. A country has to be able to plan years ahead to know what it is doing when discussing the legal framework for the protection of IPRs. It must be in a position to manage complex transversal innovation public policies, that require the articulation of public finance, tax incentives for research, funding of labs and universities, adequate educational curricula emphasising the more expensive science courses, anti brain-drain policies and laws, in addition to an IP culture, which many in the developing world have not yet acquired or developed. In a developing country, it is easier to be a secondary purchaser of technology from the North than to run the risk, against many odds locally, to innovate, produce and attempt to market your own.

It is not the purpose of this chapter to judge the Uruguay Round outcome in light of other possible developments. But a significant lack of pro-development content was widely recognised shortly thereafter, when the difficulties of internalising the legally binding elements of those lengthy documents arose.

The impact of the TRIPs "minimum" standards was much more of a burden for non-innovating developing countries than they were for the developed ones. Basically, those standards globalised one-size-fits-all solutions for the protection of IPRs, ignoring the fundamental lack of balance between IP-assets haves and have-nots.

The consequences were not just theoretical. More affordable generics for treating HIV/AIDS and other life-threatening illnesses in poor developing countries, as well as patent-expired trademarked drugs, suddenly were out of reach in many national societies, thanks to the TRIPs extension/reinstatement of enforceable monopolies in third markets.

There were in fact serious "implementation issues" for developing countries, and a listing of them was actually spelled out in the post-Uruguay Round period of WTO discussions, during the run-up to the launching of the Doha "development" Round in 2001 – more than 100 of them. At that point, many developing country delegates believed it was high time for those implementations issues to be addressed, especially the ones left "outstanding."

Unable to resist and perhaps focussing their priorities in other areas, developing countries went along with an extremely ambiguous mandate (another one of those WTO sleights of hand) for addressing the so-called outstanding implementation issues as part of the Doha work programme.

One of them was of major interest to developing countries: the relationship between the TRIPs Agreement and the Convention on Biological Diversity (CBD). For developing countries, this was supposed to be an opportunity to discuss rampant global bio-piracy (by scientific institutions, multinational companies and laboratories from the North) preying on the vulnerable, though unique and abundant biodiversity riches located mainly in the South.

For once, the possibility of the WTO TRIPs Agreement protecting an asset widely held by many in the developing South from misappropriation through undisclosed patenting of bio-pirated subject matter in the developed North held the promise of a concrete deliverable of interest to a majority of developing countries.

Unfortunately, much negotiating time has been spent since 2001 on sterile discussions as to whether the negotiating mandate for a disclosure of origin requirement in TRIPs is part of the Doha Round's single undertaking, or just an issue on the regular agenda of the TRIPs Council, where it can be left to stagnate through years of uncommitted back and forth.

The mandate for TRIPs and CBD should have been delivered to a TRIPs Council in "special session" where negotiations under the Doha mandate are taking place in order for it to be irrefutably an integral part of the "single undertaking," thus obliging all parties to engage. But, the language churned out in the Doha Declaration was not clear enough to this effect, so countries have to make additional efforts simply to get a straightforward discussion going.

To overcome such obstacles, a group of developing countries together with European countries interested in the protection of GIs and less resistant to the idea of a TRIPs amendment on disclosure of origin of genetic resources (the EU and Switzerland) joined forces. Together, they managed to bridge one of the challenging North-South divides in the TRIPs Doha discussions by putting forth the breakthrough submission TN/C/W/52, of July, 19, 2008.

The proposal reflected one of the few instances during the course of the Doha Round when a significant part of the North met a significant part of the South to converge on substance and process in three different but related issues, presenting draft modalities for their parallel negotiation as part of the Doha Round single undertaking:

a) the establishment of a registry for wines and spirits;
b) a mandatory requirement in TRIPS for the disclosure of origin of genetic resources and/or associated traditional knowledge; and
c) the extension of GI protection under Article 23 of TRIPs to all products (not just wines and spirits).

Developments taking place after the submission are captured more or less comprehensively in the reports put out by Ambassador Trevor Clark of Barbados (TN/

IP/19, of November, 25, 2009), and Ambassador Darlington Mwape of Zambia (TN/IP/20, of March, 22, 2010).

Over 100 countries co-sponsored document TN/C/W52. Few other submissions enjoy such broad-based support. In it, a balanced trade-off was pre-negotiated among over two-thirds of the WTO membership, setting the baseline for moving negotiations towards a final outcome with respect to the GI register, the TRIPs disclosure of origin requirement, and the GI extension.

Negotiating parameters are fairly self-explanatory in the draft modalities text contained in document W/52, though one must never underestimate the capacity of the opposing minority to filibuster by endlessly splitting hairs over technicalities, especially when the IP-obsessed corporations of the majors, their infatigable associations and federations, close ranks with them.

Tackling the TRIPs Mandates

The TRIPs negotiating mandates for the Doha Round are broken down into parallel formal tracks, making it more difficult to negotiate a package deal that could promote a bargain between (a) a clear majority of developing countries dissatisfied with the little that was achieved in their national interest through the Uruguay Round TRIPs Agreement in general. (In particular they resent the absence of clauses that would prevent misappropriation of their biodiversity through patenting and discourage the use of traditional knowledge associated with those increasingly valuable resources without the prior informed consent of holder communities and benefit sharing, in accordance with applicable national legislations or an international regime under the CBD); (b) European countries wishing to secure better protection for GIs through a multilateral system of notification and registration, and generally wanting to extend the higher protection afforded by Article 23 of TRIPs to products other than wines and spirits (GI extension); and (c) a minority group of mostly "New World" developed countries, amalgamated around the US's anti-GI extension position, which for strategic purposes tend to rally behind the entrenched position of the US IP-based industry, ideologically opposed to an Amendment to TRIPs for a biodiversity disclosure of origin requirement. The United States resists engaging in a more open, substance-driven debate on TRIPs reforms considered either to "weaken" the patent system in favour of bio-diverse countries (mostly developing countries) or to increase protection for products better known the world over for their European origins, and thereby coveted on the understanding that their brand name provides a reliable indication as to the true geographic origin of their production in accordance with age-old traditional manufacturing techniques and local conditions intrinsic to the quality expected of them.

Paragraph 12 of the Doha Work programme on implementation related issues and concerns makes a subtle procedural distinction between issues that "have been provided a specific negotiating mandate in the Declaration" and those to be dealt with "as a matter of priority by the relevant WTO bodies." This wording has been the object of much debate and polarisation since the Round was launched in 2001; and, in fact, it was a last minute formulation that left the outstanding implementation issues of interest to developing countries on a separate negotiating track as agenda items for regular meetings of the respective WTO bodies to which they are ascribed. The relationship between the TRIPs Agreement and the CBD, which provides the basis for discussions on Article 27.3.b of TRIPs (protection of plant varieties and other life forms) and the proposal on a TRIPs disclosure of origin requirement is formally allocated to the regular sessions of the TRIPs Council. Opposing members rely on the wording of Doha Declaration paragraph 12 to refuse taking up these issues during a TRIPs Council meeting in Special Session (jargon for a session that directly negotiates matters within the Doha Round single undertaking). The same applies to GI extension. But the multilateral system of notification and registry of GIs for wines and spirits was subjected to a specific negotiated mandate and therefore is the only issue accepted by all as an integral part of the Doha Round single undertaking.

One way to overcome this break-up of the TRIPs mandates was explored by countries that have offensive interests in the TRIPs mandates indicated in the (a) and (b) categories above: that is, Brazil, India, the EU, Switzerland and most developing countries from Africa, Latin America and Asia, totalling more than 108 members out of 153. In 2008, this group first entered into an informal substance-driven process of approximation among their respective positions on the GI register, on the disclosure of origin requirement and on GI extension. The question of mandates was temporarily set aside in favour of reaching common ground among over two thirds of the WTO membership and making progress. The outcome of this groundbreaking initiative was formalised as document TN/C/W52, of July, 19, 2008. Thanks to this effort, the TRIPs issues gained much greater traction and were discussed at higher levels in several Green Room discussions led by the Director-General Pascal Lamy himself, as per the mandate entrusted to him under the 2005 Hong Kong Ministerial Declaration. If an understanding can be reached that makes the Doha Round move forward taking on board the position of 108 members, there are ways to overcome the "parallel mandates problems" by a decision of the Trade Negotiations Committee to take up the issues for text-based negotiations under the Doha Round single undertaking process.

Basic Elements of Document W/52

GI REGISTER

Proposed modalities for the GI register appear as the first of the three TRIPs related issues in document W/52, in recognition of the fact that this issue possesses the clearest negotiating mandate, as per Article 23.4 of the TRIPs Agreement.

The first paragraph emphasises that the proposal is valid for wines and spirits only. Whether or not the registry would apply to other products is a decision that would be considered in the context of the paragraph for modalities on GI extension. The register would be multilateral (meaning non-voluntary). The system of GI notification would be straightforward and automatic, and the WTO Secretariat would not be required to verify validity of information provided. The information to be included and its format would be defined in the course of drafting the final legal text.

The second paragraph of submission W/52 stipulates an obligation of national authorities to consult the multilateral registry with the WTO and to take it into account when deciding on registration of trademarks and GIs in accordance with their domestic procedures. This solution is similar to the one in the so-called Joint Proposal.

The sentences that follow define the main substantive effects of the register: (a) in the absence of proof to the contrary, the presence of a GI in the WTO multilateral register will constitute *prima facie* evidence that it meets the definition of a GI in accordance with Article 21.1 of TRIPs; (b) claims to the effect that a name is or has become generic, within the exceptions provided for by TRIPs Article 24.6, would have to be "substantiated." These two requirements would increase the basis for actions at the domestic level within the national jurisdiction of WTO members with a view to protecting GIs. They are clearly less intrusive options than the one first put forth by the EU, which had the aim of establishing a "rebuttable presumption" of validity of any GI included in the register without opposition within a certain time frame. Since the EU´s baseline position was softened, it seemed no longer necessary to create a time frame for opposition to notifications.

TRIPs and CBD: "Disclosure Requirement"

In submission W/52 the EU and Switzerland took the critical step of accepting an amendment to the TRIPS Agreement, with a view to establishing a mandatory requirement to disclose the country providing/source of genetic resources and/or "associated traditional knowledge" used in an invention claiming patent protection. It is proposed that a functional legal definition would have to be agreed for the term "associated traditional knowledge," so as to promote greater judicial predictability. The term "source," used in Switzerland, but not in the CBD (based on the notion of sovereignty and, therefore, on the idea of "country providing"), would be more flexible and probably find greater acceptance.

The sensitive issue of the legal effects of lack of compliance with the mandatory disclosure requirement would be relegated to the pre-grant phase of the patent procedure, and the sanction would be interruption of administrative processing of the patent claim until the requirement is fulfilled. Revocation of patents for lack of compliance with the disclosure requirement is not therefore included in the proposal, but the submission states the possibility of additional elements contained in members' proposals being raised and considered, "such as PIC (Prior Informed Consent) and ABS (Access and Benefit Sharing) as an integral part of the disclosure requirement and post grant sanctions." The language does not prejudge the outcome of negotiations on these elements.

As the GI register already falls under the purview of the TRIPs Council in special session, a reference was made to "intensification of negotiations" in that format. But for the disclosure requirement and GI extension, still discussed under the TRIPs Council in regular sessions, a phrase was added to elucidate that "text based negotiations shall be undertaken, in Special Sessions of the TRIPs Council, and as an integral part of the Single Undertaking," making it clear that the three elements of the W/52 submissions would be negotiated as a package, notwithstanding the different interpretations members may have on the nature of their respective mandates when the Doha Round was launched in 2001.

GI Extension

The proposed draft modalities text for GI extension is quite straightforward, and simply states that members agree to extend to all products the protection of Article 23 of the TRIPs Agreement afforded to GIs by Article 23 of the TRIPs Agreement, including the extension of the register, as well as to apply to these the exceptions provided in Article 24 of the TRIPs Agreement *mutatis mutandis*.

Special and Differential Treatment

A catch-all phrase was added at the end of the W/52 submission stating that "Special and Differential treatment shall be an integral part of negotiations in the three areas above, as well as special measures in favor of developing countries and in particular least-developed countries."

Opponents First Informal Reaction to Submission W/52

The group that has taken a defensive position on the TRIPs issues remained opposed to the idea of parallelism among the multilateral system of notification and registry of GIs, the TRIPs disclosure of origin requirement, and GI extension, as proposed in submission TN/C/W52. In their first informal reaction, they articulated a non-paper in order to better reflect their position in the report that was to be prepared by WTO Deputy Director-General Rufus Yerxa on implementation issues, in 2008:

> **Non-paper on GI-extension and TRIPs-CBD as Outstanding Implementation Issues**
>
> Communication from Australia, Canada, Chile, the Republic of Korea, Mexico, New Zealand, the Separate Customs Territory of Taiwan, Penghu, Kinmen and Matsu and the US
>
> We are WTO Members with significant interests in intellectual property issues. Among us are developed and developing countries, representing a broad geographical diversity and substantial proportion of world trade, particularly in products potentially affected by TRIPs proposals under discussion. We are united by a joint concern that the current delicate stage in the DDA negotiations should not be unnecessarily disrupted by efforts to rush, revisit, reinterpret or change our existing negotiating mandates. On May, 30, at a meeting organised by Deputy Director General Yerxa pursuant to the Director General's authority under paragraph 39 of the Hong Kong Declaration, Switzerland introduced a "draft text" in the form of a "non-paper." Dated May, 26, the paper was submitted by "proponents of TRIPs issues"[(1)] and supported at the meeting by a number of delegations. The paper requests that reports to the Trade Negotiating Committee reflect the agreement of its authors to include the issues of "GI Register, GI extension and TRIPs disclosure requirement" as "part of the horizontal process in order to have modality texts that reflect Ministerial agreement on the key parameters for negotiating final draft legal texts as part of the single undertaking" for each of these issues. We, like others who spoke at the meeting, wish to express our strong opposition to this proposal, and our conviction that it would

substantially set back efforts to arrive at a viable way forward for the Doha negotiations. We reject the artificial parallelism in the May, 26 Paper. Each of the TRIPs issues cited in the non-paper has its own terms of reference (2), and particular subject matter. Many technical issues remain, and the extent and interest of Members in the content and potential outcomes for each issue varies considerably. For example, on the issue of extension, even basic objectives are far apart, discussions have revealed no consensus, and the suggested draft modalities text presented by the *demandeurs* prejudges an outcome. We understand that some Members require assurances that matters such as the TRIPs Implementation issues will not be left behind. However, asking Ministers, in today's highly sensitive context, to address these distinct, divisive and highly technical TRIPs issues in the way suggested in the 26 May paper, goes well beyond such assurances.

Note:

(1) This description is inaccurate as there are delegations that have made formal proposals on "TRIPs issues," but who do not support the May, 26 paper.

(2) We note that "the GI Register" does not fall within the purview of the Director General's authority under paragraph 39 of the Hong Kong Declaration, has a distinct mandate under paragraph 18 of the Doha Declaration and Art. 23.4 of the TRIPs Agreement, and has been the sole subject of negotiations in the TRIPs Special Session. The sponsors of this statement are fully committed to fulfilling the Doha mandate on the GI register for wines and spirits as part of the Doha Single Undertaking.

Final Comments

One must bear in mind that the more radical elements of the proponents' original positions on the three issues encompassed by document W/52 were smoothed over among its 108 supporters so that compromise could be reached in a commendable display of constructive flexibility.

Document TN/C/W/52 was negotiated in Geneva basically among delegates of Brazil, the EU, India, Switzerland, representatives of the African, Caribbean, and Pacific (ACP) and the African Group, and was thereafter cleared by the respective capitals. Additional co-sponsors were added subsequently. The sheer critical mass of support it received demonstrated that the draft modalities text for the three TRIPs issues could not continue to be discussed only at the technical level. DG Pascal Lamy decided in mid-2008 to include these issues in Green Room consultations on draft horizontal modalities for the Ministerial Meeting in July of that year. Consultations were presided over by the Director General himself initially, then by the Foreign Minister of Norway, Jonas Store, and later, for technical clarification purposes, by former Head of the TRIPs Division at the WTO, Adrien Otten, who coordinated a couple of sessions. After the Ministerial Meeting of July 2008 broke down for reasons to do with agriculture and NAMA, the Doha Round as a whole entered into a much less promising phase, which of course was not helpful to the cause of TRIPs issues. Nevertheless, the GI register, TRIPs and CBD and GI extension are still on the table and have been the object of ongoing activity, as is clearly informed in the DG´s report to the General Council and to the Trade Negotiations Committee of April, 21, 2011, documents T/GC/W/633 and TN/C/W/61 (document TN/IP/21, also of April, 21, 2011, contains the report of the Chair of the TRIPS Council in Special Session on the GI register).

Even though there is still no consensus on negotiating a disclosure requirement as an integral part of the Doha single undertaking (or on doing it through an amendment to TRIPs), the mere fact that over 100 members are willing to go along with it bodes well for negotiations in this area of critical importance to megabiodiverse and traditional knowledge (TK) endowed developing countries.

The critical mass of support reflected in W/52 has already produced the effect of raising the three TRIPs-related issues to the level of Green Room, DG-led informal consultations. Ambassadors were forced to better acquaint themselves with issues that were, until then, the concern of second-ranking Geneva-based negotiators only. To the extent that the Doha Gordian knot is at some point cut loose, it would be foolish not to prepare for the possibility of an outcome on the basis of W/52.

"Specialised work" hasn't stopped. During winter of 2011 in the northern hemisphere, much was made of a breakthrough in respect of the GI register negotiations. The announcement on the WTO website of January 13 reads: "For the first time in over 13 years of talks, WTO intellectual property negotiators have started work on producing a single draft text for setting up a multilateral geographical indications register for wines and spirits. A draft on notification — the first of six broad topics of the system to be discussed — was circulated by chairperson Darlington Mwape at an informal meeting of the full membership on January, 13, 2011". Interestingly, positions on this issue for two thirds of the membership are defined by their agreed modalities in the W/52 document.

Progress on the registry should be a call to arms for the broad W/52 grouping of nations. They must remain united and stick to the essential: a requirement to disclose genetic resources and/or associated TK in patent claims must be made obligatory for all WTO Members through a TRIPs amendment containing elements spelled out in the W/52 draft modalities text; a GI register, along the lines of W/52 should be acceptable, together with the idea of extending GI protection for products beyond wines and spirits.

The devil is in the details and there is much to negotiate. But, the lack of outcome on proposals supported by an absolute majority of WTO members would really make the organisation and its negotiating procedures look bad. From the perspective of developing country negotiators, it would constitute a major blow to the "development" component so loudly proclaimed as the Doha Round guiding principle.

Endnotes

1 See 'WIPO: India Rejects Outcome of Casablanca Patent Harmonisation Meeting', Bridges Weekly, April 13, 2005, http://ictsd.org/i/ip/39678/, and 'General Assembly Bypassed in Informal WIPO Talks on Patent Harmonisation', Bridges Weekly, February, 23, 2005, http://ictsd.org/i/ip/39684/. Both articles refer to the Casablanca informal consultations of February 2005, convened by the Director-General of WIPO with a group of representatives acting on their own behalf, cherry-picked on the basis of their willingness to support a "global patent" deal within WIPO´s Standing Committee on the Law of Patents. The Brazilian invitee was the only member not aligned with the DG´s proposal, as was made clear in WIPO press update 241, of February, 18, 2005, http://www.wipo.int/pressroom/en/prdocs/2005/wipo_upd_2005_241.html.

2 Liberti, L. 2010. Intellectual Property Rights in International Investment Agreements: An Overview, OECD Working Papers on International Investment, No. 2010/1, http://www.oecd.org/document/24/0,3343,en_2649_33783766_45219352_1_1_1_34529562,00.html.

3 In December 2008 Dutch customs officials seized a shipment of the generic pharmaceutical product Losartan used to treat high blood pressure. Produced in India, the product was in transit for Brazil. The active principle is considered generic both in India and in Brazil, but was allegedly under patent protection in Europe. The seizure defies the national territorial jurisdiction of the patent system, and one could claim that it ignores TRIPs Part III, Article 41.1, which states members shall avoid the creation of barriers to legitimate trade. Brazil and India requested formal consultations with the EC and the Netherlands as a first step in a dispute settlement procedure regarding the violation of GATT 94 and of the TRIPs Agreement.

4 WIPO Copyright Treaty (WCT) and WIPO Performances and Phonograms Treaty (WPPT).

5 Extension of copyright protection term in Europe was achieved through European Council Directive 93/98/EEC of October, 29, 1993 harmonising the term of protection of copyright and certain related rights, and in the USA through the Sonny Bono Copyright Term Extension Act of 1998, adopted on October, 27, 1998.

6 WTO document WT/MIN(01)/DEC/2.

7 See WTO document WT/L/540, September, 02, 2003, "Decision of August, 30, 2003*". The footnote associated with the asterisk added onto the title of the Decision states: "This Decision was adopted by the General Council in the light of a statement read out by the Chairman, which can be found in JOB (03)/177. This statement will be reproduced in the minutes of the General Council to be issued as WT/GC/M/82."

7 Rules Negotiations – Anti-Dumping, Subsidies and Countervailing Duties, Fisheries Subsidies and Regional Trading Agreements

Guillermo Valles Galmes
Former Ambassador of Uruguay to the WTO

Introduction: Background of the Negotiating Group on Rules and its Mandate

Since this chapter is being written presumably during the closing phase of the Doha Round[1] and more than ten years have passed since the preparations for this multilateral negotiation, it seems important to start analysing the negotiations on rules, by contrasting what were the original facts and positions at the time of the launching of the Round with those prevailing in present circumstances. This approach will help address this complex area of the negotiations with the greatest degree of realism - an important ingredient to successfully conclude any negotiation.

A pragmatic analysis is required in the case of rules also for the following reasons:

- In contrast to what happened in other areas of the negotiations, in which the original political aims were clear, the mandate on rules, emanating from Doha in 2001 was crafted with very general and abstract language, mainly referring to the need to "clarify and improve" the rules on anti-dumping and subsidies[2].
- The scope of the negotiations in this group is particularly broad, since it covers four wide areas. Each of these areas is technically very intricate and differentiated from the rest, therefore requiring diverse expertise.
- Political and economic interests in each of these areas vary greatly within the WTO membership, ranging from "peripheral interest" to "high sensitivity," They also changed over time and according to members' evolving concerns.

Negotiations on Anti-Dumping

The Motivations

To begin, it should be noted that in the field of anti-dumping there were, formally, no pending negotiations from the Uruguay Round that could prompt, *per se*, another multilateral round, as was the case with agriculture and services. In 1994, the only negotiations in this field that were to be continued, since agreement was not reached at the time of the conclusion of the Uruguay Round, were specifically on anti-circumvention. Also, a review of the dispute settlement articles for anti-dumping was mandated, but in Marrakech 1994 no reference to an overall review of all anti-dumping rules and no formal "built-in agenda" was made.[3]

Moreover, at the conclusion of the Uruguay Round at the Marrakech Ministerial Conference in 1994, although many ministers referred to their concerns about unilateralism, the only two who directly alluded to the need to further improve the anti-dumping rules, were the Japanese and the Chilean Ministers[4]. This picture changed by the time of the Ministerial Conference in Seattle when no less than 10 ministers strongly called for negotiations in the area of anti-dumping and 14 proposals were presented by 32 members.

What had changed from 1994 to 2001 was the concern about the annual increase in anti-dumping investigations being initiated (Chart 1) and the perception among some members that, since they were entering a new multilateral trade round, it was convenient to include negotiations on anti-dumping in the overall package to be covered by the single undertaking rule. In the view of these members, the market access gains obtained with tariff reduction in the Uruguay Round were being ultimately denied through the misuse of anti-dumping measures. If they were entering a new multilateral round of trade negotiations, searching for new market access, it was just natural to seek a further discipline in the ever-increasing use of anti-dumping. Nevertheless it should be noted from the outset that the trend in anti-dumping usage has turned downward since 2001 (dotted line in Chart 1), even as countries experienced the biggest trade and economic crisis in the past 50 years.

Chart 1:

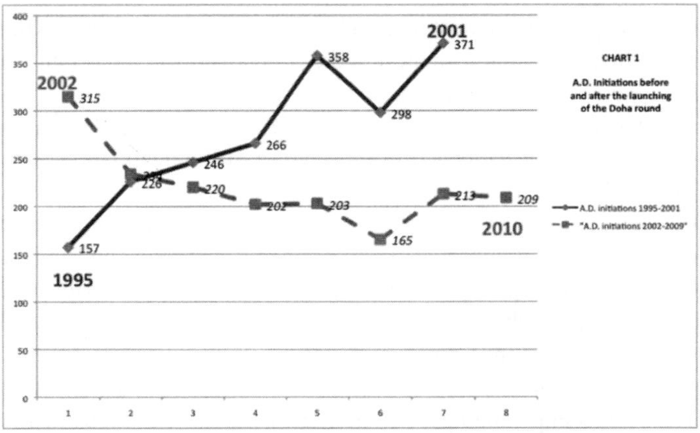

Source: Guillermo Valles on the basis of WTO anti-dumping statistics.

The "Demandeurs"

The annual increase of anti-dumping investigations from 1995 to2001 prompted a number of developing and developed countries to push for the inclusion of anti-dumping in the multilateral negotiations starting in Doha. They eventually formed a negotiating group - the Friends of Antidumping Negotiations (FANs) - lobbying for more restrictive use of anti-dumping remedies.

It should be noted that this group includes WTO members concerned about the abuse of anti-dumping investigations and measures, but it does not represent a developing country perspective *per se*. The Group is a mix of small and large economies, developed and developing concerned about exports.

The exporter's view is prevalent in the Group position and its members have very diverse experiences in the use of this trade remedy. As Table 2 shows, some of them are extensive users of anti-dumping themselves. Others do not have any anti-dumping domestic legislation and have suffered few (though relevant) measures affecting their exports.

Table 1: FANs as users and targets of anti-dumping (by December 2009)

FANs	Anti-dumping Initiations against:	Anti-dumping Initiations by:	Disputes on Anti-dumping (as complainant)	Disputes on Anti-dumping (as defendant)
Brazil	108	179	8	2
Chile	27	17	1	1
China	761	178	4	2
Colombia	5	48		
Costa Rica	2	10	2	
Hong K., China	28			
Israel	10	32		
Japan	155	6	5	
Korea	264	108	6	1
Mexico	47	97	11	4
Norway	6		1	
Singapore	45			
Switzerland	7		1	
Taipei, Chinese	198	22	1	
Thailand	150	41	5	
Turkey	45	144	2	1
S.T. FANS	***1858***	***882***	***47***	***11***
TOTAL	**3675**	**3675**	**84**	**84**

While these sixteen members constitute the core of the proponents of negotiations on anti-dumping, many initiatives also came from other active participants.

Developing Country Members: Practice of Anti-dumping and Approach to the Negotiations

A distinctive feature of negotiations in this area is that there are no visible common strategies from the developing countries, and there is no formal "group" of developing countries as such. This is mainly because their trade interests, institutional capacity and experience with anti-dumping vary quite largely.

Of course many developing (and developed) members claim, with all reason, that they do not want to be abused through the imposition of anti-dumping measures against their exports. But, what is the case when those measures are applied among developing countries? The question is relevant because the number of users of anti-dumping has extended from a handful of developed countries in the mid-1980s, at the time of the launching of the Uruguay Round, to more than 40 today, including many developing countries.

As a matter of fact, by December 2009 more than 61 percent of the investigations had been initiated by developing countries. Moreover, the use of anti-dumping in South-South trade has increased dramatically, with 64 percent of the investigations by developing countries directed against, presumed, dumped exports of other developing countries. This situation makes it difficult to define the developing countries' common needs *per se*. Beyond the concern for market access, the main worries expressed by many ACP countries were connected to the difficulty of using the complex anti-dumping system set in the WTO rules. This perspective is reflected in the Kenyan proposal on S&D treatment originally contained in document TN/RL/GEN/143,[5] which is referred to later.

Key Issues and Problems in Negotiations on Anti-dumping

Literally, hundreds of proposals covering all the phases of an anti-dumping process were introduced in the ensuing years after the Doha Declaration. They included a myriad of projects and ideas for changing the existing language on initiation of an anti-dumping investigation, calculation of dumping margins, determination of injury, due process, transparency, imposition of measures, termination, and reviews and dispute settlement.

A Broad Ministerial Mandate and no Common Political Direction

Beyond the wide number of proposals another difficulty present in the negotiations was (and still is) the unclear policy direction of the original Ministerial mandate. This was not the case in other areas of negotiation. In agriculture, for example, there is no question that, notwithstanding all the caveats and conditions, the overall direction of the negotiation from the outset was to make agricultural trade freer and more equitable. In the case of services and NAMA the direction is, again, to attain more market access in a framework of S&D treatment for developing countries. In anti dumping such a direction was unclear from the beginning, as a result of the broadness of the original mandate.[6]

The FANs proposed in 2005 six political objectives in order to clarify the goals and therefore make the negotiations more focused.[7] Those were:

> *mitigating the excessive effects of anti-dumping [sic]measures; preventing AD measures from becoming permanent; strengthening due process and enhancing transparency; reducing costs for authorities and respondents; terminating unwarranted and unnecessary investigations at an early stage; and providing disciplines to improve and clarify substantive rules for dumping and injury.*

No consensus was reached on those goals and the Ministerial mandate, although somehow streamlined in Hong Kong (2005), remained as broad as the original. Moreover, the view that the negotiations were not seeking a fundamental change of Article VI was reflected in the Hong Kong Declaration:

> *(Ministers)...call on Participants, in considering possible clarifications and improvements in the area of anti-dumping, to take into account, inter alia, (a) the need to avoid the unwarranted use of anti-dumping measures,* ***while preserving the basic concepts, principles and effectiveness of the instrument and its objectives where such measures are warranted****; and (b) the desirability of limiting the costs and complexity of proceedings for interested parties and the investigating authorities alike,* ***while strengthening the due process, transparency and predictability of such proceedings and measures****.*

It was, therefore, clear at that time that the process would need to be guided by the Chair through a series of proposals under his own responsibility and authority in a sort of top-down approach.

That process started in 2008 with a first draft from the Chair (contained in document TN/RL/W/213) that was strongly objected from every side of the negotiation. Nevertheless, it served the purpose of clarifying members' positions and intentions. Eventually, this first draft led to the identification of three broad categories of issues (see Table 2).

In the first category are those issues that have a rather clear potential for consensus. These are mainly related to due process and transparency, and in the latest Chair´s documents they appear without brackets, although there is no agreement on the issues or on the language so far drafted.

The second category contains issues that are not showing any consensus or any easy solution at the moment and might require some sort of arbitrated solution. This intervention will presumably be a new draft by the Chair - when the political time is ripe- in order to advance and conclude the negotiations.

There is a third category of issues that were not addressed in the Chair's proposals.

Table 2:		
Issues with potential consensus	**Relevant issues without consensus**	**Unaddressed Issues by 2009**
Cost allocations (Art. 2.2.1.1)	Zeroing (Art.2.4.2.)	*De Minimis* Margins
Model matching (Art. 2.4.4)	Sunset reviews (Art.11.3)	Negligible Import Volumes
Exchange rates (Art. 2.4.1.1 and 2.4.1.2)	Public interest/lesser duty	Mandatory Preliminary Determinations
Threat of injury (Art. 3.7)	Anti-circumvention (Art. 9*bis*)	Standing
Dumped imports (footnote 11)	Causation of injury (Art. 3.5)	Seasonal/ Perishable Products
Contents of application (Art. 5.2)	Product under consideration (Art.5.6.)	Compliance
Standing (Art. 5.4)	Material retardation (Art. 3.9)	
Pre-initiation provision of application (Art. 5.5)	Domestic industry – related parties (footnote 17)	
Identification of parties (footnote 21)	Third-country dumping (Art. 14.4)	
Back-to-back investigations (Art. 5.10)	Info requests to affiliates (Art. 6.1 & 6.8.1)	
Official translations (footnote 25)	Special & Differential Treatment & Technical Assistance	
General due process rights (Art. 6.4)		
Non-confidential file (Art. 6.4*bis*)(but for interested parties only)		
Non-confidential summaries (Art. 6.5.1)		
Post-determination calculation disclosure (Art. 6.9*bis*)		
Disclosure (Art. 6.9)		
Sampling (Art. 6.10)		
Clarification of questionnaires (Art. 6.13)		
Provisional measures (Art. 7.1)		
Price undertakings (Art. 8)		

Contd...

Issues with potential consensus	Relevant issues without consensus	Unaddressed Issues by 2009
Duty assessment (Art. 9.3)		
Changed circumstances (Art. 11.2)		
New Shipper (Art. 9.5)		
Public notice (Art. 12)		
Notifications (Art. 16.4)		
Transition (Art. 18.3*bis*)		
Verifications (Annex I)		
Best information (Annex II)		
AD Review (Annex III)		

The Most Problematic Issues and their Status in the Negotiation

Zeroing

Dumping exists when the export price of a product is less than the normal price of a product in the home country. Article 2.4.2. of the Anti-dumping Agreement (ADA) establishes that the dumping margin should be calculated based on a number of fair comparisons between these two prices. Zeroing happens in the process of comparing prices when, the so-called negative margins (i.e. when the export price is higher than the normal price) are not offset against the positive margins, but instead treated as zero. This practice, in the view of the FANs and many others, artificially inflates the existence and margins of dumping.

One of the difficulties is that zeroing may occur not only in the original investigation leading to the imposition of measures and in reviews, but also when collecting anti-dumping duties. This happens since many countries –including several developing countries – do not apply the additional customs duties as *ad valorem*, but rather impose minimum price duties. The anti-dumping duty collected is the difference between a minimum benchmark price and the actual import price of the product. There is never an offset (or credit) for imports above the minimum price; and therefore zeroing occurs also at this stage.

The most important proposals calling for a complete prohibition of zeroing are contained in documents TN/RL/GEN/8, TN/RL/GEN/ 126, TN/RL/GEN/ 137, TN/RL/GEN/214 rev.3, TN/RL/GEN/233 and TN/RL/GEN/215. The main proposal opposing this prohibition is contained in TN/RL/GEN/147.

It should also be noted that to date 13 cases on this topic have been brought before the Dispute Settlement Body (DSB). Also, while the negotiation were ongoing, several Appellate Body rulings prohibited zeroing. These decisions greatly impacted the discussion among the members on this particular issue and dramatically changed the political dynamic of the negotiations.

The Chair in his first Draft Text in TN/RL/GEN/213 proposed to partially prohibit the practice of zeroing in some original investigations, through a specific language in Article 2.4.3. (i). In that draft, zeroing was nevertheless specifically authorised when calculating dumping by making multiple comparisons on a transaction-to-transaction basis or a weighted average normal value to multiple export price transactions (Article 2.4.3. (ii) (iii). It was also authorised in duty assessment proceedings (Article 9.3.1.).

The result was that almost all delegations expressed disappointment with this first Chair's draft. A clear overwhelming majority is of the view that zeroing should be prohibited in all proceedings. The US on the contrary has insisted that a restoration of zeroing in all contexts and proceedings is absolutely necessary to return to what, in its view, was the explicit status quo of the matter emerging from the Uruguay Round. It has also raised several questions about how a complete prohibition could affect not only its own, but also others' duty assessment systems.

Some countries, including developing countries, have expressed the view that zeroing should be permitted in the context of so-called targeted dumping, when a weighted average to transaction methodology is used. Others, including developing members, are also concerned with the impact of any broad prohibition to their duty collection systems. Those members that have prospective normal value systems (like the minimum prices referred to above) would like to ensure that they are not affected by any zeroing prohibition. There are, therefore, a number of countries, including developing ones, that do not see an outright prohibition or authorisation of zeroing as the way forward. But no concrete middle ground alternatives (other than the first Chair´s attempt) have been proposed thus far.

Considering this overall situation, as well as the very strong position held by a large number of members of the U.S. Congress, it is hard to imagine what sort of accommodation the US could finally provide for this negotiation to move forward in this crucial field. The general perception in the U.S. Congress is that the Appellate Body has wrongly interpreted the clear outcome of the Uruguay Round (i.e. zeroing was to be permitted). Notwithstanding this strong political view, the necessary implementation of several Appellate Body decisions is taking the discussion of the prohibition of zeroing beyond the realm of the rules negotiations. If past experience could count, it should be remembered that the EC ultimately changed its anti-dumping system to implement an Appellate Body ruling on zeroing.[8] In this case, however, it would be naïve to think that the US's eventual implementation (or lack of it) would be without any major consequences for the rules negotiations.

Sunset Reviews

In the final stages of the Uruguay Round, specific reforms were made in the anti-dumping process. One of these pertains to the sunset reviews of anti-dumping duties. The pre-WTO GATT rules were relatively vague with respect to when governments were required to terminate anti-dumping duties. Some anti-dumping measures remained in place for decades and, in the view of many members, this actually shows that "for anti-dumping measures the sun never sets." The commitment undertaken by members in the Uruguay Round imposed an obligation requiring that all anti-dumping orders be terminated five years after their initiation, unless the importing country government makes a determination that revocation would lead to renewed dumping and material injury to the domestic industry.

In the DDA the demandeurs proposed to clarify the rules applied to the sunset reviews (Article 11 of the ADA) through a series of proposals, included in TN/RL/GEN/ 104, TN/RL/GEN/61, TN/RL/GEN/ 74, TN/RL/GEN/149.

In the view of the proponents, anti-dumping measures are often imposed for more than five years, some considerably longer, even when those measures are not warranted by the likelihood of recurrent dumping and injury. This, from their viewpoint, is a result of the lack of guidance provided by the ADA on how to assess whether anti-dumping measures are still necessary after five years. In this area, since 1995 there have been four relevant disputes related to the sunset review brought to the DSB

The Chair's first draft made some procedural, due process and substantive proposals to clarify the language of Article 11 on sunset reviews. It established the type of information that should be included in the written application for a sunset review. It also proposed a standing requirement ("by or on behalf" of the domestic industry) and an initiation standard of sufficient evidence. It restrained the possibility of *ex officio* initiations to "special circumstances" where warranted by sufficient evidence. It also prescribed a number of precise process lengths and deadlines for the review. It clarified the requirements for determinations (i.e. determinations should be based on positive evidence and objective examination of all relevant factors and presumptions that assign decisive weight to particular factors would not be allowed). It established a firm ten-year automatic termination, while allowing for existing anti-dumping measures to be deemed to be imposed as of entry into force of the Doha Development Round (i.e. the ten-year clock would start from the date of the entry into force of the DDA). On none of the issues related to sunset review is it possible to point-out a specific developing country perspective. In many cases, developing countries have represented their export interests, but several of them have also taken the opposite view (i.e. as importers), indicating their concerns about the adoption of overly complicated standards that could render this trade remedy inapplicable in a developing country context.

Lesser Duty

The ADA already establishes in Article 9.1 that it is desirable for members to impose a duty less than the margin of dumping where such a lesser duty is adequate to remove the injury, but actually does not require it. Being a best endeavour clause, the FANs and others have proposed (in TN/RL/GEN/1 as well as GEN/32, 43 and 99) that the lesser duty rule be made mandatory. Some developing countries have proposed that this rule be made mandatory only where a developed country investigates imports of a developing member. The FANs have proposed a new annex to the ADA, setting forth three alternative methodologies for calculating the lesser duty. Some developing countries have not favoured the mandatory rule. Nevertheless, assuming a mandatory rule is agreed to in principle, the critical issues would be whether the ADA sets out methodologies for applying the rule; what would be the specifics of such a methodology (i.e. a "price undercutting," "non-injurious price," "non-dumped import price" or other benchmarks); how intricate and applicable they would be and whether the application of such methodology would be reviewable in WTO dispute settlement.

Public Interest

Closely connected to the previous topic is the issue of a public interest test. Several members of the FANs presented a proposal that would force the investigating authorities to take due account of the representations of domestic parties (other than the producers themselves) when deciding whether to impose an anti-dumping duty and at what level. The proposals are contained in TN/RL/GEN/53, 85 and 222. The Chair in his first draft included a provision to require procedures in national laws and regulations that would enable investigating authorities, in the original investigations, to take due account of representations of domestic interested parties whose interests could be affected by the anti-dumping duty. Several members, including developing countries, have considered such a proposed obligation as intruding on member's sovereign jurisdictions or being too costly to implement.

Product under Consideration (PUC)

This issue relates to the scope of the investigation and in the view of the proponents is relevant since:

> the selection of the product under consideration is fundamental to determining the scope of both anti-dumping and countervailing investigations and of any resulting measures...(and)... the lack of guidance in the Agreement creates systemic problems, such as Members capturing, in a single investigation, determination and remedy, products that can be completely different in terms of their physical characteristics, end uses, and channels of distribution.[9]

The FANs made several proposals to address this. The original language can be found in TN/RL/W/ 7, 10, GEN/50 as well as 66 from China and 26 and 73 from Canada. A useful background paper on this issue is G/ADP/AHG/W/121/Rev. 4 from the working group on implementation in the Anti-dumping Committee.

In the Chair's first draft, 'product under consideration" is defined in Article 2.6 as "*the imported product subject to investigation or review,*" which may be constituted by multiple imported products, different in terms of models, types, grades and quality, provided they all "share the same basic physical characteristics." It also establishes that all relevant factors (such as similarity in use; interchangeability; competition in the same market and distribution through the same channels) should be taken into account in assessing whether differences between imported products are so significant to preclude their inclusion within a single PUC. Moreover, in Article 5.6*bis,* the Chair's first draft prescribes that the investigating authority must amend the PUC if during the course of investigation evidence obtained indicates that certain imported products should not form part of the PUC.

In determining the PUC, differences of view exist among all participants, including developing countries, on the role of physical and market characteristics, as well as on when and how the PUC should be determined.

Circumvention

Closely related to the previous issue of PUC is the question of how to address marginal modifications or alterations of the physical characteristics, production or shipment of merchandise otherwise subject to an anti dumping or countervailing duty measure, where such modifications or alterations are done in a manner that undermines the purpose and effectiveness of remedies provided for under the WTO agreements.

As mentioned at the beginning of this chapter, the question of circumvention was unresolved in Marrakech, and the Ministers instructed the Committee on Anti-Dumping Practices to find uniform rules in this area "as soon as possible." Sixteen years have passed and no common definition of what constitutes circumvention has been reached. Nevertheless, a number of members, including developing countries, have adopted measures to prevent the evasion of anti dumping and countervailing measures through circumvention. The proponent of this topic in the Negotiating Group on Rules (NGR) has been the US to which the issue is of crucial political importance. China, Korea and others strongly insist that no special provision should be authorised, as the only appropriate approach to alleged "circumvention" is to initiate a complete new investigation. Although not being proponents, several developing countries have indicated that circumvention is a fact and therefore common rules should be set in order to attain predictability and consistency.

As a mirror to Article 2.6 on PUC, the Chair´s first draft authorises extending the scope of existing anti-dumping duty to products not within the investigation. That draft includes three types of circumstances in Article 9*bis: a)* where imports of the PUC have been supplanted, in whole or in part, by imports of

- parts or unfinished forms for assembly or completion into a product that is the same as the PUC in the country of import; or
- a product that is the same as the PUC and that has been assembled or completed from parts or unfinished forms in a third country; or
- a "slightly modified product" from the country subject to the anti-dumping duty.

The draft also included stringent conditions for that extension of the scope to take place, including the requisite that products subject to any anti-circumvention measure must also have been dumped. In the author´s view it is hard to imagine that a solution for PUC is found without coming to some kind of understanding in relation to circumvention as well.

Lessons for Developing Countries

The following are some reflections "from the trenches." The author's view is that a non-conclusion of the DDA will be of greater cost for developing countries; therefore, these suggestions are provided with a view toward concluding and to help "everyone move from its comfort zone" as the Director General of WTO has recently called for.

On the Need to Review the Perspective of Anti-dumping Negotiations

The days when only the US, the EC, Australia and Canada were the only users of anti-dumping measures are long past. The anti-dumping problem is not any longer a North-South issue. Domestic laws and regulations on anti-dumping as well as investigating authorities can be found now in no less than 70 countries. Notwithstanding the clear global decline in the use of anti-dumping, the large number of anti-dumping users will be a permanent feature of international trade in the future. Therefore, anti-dumping is, and will remain, present in South-South trade as well.

The use of anti-dumping (coupled with safeguards) has played an important role as an instrument of trade policy in many developing countries.[10] Both devices were relevant escape valves not only to protect newly exposed industries from un-fair pricing practices, but also, domestically, to contain the neo-protectionist pressures in their own constituencies. These escape valves are of extreme importance when, on top of trade liberalisation, developing countries face downturns in their economic cycles as well as currency misalignments.

From a global perspective one could say that the use of anti-dumping is also playing a historical role in helping integrate the Chinese economy into the world (and the world with China). The prevalence of China as the main target of anti-dumping investigations and the permanent global increase of initiations against China, sustain this view. China itself, by the way, has also become an important anti-dumping user.[11]

Contrary to the post-Uruguay Round period (and particularly before the launching of the DDA) the evidence of the declining trend in the number of anti-dumping initiations in the past decade could constitute the basis to approach these negotiations on anti-dumping in a less dramatised way.

All parts in the DDA would benefit if, from all sides, a pragmatic view of these factors is clearly present in their negotiating strategies. The message is, therefore, negotiate anti-dumping (and for this matter all areas) with a view toward the future, not the past. The prevalent view has been to negotiate from what was or was not achieved in the Uruguay Round. Circumstances have changed dramatically and they need to be taken into account. Those who have negotiated anti-dumping merely from an exporter perspective need to look after their import interests as well. The same is true for those who, in the Doha negotiations, have only cared to keep their anti-dumping practices and domestic regulations unchanged (i.e. "care also for your own exports and watch-out for the new anti-dumping users").

For those developing countries that have so far focussed on these negotiations only from an exporter perspective, the question is whether a more stringent, but also complex, anti-dumping agreement will benefit them, particularly when they could be required to use it to protect their own markets.

Therefore, two objectives should be kept in mind. First, try to "clarify and improve" the ADA in such a way that the system itself does not ultimately become more costly and intricate for smaller developing countries. Second, the outcome of the anti-dumping negotiations must include a strong, credible and effective capacity building project for developing countries. Perhaps it should be embedded in the Aid for Trade outcome and South-South cooperation should also be part of it.

The original Kenyan proposal on S&D treatment contained in TN/RL/GEN 143 item 4 could be articulated and expanded. Such a programme could be the result of a special decision by the ministers and it could envisage technical and financial support for:

- the establishment of legal domestic frameworks to enable smaller economies to make an effective and transparent use of anti-dumping and countervailing measures:
- permanent capacity building and training activities for investigating authorities of smaller economies: and
- the institution and development of regional investigating authorities.

The Right Tactics, Logistics and Process to Conclude the Round

First, the complexity of rule-making in the area of anti-dumping makes it unrealistic to pretend to conclude anti-dumping negotiations without the investigating authorities present in the negotiations.

Second, negotiate those issues with potential consensus and the "core" ones in parallel. This categorisation to a certain extent is arbitrary, so do not expect the first list to become any easier than the crucial or "core" issues.

Third, encourage small group discussions to take place. Unlike market access negotiations in which national direct presence and representation cannot be easily substituted, in anti-dumping there are no life-threatening issues that demand permanent and continuous presence in all small groups. Drafting would need to be encouraged when the political time is ripe. Rules demand detail and careful technical drafting, which take place better in small and transparent formal drafting groups.

Fourth, allow time to work on the harmonisation of texts between anti-dumping and the subsidies and countervailing measures.

Five, create some non-negotiating environment among investigating authorities. In the author's experience, a technical group composed of the investigating authorities that could gather in parallel to the negotiations benefited the necessary synergies. In the past they met to discuss experiences, problems and challenges in the process of investigating anti-dumping or assessing injury. These meetings could be continued and fostered provided they do not intrude on the negotiating process, but rather support it by creating a cooperative environment of technical exchange.

Some Questions for the Future

From a theoretical perspective, one could say that negotiations on rules should be permanently continued since norms need permanently to be adapted to an ever-changing reality. So when should rules (especially anti-dumping) start and conclude?

WTO rules on anti-dumping would always need to be "clarified and improved" since they are a common set of norms implemented in different legal and economic environments and jurisdictions. One could argue, therefore, that the necessary harmonious implementation of those rules could call for a permanent negotiation. Contrary to what could once happen when all tariffs could be removed, the rules will always stand for further improvement because of their non-quantitative nature. In other words, in the vast domain of "rules" one will never reach level zero as with tariffs.

The question, therefore, is whether the multilateral trading system requires a multilateral and comprehensive "round" for this permanent task of clarifying, improving and harmonising the implementation of rules.

Another question is the suitability of seeking new legislation (i.e. more specific anti-dumping rules) to limit the abuse of anti-dumping duties being imposed when they are not really warranted. One could wonder whether some of the proposed amendments would actually restrain investigating authorities in their potential abuse of the norms. Of course limiting the "administrative space" of the investigating authorities by having more detailed WTO rules could help, but it could also render the system highly complex or even inefficient for smaller developing countries.

The question of the "abuse of anti-dumping measures" perhaps could be addressed more effectively, if really needed, by a combination of more active and concerted participation in the DSM, as well as more often and efficient use of regular bodies, such as the Committee on Anti-Dumping, the Trade Policy Review Mechanism and Ministerial Conferences.

Negotiations on Horizontal Subsidies

The Doha Ministerial mandate on rules also encompasses negotiations for the "clarification and improvement" of the Agreement on Subsidies and Countervailing Measures (ASCM). Nevertheless, in this area there was a far lower number of proposals and less interest for major changes than was the case of anti-dumping. This could be a reflection of the fact that, in general terms, the ASCM has been less used as a trade remedy than the Anti-Dumping Agreement. Although targeting different practices (private in the case of anti-dumping and public policies in the case of ASCM) it is interesting to acknowledge the wide discrepancies in the use of each trade policy instrument, in terms of number of initiations, tendencies and use by developing countries.

The total number of WTO members that have initiated countervailing procedures is 20 (13 of which are developing countries), while in the case of anti-dumping it has been more than double that number.[12] Moreover, of a total of 250 initiations to date, only 47 were from developing members and (contrary to what happened in anti-dumping) the percentage of initiations undertaken by developing members has not increased over time.[13]

Still, the number of cases brought to the DSM in the case of anti-dumping and subsidies and countervailing measures almost coincide: 86 cases cite the Anti-dumping Agreement in requests for consultations and 87 do it in relation to the ASCM.

Chart 2

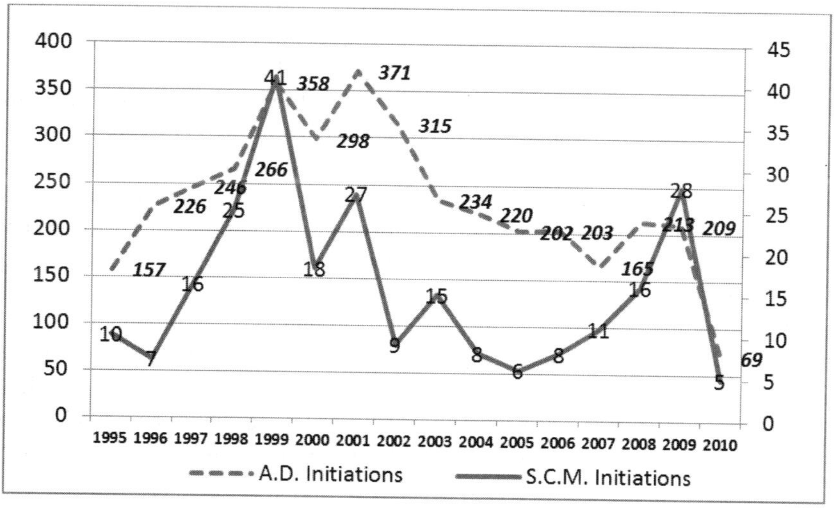

Author's elaboration on the basis of WTO statistics, as reported by February 2011

In any case, in the rules negotiations there were several proposals from some developing countries that reflect what, in their views, are ways to prevent unfairness against their trade interests and against S&D treatment as a whole.

India has proposed (with the support of Egypt, Kenya, and Pakistan) some amendments to Articles 27.5 and 27.6 regarding export competitiveness. In the ASCM developing countries are allowed to provide export subsidies to a product, contingent on export competitiveness not having been achieved in respect of that product. These proponents would like to amend the ASCM to make sure that the S&D treatment remains available for them even when for any temporary volatility in global markets they might appear to have gained export competitiveness. They therefore propose to change the simple threshold trigger of two years and 3.5 percent of world trade to a longer period or a moving average. Many delegations support, in principle, clarifying the provisions on the determination of export competitiveness in a product. Views among the members, however, differ considerably as to the best way to do this, including changing the period and/or methodology for calculating share of world trade in a product or clarifying the definition of a "product" for this purpose. The opinions are even more split regarding the Indian proposal to allow the reintroduction of export subsidies if export competitiveness is lost after having been reached.

Brazil has been one of the most active proponents of clarifications to the ASCM. It has made very specific proposals with respect to export credit guarantees, reflecting its industrial export interests and the perceived unequal footing it has *vis-à-vis* developed countries. In Brazil's view items j) and k) of the illustrative list of prohibited subsidies contained in Annex I of the ASCM provide a biased safe haven to developed countries. Item j), prohibits governments from providing export credit guarantees at premium rates that are inadequate to cover "long-term operating costs and losses of the programmes." Due to the fact that developed countries generally have higher credit ratings than developing countries, item j) ultimately provides developed countries a much larger safe harbour than is provided to developing countries. Brazil is of the view that, based on their normally higher credit ratings, developed countries are able to provide export credit guarantees that lower the overall interest rate to below market levels, if compared with the overall interest rate offered by international capital markets without that guarantee. In a similar sense, Brazil raised its concerns about item k) of Annex I, citing the bigger disadvantages of developing countries in financing for sales of large capital goods. The last proposal Brazil has made is related to the fact that, according to item k) of Annex I, an export credit practice will not be considered a prohibited subsidy if it is in conformity with the provisions of an international undertaking, to which at least 12 members of the WTO are parties. The problem here is clearly with the OECD evolving regulations being introduced in the WTO as benchmarks. In the view of many developing countries, non-participants of an international undertaking cannot be bound by rules established outside the organisation and without their consensus.

Members' views differ widely as to whether the second paragraph of item k) should be amended, such that any changes to the OECD export credit arrangement would not automatically take effect for purposes of the WTO ASCM. At one end of the spectrum, some delegations consider that only amendments not opposed by any member within a certain period should have legal effect under the second paragraph of item (k). This is a similar approach to the one taken in the Chair's first draft. At the other end of the spectrum, some developed countries consider that members should not have any basis to veto decisions taken by participants to the arrangement.

With regards to their defensive interests, several developing countries have shown concerns about the proposal made by some developed countries regarding regulated prices. The thrust of the proposal is that the presence of regulated prices should be taken into account when considering whether a subsidy is specific and when calculating the amount of such subsidy. More specifically, the EC and other members have proposed that specificity could be considered to exist when (foreign) firms are excluded from access to goods or services at regulated prices. Their main concerns seem to be in the chemical and fertiliser industry, where certain governments provide their national industries with access to much cheaper energy resources, through regulated prices. This approach has confronted a strong rejection from some developing members that are important producers of oil and gas and perceive a great danger of any changes to Articles 2 (specificity) and 14 (calculation of amount of subsidy).

Beyond these proposed amendments, there are also other important issues, which could be a matter for consensus and benefit the interests of developing countries, such as: existence and amount of benefit, benefit pass-through and subsidy allocation. Finally, the possible transposition of potential amendments to the anti-dumping text into the countervailing duty rules and amending the existing differences between the existing ADA and countervailing duty rules also seem important.

Appraisal

It is difficult at this point to elaborate on the perspectives of this sector of the negotiations, if the DDA is required to be finished soon. On top of the reduced number of proposals and lack of strong political attention, the experience of developing countries with respect to the ASCM is less, compared to their familiarity (as investigators and as targets) with anti-dumping. Moreover, the recent bailouts and stimulus packages adopted, mainly by developed countries, as counter-cyclical measures to confront the economic crisis, have somewhat altered the attention and the direction of this sector of the negotiations.[14] In view of these measures and the new paradigms on state intervention, it is hard to anticipate any major reform of the ASCM that would strengthen rules against subsidisation or further relax the permissible public financing of industries. Developing countries, perhaps, could do well in putting all their political and technical strength in the subsidies committee to make sure that these huge interventions are really time limited, justified and legitimate.

Negotiations on Fisheries Subsidies

As was the case with the negotiations in other areas of rules, in fisheries subsidies, the Doha Ministerial mandate was quite broad[15] and lacked clear political orientation. It stated only that fisheries subsidies negotiations form part of the rules negotiations and that they are related to the trade and environment negotiations. Thus, in order to understand why and with what purpose, these negotiations form part of the Doha Declaration in 2001 and the Rules Negotiations Group, one has to recall three interlinked factors: the incremental interest and legal competencies of the GATT/WTO multilateral system in trade and environment issues; the growing awareness of the over-exploitation of the most traded fish stocks, and the increasing international pressure against certain forms of fisheries subsidies.[16]

The links between trade and environment are not new in the GATT/WTO system. An early interest of GATT in environmental issues can be found in the special report [17] prepared in 1971 by the Director General, Olivier Long, at the request of the Secretary General of the UN Conference on Human Environment, convened in Stockholm in 1972. This pioneer work made no reference to the issue of fisheries since it concentrated on pollution and waste and less focus was provided to the question of exhaustion of natural resources. It, nevertheless, led to the creation in November 1971 of the Group on Environmental Measures and International Trade (EMIT). After being dormant for more than 20 years, this group was convened on the occasion of the preparations of the 1992 UN Earth Summit in Rio de Janeiro.[18] At this historical Conference, the UN was called to hold talks on preventing the depletion of certain fish stocks. One year later, the Food and Agriculture Organisation (FAO) of the UN published a milestone study that warned of the critical situation of certain fish stocks and the sustainability problem caused by overfishing.[19] The Earth Summit in 1992, the Cancun Declaration on Responsible Fishing the same year, the Rome Consensus on World Fisheries and particularly, the UN Code of Conduct for Responsible Fishing in October 1995, show a trend of international concern and action with respect to the sustainability of world fisheries. In the GATT domain there was also an increasing interest in sustainable development and environment.

Thus, in the Preamble of the Marrakech Agreement Establishing the WTO members recognised that trade, environment and sustainable development objectives could be mutually supportive. The ministers also signed a Decision on Trade and Environment and called for the establishment of the Committee on Trade and Environment as a permanent subsidiary body of the new WTO. It was in this specific committee where in May 1997 the US and New Zealand tabled two separate documents advocating, for the first time, the removal of fisheries subsidies.[20] That year showed a particular political momentum in the struggle against harmful fisheries subsidies. In fact, the UN General Assembly adopted the "Programme for Further Implementation of Agenda 21," which called for the consideration of the negative impact of fisheries subsidies and the need to take appropriate action against them. In the ensuing 24 months, the International Plan of Action for the Management of Fishing Capacity was negotiated in the FAO`s Fisheries Committee.[21]

Within this political context, in August 1999, and in preparing for the "Millenium Round" expected to be launched at Seattle, six countries presented a proposal to the General Council. Document WT/GC/W/303, sponsored by the US, Australia, New Zealand, Norway, Peru, and the Philippines was the first call for the elimination of subsidies that contribute to fisheries overcapacity "*to be part of the upcoming WTO negotiations.*" Some developing countries including Argentina, Brazil and Chile showed immediate interest in the issue. It is interesting to recall that, although the negotiations at Seattle failed, the paragraphs on subsidies were tentatively approved and they included an extensive mandate to negotiate "*certain subsidies that may contribute to over-capacity in fisheries and over-fishing or cause other adverse effects to the interest of Members....*" Meanwhile, outside the WTO there were parallel analytical, technical, legal and diplomatic efforts being undertaken in intergovernmental organisations, such as the FAO, the United Nations Environment Programme (UNEP), Asia-Pacific Economic Cooperation (APEC), the OECD, the World Bank and nongovernmental organisations, such as the World Wildlife Fund (WWF) and the International Centre for Trade and Sustainable Development (ICTSD). Therefore, it was not a surprise that fisheries subsidies was retained as part of the negotiating mandate when the multilateral trade negotiations were finally launched in Doha in 2001. The following milestone in the negotiation of fisheries subsidies came in December 2005 when, at the Hong Kong Ministerial, the mandate was further refined and more clear political direction was provided, through the call to ban certain forms of fisheries subsidies that contribute to over-capacity and over-fishing.[22]

In conclusion, the fisheries subsidies negotiations are not new to the WTO, and they take place within a broad context of increasing political interest, refined technical research and policy analysis by international organisations and public awareness and concern for sustainability of fish resources. For these reasons, if the DDA is to conclude soon, this area of negotiation is certain to be one of the dealmakers.

The importance of the fisheries sector and S&D treatment

Special and differential treatment for developing countries has been central to the Group's mandate and from the inception of this Negotiating Group, a crucial chapter of the negotiations. A level playing field can be attained only by crafting rules that take into consideration different capacities and development levels. Those rules should reflect the extraordinary importance that the fisheries sector has for developing countries in terms of livelihood, employment, export revenues, food security, social integration and even gender relations.

The FAO estimates the number of fishers and fish farmers in 2008 at 44.8 million, with the vast majority coming from developing countries. It also estimates that for each fisher employed, three indirect jobs are created and three family members or dependents are provided for. "*..Thus, fishers, aqua culturists and those supplying services and goods to them assure the livelihoods of a total of about 540 million people, or 8.0 percent of the world population*" (FAO's SOFIA 2010).

In terms of food security, fish is a strategic staple food in many developing countries. In 2007, it accounted for 15.7 percent of the global population's intake of animal protein. This figure rises to 50 percent in several LDCs and small and island developing countries.

Fish trade also plays a very important economic role for a large number of developing members. Trade in fish accounted for about 10 percent of total agricultural exports (excluding forest products) or one percent of world merchandise trade in 2008, reaching a record of US$102bn. This figure nearly doubles the US$51.5bn corresponding value in 1998.

Defining the Problem

As mentioned above, a large number of international instruments and high-level political declarations, such as the Hong Kong Ministerial Mandate, show an increasing public concern for the overfishing that is taking place and the over-capacity present in the fishing sector. While the underlying causes for overfishing and overcapacity are multiple and complex, it is increasingly clear that certain forms of subsidies are linked to these two phenomena and produce highly negative externalities.

The urgent need to curb them is a result of the worrying situation and trend of the most traded fish stocks. The FAO estimated that in 2008[23], 82 percent of the fish stock monitored fell into the compound category of: fully exploited (50 percent); overexploited (28 percent); depleted (3 percent) or recovering from depletion (1 percent). It also calculated that only 15 percent of the stocks were underexploited or moderately exploited and, therefore, able to produce more than their current catches. The declining trend of this "safe" category can be illustrated by recalling that the corresponding figure in 1974 was 40 percent and by the time fisheries subsidies were first discussed in the Committee on Trade and Environment in the WTO (1997) it amounted to 35 percent.

Since the early 1990s several studies have been undertaken to estimate the magnitude of subsidies in the fisheries sector. The results show wide variations mainly due to the different definitions of subsidies and the lack of transparency. Estimates vary widely as can be seen in the following table, but the order of magnitude is significant in any case.

Table 3: Global Estimate			
Date	Institution	(US$bn)	
1998	World Bank	11-20	20-25% of catch value
2000	APEC	12.6	
2001	WWF	8.00- 8.32	
2003	OECD	6.3	
2006	University of B. Columbia	30-34	

From an economic point of view, it should also be recalled that the study by the World Bank and the FAO in October 2008, in justifying the need for reform in fisheries policies, estimated the global rent loss at USD 51 bn[24]. Also, in pointing to the massive overcapacity of the sector, this research indicated that the current marine catch could be achieved with approximately half the current global fishing effort.

Key Issues in Fisheries Subsidies Negotiations

The first draft by the Chair in 2007[25] has become the axis of present negotiations, regardless the positions of the members toward it. In simple terms the discipline proposed is based on the following five pillars: a) a list of prohibited subsidies; b) general exceptions; c) S&D treatment; d) fisheries management conditionalities and e) enforcement and implementation requirements. The new disciplines will apply only to marine wild capture, therefore leaving outside its scope all subsidies related to fisheries in internal waters and aquaculture. The present consensus around this approach should be maintained for the benefit of many developing countries and the negotiations as a whole.

The prohibition tries to comply with the Hong Kong Ministerial mandate, in terms of addressing subsidies that contribute not only to over-capacity but also over-fishing. Hence, it covers subsidies for:

- acquisition/construction/renewal of vessels;
- operating costs;
- port infrastructure predominantly for fishing and related activities;
- income and price supports;
- onward transfer of access rights to fisheries; and
- illegal, unreported and unregulated (IUU) fishing

Beyond this positive list the proposal also includes two general disciplines: a broad prohibition for any subsidies for fishing patently over-exploited stocks and a general discipline making actionable any non-prohibited subsidy that harms stocks in which another member has identifiable fishing interests.

The exceptions cover "green" subsidies for: environment and sustainability, crew safety, re-education or redeployment of fish workers and vessel decommissioning.

The S&D treatment the ministerial mandate calls for was structured in this first Chair´s draft around three areas: a) a set of differentiated obligations for developing countries; b) different deadlines for entry into force and compliance and c) the obligation to establish mechanisms for technical assistance. In brief, the core S&D treatment in this first draft was provided by:

- exempting all LDCs (without any conditions) from all prohibitions of subsidization
- allowing all subsidies for subsistence (artisanal) fisheries, under a flexible condition of submitting them to some kind of fisheries management system[26]
- allowing all subsidies for commercial fisheries (with the exception of construction and operating subsidies for large vessels fishing outside the member´s exclusive economic zone (EEZ) with the condition of a mandatory fisheries management system (national or regional) to be established by the developing member according to internationally recognised best standards.

Table 4: Scheme of S&DT in Chair´s first draft

Category of Developing member	LDC	Non LDC			
Types of fisheries	*All*	*Subsistance*	*Commercial-small*	*Commercial-large*	
Subsidies				Within EEZ	Outside EEZ
Construction	Allowed	Allowed	Allowed	Allowed	Not allowed
Transfer	Allowed	Allowed	Not allowed	Not allowed	Not allowed
Operating	Allowed	Allowed	Allowed	Allowed	Not allowed
Infrastructure	Allowed	Allowed	Allowed	Allowed	Allowed
Income	Allowed	Allowed	Allowed	Allowed	Allowed
Price	Allowed	Allowed	Allowed	Allowed	Allowed
Access	Allowed	Allowed	Allowed	Allowed	Allowed
Conditions	NONE	Flexible[27] & subject to an indicative Fisheries Management System	Mandatory Fisheries Management System based on internationally-recognised best practices		

Participation and Concerns of Developing Countries: An Evaluation

General Considerations

With respect to the general objective of the negotiation, developing countries have shown a great deal of convergence in their positions on the need for an ambitious outcome in fisheries subsidies negotiations. Nevertheless, contrary to what has happened in agriculture, they have not presented a unified front against subsidisation. Some of them are members of the informal group "Friends of Fish" and many have expressed views close to the Friend´s approach, with high demands to curb harmful subsidies. None of the developing countries have formally supported the defensive positions of Japan, Korea or Chinese Taipei, for whom the issue of overfishing is closely linked (and could be coped) with an efficient fisheries management system.

With respect to their own defensive interests, as early as 2006, developing countries agreed that S&D treatment should not constitute a "blank check"[28] and, although with differences among themselves, these countries have accepted the idea that exceptions granted on the basis of development condition should nevertheless be subject to some sustainability criteria.

Specific Concerns and Proposals from Developing Members

Brazil, China, India and Mexico have voiced their concerns regarding several aspects of the Chair's proposed S&D treatment and their willingness to see some of the conditionalities and limits relaxed or eliminated.[29] In particular, they have emphasised their right to access subsidies for construction and operation of vessels; fishing beyond their respective EEZs to exploit stocks over which they have jurisdiction, sovereignty or sovereign rights, fishing quotas or any other fishing rights. These very important fishing nations have indicated their interest to nevertheless condition these subsidies to sustainability criteria, determined ultimately by a stock assessment and respect of their maximum sustainable yields. This stock assessment, apparently, would be self-undertaken and not subject to any peer review.

Taking a different view, Argentina, Chile, Egypt and Uruguay have recently proposed to reaffirm the sustainability criteria under which subsidies could be provided, even for fisheries within an EEZ. Under this proposal, members who wish to have the right to subsidies will be required to prove the existence of under-exploited or unexploited fisheries resources within their jurisdictions (exclusive economic zones) and actual lack of enough fishing capacity to exploit those natural resources in a sustainable way.

SVEs have been particularly active and have taken a rather strong position in demanding a broad elimination of subsidies. With respect to their own defensive interests, the SVEs have proposed to be exempted from the prohibition based on their small participation in the world´s fish catch, which eventually would reintroduce the discussion of a "*de minimis*" and differentiation among developing members.

Mexico, sustaining an ambitious approach to curb fisheries subsidies, has recently raised concern about the potential inequity of prohibiting certain subsidies that by WTO definition should be specific, while allowing other general financial support by developed members and with presumably greater economic impact in the fishing sector.

The implication of this proposal is that the very definition of subsidy within the WTO will be put in question, therefore broadening the discussion. To avoid this situation, Mexico has expressed interest in circumscribing the discussion of the specificity requirement, only to fisheries subsidies.

Small islands are, in general terms, supportive of an ambitious outcome. However, they have raised concerns about the conditionalities as well as the impact of new disciplines in fishing access agreements.

In more general terms, many developing members have expressed concern about the possible burden (in institutional, technical and financial terms) that sustainability requirements could imply for them.

Concerns from Some Developed Countries

The interest and concerns of the developed countries need to be taken into account by the developing members at the time of strategic design and tactical definition. First, the political economy, the real social dimension, the domestic politics and even the geographical location of the three most defensive members (Japan, Korea and Chinese-Taipei) should be understood in order to find a consensus solution. The question of the potential "imbalance" between too loose requirements for developing countries and too tight for developed, is immediately understood in that fishing area.

It should, therefore, be kept in mind that the crucial question for many developed members is the treatment of the so-called small fisheries programme, their coastal fisheries or their own version of "artisanal" fisheries.

Final Reflections and Recommendations

After such a long march and so dark perspectives ahead if no solution is found, there should be hope for a successful and rather short negotiation, but for this to happen, members would have to accept the idea that:

- Notwithstanding the past responsibility in the depletion of the seas, no developing nation has the right to continue doing the wrong thing for reasons of "equity".
- A suitable balance between socio-economic and environmental objectives will be crucial for the successful conclusion of the negotiations. Ultimately protecting fish also means protecting jobs. The false logic of being "friend of fish" or "friend of fishers" as if they were mutually exclusive should be prevented.
- It will be irrational and ineffective for some developed countries to maintain the pretence that overcapacity and overfishing can be solved by mere fisheries management requirements and strong notification obligations. Sustaining this logic amounts to denying their own most recent history, as well as their own direct responsibility in the bad state of many fish stocks around the world.
- The long experience gathered by a large number of developing countries in their adherence to and use of renowned international instruments (such as the Convention on the Law of the Sea, and FAO´s Code of Conduct for Responsible Fisheries, and International Plans of Action on Illegal Unregulated and Unreported Fisheries and Capacity) should be taken into account and reflected in the texts,

particularly on fisheries management. This will require among other factors, building strong national negotiating teams made up of national/regional fisheries authorities and WTO subsidies experts.

- The reality of coastal "artisanal" fisheries in developed countries will have to be accepted. Nevertheless, the summing-up of all exceptions requested is no exit to this negotiation. In other areas of the DDA, members could be tempted to lower ambition and look for a minimum common denominator. In fisheries subsidies it will not work, or worse it could work counter to the mandated objectives.

In retrospect, WTO negotiations and UN legislation in this field have advanced quite a long distance. Yes, there is a lot to be done yet, but the public and general awareness of the sustainability crisis in the fisheries sector should remind everyone that there is no way back and that the clock is ticking.

Negotiations on Regional Trade Agreements

The Ministerial Mandate and the Ensuing Debate

As was the case in other areas of the rules negotiations, the original mandate with regard to regional trade agreements was broad and lacking clear objectives.[30] Furthermore, in the following Ministerial meetings this deficiency of political direction was not mended and the ensuing declarations coming out of Cancun and Hong Kong did not make it any clearer.

The uneasiness with the fact that regional trade agreements are growing in number, scope and complexity is certainly not new and it is a sensible concern, since there would be legal, economic and political implications of huge proportions if the fragmentation of the multilateral trading system were to continue.[31]

The founding principle of the post World War II trading system was non-discrimination, embodied in the most favoured nation clause and the national treatment obligation. The departure from this principle was only meant to be an exception, in order to promote further and more rapid trade liberalisation. In other words, to make sure that those exceptional regional trade agreements would be "building blocks" not "stumbling blocks" for freer trade, they were ruled by Article XXIV of GATT and later by the enabling clause[32], the Uruguay Round Understanding on Article XXIV and Article V of the General Agreement on Trade and Services (GATS). In February 1996 the Committee on Regional Trade Agreements (CRTA) was established, mainly, to examine those agreements, consider the systemic implications for the multilateral trading system and make appropriate recommendations to the General Council.[33]

The problem was supposed to be (and presumably still is) that those norms impose obligations on members of WTO in terms of notifications[34], provision of information and periodic reporting; but they are unclear on the scope and characteristics of that information. Furthermore, the link between the notification, the CRTA examination and the DSM became a vicious circle, since members were reluctant to provide detailed and periodic information that eventually could be used against them.

Members were therefore wise to simplify this issue by separating the transparency issue from the systemic implications posed by regional trade agreements. In 2006 the WTO reached consensus on the provisional application of a new Transparency Mechanism that clarifies greatly the procedural rules regarding the time, scope and even purpose of notification and reporting.[35]

Both from the perspective of the multilateral trading system's interests and the standpoint of developing countries, this was an important achievement. Enhancing transparency on the "spaghetti bowl" can only help weaker members with greater information deficits. With that in mind, members, particularly developing ones, could do well in pressing for a quick review of the mechanism and a final and permanent approval of it this year and notwithstanding the results of the DDA.

That being said, it should be recalled that, beyond the rules of transparency, there was a very long debate on the possible clarification of the substantive rules of Articles GATT XXIV and GATS V. The debate followed an early and excellent identification of the systemic issues at stake undertaken by the Secretariat in 2000 and revised two years later.[36]. Several proposals were made and the debate soon became very active, profound and technical, in many aspects even academic. Two road maps were offered by the Chair to guide the debate and the discussions focussed on a core set of issues, in particular: the clarification of the "substantially all the trade" (SAT) concept in Article XXIV; the length of transition periods; and regional trade agreements' development dimension (inclusion of S&D provisions in Article XXIV of the GATT 1994).

The main thrust of the discussions was on the clarification and calculation of substantially all trade (SAT). The quantitative elements of SAT were discussed in detail. Consideration was given to the pros and cons of tests based on trade and on tariff lines, their respective benchmarks, how to combine them, the level of HS disaggregation for the calculations, the non-exclusion of "major sectors" and the relationship of "other restrictive regulations of commerce" with SAT.

Views diverged widely among those members favouring a trade-based test, a tariff line test and a combined one. Differences were equally big on the weight to attribute to each benchmark and on how to combine them. Some participants favoured an approach to SAT that would include "other restrictive regulations of commerce" as well as preferential rules of origin. Qualitative benchmarks to complement the SAT evaluation were also discussed.

Evaluation and Suggestions

Overall there was no lack of technical insight and expertise in the debate, but what was (again) missing was a clear political objective. For this reason, notwithstanding the recognised importance of the systemic implications of regional trade agreements, the number of proposals started to decline and the interest in this area of the negotiation subsided to the point that, now, it is not easy to determine who is the demandeur of these negotiations. Why would WTO members seek a common "golden standard" of regional trade agreements when each thinks its own way is best and the least disturbing for the multilateral trading system? Why confront the "constructive ambiguity" of GATT

Article XXIV with a "disruptive clarity" that would only strengthen the scrutiny of regional trade agreements? Is it politically logical to demand those who have opted for the "second best" to legislate against their own trade policies and have more rules that would self-restrain them? Yes, the fragmentation of the trade system could be a real danger in institutional terms, highly costly for national administrations and a promoter of inefficiencies, asymmetries and inequities. But, the overly legalistic (and ultimately punitive) approach does not seem to be the most effective way to strengthen multilateralism.

The paradox is that this area of the DDA would become even more relevant if the rest of the DDA fails. Therefore, a cautious path is advised to avoid the contradiction of demanding clearer (and stricter) WTO rules on regional trade agreements precisely when the WTO is proving to be ineffective in further liberalizing trade in goods and services.

Historical experience shows that convergence of regional trade agreements cannot be imposed. In many regions this normative approach has not gone beyond declarations of intent or vacuum resolutions. To reduce the negative elements of neo-regionalism and promote convergence perhaps a less formalistic approach is needed, where incentives for multilateralisation could be identified and costs of fragmentation exposed.

Therefore, instead of a legislative approach, perhaps an extended and permanent work programme on regional trade agreements for the General Council and Ministerial Conference could be envisioned. The reinforcement of the CRTA, in terms of high-level participation, composition and regularity could be considered. Likewise, an institutional tripartite dialogue between governments, academics and the private sector could provide useful permanent analysis and insight. Would not this be a more effective way, say, to promote benefits of accumulative rules of origin or publicly expose the high cost of administrating a fragmented trade system?

Probably this is one of the most crucial areas for the WTO since it touches upon the basic principle of non-discrimination and the effectiveness to promote trade liberalisation. For many what is at stake is the very relevance of the institution. The previous ideas are just some thoughts and suggestions based on experience gathered in the trenches of trade policy formulation and negotiation. They could be controversial but ultimately the unquestioned truth, with which everyone should agree, is that the best incentive for multilateralism would be a prompt conclusion of the DDA.

Endnotes

1 The G20 Seoul Summit refers to "*our strong commitment to direct our negotiators to engage in across-the-board negotiations to promptly bring the Doha Development Round to a successful, ambitious, comprehensive, and balanced conclusion consistent with the mandate of the Doha Development Round and built on the progress already achieved. We recognise that 2011 is a critical window of opportunity, albeit narrow, and that engagement among our representatives must intensify and expand. We now need to complete the end game. Once such an outcome is reached, we commit to seek ratification, where necessary, in our respective systems.*"

2 The original Ministerial mandate for negotiations on anti-dumping is contained in paragraph 28 of the Doha Declaration, which states: "*28. In the light of experience and of the increasing application of these instruments by members, we agree to negotiations aimed at clarifying and improving disciplines under the Agreements on Implementation of Article VI of the GATT 1994 and on Subsidies and Countervailing Measures, while preserving the basic concepts, principles and effectiveness of these Agreements and their instruments and objectives, and taking into account the needs of developing and least-developed participants.*"

3 "**DECISION ON ANTI-CIRCUMVENTION** *Ministers,* Noting that while the problem of circumvention of anti-dumping duty measures formed part of the negotiations that preceded the Agreement on Implementation of Article VI of GATT 1994, negotiators were unable to agree on specific text, *Mindful* of the desirability of the applicability of uniform rules in this area as soon as possible, *Decide* to refer this matter to the Committee on Anti-Dumping Practices established under that Agreement for resolution."

4 See MTN.TNC/MIN (94)/ST/100 for Japan and MTN.TNC/MIN (94)/ST/92 for Chile. Secretary Chau Tak Hay on behalf of Hong Kong China also referred to anti-dumping but in the context of the need for new rules on competition and trade. See MTN.TNC/MIN (94)/ST/9. Also see "Keeping animal spirits asleep: the case of Chile" within Safeguards & Anti-dumping in Latin American Trade Liberalization, ISBN-10:0-8213-6308-5.

5 "*...The experience of Kenya and some of the other African countries in the region which have some inadequate legal framework and have been unable to establish institutional framework for the investigations of complaints, shows that manufacturing industries and agricultural producers in their countries which are being injured by dumped or subsidised imports are not able to take full advantage of the right which the two agreements confer on them to petition for investigations for the following reasons...*"

6 See note 2 above.

7 For further information see document TN/RL/W/171.

8 See DS 141 India vs. European Communities.

9 Canada TN/RL/W/ 26 and 73.

10 For an in-depth view of the use of anti-dumping in Latin America (Argentina, Brazil, Chile, Colombia, Costa Rica, Mexico and Peru) see "*Safeguards and Anti-dumping in Latin American Trade Liberalization, Fighting Fire with Fire*" Edited by Michael Finger and Pablo Nogués and published jointly by World Bank and Palgrave Macmillan with ISBN-10:0-8213-6308-5.

11 For in-depth economic analysis of the use of anti-dumping against and by China see "*China's WTO Entry Antidumping, Safeguards, and Dispute Settlement*" by Chad P. Bown.

12 The three most active developing countries initiating investigations under the ASCM have been South Africa, Peru and Chile. The most investigated members under the ASCM have been India and China, accounting to around 25percent of the initiations.

13 As we have seen in the previous section, the overall number of anti-dumping initiations has been much larger, amounting to an accumulated total of 3752 from 1995 to 2010.

14 For an economic and legal appraisal of this huge intervention, see the WTO special reports as well as the following articles: "WTO subsidies discipline during and after the crisis" by Gary N. Horlick and Peggy A. Clark in the *Journal of International Economic Law*; "The collapse of global trade; murky protectionism and the crisis: recommendations for the G20" edited by Simon Evenett and Richard Balwin.

15 See paragraphs 28 and 31 of the Doha Ministerial Declaration.

16 For the five phases distinguished in the history of these negotiations s*ee Chapter 4 of Fisheries Subsidies, Sustainable Development and the WTO, published by Earthscan, UNEP, ISBN: 978-1-84791-135-7.*

17 L/3538 "Industrial Pollution Control and International Trade" dated June, 09, 1971.

18 Document Spec(91)21 of April, 29, 1991 the Chairman prepared an 'Outline Of Points For Structured Debate On Environmental Measures And Trade' which included fish and fish products as a sector of particular interest to developing countries, taking into account their trade, financial and development needs, "in which trade may be affected as a result of environmental policy measures".

19 See FIDI /C853 FAO Fisheries Circular 853 "Marine Fisheries and the Law of the Sea: A Decade of Change".

20 WT/CTE/51 by U.S. and WT/CTE/52 by New Zealand.

21 Paragraph 26 Section II of the IPOA reads: "States should reduce and progressively eliminate all factors, including subsidies and economic incentives and other factors which contribute, directly or indirectly, to the build-up of excessive fishing capacity thereby undermining the sustainability of marine living resources, giving due regard to the needs of artisanal fisheries."

22 See Annex D Para. 9 of the Hong Kong Ministerial Declaration.

23 See FAO SOFIA 2010.

24 See World Bank, FAO (2008) The Sunken Billions.

25 See document TN/RL/213.

26 The flexibility of the condition to access subsidies otherwise prohibited is the following "*Fisheries management measures aimed at ensuring sustainability...* ***should*** *be implemented in respect of the fisheries in question,* ***adapted as necessary to the particular situation****, including by making use of indigenous fisheries management institutions and measures*."

27 *Ibid.*

28 This was expressed in the presentation by the Brazilian Minister for Fisheries at the NGRules. Later on similar concept can be found in document TN/RL/W/210/Rev.2 by the SVEs and TN/RL/W/234 from Argentina, Chile, Colombia, Ecuador, Mexico and Peru.

29 See TN/RL/GEN/163.

30 Paragraph 29 of the Doha Declaration states *"We also agree to negotiations aimed at clarifying and improving disciplines and procedures under the existing WTO provisions applying to regional trade agreements. The negotiations shall take into account the developmental aspects of regional trade agreements."*

31 For updated statistics on regional trade agreements see the WTO Regional Trade Agreements Information System at http://rtais.wto.org/UI/PublicMaintainRTAHome.aspx and for a further reading of these implications see Chapter II of "The Future of WTO" , by the Consultative Group to the WTO's Director General, WTO 2005 and "Termites in the Trading System" by Jagdish Bhagwati.

32 Short name for the 1979 GATT Contracting Parties Decision on Differential and More Favourable Treatment, Reciprocity and Fuller Participation of Developing Countries.

33 See General Council's decision WT/L/127 7 of February 1996.

34 GATT Article XXIV:7(a), Paragraph 4(a) of the Enabling Clause, GATS Article V:7(a) and Paragraph 11 of the Understanding.

35 See WT/L/671.

36 WT/REG/W/37 Synopsis of "Systemic" Issues Related To Regional Trade Agreements and TN/RL/W/8/Rev.1.

8 Special and Differential Treatment – Continuing Saga of Stalled Negotiations

Nelson Ndirangu
Programme Director ACP MTS Programme
Former Negotiator, Kenya Mission to the WTO

Introduction

The debate on the need to review the provisions on S&D treatment contained in the various WTO agreements emerged during the preparatory process for the third WTO Ministerial Conference that was held in Seattle, US in 1999. The review of S&D treatment provisions was raised by many developing country members who pointed out that they had not benefitted from those provisions in the WTO agreements because of inherent shortcomings. Therefore, they wanted the WTO members to address the problems they were experiencing in the implementation of the Uruguay Round Agreements before they could undertake any further trade liberalisation measures.

Many developing country members argued that the S&D treatment provisions were not effective and, therefore, had not facilitated the implementation of the obligations arising from the Uruguay Round Agreements; and hence they were unable to integrate into the multilateral trading system. They pointed out that the adjustment measures provided by the S&D treatment clauses were not appropriate in assisting developing country members attain the required capacity. For instance, the transition periods granted to developing country members were not based on their levels of development and capacities and hence did not help in achieving the capacity required to comply with certain provisions of the Uruguay Round Agreements. It was also pointed out that most of the S&D treatment provisions were "best endeavour" clauses and therefore enforcement of such non-binding clauses was a big challenge.

At the Seattle Ministerial Conference, the developing country members wanted the ministers to address their "implementation-related issues and concerns," which included the review of S&D treatment provisions while the developed country members wanted a decision to negotiate particularly on "new issues" i.e. investment, competition, trade facilitation and government procurement, commonly referred to as the "Singapore issues." The developing country members were opposed to the introduction of the Singapore issues, arguing that they did not constitute the core mandate of the WTO and therefore were not a priority over their "implementation-related issues and concerns." The difference in position on a number of issues between the developed and developing country members led to the collapse of the Seattle Ministerial Conference and hence no decision on the implementation issues and concerns, including S&D treatment was made.

After Seattle, the developed country members expressed their willingness to address "implementation issues and concerns" that had been raised by the developing country members. As a result, the CTD began discussions on S&D treatment provisions. This was part of the strategy by the developed country members to woo the developing country members and have them agree to a new Round of trade negotiations that would include the Singapore issues. Further to this strategy, the developed country members pointed out that a "development round" was necessary to address the development needs and concerns of the developing country members, which included the "implementation-related issues and concerns." It was on this premise that a development round" was launched during the fourth WTO Ministerial Conference held in Doha, Qatar in November 2001.

With respect to S&D treatment provisions, the ministers at Doha recognised that problems existed and set out a work programme in paragraph 44[1] of the Doha Ministerial Declaration, in which they reaffirmed that S&D treatment is an integral part of the WTO rules. The declaration also expressed concerns about the implementation of S&D treatment provisions and directed that all S&D treatment provisions be reviewed with a view to strengthening them and making them more precise, effective and operational.

Paragraph 44 was also linked to the Ministerial Decision on "implementation-related issues and concerns,"[2] in particular paragraph 12, which mandated the CTD to identify the S&D treatment provisions that would be made mandatory and examine additional ways to make S&D treatment more effective with clear recommendations to the General Council by July 2002. The decision also mandated members to consider how S&D treatment could be incorporated into the future architecture of the WTO rules.

In fulfilling the mandate on S&D treatment, the decision also highlighted the need to fully take into consideration the previous work of the CTD particularly the WTO typology of 155 S&D treatment provisions that had been identified by members at the time.[3] The typology identified six categories of S&D, each one of them raising specific implementation difficulties. The six categories were:

i) provisions aimed at increasing the trade opportunities of developing country members;
ii) provisions under which WTO members should safeguard the interests of the developing country members;

iii) flexibility of commitments, of action and use of policy instruments;
iv) transitional time periods;
v) technical assistance; and
vi) provisions relating to LDC members.

Developing Country Proposals on S&D Treatment Provisions

The negotiations to implement the Doha Mandate on S&D treatment began in March 2002 after the establishment of the Trade Negotiations Committee (TNC) and were conducted in the CTD-SS. Members started the negotiations on S&D treatment by exchanging views on principles and objectives related to S&D treatment provisions and the need for strengthening them. This was followed by discussions on the identification of non-mandatory S&D treatment provisions, which members considered, should be made mandatory, and on the legal and practical implications of doing so.

By July 2002, the members had tabled 14 submissions before the CTD-SS for discussion.[4] The joint communication from the African Group[5] had the highest number of proposals and was submitted on June 07, 2002. It was subsequently introduced during the informal meeting of the CTD-SS held on June 10, 2002. The members requested more time beyond the deadline of July 2002 set out in the Doha Declaration in order to allow for in-depth analysis and discussion of the proposals submitted as well as the possibility for submission of new proposals.

In July 2002, the General Council extended the deadline and instructed the CTD-SS to proceed expeditiously to fulfill its mandate, as contained in paragraph 44 of the Doha Ministerial Declaration and paragraph 12 of the Decision on Implementation-Related Issues and Concerns, in order that clear recommendations for a decision could be made to the General Council by December, 31, 2002. The General Council gave further instructions regarding, *inter alia,* the consideration of agreement-specific proposals, the analysis and examination of cross-cutting issues, the establishment of the monitoring mechanism, the consideration of proposals on institutional arrangements and on technical and financial assistance and training, the consideration of how S&D treatment may be incorporated into the architecture of WTO rules.

Cross-cutting issues

On cross-cutting issues the main proposals by the developing country members were related to institutional issues, including on:

(i) a monitoring mechanism;
(ii) an Annual Special Session of the General Council on LDCs' participation;
(iii) a facility under the DDA Trust Fund; and
(iv) proposals on technical assistance and training.

A listing of these issues together with references to relevant written submissions is contained in Annex I at the end of this chapter.

The African Group made the proposal for the establishment of a monitoring mechanism. In the Group's view, among the main functions of the mechanism would be:

(i) the regular evaluation of the utilisation and effectiveness of the S&D treatment provisions, with a view to ensuring that they are duly utilised and any problems are effectively addressed, and

(ii) provision of a framework for initiating and considering recommendations that the CTD could make to members on complying with obligations under S&D treatment provisions, as well as best practice for utilisation of the provisions.

The LDC Group made the proposal for an Annual Special Session of the General Council on the participation of the LDCs in the multilateral trading system (MTS). They proposed that the agenda of such an annual session could encompass:

(i) the implementation of the Decision on Measures in Favour of Least-Developed Country members and its overall objectives in favour of LDCs;

(ii) the review of the implementation of the specific special and differential provisions included in the WTO agreements, decisions and declarations; and

(iii) the overall review of S&D treatment.

Some members were of the view that should a monitoring mechanism be established, its role and functions could include the proposed Annual Special Session of the General Council on the participation of the LDCs in the multilateral trading system and emphasised that it would have to be without diluting the concerns of the LDCs. Other members suggested that the various proposals and their role and functions would need to be assessed in the context of existing machinery such as the Sub-Committee on the LDC members and the Integrated Framework (IF).[6]

Finally, the African Group proposed the establishment of a facility under the Doha Development Agenda Trust Fund to ensure the financial underpinning/backing necessary for the effective utilisation of S&D treatment provisions under the various agreements, and that it would be a permanent financial arrangement for S&D treatment provisions. The African Group also outlined criteria for technical and financial assistance and training in the annex to its submission. However, some members, particularly the developed country members were of the view that the proposal could be given further consideration in the context of the development of technical assistance plans.

Developed country members also made submissions on cross-cutting issues but these were limited to a number of systemic issues, including the principles and objectives of S&D treatment, including the utility of a clearer definition and understanding on these principles in assessing the effectiveness of S&D treatment provisions; a single or multi-tiered structure of rights and obligations; coherence; bench marking; transition periods; utilisation; and universal or differentiated treatment, including graduation.

Agreement-specific proposals

The agreement-specific proposals were largely submitted by the developing and LDC members that were keen to introduce specific drafting language into S&D treatment provisions contained in various WTO agreements in order to make them more precise, effective and operational.

A total of 88 agreement-specific proposals were submitted to CTD-SS to address S&D treatment related issues. These proposals came from individual developing country members, the Like-Minded Group (LMG), the LDCs and the African Group. A synoptic table indicating the proposals made on specific provisions under the various agreements is contained in Annex II at the end of this chapter. The agreement-specific proposals mainly focused on the following most important areas for the developing country members:

(i) improved preferential access to developed country markets;
(ii) exemptions from certain WTO rules aimed at increasing policy space in order to address developmental concerns of the developing country members;
(iii) binding and enforceable commitments for technical and financial assistance; and
(iv) more and predictable development aid.

The developed country members did not submit agreement-specific proposals. They appeared to be interested in systemic issues of cross-cutting nature.

Participation of Developing Country Members in the Negotiations

The African Group and the LDCs were the major players in the negotiations on S&D treatment. These two groups of countries had the highest number of proposals that were submitted for discussion in the CTD-SS.

In the discussions, the African Group and the LDCs pointed out that they were having difficulties using the WTO framework properly in order to fully benefit from the market access opportunities available to them. In addition, they were experiencing difficulties in complying with the many existing multilateral trade obligations, since their countries operated under enormous financial, institutional and human resource constraints. The African Group and the LDCs further observed that WTO members were not equal in terms of resources and capacity and hence were similarly unequal in their participation in the WTO system, especially with regard to meeting their implementation and compliance requirements. In this respect, therefore, they needed assistance and flexibility in implementing and complying with their multilateral trade obligations, as well as supporting measures that would enable them to benefit from the market access opportunities. They highlighted that it was against this background that S&D treatment was accorded to developing country and LDC members as a means of facilitating their integration into the multilateral trading system. The CTD-SS was, therefore, required to consider how to strengthen the S&D treatment provisions and make them more precise, effective and operational. It was also required to find additional measures for that purpose, where necessary, and to consider how to include S&D treatment provisions in the architecture of the WTO Agreement in the context of the Doha Work Programme.

The African Group and the LDCs were followed by the LMG in terms of the number of proposals that were submitted. While the African Group submitted proposals in almost all areas of the WTO Agreements,[7] the LMG submitted nine proposals that were limited to S&D treatment provisions in the WTO Agreements on SPS measures,[8] TBT,[9] SCM, and the WTO DSM.[10]

The submissions from individual developing country members came from India,[11] Paraguay,[12] St. Lucia,[13] and Thailand.[14] While the proposals by India, St. Lucia and Thailand were generally acceptable among the African Group, the LDCs and the LMG members, the submission by Paraguay raised divergent positions among the proponents of the mandate on S&D treatment.

The submission by Paraguay was related to the Decision on Differential and More Favourable Treatment, Reciprocity and Fuller Participation of Developing Country Members, more commonly known as the "enabling clause," as contained under the GATT 1994. The submission by Paraguay raised concerns that the implementation of the enabling clause had encouraged discrimination among the developing country members in terms of accessing benefits accorded to them by the developed country members. Paraguay pointed out that while the developed country members had the right under the enabling clause to accord preferential market access to developing country members on a unilateral basis, such benefits should be available to all other developing country members without discrimination. It pointed out that the requests for WTO waivers by the developed country members under Article 1 of the GATT 1994 to accord privileges and benefits to some specific developing country members to the exclusion of the rest was a violation of the MFN principle and the enabling clause. Paraguay further observed that those who ended up paying for the concessions provided to some developing country members by means of such waivers were generally the developing country members excluded from such preferential treatment.

The paper, therefore, proposed that the implementation of the enabling clause should not give rise to discrimination among developing country members except where only the LDCs were the beneficiaries. Other developing country members, such as Argentina, Chile, Hong Kong, SAR, India, the Philippines, and Thailand, supported the submission by Paraguay. This group of developing country members argued that they had also suffered from the selective administration of the enabling clause by some developed country members and wanted the issue addressed in the negotiations on S&D treatment.

The ACP countries and the African Group considered the submission by Paraguay as an attack on the WTO waiver under the Cotonou Agreement and the AGOA arrangement granted to these groups of countries respectively. The AGOA is a preferential scheme granted by the US to the African sub-Saharan countries, while under the Cotonou Agreement, the EU granted preferential market access to the ACP Group. The Groups argued that the implementation of the enabling clause should also take into account the principle of equity in order to ensure that the weak members were supported in their efforts to integrate into the multilateral trading system. They observed that the developing country members were no longer a homogeneous group in terms of levels of development, since some had advanced more than others. The enabling clause, therefore, provided an important avenue for putting in place measures aimed at assisting those who were economically weak and vulnerable to fully participate in the multilateral trading system. The African and the ACP Groups were supported by some developed country members, such as Canada, the EU, and the US, which expressed sympathy to the economic and development situation of those groups of countries and urged other members to provide assistance to them so that they too can reap the benefits of the multilateral trading system.

Progress on Proposals on S&D Treatment

During negotiations the discussions on S&D treatment provisions generated many divergent views among members that delayed progress in this important area. One major area of differences was the interpretation of some aspects of the Doha mandate. The majority of developing country members considered that one way to make S&D treatment provisions more precise, effective and operational was to make them mandatory by changing the existing language of some of the 'best endeavour' provisions. However the developed country members did not wish to consider amending the text of the agreements as it would alter what they considered to be the existing delicate balance of rights and obligations.

Consequently, the developed country members expressed the need to seek clarification of the mandate contained in paragraph 44 of the Doha Ministerial Declaration and paragraph 12 of the Decision on Implementation-Related Issues and Concerns, while many developing country members were of the view that the mandate was clear and interpreted the views of the developed country members as a lack of political goodwill to resolve the problems related to S&D treatment provisions. While developing country members considered the mandate as a negotiating issue and, therefore, demanded a special session to handle the issue, developed country members insisted on the matter being discussed in an existing WTO body. After some delays, the developing country members' demand to establish the CTD in special session carried the day. The initial exchange of views on principles and objectives related to S&D treatment provisions and the need for strengthening them brought out differences that were not easy to resolve. The differences related to the mandate, the understanding and purpose of the subject matter and how to resolve the issues identified by the ministers in Doha. Because of such differences and the developed country members' unwillingness to be flexible on the agreement, progress became extremely slow, and many deadlines set by the General Council for the conclusion of the negotiations on S&D treatment provisions were missed.

On cross-cutting issues, the only proposal on which some progress, albeit minimal, was achieved was on the establishment of the monitoring mechanism. In July 2002, the General Council agreed to establish a monitoring mechanism for S&D treatment. However, it instructed the CTD-SS to further elaborate for the Council's approval, the functions, structure and terms of reference of such a mechanism. A number of new submissions were introduced, and possible elements relating to the establishment of the monitoring mechanism were discussed. There was a convergence of views on some elements, such as the structure and possible role of the mechanism and the sources of information for the conduct of its work. However, there were also some areas of major differences, including on the institutional structure of the mechanism and the timing for its coming into force that remain outstanding. While the African Group proposed that the mechanism should come into force after the review and strengthening of all the S&D treatment provisions, developed country members wanted it to be made operational as soon as possible. The developed country members viewed the mechanism as another review, as opposed to the African Group which wanted the mechanism to establish the implementation difficulties that would be encountered during the application of strengthened S&D treatment provisions and the ways to overcome them.

With respect to agreement-specific proposals, inspite of the considerable time that had been spent trying to agree on these proposals, very little progress had been achieved by the end of 2002, which led to frustration among members, particularly the African Group and the LDCs, which were the main proponents. Consultations in December 2002 and later in January-February 2003, resulted in an agreement in principle on 12 agreement-specific proposals.[15] In order to enhance progress, a new approach was proposed by the then-Chairman of the General Council.[16] He came up with an informal categorisation of the 88 Agreement-specific proposals in April 2003. These proposals were classified into three categories[17].

Category I contained 38 proposals on which, based on the discussions that had taken place and the responses given by members, there appeared to be a greater likelihood of reaching an agreement. This category included the 12 agreement-specific proposals, which were already agreed in principle by members in February 2003 and set out in Annex III of document TN/CTD/7. Category II contained 38 proposals that in his view were made in areas under negotiation as part of the DDA or could be considered in other WTO bodies, in order to get better responses within the framework of the negotiations or at the technical level. Category III contained proposals on which there were wide differences of views among members. These proposals according to the assessment of the chairman required a certain degree of redrafting in order to achieve a positive outcome. The African Group was opposed to the idea of categorisation of proposals and scattering them to various WTO bodies because it considered that discussing S&D treatment provisions under a single body would attract the necessary focus and attention that was required to make progress. It also argued that the African Group did not have sufficient capacity to participate in the negotiations on S&D treatment provision that would be placed before various bodies. Africa's plea to continue negotiations in the CTD-SS received lukewarm support from other developing country members.

To appease the African Group and in a bid to make substantial progress prior to the Fifth Ministerial Conference, the Chairman formed a small group of six countries to work informally on S&D treatment and report back to the CTD-SS. The six countries were the US; the EC; Norway (representing the developed country members); Kenya (representing the African Group); Bangladesh (representing LDCs) and Brazil (chairing the informal group). The fact that the Chairman of the CTD-SS picked Brazil to chair the small group meant that Kenya and Bangladesh had to face the US, the EC and Norway, whose interests on the issues were diametrically opposed to those of the African Group and the LDCs. The Chairman's main interest was to conclude on as many agreement-specific proposals as possible, but not the economic value of the strengthened provisions. This can be seen in the 25 agreement-specific proposals that were concluded in a pressure cooked manner by the heads of delegation of the small group. Resistance from Kenya and Bangladesh did not count in the decision-making process. The recommendations from the small group were reflected in Annex C to the draft Cancun Ministerial text.[18] Further recommendations for three agreement-specific proposals were included in Annex C at Cancun, which came to 28 proposals. The draft Ministerial text[19] also provided for work on the remaining agreement-specific proposals and on the proposals referred to negotiating or other WTO bodies, including all outstanding issues to be continued under the close supervision of the General Council. The Ministerial Conference in Cancun was a failure and as such the package of the 28 agreement-specific proposals on which there was agreement in principle, was not adopted.

The failure of the Cancun Ministerial Conference may have been seen as a serious setback by developed country members, but it was a relief for the African Group and the LDCs, because it afforded them more time to evaluate progress in this respect.

Notwithstanding this and after a pause in negotiations at the WTO, members agreed to resume business through the framework agreement reached in July 2004. Subsequent discussions did not yield any meaningful progress and as a result, there was no concrete decision during the Sixth WTO Ministerial Conference held in Hong Kong in 2005. Instead, ministers at Hong Kong, instructed the CTD-SS to expeditiously complete the review of all the outstanding agreement – specific proposals and report to the General Council, with clear recommendations for a decision.[20] The 28 agreement-specific proposals on which there was agreement in principle were not adopted at the Hong Kong Conference, since according to the proponents they did not constitute a meaningful commercial value. An assessment done by the African Group had revealed that those proposals did not have any meaningful commercial value. However, the ministers at Hong Kong adopted five decisions[21] in favour of the LDCs arising from the proposals[22] submitted by this Group of countries.

After the Hong Kong Ministerial Conference, work on agreement-specific proposals continued, but very little progress had been made and by March 2010 members had narrowed the areas of divergence to a few brackets in only six proposals.[23] The language on the six agreement-specific proposals is exactly the same as that proposed and negotiated in 2007, the date when negotiations seem to have come to an unexplained end. The last language tabled relating to the six agreement-specific proposals is markedly different from the original proposals and as such adds very little, if any, value.

Lessons for Developing Country Negotiators

Differences in positions among the WTO members emerged immediately. The negotiations on S&D treatment provisions began in the Special Session of the CTD in early 2002. The developed country members had no strategic interest in S&D treatment provisions other than using it to entice developing country members to agree to launch negotiations and thereafter focussed on issues of interest to them. Hence, although the developed country members agreed to make all S&D treatment provisions more precise, effective and operational, they tactfully expressed divergent views when it came to the practical modalities for implementing the mandate. For instance, the issue of changing non-binding S&D treatment provisions or "best-endeavour" provisions to mandatory provisions without reference to the level of development was not acceptable to the developed country members, since they were of the view that it would favour advanced developing country members over weaker developing country members.

The heterogeneous character of the developing country members, which ranges from LDCs to economically advanced developing country members, presented one main difficulty in the negotiations. It became difficult to obtain a meaningful package on S&D treatment provisions for all developing country members, because members could not reach an agreement to provide the same strengthened provisions to all developing country members. The developed country members could not accept to grant the same favourable provisions to both small, weaker economies and comparatively advanced developing country members that enjoyed high economic growth and development.

Another challenge faced in the negotiations was the lack of unity among the developing country members. This was revealed during the submission of proposals and the subsequent discussions that took place in the CTD-SS. The African Group, the LDCs, the SVEs, the ACP Group and other individual developing country members could not come together to submit joint proposals. Each of these groups of countries had their own individual submissions. This weakened the necessary political weight that was needed to have a positive bearing on the progress of the negotiations. This weakness among the developing country members was compounded by the fact that the advanced developing country members were not keen to take the lead in the negotiations. Their advantage lied in not supporting differentiation among the developing country members, meaning that they would still benefit from any positive outcome even if they did not take a lead in the negotiations.

The effective participation in the negotiations by the proponents of S&D treatment was negatively affected after categorisation of agreement-specific proposals and subsequent distribution of these proposals to various negotiating groups and other WTO regular bodies. For instance, the limited capacities in terms of human resources experienced by the African Group and the LDCs meant that they were unable to spread themselves adequately and participate effectively in the S&D treatment negotiations that took place simultaneously in various bodies.

Throughout the negotiations, it was observed that advanced developing country members and probably some developed country members would not accept the emergence of new categories among developing country members in order to make progress in the negotiations on S&D treatment proposals. It was also observed that a "one-size-fits-all" approach was not appropriate as far as S&D treatment was concerned in the WTO since there were wide differences between advanced developing country members and small developing country members.

It is, therefore, important for the WTO members to consider an alternative way of ensuring that each developing country member has access to flexibilities commensurate with its individual development, financial and trade needs. Building on current development provisions in the WTO agreements, members may wish to initiate key elements of a framework on trade and development that would include the following:

a. elaboration of the conceptual and practical relation between trade and economic development, and the adoption of principles to facilitate the role of trade in the promotion of the social and economic development of developing countries; and
b. elaboration of overarching rules on S&D treatment that would govern the negotiation, conclusion, and implementation of WTO rights and obligations as well as compliance with them, building upon the Doha mandate under paragraph 44 of the Doha Ministerial Declaration

The establishment of the framework on S&D treatment would not lead to the creation of new categories of developing countries, as some members and scholars have argued, but would ensure that S&D treatment is customised to address the specific needs of individual developing country members. The EC-India generalised system of preferences (GSP) case[24] provides us with a solid basis to advance this argument. The DSB examined the meaning of developing countries under the enabling clause and the legality of conditional GSP schemes. The outcome of the case was that developed countries may discriminate among developing countries as long as they do so based on an objective criterion. The Appellate Body reaffirmed the decision by stating that footnote 3 of the enabling clause creates a binding legal obligation requiring generalised, non-reciprocal and non-discriminatory preferences but that nevertheless, preference-giving countries may afford differential treatment to beneficiary countries if it is based on differences in their 'development, financial and trade needs', i.e. objective criteria.

In addition to the above, the current Doha texts on NAMA and agriculture go towards responding to specific needs of groups of different developing countries. For instance, different flexibilities are proposed for various developing country members subject to the formula, while different flexibilities are proposed for developing country members with low tariff binding coverage; SVEs; and RAMs (RAMs in the NAMA document TN/MA/W/103Rev.3/Add.1). This principle should be extended to other WTO subjects, including S&D treatment.

Hence, in order to overcome the current impasse in the agreement-specific proposals, members should now focus on developing specific objective criteria that would respond to the needs of countries that are in similar economic situations on the basis of the DSB decision on the EC-India GSP case and along the lines of DDA negotiating texts on NAMA and agriculture. In this respect, S&D treatment could be linked to certain parameters, for example, on the basis of trade performance over an appropriate period, which would reflect vulnerability so that those developing country members that are economically weak and vulnerable may enjoy more flexibility than others. This would be in line with the submission made by some developing country members in the preparatory process for the Fourth WTO Ministerial that proposed a Framework Agreement on Special and Differential Treatment[25] and in essence captured in paragraph 44 of the Doha Ministerial Declaration.

This approach will enable developing country members to pursue their development goals by applying appropriate flexibilities provided according to their individual finance, trade and development needs and hence participate fully in the multilateral trading system.

Endnotes

1 See WTO document: WT/MIN(01)/DEC/1

2 See WTO document: WT/MIN(01)/17

3 Following a request by the WTO members, the WTO Secretariat produced a number of documents: mandatory and non-mandatory special and differential provisions (WT/COMTD/W/77/Rev.1/Add.1), a review of mandatory S&D treatment provisions (WT/COMTD/W/77/Rev.1/Add.2), non-mandatory S&D treatment provisions (WT/COMTD/W/77/Rev.1/Add.3) and information on the utilisation of S&D treatment provisions (WT/COMTD/W/77/Rev.1/Add.4)

4 Fourteen submissions tabled by July 2002 were as follows: TN/CTD/W/1 from Cuba, Dominican Republic, Honduras, India, Indonesia, Kenya, Pakistan, Sri Lanka, Tanzania and Zimbabwe; TN/CTD/W/2 from Cuba, the Dominican Republic, Egypt, Honduras, India, Indonesia, Kenya, Mauritius, Pakistan, Sri Lanka, Tanzania and Zimbabwe; TN/CTD/W/3/Rev.1 and TN/CTD/W/3/Rev.1/Add.1 from the African Group; TN/CTD/W/4 and TN/CTD/W/4/Add.1 from the Group of LDC members; TN/CTD/W5 and TN/CTD/W/5/Add.1 from Paraguay; TN/CTD/W/6 from India; TN/CTD/W/7 from Thailand; TN/CTD/W/8 from St. Lucia; TN/CTD/W/9 from the United States; TN/CTD/W/10 from Hungary; and TN/CTD/W/11 from Japan

5 Contained in the WTO document TN/CTD/W/3

6 This is a programme that aims to enhance the capacity of LDCs to integrate into the multilateral trading system in order to reduce poverty and benefit from increased market access. Its mandate includes: mainstreaming trade into LDCs' national development plans, such as PRSPs; assisting to coordinate the delivery of trade-related technical assistance to respond to the needs identified by LDCs and developing the capacity of LDCs to trade, including through capacity building and addressing supply side constraints.

7 Contained in WTO documents TN/CTD/W/3/Rev.1 and TN/CTD/W/3/Rev.2

8 Three proposals pertaining to Articles 9.2, 10.1, 10.3 of the Agreement on Sanitary and Phytosanitary Measures contained in WTO document TN/CTD/W/1, which is a joint communication from the delegations of Cuba, Dominican Republic, Egypt, Honduras, India, Indonesia, Kenya, Mauritius, Pakistan, Sri Lanka, Tanzania and Zimbabwe

9 Proposal contained in document TN/CTD/W/2 on Article 12.3 of the Agreement on Technical Barriers to Trade

10 Proposal contained in document TN/CTD/W/2 on Article 12.10 on the Understanding on Rules and Procedure Governing the Settlement of Disputes

11 Proposals contained in WTO document TN/CTD/W/6 on Article 10.2 of the Agreement on Sanitary and Phytosanitary Measures and Paragraph 3.1 of the Decision on Implementation-Related Issues and Concerns; Article 10.4 of the Agreement on Sanitary and Phytosanitary Measures & Paragraph 3.5 of the Decision on Implementation-Related Issues and Concerns; Article 3.5 (j) of the Agreement on Import Licensing; Articles 4.10 and 21.2 on Understanding on Rules and Procedures Governing the Settlement of Disputes

12 Proposal contained in WTO document TN/CTD/W/5 on Differential and more favourable treatment, reciprocity and fuller participation of developing countries (enabling clause): Decision of November 28, 1979

13 Proposal contained in WTO document TN/CTD/W/8 on Article XVIII:C of the GATT 1994

14 Proposal contained in WTO document TN/CTD/W/7 on Article 3.5 (a)(iv) of the WTO Agreement on Import Licensing

15 The proposals are contained in Annex III of document TN/CTD/7

16 Ambassador Carlos Pérez del Castillo of Uruguay

17 The specific proposals that were divided into three categories can be found in WTO document JOB(03)/68

18 WTO document JOB(03)/150/Rev.2

19 The decision relating to S&D treatment reflected in paragraph 12 of the Draft Ministerial Text reads as follows: "We reaffirm that provisions for special and differential treatment are an integral part of WTO Agreements. We recall our decision in Doha to review special and differential treatment provisions with a view to strengthening and making them more precise, effective and operational. We note the progress that has been made towards meeting these objectives and adopt the decisions in Annex C to this document. We instruct the General Council to continue to monitor closely work on the proposals referred to negotiating groups and other WTO bodies, and direct these bodies to report to the General Council no later than [...]. We instruct the Committee on Trade and Development in Special Session to pursue expeditiously, within the parameters of the Doha mandate, the work on remaining agreement-specific proposals and other outstanding issues referred to in TN/CTD/7 and report with recommendations, as appropriate, to the General Council by [...]. The General Council shall submit a report on all these issues to our next Session."

20 Paragraph 35 to 38 of the draft document WT/MIN(05)/W/Rev.2

21 Contained in Annex F of the draft document WT/MIN(05)/W/Rev.2

22 The five proposals were the result of the work of a Dedicated Special Session of the CTD that was initiated in July 2005 to discuss agreement-specific proposals particularly submitted by the LDCs

23 These include one proposal on Article 10.2 of the SPS Agreement; two proposals on Article 10.3 of the SPS Agreement; and three proposals on Article 3.5 of the Agreement on Import Licensing.

24 WT/DS246/R and WT/DS246/AB/R

25 Communication from Cuba, Dominican Republic, Honduras, India, Indonesia, Kenya, Malaysia, Pakistan, Sri Lanka, Tanzania, Uganda and Zimbabwe (WT/GC/W/442), September 19, 2001.

ANNEX I:
Table of Submissions by Some Members on Crosscutting Issues

Issue	Proponent & Document Symbol
Principles & objectives	African Group – TN/CTD/W/3/Rev.1 and TN/CTD/W/3/Rev.2 African Group – TN/CTD/W/3/Rev.1/Add.1 LDCs – TN/CTD/W/4 US – TN/CTD/W/9 Japan – TN/CTD/W/11
Single-tiered, two-tiered or multi-tiered structure of rights and obligations?	African Group – TN/CTD/W/3/Rev.1 and TN/CTD/W/3/Rev.2 LDCs - TN/CTD/W/4
Coherence	African Group – TN/CTD/W/3/Rev.1 and TN/CTD/W/3/Rev.2 LDCs – TN/CTD/W/4
Bench marks	LDCs – TN/CTD/W/4
Technical assistance and capacity building	African Group – TN/CTD/W/3/Rev.1 and TN/CTD/W/3/Rev.2 United States - TN/CTD/W/9
Transition periods	African Group – TN/CTD/W/3/Rev.1 and TN/CTD/W/3/Rev.2 US - TN/CTD/W/9
Utilisation	US - TN/CTD/W/9 Japan– TN/CTD/W/11
Trade preferences and related issues, including the enabling clause	Paraguay – TN/CTD/W/5, TN/CTD/W/5/Add.1 and TN/CTD/W/5/Add.2 African Group – TN/CTD/W/3/Rev.1 and TN/CTD/W/3/Rev.2 LDCs – TN/CTD/W/4/Add.1 Hungary – TN/CTD/W/10
Universal or differentiated treatment?	African Group – TN/CTD/W/3/Rev.1 and TN/CTD/W/3/Rev.2
Issues related to graduation	US – TN/CTD/W/9

ANNEX II:
Table of Submissions by Some Members on Specific Agreements and Decisions

Number of Proposals	Proponent	Article /Paragraph (Document Reference)
General Agreement on Tariffs and Trade 1994 (GATT 1994)		
6	African Group	Whole Agreement (TN/CTD/W/3/Rev.1 and TN/CTD/W/3/Rev.2) Article XVIII:A (TN/CTD/W/3/Rev.1 and TN/CTD/W/3/Rev.2) Article XVIII:B (TN/CTD/W/3/Rev.1 and TN/CTD/W/3/Rev.2) Article XXXVI (TN/CTD/W/3/Rev.1 and TN/CTD/W/3/Rev.2) Article XXXVII (TN/CTD/W/3/Rev.1 and TN/CTD/W/3/Rev.2) Article XXXVIII (TN/CTD/W/3/Rev.1 and TN/CTD/W/3/Rev.2)
1	St. Lucia	Article XVIII:C (TN/CTD/W/8)
1	LDCs	Article XVIII:C (TN/CTD/W/4/Add.1)
Understanding on the Interpretation of Article II:1(B) of the GATT 1994		
1	African Group	Proposal (TN/CTD/W/3/Rev.1 and TN/CTD/W/3/Rev.2)
Understanding on the Interpretation of Article XVII of the GATT 1994		
1	African Group	Proposal (TN/CTD/W/3/Rev.1 and TN/CTD/W/3/Rev.2)
Understanding on Balance-of-Payments Provisions of the GATT 1994		
1	LDCs	Paragraph 8 (TN/CTD/W/4/Add.1)
1	African Group	Proposal TN/CTD/W/3/Rev.1 and TN/CTD/W/3/Rev.2
Understanding on the Interpretation of Article XXIV of the GATT 1994		
1	African Group	Proposal TN/CTD/W/3/Rev.1 and TN/CTD/W/3/Rev.2
1	LDCs	Proposal TN/CTD/W/4/Add.1
Understanding in Respect of Waivers of Obligations Under the GATT 1994		
1	African Group	Proposal TN/CTD/W/3/Rev.1 and TN/CTD/W/3/Rev.2
1	LDCs	Proposal TN/CTD/W/4/Add.1
Understanding on the Interpretation of Article XXVIII of the GATT 1994		
1	African Group	Paragraph 1 (TN/CTD/W/3/Rev.1 and TN/CTD/W/3/Rev.2)
Agreement on Agriculture		
4	African Group	Article 6.2 (TN/CTD/W/3/Rev.1 and TN/CTD/W/3/Rev.2) Article 14 (TN/CTD/W/3/Rev.1 and TN/CTD/W/3/Rev.2) Article 15.1 (TN/CTD/W/3/Rev.1 and TN/CTD/W/3/Rev.2) Article 15.2 TN/CTD/W/3/Rev.1 and TN/CTD/W/3/Rev.2
1	LDCs	Article 15.2 (TN/CTD/W/4)
Agreement on Sanitary and Phyto-Sanitary Measures (SPS)		
2	LMG	Article 9.2 (TN/CTD/W/2); Article 10.1 (TN/CTD/W/2)

Contd...

Number of Proposals	Proponent	Article /Paragraph (Document Reference)
4	African Group	Article 9.2 (TN/CTD/W/3/Rev.1 and TN/CTD/W/3/Rev.2) Article 10.1 (TN/CTD/W/3/Rev.1 and TN/CTD/W/3/Rev.2) Article 10.3 (TN/CTD/W/2, TN/CTD/W/3/Rev.1 and TN/CTD/W/3/Rev.2) Article 10.4 (TN/CTD/W/3/Rev.1 and TN/CTD/W/3/Rev.2)
2	India	Article 10.2 and Paragraph 3.1 of the Decision on Implementation-Related Issues and Concerns (TN/CTD/W/6) Article 10.4 and Paragraph 3.5 of the Decision on Implementation-Related Issues and Concerns (TN/CTD/W/6)
Agreement on Textiles and Clothing		
1	LDCs	Paragraph 2 of Article 1 and Paragraph 18 of Article 2 (TN/CTD/W/4/Add.1)
1	African Group	Articles 2.18 and 6.6 (TN/CTD/W/3/Rev.1 and TN/CTD/W/3/Rev.2)
Agreement on Technical Barriers to Trade (TBT)		
1	African Group	Articles 11 and 12 (TN/CTD/W/3/Rev.1 and TN/CTD/W/3/Rev.2)
1	LMG	Article 12.3 (TN/CTD/W/2)
Agreement on Trade-Related Investment Measures (TRIMs)		
1	LDCs	Whole Agreement (TN/CTD/W/4)
3	African Group	Article 3 (TN/CTD/W/3/Rev.1 and TN/CTD/W/3/Rev.2) Article 4 (TN/CTD/W/3/Rev.1 and TN/CTD/W/3/Rev.2) Article 5.3 (TN/CTD/W/3/Rev.1 and TN/CTD/W/3/Rev.2)
Agreement on Implementation of Article VI of the GATT 1994 (Anti-Dumping)		
1	African Group	Article 15 (TN/CTD/W/3/Rev.1 and TN/CTD/W/3/Rev.2)
Agreement on the Implementation of Article VII of GATT 1994 (Customs Valuation)		
2	African Group	Article 20.1-2 (TN/CTD/W/3/Rev.1 and TN/CTD/W/3/Rev.2) Article 20.3 (TN/CTD/W/3/Rev.1 and TN/CTD/W/3/Rev.2)
Agreement on Preshipment Inspection (PSI)		
1	African Group	Article 3.3 (TN/CTD/W/3/Rev.1 and TN/CTD/W/3/Rev.2)
Agreement on Rules of Origin		
1	African Group	Proposal (TN/CTD/W/3/Rev.1 and TN/CTD/W/3/Rev.2)
Agreement on Import Licencing		
2	African Group	Article 1.2 (TN/CTD/W/3/Rev.1 and TN/CTD/W/3/Rev.2) Article 3.5 (TN/CTD/W/3/Rev.1 and TN/CTD/W/3/Rev.2)
1	Thailand	Article 3.5 (a)(iv) (TN/CTD/W/7)
1	India	Article 3.5 (j) (TN/CTD/W/6)

Contd...

Number of Proposals	Proponent	Article /Paragraph (Document Reference)
Agreement on Subsidies and Countervailing Measures		
1	LDCs	Paragraph 1 of Article 2 1 and Paragraph 4 of Article III of GATT 1994 (and paragraphs 1 (b) and 27.3 of the Subsidies Agreement) (TN/CTD/W/4)
1	Some of the LMG members	Article 27.1 (TN/CTD/W/1)
5	African Group	Article 27.1 (TN/CTD/W/3/Rev.1 and TN/CTD/W/3/Rev.2) Article 27.4 (TN/CTD/W/3/Rev.1 and TN/CTD/W/3/Rev.2) Article 27.8 (TN/CTD/W/3/Rev.1 and TN/CTD/W/3/Rev.2) Article 27.9 (TN/CTD/W/3/Rev.1 and TN/CTD/W/3/Rev.2) Article 27.13 (TN/CTD/W/3/Rev.1 and TN/CTD/W/3/Rev.2) Article 27.15 (TN/CTD/W/3/Rev.1 and TN/CTD/W/3/Rev.2)
Agreement on Safeguards		
1	African Group	Article 9.1-2 (TN/CTD/W/3/Rev.1 and TN/CTD/W/3/Rev.2)
General Agreement on Trade in Services (GATS)		
3	African Group	Article IV (TN/CTD/W/3/Rev.1 and TN/CTD/W/3/Rev.2) Article V:3 (TN/CTD/W/3/Rev.1 and TN/CTD/W/3/Rev.2) Article XXV (TN/CTD/W/3/Rev.1 and TN/CTD/W/3/Rev.2)
4	LDCs	Article IV (TN/CTD/W/4/Add.1) Article IV:1 (TN/CTD/W/4/Add.1) Article IV:2 (TN/CTD/W/4/Add.1) ; Article IV:3 (TN/CTD/W/4/Add.1)
Annex on Telecommunications		
1	LDCs	Paragraph 6 (TN/CTD/W/4/Add.1)
Agreement on Trade-Related Aspects of Intellectual Property Rights (TRIPs)		
2	African Group	Articles 65, 66.1, 70.8 and 70.9 (TN/CTD/W/3/Rev.1 and TN/CTD/W/3/Rev.2); Articles 7, 8 and 66.2 (TN/CTD/W/3/Rev.1 and TN/CTD/W/3/Rev.2)
2	LDCs	Article 66.1 (TN/CTD/W/4/Add.1) Article 67 (TN/CTD/W/4/Add.1)
Under-Standing on Rules and Procedures Governing the Settlement of Disputes (DSU)		
2	India	Article 4.10 (TN/CTD/W/6) ; Article 21.2 (TN/CTD/W/6)
6	African Group	Article 4.10 (TN/CTD/W/3/Rev.1 and TN/CTD/W/3/Rev.2) Article 8.10 (TN/CTD/W/3/Rev.1 and TN/CTD/W/3/Rev.2) Article 12.10 (TN/CTD/W/3/Rev.1 and TN/CTD/W/3/Rev.2) Article 12.11 (TN/CTD/W/3/Rev.1 and TN/CTD/W/3/Rev.2) Articles 21.2, 21.7 & 21.8 (TN/CTD/W/3/Rev.1 and TN/CTD/W/3/Rev.2); Article 24.1 (TN/CTD/W/3/Rev.1 and TN/CTD/W/3/Rev.2)
1	LMG	Article 12.10 (TN/CTD/W/2)

Contd...

Number of Proposals	Proponent	Article /Paragraph (Document Reference)
Decision on Measures in Favour of Least-Developed Country Members		
1	African Group	Paragraph 1 (TN/CTD/W/3/Rev.1 and TN/CTD/W/3/Rev.2) and Paragraph 2 (TN/CTD/W/3/Rev.1 and TN/CTD/W/3/Rev.2)
1	LDCs	Paragraph 2 (ii) (TN/CTD/W/4)
Decision on Measures Concerning the Possible Negative Effects of the Reform Programme on Least-Developed and Net Food-Importing Developing Country Members		
1	African Group	Proposal (TN/CTD/W/3/Rev.1 and TN/CTD/W/3/Rev.2)
Differential and More Favourable Treatment, Reciprocity and Fuller Participation of Developing Country Members (Enabling Clause): Decision of November 28, 1979		
2	LDCs	Paragraph 1 and 2(d) (TN/CTD/W/4/Add.1); Paragraph 3 (d) (TN/CTD/W/4/Add.1); Whole Decision (TN/CTD/W/4/Add.1)
1	African Group	Proposal (TN/CTD/W/3/Rev.1 and TN/CTD/W/3/Rev.2)
2	Paraguay	Whole Decision (TN/CTD/W/5, TN/CTD/W/5/Add.1 and TN/CTD/W/5/Add.2)

9 Preference Erosion – Negotiating with Steadfast Pragmatism

Shree B. C. Servansing
Ambassador of Mauritius to the UN and other International Organisations including WTO

Introduction

Trade preferences as instruments to provide enhanced market access opportunities for developing countries have existed for a long time in the global trading system. Many of the great trading countries of today, like Australia, Canada and New Zealand, have at one time benefitted from preferential schemes that helped their economic development to a large extent. Some of these preferential arrangements, like the Commonwealth System of Preferences, even pre-date the system established under the GATT. However, it was only in 1971 that in GATT, following the creation of the GSP by UNCTAD in 1969, the issue of non-reciprocal preferences was institutionalised formally as it was acknowledged that the global trading system was not a level playing field for all countries. In order to create greater universal ownership and legitimacy for GATT, it was deemed necessary to reinforce its S&D treatment provisions to assist poorer developing countries that could not operate on the MFN principle.

Hence the "enabling clause"[1] was endorsed in 1979 to legally allow for the creation of GSP schemes by developed countries to provide preferential market access for goods from developing countries in their markets on a non-reciprocal basis. Many such unilateral schemes are operated today by developed countries and they provide different levels of market access. The nature and coverage of preferential schemes differ widely in terms of their product coverage, depth of tariff preferences, which can range from a preferential tariff to duty free concessions, preferential tariff rate quotas (TRQs) and preferential rules of origin.

However, over the years, many limitations have been introduced to curtail access enjoyed by developing countries through a system of graduation of countries and of sectors within countries and other eligibility criteria. The LDCs for example benefit from the most generous of such schemes in the EU through the "Everything but Arms" (EBA) initiative. The unilateral nature of these schemes and their best-endeavour nature, wide variations, subjective criteria of eligibility for participation and their frequent modifications over time have led critics to question their real value. Trade cannot prosper if there is no predictability, security and sustainability. Nonetheless, one cannot deny the value of trade preferences for the development and growth of SVEs that are not rich natural resource-endowed and that very often are dependent on one or two commodities.

The GSP schemes falling under the enabling clause have not been controversial in the WTO because they do not pose a problem among developing countries. They operate on the principle of MFN for developing countries or are dispensed on the basis of universally agreed objective criteria that do not allow for undue discrimination among developing countries.[2] Moreover developed countries can unilaterally modify the schemes to suit their domestic and foreign policy interests. However, other types of non-reciprocal trade preferential schemes became very problematic in the GATT/WTO system as they were exclusive to only a group of developing countries which had to obtain a waiver from Article I of GATT to gain legal cover. In this category, one could find among others preferential trading arrangements like the Cotonou Agreement between the EU and the ACP group of countries or the AGOA between the US and sub-Saharan African countries.

In spite of the enabling clause, the issue of preferences was almost taboo in the WTO for a long time. The deep scars left by one of the longest and most bitter trade conflicts between the EU/ACP and a group of Latin American countries over banana trade was perhaps instrumental to this state of affairs. But, the reality is perhaps politically and substantively deeper than this as we shall see below. Moreover, with the launching of the DDA in 2001, it is not only the systemic implications of trade preferences *per se* that pose the problem, but also how to address the issue of preference erosion in a round where trade liberalisation is the prime objective.

This chapter will evaluate how the issues of trade preferences and preference erosion were introduced and treated over the years in the DDA, the debate among members over systemic issues relating to preferences, its value as a tool for development and the strategies adopted by the ACP, the African Group and the LDCs to seek a solution to this problem.

The Uneasy Status of Trade Preferences in the WTO

The WTO pursues trade liberalisation as its main objective and is founded on the principle of MFN. The discomfort about trade preferences in the system is understandable as the latter goes against the GATT/WTO's founding principle. But, it is not the systemic implications of discriminatory treatment in favour of a sub-set of developing countries that creates the biggest concern. It is the view that some developed countries to prevent preference erosion should stall MFN trade liberalisation on preferential tariff lines to benefit preference-beneficiary developing countries and hence deny market access to non-preference beneficiaries that poses the problem. These non-preference receiving countries argue that having been victims of discrimination before, they will have to pay a double price if denied market access again through the blocking of MFN liberalisation. Many such countries, which are developing countries as well, contend that the reason for their participation in the DDA Round is to obtain greater access in developed country markets.

Opponents of trade preferences in the WTO have always emphasised the negative costs of trade preferences to the economy and questioned its validity as a tool for development. They have pointed to their welfare-reducing effects as they can potentially create trade diversion; allocate scarce resources to inefficient production structures, which thrive on rents; and create dependence on preferences, hence preventing diversification. Preferences also remove the incentive for domestic reform arising from growing multilateral and bilateral trade liberalisation. The benefits of preferences are sometimes exaggerated because the rents are captured by or at least shared with the importers and exporters and face increased transactional costs due to additional administrative burdens and complex rules of origin. Most important, it is believed that preferences provide a safety net for the beneficiaries and act as a disincentive to multilateral trade liberalisation.[3]

Moreover, many trade economists have stated that the purported aim of granting trade preferences is to spur export-driven economic development. However, there is little empirical evidence of meaningful preference-led economic development among developing countries.[4] In contrast the success stories of many developing countries in Asia and Latin America that have relied on trade liberalisation and anchored their trade policies on a model of global competitiveness are portrayed against the poor performance of preference beneficiaries.

It is true that benefitting from trade preferences does not correlate to consistent and sustained success in beneficiary countries. The performance has been very mixed with a few good performers. But, the real question is whether we can explain this negative correlation between preferences and poor development records by a causal relationship that pins down preferences as the culprit. The issue is in fact more complex and needs greater analytical study by researchers. The views of economists related to welfare loss for the trading system and the community may make academic sense, but it is useless for policy makers confronted with the constraints of reality on a daily basis. Producers in small island states, like Solomon Islands in the Pacific, would probably not be competitive in anything or the Windward Islands, like St Lucia, need the export earnings from preferential banana sales to be able to diversify into anything else. Preferences in such situations are a necessity to survive or at least to transition to more competitive trade. There is, therefore, a political reality to preferential trading schemes in the global economy, and it would be a mistake for the WTO to deny this if we do not want the system to polarise into winners and losers.

We have to ask ourselves whether the poor performance is the consequence of factors intrinsic to the system of preferences, attributable to shortcomings in the design of particular schemes, or caused by extraneous factors. It is crucially important to distinguish between the concept of trade preferences and the nature of preference schemes. The latter may have defects that prevent the proper harnessing of trade preferences, like constraints related to RoO, product exclusions, shallow preferences, etc. Moreover, many empirical studies have shown how countries have been using preferential schemes to achieve some degree of economic development and the relevant question is what would have been the fate of these countries in the absence of such preferential schemes.[5]

Criticisms relating to the conflictual interface between preference schemes and preference erosion on the one hand and the multilateral trading system and the DDA negotiations on the other are difficult to disentangle. While the WTO's objective is to promote greater trade opening through liberalisation of tariffs and removal of trade distortions, it is crucial to remind ourselves that the WTO operates in the real world constrained by the political decisions of member states. As such, we are far from the ideal situation of a non-trade-distorted world. Moreover, can the WTO disregard the needs of a large number of small developing countries and yet claim universal legitimacy? Or can a group of countries wilfully negotiate to be losers in a round? The comments of Kathy-Ann Brown, representative of St Lucia to the WTO clearly reflect this concern:

> The first fundamental divergence noted is one of ideology and philosophy in terms of the economic advice presented. The model advocated is that of total liberalisation which does not lend itself to any societal structure, national or global, unless there are sufficient safeguards in place for ensuring the survival of the most vulnerable sector of the community – a sector which will be forced to pay the highest price in terms of its survival. It may be timely to recall the notion that only the strong survive and to question whether this is the appropriate model for fashioning our multilateral trading system.[6]

Kathy-Ann Brown goes further, arguing that there is need for greater recognition that some developing countries are less disadvantaged than others and she does not understand "why so self-evident a reality continues to be denied, quite apart from the situation of LDCs in the WTO rules-based system."

The practical issue is one of negotiations. It behoves the developing countries concerned with the issue of trade preferences to answer the above questions and factor their concerns in the DDA negotiations to secure an outcome that does not marginalise them. The strategies adopted and the success achieved is analysed below. It should be noted that while the issue of trade preferences concerns a wide spectrum of developing countries, it was mostly the ACP within the alliance of the G-90 (ACP, African Group and LDCs) that provided the leadership on this issue. At the risk of oversimplifying, schematically the proponents focused on three issues in the DDA negotiations:

(a) how to multilateralise and deepen the regime of preferences for greater security and benefit;

(b) how to create a legal basis within the WTO rules-based system to enable continued and sustainable preferences to some small developing countries through schemes that are not covered by the GSP, like the ACP-EU Cotonou Agreement, AGOA, etc; and

(c) how to address the important issue of preference erosion so as to provide comfort to G-90 members standing to lose access in their traditional markets through MFN liberalisation.

Good Intentions, Bad Strategies

The defence of preferential trading arrangements in favour of developing countries took a more combative form in the agriculture track of the negotiations in the early phase. While in NAMA there was mostly a general advocacy for preferences and their importance for the development of vulnerable countries, in agriculture there was a more elaborate and intellectually cogent attempt to make a case for preferences. In fact, it started even before the launch of the DDA in the in-built negotiations on agriculture of the Uruguay Round[7] - AIE process - in 1999 and in the CoA-SS in 2000.

It should be recalled that on the basis of Article 20 of the AoA, there was already an in-built agenda to continue the reform process in agriculture. Negotiations to comply with Article 20 started in 2000 before being merged in the single undertaking of the DDA mandate on the basis of Paragraph 13 of the Doha Declaration.[8] These mandates did not define any specific reference to preferences or preference erosion. Thus, the concerns of proponents of preferences in the earlier stages of the negotiations were how to conceptually anchor the issue of preferences in the process and eventually frame the agenda for negotiations on the issue.

This proved to be a very difficult enterprise primarily because the nature of the tariff-cutting modality to be used in agriculture was not prescribed in the mandate. In NAMA, the level of ambition was prescribed through a harmonising approach that will reduce or eliminate tariff peaks, high tariffs and tariff escalation. In agriculture, the type of tariff cutting modality and the level of ambition became the issues that engaged negotiators for years. Obviously, in this context, the proponents could not gauge the extent of preference erosion and could not discuss specific proposals to address the issue. The only option for them was to engage in the three pillars of the negotiations, namely market access, domestic support and export competition in a defensive manner to emphasise the interface of the three pillars with preference erosion and the need to sustain preferential market access for the development of their economies.

As mentioned above, negotiating the type of tariff-cutting formula and subsequently the numerical parameters of the agreed formula became the central issue in the agriculture negotiations. It pitched the offensive interests of exporters against the defensive interests of importers. Exporters tabled tariff-reducing formulas with a high ambition while the importers wanted a moderate formula, which protects their sensitive agricultural sectors. A number of proposals on tariff-cutting modalities in agriculture were tabled by members ranging from a most ambitious Swiss formula with a coefficient of 25 to the moderate Uruguay Round modality of an average tariff cut with minimum line-by-line cuts.[9]

As agricultural tariffs were generally very high in developed countries, like Canada, the EU, Japan, Norway, Switzerland, and even the US, as opposed to developing countries, the exporters' demands for rebalancing global agricultural markets and removing trade distortions quickly became a development issue. However, in reality it was not just a north/south divide in the negotiations. This was reinforced by developing country think-tanks, like the South Centre and the Third World Network, which emphasised only the perspectives of big exporting developing countries like Argentina, Brazil, and the like and ignored the claims of a group of smaller ACP countries on preference erosion.

Thus, proponents of preferences became a 'nuisance' in that neat projection of a development round symbolised by an ambitious, offensive and anti-developed country approach in agriculture against defensive and protectionist developed countries. While not totally devoid of truth, this was an oversimplification of the development dimension of the round.

The aim of proponents of preferences was to maintain or if possible deepen their preferential access and prevent erosion. In doing so, the proponents adopted mostly a defensive approach in the market access pillar of the negotiations and rallied around the platform of NTCs which became the conceptual framework through which a group of defensive countries led by the EU constructed a defence against aggressive market access opening in agriculture. In the first phase of the built-in negotiations in agriculture, which was based on Article 20 of the AoA, a large number of notes and proposals on NTCs were tabled by the members.[10] Proponents of NTCs argued that agriculture must not be conceived from a purely mercantilist perspective in the WTO negotiations, as it plays a multifunctional role in society and has positive externalities that are not accounted for in normal trade exchanges. They emphasise the food security, rural development and environmental preservation roles of agriculture, which are common concerns for both developed and developing countries. As such, they argue that there is a wide variety of agricultural systems and situations worldwide, and often the positive externalities of agriculture are as important as the mere production of food and fibre. This is why the conduct of agricultural activity cannot be based on rules that govern trade in the industrial sector. In other words, in order to allow states to compensate the agricultural sector for its non-trade services to the community, they must be allowed to protect their agriculture to a certain extent and modulate agricultural trade liberalisation. It is not the purpose of this chapter to discuss the merits of this approach but it was this framework that would shape the position of its proponents on the three pillars of the agriculture negotiations.

Thus, the proponents of NTCs tabled their proposals which were aimed at allowing for a gradual process of agriculture reform.[11] Essentially in market access, they were in favour of a linear formula of the Uruguay type that would not cut tariffs deeply. In domestic support, while arguing for the continuation of the Blue and Green Boxes without limitations, they were proposing low levels of reduction in the Amber Box and in the export subsidies pillar. Some preference beneficiaries argued for the exemption of sensitive preferential products from reduction commitments in the domestic support and export subsidies pillars.[12]

At varying levels, proponents of preferences identified with the NTCs framework as it objectively leads to an outcome that maintains their market access and prevents preference erosion. The extreme case of complete identification of a preference proponent with NTCs was Mauritius.[13] In some way, Mauritius took over the mantle of defence of preferences on behalf of the ACP. Eventually Mauritius did become the ACP focal point in agriculture in the initial phase of the negotiations and up to the July 2004 Framework Agreement. Mauritius put forward the case of SIDS as a variant of the diversity of agricultural systems and situations worldwide. SIDS are small and vulnerable entities with many structural and intrinsic constraints relating to their physical characteristics, namely isolation, smallness, proneness to natural catastrophes and economic constraints, like lack of competitiveness and economies of scale. In agriculture, they were mostly low potential, single commodity dependent exporters and NFIDCs. Historically, their agricultural trade was dependent on preferential trading arrangements, like the Sugar Protocol, the Banana Protocol, the Lome /Cotonou Agreements, EBA and the AGOA.

A deep liberalisation of agricultural markets will therefore erode their competitive advantage in their traditional markets. Maintaining such preferential access was, therefore, vital for their survival as preferential trade ensured much needed export earnings, which in turn enabled access to food. Preferential access was therefore the key to the SIDS' food security in view of the fact that SIDS were food deficit countries, a result of their topographic and agro-climatic constraints and inability to produce their food requirements and preferences.[14]

Thus, for Mauritius, NTCs became the general framework to emphasise the specificity of the agricultural systems of SIDS as opposed to huge competitive high potential exporting countries, which were naturally better endowed. The concept of SIDS became the instrument through which these states could call for greater flexibility or more advantageous treatment in the negotiations. The limitation conveyed by the wording, SIDS, in terms of their geographical coverage very soon led the Caribbean countries and some African countries which supported the approach to talk in terms of small and vulnerable countries and hence the replacement of SIDS by SVEs.[15] However, while Mauritius continued to present a case in defence of preferences, using the specificity of SIDS as a vehicle to justify lower ambition in the three pillars of market access, domestic support and export competition, other SIDS mostly restricted the scope of their demands within the market access pillar only for the defence of preferences. Some were even very critical of developed country policies on the domestic and export competition pillars demanding deeper disciplines.[16]

The proponent of preferences also made SIDS the vehicle through which to multilateralise and deepen the regime of preferences at par with LDCs.[17] Thus, in the phase of preparing for modalities in 2002, the representative of St Lucia, in stressing the importance of trade preferences for the SIDS, proposed: [18]

- preferences to these countries should be accepted as legitimate instruments to assist their development;

- all members, developed and developing, should be able to offer non-reciprocal preferences to LDCs as SIDS;

- in areas where SIDS, LDCs and small developing countries benefited from preferences, tariff reductions should be gradual, give adequate time for adjustment and compensation should be provided to these countries for any erosion of preferences; and

- where a tariff quota existed for a product that was also subject to preferences for SIDS and LDCs, a minimum share of the tariff quotas should be reserved for these countries.

In his summary report of the 15th meeting of the CoA-SS of December 16, 2002, the Chairman summed up the demands of the proponents in a succinct manner:[19]

> Regarding preferences, the co-sponsors indicated that given their inherent lack of competitiveness and limited supply capacity, they were not realistically in a position to gain from new trading possibilities from the global improvement in market access conditions and further, their ability to continue agricultural exports was in many instances dependent on non-reciprocal market access provided by developed countries. They proposed "grandfathering" of existing non-reciprocal preferential trading arrangements between developed and developing countries and the extension to SIDS agricultural exports of the facility currently available to LDCs that enabled special WTO compatible market access arrangements with developed countries on terms that did not require extension of reciprocal preferences.

The proactive stance of the proponents did not fall on deaf ears. The "First Draft Modalities for Further Commitments" did make provision for a specific modality to address the issue at paragraph 14 as follows:

> In implementing their tariff reduction commitments, participants undertake to maintain, to the extent possible, the nominal margins and other terms and conditions of tariff preferences they accord to their developing trading partners. As an exception to the modality under paragraph 7 above, tariff reductions affecting long-standing preferences in respect of products which are of vital export importance for developing country beneficiaries of such schemes may be implemented in equal annual instalments over a period of [eight] instead of [five] years by the preference-granting participants concerned. The products concerned shall account for at least [25] percent of the total merchandise exports of any beneficiary concerned on average of the most recent three years for which data are available. Interested beneficiaries shall notify the CoA-SS accordingly and submit the relevant statistics. In addition, any in-quota duties for these products shall be eliminated.[20]

However, this relative success of the proponents was not without costs. It spurred a bitter division among a subset of developing countries, which argued that extension or preservation of such preferences are discriminatory as is the attempt to create a new category of countries of SIDS/SVEs. It was mostly the banana exporting countries of Latin America that put forward the strongest objection. Ecuador went to the extent of requesting the deletion of Paragraph 14 from the draft modalities text. Costa Rica argued that non-reciprocal preferences adversely discriminate against its exports and any legal cover through a process of multilateral binding would foreclose the scope of fullest liberalisation of tropical products, which is a requirement of the WTO mandate. The basis was thus laid for an extension of the long-lasting banana conflict to the preferences and tropical products groups of countries, more precisely the Latin American Tropical Products Group (TPG) against the ACP group of countries.

On the broader front, the preference issue did generate a sense of discomfort among developing countries. This was not for lack of sympathy for the plight of such SVEs, but because of the implicit stand of many preference proponents against trade liberalisation to preserve preference schemes. This created a perception that this group of developing countries was in a tacit manner morally cushioning the stand of developed countries in the agricultural negotiations. The past colonial links between the ACP countries and the EU reinforced the perception of ACP tutelage by the EU. The sympathy of many ACP countries towards NTCs and the extreme position of Mauritius further compounded this perception of lack of solidarity with developing countries on the part of preferences proponents. Evidently developed countries seized on the opportunity and openly declared their support for the cause of preference proponents to give the impression that they were championing the cause of development as well, mainly of small developing countries. Their negotiating proposals clearly illustrated this posture. The EU in its negotiating proposal of December 2000 stated:[21]

> The EC propose, in addition to multilateral liberalisation and in order to increase market access to products, originating in developing countries, that developed countries and the wealthiest developing countries provide significant trade preferences to developing countries, and in particular the least developed ones. The EC propose that an examination is undertaken on ways to ensure that these trade preferences are rendered stable and predictable, in order to create the appropriate conditions for further investment in, and developing of, the agricultural and agri-food sectors in developing countries.

Preferences were clearly in the first phase of the negotiations a very divisive issue among developing countries. The division arose not only because of divergent and competing trade interests, but also due to a lack of coherence and strategic unity among developing countries in general. In fact, the G-90, G20 or G-33 alliances were not yet formed and developing countries were left without real leadership either to steer an agreed agenda or manage differences. This vacuum led to questionable strategies and even to instrumentalisation of some developing countries by some developed countries at times. While NTCs and the multifunctional role of agriculture was and is a valid policy concept, its abuse to justify protectionism in agriculture cannot be overlooked.

Non-Agricultural Market Access

In the NAMA track of the negotiations, the Doha mandate as framed in 2001 was not explicit on the issue. Subsequent treatment of this issue in the Girard text was limited to non-trade solutions through technical assistance and capacity building in the process of adjustment to MFN liberalisation.[22] The proponents of preference erosion were also in the early phases of the negotiations more in a protest mode in their advocacy rather than developing a clear negotiating strategy and tabling concrete proposals. For example, Mauritius in July 2003 in a communication on market access for non-agricultural products stated:

> It is, therefore, imperative that appropriate modalities be developed to address this issue with a view to achieving balanced outcomes in these negotiations.

While it is believed that average tariff reduction could be an appropriate means to address the question of preference erosion, our delegation remains nonetheless open to the possibility of considering other modalities.[23]

Similar communications, which emphasised either the creation of an adjustment fund, staging of liberalisation or exemption of preferential tariff lines from any liberalisation, were being canvassed.[24] It should also be recalled that the dynamics of the negotiations on preferences in NAMA was quite different from that in agriculture. In agriculture the interests of the proponents and some developed countries coincided so that they could rely on some powerful allies. Likewise, not all developing countries (e.g. India) had offensive interests in agriculture and were careful not to push ambition in the market access pillar too far. On the other hand, in NAMA, the proponents of preferences were quite isolated. The preference-givers were the biggest demanders in NAMA liberalisation and wanted a high level of ambition. Proponents of preference erosion were clearly a nuisance on their way. Other major developing countries wanted lower liberalisation in their own markets through S&D but greater market access in developed countries, which contradicted the interests of preference proponents as such liberalisation would erode their competitive edge. Moreover, they had to face stiff opposition from another subset of developing countries who felt discriminated against, and they feared that any further trade solution could affect their interests mainly in textiles and clothing, fish and fish products and gems and jewellery.

Post 2005 - Change in Strategy

Unfortunately the failure of the Cancun meeting did not allow for either the development of modalities on preferences or any in-depth discussion of the issue. The relevant documents in agriculture remain the revised draft Modalities for Further Commitments by Chairman Stuart Harbinson. In NAMA there was no appropriate modality in the Girard/Derbez text on preferences. However, the proponents of preferences came out of the Cancun meeting politically much stronger, as they were able there to build a strong coalition of the most vulnerable countries through the G-90 alliance, which grouped the ACP, AU and the LDC groupings. The G-90 became a major actor not because of its weight in global trade, but because of its numbers and its moral high ground as representing the poorest of the world.

The G-90 was able to force the issue of preferences on the agenda of both agriculture and NAMA negotiations in the July Framework Agreement in 2004. In NAMA, preferences were added to the list of areas where "additional negotiations are required to reach agreement on the specifics of some of these elements."[25] This mandate was further elaborated in the Hong Kong Ministerial meeting where Ministers "instruct(ed) the Negotiating Group to intensify work on the assessment of the scope of the problem with a view to finding possible solutions."[26] In agriculture, Annex A of the July Framework Agreement gave a more positive orientation for the treatment of preference erosion in Paragraph 44, which states:[27]

The importance of long-standing preferences is fully recognised. The issue of preference erosion will be addressed. For the further consideration in this regard, paragraph 16 and other relevant provisions of TN/AG/W/1/Rev.1 will be used as a reference.

In the view of the G-90, both these mandates on NAMA and agriculture meant that henceforth a trade solution to preferences is possible and it is only a question of negotiating its parameters.

However, in Hong Kong a few important changes occurred in the political dynamics of the DDA negotiations from a developing country perspective. The developing countries started to get their act together and in the margins of the Hong Kong Ministerial Conference, the developing country groupings formed a common alliance loosely dubbed the G-110.[28] That new development brought some closer collaboration among developing countries and a tacit understanding to mutually support one another where possible or at least not to overtly attack each other's positions where there may be divergences. For the preference proponents, that was an important development as both the G-20 and NAMA-11 began to support a trade solution for preference erosion. The G-20 insisted that any such solution must also take into account the interests of tropical products proponents in agriculture. Conversely, it meant that after the Hong Kong meeting, the ACP including Mauritius distanced itself from the NTCs platform and concentrated more on their ACP-specific issues. The substance of their dialogue with the EU changed to an issue-based one concentrating on ACP concerns of which preference erosion was primary. Mauritius was no longer an active member of the G-10, a very defensive coalition in agriculture. The preference issue was no longer being moved as a SIDS/SVE demand, but under the G-90 banner with the ACP as its main coordinator. The SIDS concept was abandoned in favour of the broader SVE one and to garner consensus within that group, the issue of preferences was suspended from its agenda.[29]

The substance of the negotiations in agriculture also changed from general approaches to the negotiation of modalities specifically after Hong Kong. In the market access pillar, the priority was more now on fixing the numerical parameters of a tiered approach as the tariff-cutting modality. The simple Uruguay approach was no longer an option. The focus of the defensive developed countries switched from the formula *per se* to the flexibilities, more particularly the sensitive products to shelter their sensitive lines. Such an approach excluded the taking into account of most preference products and hence preference proponents realised that a blind support of developed countries was not going to serve their interests. At the same time it also became clear to them that if avoidance of preference erosion could not be the function of a low tariff-cutting formula as they had hoped, it could only be achieved through a derogation from the formula. This will demand the negotiation of a specific modality for preferences as opposed to supporting a low tariff-cutting modality, which was the option earlier. In this regard, the support of those who will be the victims of this derogation becomes politically important and they are mainly developing countries. Hence the need for the ACP to change its approach in the modalities phase of the negotiations after 2005.

The NAMA Preference Erosion Negotiations

In the context of these new developments, the ACP after a long process of internal reflection in 2005/2006 developed a strategy and submitted its proposals to address the issue of preferences. The underlying rationale of the strategy was the same in both NAMA and agriculture but the negotiating routes taken for each were different. It was a difficult decision for the ACP because it should be remembered that the ACP was a group that was historically conceived on the basis of non-reciprocal preferential trading agreements since the first Lome Convention with the EU in 1975. The ACP came to the conclusion that preferences were not a sustainable strategy on which to build its trade policy and anchor its long-term development in view of inevitable preference erosion through multilateral trade liberalisation and regional free trade agreements. In this context, the ACP proposed the following:

(i) a methodology, through the development of a vulnerability index, to identify the preference tariff lines and determine the scope of the problem;[30]

(ii) the proposal of a transitional period for the longer staging of tariff reductions in the market of the EU and the US for the identified tariff lines; and

(iii) the need to provide adjustment assistance during the transition period through aid for trade to build competitiveness in the ACP countries.

The strategy that the ACP used was to make this proposal a common G-90 one with the support of the African Group and the LDCs. The ACP also decided to secure greater buy-in from other major developing players by lobbying support from Brazil, Chile, China, India and others in the context of the G-110 alliance. The NAMA-11 group also supported the ACP proposal. Through an outreach campaign, even the opponents of preference erosion were targeted, and the proposal was skilfully sold as, in fact, a strategy to exit discriminatory non-reciprocal preferences from the multilateral trading system for good. It was also explained to the developed countries that if such an approach was not accepted by them, the G-90 would have no other choice than to raise the rhetoric of its opposition to the Swiss formula, which would erode its preferences if it was too ambitious. This tactical argument convinced many that the ACP proposal was worth considering. From then on, the negotiations on this issue changed character completely and the hardcore group intrinsically opposed to preferences was reduced to a tiny group of Latin American countries that were still obstinately opposing the principle of a trade solution to non-reciprocal preferences. The main reason obviously was because of its implications for bananas in the agriculture negotiations. The objections of other opponents mainly from the ASEAN and South Asian countries were on certain specific tariff lines on the list rather than on the overall architecture of the proposal.

It was on the basis of this approach that the WTO membership by and large agreed to the architecture proposed by the ACP, which became the basis of discussions in the different draft modalities texts. The NAMA chair also was convinced that this approach was the only acceptable one, but his problem was to find a more objective way to determine the coverage of tariff lines to be set aside for longer tariff phase-down periods as there was no consensus over the ACP list. In his draft modalities text of July 2007, he drew a very restricted list of 23 lines on the EU market and 16 lines on the US market under Annex 2 and 3 for a longer tariff phase-down period of seven years.[31] Both the restrictive nature of the list and the short duration of the transition period were rejected by the proponents.

Intensive negotiations followed in different formats over the numbers in the architecture, namely over the length of the transition period and the coverage in the list of preferential tariff lines for staging in Annex 2 and 3 of the Chair's texts. Some of these negotiations were carried out bilaterally between the ACP and specific countries while others took place under the Chair's guidance either in Room E format, confessionals or with specific delegations that had problems with specific lines. Much progress was achieved in the first part of 2008. The modalities for treatment stabilised and an implementation schedule of nine years to reduce tariffs on preference-benefitting lines was proposed in the modalities text. The coverage was also increased under pressure from the ACP. However, final agreement on coverage as is contained in Annex 2 and 3 of the December 2008 text was only reached in the margins of the 2008 mini-Ministerial meeting in restricted meetings brokered by the Director-General and the NAMA Chair with ministers of the G-90 and ministers from the EU, the US and China. That consensus as reproduced in the December 2008 Chair's text still holds today.[32]

Disproportionately Affected Countries

The July package also consisted of Annex 4 on disproportionately affected countries (DAC). This is based on a mandate obtained by Pakistan in the Hong Kong Ministerial meeting when DFQF market access for 97 percent of tariff lines for LDCs were agreed upon. The mandate directs members to address the concerns of other developing countries whose market share will be affected by this decision.[33] The basis of the problem was that Pakistan complained that its exports would be threatened if a powerful and big exporter like Bangladesh gets preferential access on a third-party market and Pakistan is disadvantaged by being denied even normal MFN tariff conditions through the longer preference staging modality in that same market.

Annex 4 of the July draft Modalities text lists a limited number of tariff lines for Pakistan and Sri Lanka, which are also on the preferential lists in Annex 2 and 3 for which the pace of tariff reduction would be over six years instead of nine years for these two countries. The issue of DAC was discussed for a long time between the ACP, the Chair and the two requesting countries, namely Sri Lanka and Pakistan. It was only just before the issue of the July texts that Bangladesh pushed the DAC issue to the forefront from a different perspective. The divergence pitches two sets of LDCs, namely the African LDCs on the one hand and the Asian LDCs like Bangladesh, Cambodia and Nepal on the other. The latter want to have the same DAC treatment as Sri Lanka and Pakistan. The Asian LDCs argue that they will be adversely affected by the advantages given to those two developing countries in view of the fact that they do not have preferential market access on the US market. It will be noted that the problem was more on the US market, because all LDCs have DFQF access on the EU market through the EBA programme.

While Bangladesh mainly argues that this is an issue of equity in that a developing country cannot get more advantageous conditions of access than an LDC, the African LDCs wanted to protect their competitive advantage on the US market against a big competitor even if it was an LDC. In the July bargaining process Bangladesh was finally given some DAC tariff lines as compensation but it protested that they were lines on which it had no significant trade with the US. As such, it wanted the same lines as those obtained by Pakistan.

Besides the commercial aspects of this differential treatment, there was the political embarrassment for Bangladesh to explain to its domestic constituency how a more developed neighbour could get a better deal than itself. Bangladesh agreed to forego the DAC status if the United States could guarantee that the 97 percent tariff lines of LDCs DFQF agreed in Hong Kong would include the lines of Annex 3 in the Modalities draft text.

The US, which was also under pressure from domestic lobbies not to open its textile market, could not give that guarantee. Moreover, non- LDCs like the Dominican Republic, Kenya and Mauritius, also realised that their market access might be compromised by too generous a disposition towards Bangladesh. Thus a larger front developed against the Asian LDCs with both the ACP and the African Group not wanting to reopen Annexes 2, 3 and 4 of the July package in order not to give any more concessions to Bangladesh. With the exception of the three Asian LDCs, the overwhelming majority of the membership does not want to reopen this issue again.

Agriculture: Overcoming the Banana Hurdle

The deployment of the ACP strategy in the agriculture tract of the negotiations followed a more tumultuous path than in NAMA. This was due to the deep-seated conflict over preferences in agriculture among two groups of developing countries. The first element that vitiated the negotiations was the long dispute over bananas and its non-resolution despite many Dispute and Appellate Body panels' reports in favour of the Latin American banana exporting countries. The second complicating factor was the conflicting mandate over how to address preference erosion on the one hand and the fullest liberalisation of tropical products on the other, as the products involved overlap with each other in large measure. The conflict spanned both the coverage of products and the treatment.

On coverage, there were not only numerous overlapping products, but also major products that were red lines for both sides. On treatment, there was disagreement on whether overlapping products could get tropical treatment after the longer transition period and the hierarchy between the two categories of products to determine their status and eventually which treatment should take priority over the other. Thus, any attempt to discuss the issue of preference erosion in a specific manner in the CoA-SS or in restricted chair-led processes, like Room E or 'Walk in the Woods' meetings were unsuccessful throughout 2006 and for most of 2007. The TPG led by Costa Rica could not accept any trade solution for preferences. This led to a stalemate in the negotiations in the CoA-SS. In reality, the TPG was delaying the discussion to gain time in view of the interlinkages of the issues under discussion, namely:

a. the level of ambition for the tariff-cutting formula in agricultural products was not yet finalised, and this was an important benchmark to know the top-up for tropical products to meet the fullest liberalisation mandate;

b. the coverage of tropical products was not settled as there was no consensus on any list (Uruguay or Cairns lists). This was important in order to know whether preference products, like sugar and bananas, would get on that list, which would weaken the preference proponents; and

c. the TPG wanted a stand-alone solution to bananas in terms of compliance by the EU to the legal recommendations of the Appellate Body's reports in their favour. Moreover, in 2008, some TPG members lodged another case against the EU, which could change the dynamics of the negotiations if the ruling was in their favour.

The ACP refused to be outsmarted by the TPG, and faced with the TPG refusal to engage, the ACP showed their readiness to do so in the negotiating groups and denied any opposition to more favourable treatment for tropical products as a matter of principle. They wanted only an accommodation for a small number of preferential tariff lines. The rest of the membership empathised more with the ACP, and politically the ACP was perceived as being more positive and solution-oriented. With this official posture in the negotiations, the ACP decided to maintain the pressure by retaining the initiative and table its proposals unilaterally. Hence, in early 2007, the ACP started working on the coverage of products that should be singled out for preference-erosion treatment.

The methodology used was to elaborate a number of criteria and filters to sift through the large universe of preference-receiving tariff lines the most important ones not only in terms of trade value, but also political importance in the ACP countries. Technical assistance from UNCTAD was used to do this work, as the ACP did not have that expertise. The starting point of this technical work was the Job(06)2004 ACP document,[34] which contained a preliminary list of 43 tariff lines at the four-digit level which corresponded to some 190 products at the six-digit level. However, many of these products were not traded. New criteria were developed based on an export revenue share of at least five percent and a preference margin of five percent which reduced the list to 32 tariff lines at the six-digit level.

At the same time, the Chair in his second set of 'challenges' paper[35] circulated in May 2007 issued a number of possible orientations that he termed a conceptual "sieve." Among other things, he identified the significance of the product for an exporting ACP member, the magnitude of the tariff cut and the real consequences of the cut. Subsequently, when he applied some of these criteria in Attachment 2 of his first draft Modalities text,[36] namely a minimum preference margin of five percent, an MFN rate above zero percent and a trade value of US$50,0000, it yielded 26 tariff lines on the EU market and 40 lines on the US market at the eight-digit level. Improving on the Chair's criteria, which the ACP thought were too restrictive, the latter came with an additional list based on criteria of three percent export revenue and a five percent preference margin, and the ACP added these new lines to the Chair's list. The ACP presented this consolidated new list in its submission of November 2007 "Draft ACP Proposal on Longstanding Preferences and Preference Erosion," which contained 54 lines at the six-digit level.[37]

However, there was concern that working with a six-digit level list would not garner broad support in the membership as it could freeze many other traded items in those lines that were not preference products. The ACP therefore realised that to be more precise and target only real ACP preferential exports, it was more appropriate to work at the eight-digit level. Moreover, at the beginning of 2008 more detailed discussions began with the EU on a line-by-line basis. The EU was working at the eight-digit level and this was the approach that was taken in NAMA as well. A number of discussions took place with the EU on both criteria for coverage and treatment.

Finally the ACP with the help of UNCTAD was able to revise its November list and convert it to the eight-digit level. However, some new filters were used on top of the previous ones, namely products with a six percent *ad valorem* duty and which contributed one percent export revenue of any ACP country were eligible. The new list was divided to contain the specific coverage on the EU and US markets, respectively, and proposed the treatment to be applied. In this regard, 62 tariff lines on the EU market and 14 on the US market were identified at the eight-digit level.

The treatment was along the lines of NAMA, namely longer staging periods with standstill periods at the start of implementation. However, the staging and grace periods were modulated depending on whether or not the product was an overlapping one. It also contained an additional modality for a preference product which would be declared sensitive to benefit from a longer period of implementation for the phase-in of the TRQ expansion and the out-of-quota tariff phase-down. This was negotiated particularly for sugar products.

It should be noted that in contrast to the NAMA negotiations, the Chair was almost totally absent in the preference/tropical products negotiations in spite of the guidelines he provided in his challenges and draft modalities paper.[38] The actual elaboration of the lists was done by the ACP and subsequently by the TPG for tropical products separately, and the real negotiations in late 2007 and 2008-09 took place without the Chair's involvement. It was brokered by the parties involved, namely the TPG, the ACP and the EU as the main preference-provider. The EU very often played the role of the intermediary. When the ACP tabled its submission in late 2007 and it became obvious that it was not a long list with hundreds of items as the TPG feared, the latter was forced to react and the Chair also pushed the TPG to engage more meaningfully. To comfort the TPG, the ACP agreed in the Room E discussions that any outcome on preferences and tropical products would be conditional upon a satisfactory resolution of the banana issue.

The TPG started to engage substantively for the first time in late 2007. Another reason that prompted it to engage was the fact that by that time it was clear that a solution to bananas had to be found in order to conclude modalities in agriculture. That solution could not be one that comes from the Doha Round exclusively because of the complex interlinkages related to bananas. As CoA-SS Chair Crawford Falconer stated:

> … Bananas will be settled or it won't be. Let's not kid ourselves: it is not going to sleepwalk to a solution through whatever generalised approach we have on tariff formulas in the Round. It will be a banana-specific outcome and it will only work as a full and final settlement by all involved.[39]

In early 2008 serious negotiations between the TPG and the EU were initiated to resolve the banana issue and to find a stand-alone solution that would settle the various facets of the dispute, including the ACP concerns, tropical product treatment, implementation by the EU of the legal rulings of the WTO banana panels and the DDA negotiation of modalities. The final understanding reached was to be formalised in the DDA modalities as the final and conclusive settlement on bananas, tropical products and preference erosion. The ACP was kept in the loop of these negotiations on bananas as their agreement was necessary to reach a final settlement that they would not veto either in the DDA modalities or in the notification on tariff rebinding in the General Council. The prospects of a mini-Ministerial meeting to be convened in July to conclude modalities and the increased pressure on the Chairs to speed up their work and issue revised texts prompted the Latin American banana exporters and the EU to look for a comprehensive deal more earnestly.

From the beginning of 2008 a series of protracted negotiations among the three parties started and culminated in the July Ministerial meeting. The TPG agreed to conclude a triangular deal that would settle the banana dispute, the preference erosion issue and the tropical products issue among the three parties, which would then be multilateralised as such. The only bone of contention was the immediate application of the banana deal demanded by the TPG and disapproved by the ACP, which wanted a longer and delayed implementation and which posed administrative problems of immediate implementation by the EU because of their internal legislative process.

On the strict preference erosion side of those trilateral negotiations, much progress was made with the TPG and the EU. Agreement was reached on many lines except some of the big-ticket issues like sugar, cut flowers, and some other additional overlapping lines. Of the 42 overlapping lines in the ACP list of 62, the TPG wanted to trade off 25 lines, which were zero rated for them as well on the EU market (being in the GSP+ scheme) against no preference treatment for sugar and tropical treatment for 12 overlapping lines. This was unacceptable to the ACP, which as mentioned earlier wanted a further modality on sugar in the event it was declared a sensitive product. The situation could not be resolved at the trilateral officials' level and was referred to a Ministerial meeting of the G-90 Ministerial coordinators and TPG Ministers arbitrated by Director-General Lamy and the CoA-SS Chair in the margins of the July mini-Ministerial meeting. Agreement was reached in that meeting on the package both in terms of coverage and treatment except for two tariff lines where the TPG had asked for more time to choose between two options. On bananas also the Geneva Agreement on Bananas was reached on July, 27, 2008 including the size of and staging period for tariff cuts and a guarantee by the EU of development assistance for adjustment in the ACP affected countries. Similarly, there was an agreement on tropical products between the EU and the TPG. The details of the agreement on preferences were as follows:[40]

a) tariff cuts by preference-granting members for tariff lines in the EU (57 lines) and US market (18 lines) to be implemented over the period agreed for developing countries (Paragraph 63 of modalities text), with a two-year grace period at the rate based on Paragraph 61 of modalities text;

b) specific provisions with regard to six specific tariff lines are also specified; and

c) the specific modality for preferential products declared sensitive proposed by the ACP was agreed to.

Unfortunately the whole package fell victim to the mini-Ministerial meeting's failure to reach a deal on modalities to conclude the round. As the agreement of the EU was contingent upon reaching full modalities in the DDA, the EU walked away from the deal leaving the TPG bitterly disappointed.

The Director-General of the WTO tried to revive the negotiations in the fall of 2008 and pressed the negotiating groups' chairs to come out with new texts in December that would capture progress made in the so-called 'July package' and propose options for resolving some of the issues on which there was deadlock in July.[41] He also stated that if enough progress was made, he would be willing to call a Ministerial meeting again in December to finalise modalities.

The objective of the ACP was to put pressure on the Chair of CoA-SS to record the convergence reached on the triangle of issues, namely preferences, tropical products and bananas in July, although it was obvious that the July failure necessitated adjustments in the staging dates of the banana package. In fact, intense negotiations took place once again both multilaterally and bilaterally to try to reach an agreement. The Chair convened dedicated sessions of the "Walk-in-the-Woods" meetings to prompt an initial multilateralisation of the July convergence on these issues and to receive confirmation from all key parties concerned - the ACP, EU, TPG and the US - on what exactly was agreed in July and whether the convergence still held.[42] While all other parties confirmed their agreement to the July convergence, the TPG raised two concerns.

First, it objected to sugar obtaining a more flexible modality if it were designated a sensitive product and second it wanted a commitment from the EU that the Geneva Agreement on Bananas of July, 27, 2008 would be signed even before or without any agreement on DDA modalities in December.

It should also be noted that some other countries not forming part of the TPG or ACP but who had, as producers of tropical products, a substantial and systemic interest on this issue, had been persistently calling for an early multilateralisation of any deal reached between the ACP and the TPG and between the latter and the EU/US. These countries (which included Brazil, China, India, Malaysia, Philippines and Thailand) were concerned over the lack of transparency surrounding such a deal and their exclusion from the process.[43]

The prospect of an impending Ministerial meeting, which was tentatively fixed for mid-December by the Director-General increased the pressure on Chairs to issue their revised texts. The CoA-SS Chair on the eve of the release of his new text convened the parties to the three interlinked issues and indicated his intention to produce a working document in which he would provide his views on likely modalities for preferences and tropical products, which could be agreed if a satisfactory deal on bananas could be arrived at. The TPG opposed such an initiative from the Chair in view of the fact that there was no consensus on some of the elements relating to preferences but most importantly because of deep disagreements with the EU over the banana deal. As it turned out eventually, no document on these issues as promised by the Chair was annexed to the revised December draft texts. In his introductory letter to his revised text, the Chair explained his decision:[44]

> On tropical and diversification products and preference erosion, the text remains the same. I had wanted to record in a separate paper the considerable progress that had been made in July. As of yesterday, I had drafted that on the basis that, if everything fell into place – and bananas was key to that – there was a deal there for the taking. And it would have been useful for everyone to see how close we were to that. But I was advised yesterday that, on bananas certain material changes had occurred which, in the view of at least one set of Members, vitiated any assumptions about what might even be hypothetically possible. I cannot ignore such a strongly held view so, yet again, all we get for the time being is the July, 10, text.

It was clear that the material changes referred mostly to the unfavourable report of the Appellate Body on bananas to the EU, which changed the dynamics of the situation in favour of the banana MFN suppliers of the TPG. The EU had fewer options than in July in dealing with the latter. Aware of this, the MFN suppliers were insisting that the July, 27, 2008 draft agreement on bananas be implemented from January 01, 2009 as a precondition for any deal on preferences and tropical products. But the EU wanted such a deal only in the context of overall DDA modalities and not as a stand-alone agreement.[45] Thus, the whole deal on preferences in December once again was held hostage by the banana hurdle.

As for the overall DDA negotiations that December, the Director-General did not convene the Ministers to Geneva in view of lack of consensus on key issues among the major players. A stalemate developed in the DDA negotiations, which is persisting to this date. Thus, waiting for modalities in the DDA was no longer an option for the EU as it had to comply with the Appellate Body ruling. A new strategy had to be designed and in the course of 2009 following long consultations, it was agreed that a comprehensive agreement will be negotiated along the following lines:

1. a stand-alone agreement on bananas agreeable to the three parties, which would be communicated to the WTO Council and formal notification on the EU's tariff rebinding will be effected immediately after the internal legislative processes of the EU would have been completed;

2. the ACP would not object to the agreement provided an agreed adjustment aid package for the ACP banana exporting countries will be guaranteed by the EU;

3. the tariff bindings agreed for bananas would be a conclusive and definitive settlement for all the legal disputes and would also constitute the modalities for tariff reduction for bananas in the DDA negotiations whenever they are concluded; and

4. an agreement on coverage and treatment of preference erosion products on the one hand and tropical products on the other among the EU, TPG and ACP would

be signed and would be multilateralised and defended by the three groups in the DDA negotiations.

Negotiations took place throughout 2009 to reach an understanding on the basis of the objectives referred to above. The preference list agreed to in July was reviewed and some adjustments were made to the modalities for treatment mainly for sugar and cut flowers to accommodate the sensitivities of each other. A comprehensive deal on all the elements of the package including the deal on bananas, preferences and tropical products was finally reached in December 2009. The agreement on bananas was communicated to the Council in December 2009 while the agreement on preferences and tropical products signed by the three parties was communicated to the Chair of CoA-SS on December, 15, 2008.[46]

The Chair then circulated the understanding reached on modalities for preference erosion and tropical products to the entire membership for purposes of transparency and multilateral discussions. That deal has not been translated into a multilateral consensus yet. However, it enjoys very wide support and a final deal will not be too far away.

Conclusion

The December 2009 accords on bananas, preference erosion and tropical products were historical achievements for the WTO. It laid to rest one of the longest and most bitter trade conflicts in the history of GATT/WTO. It also reconciled two groups of developing countries, namely the ACP and TPG countries. It also proved that however difficult an issue is, genuine negotiations can yield a win-win result if there is political will on both sides. On a broader perspective it showed that developing country solidarity provides an added strength to developing countries even if there is no unanimity among them. The G-110 alliance in Hong Kong changed the dynamics for the ACP on the issue of preferences after 2005. At a more micro level, it was a great learning experience for the small and vulnerable countries of the ACP, which had to sustain such a long negotiation in spite of their limited resources and technical capacity. Yet, their resilience and tenacity earned them a new visibility in the WTO, and the ACP coordinator was more widely recognised as a stakeholder in the Geneva landscape.

However, lack of capacity in terms of technical back-up was a major constraint although negotiating skills had improved. This confirms the need and importance of strengthening capacity building in these delegations. It also shows the importance of developmental think tanks and other technical assistance institutions for smaller developing countries. The ACP would not have been able to sustain that level of technical engagement in those negotiations had it not been for the help of ITC and UNCTAD. Moreover, the preference issue in the WTO has demonstrated that there is not a unique view on what development means in the WTO and that the developing countries are not necessarily a homogeneous group. There are varying interests and these differences will grow in the future as countries take on different development strategies. This does not mean that developing countries cannot work together in solidarity, but it will entail a more sophisticated approach that accepts the diversity of interests and greater mutual accommodation.

The agreements on preferences both in NAMA and agriculture can be considered to be stabilised although not commanding complete consensus yet. Minor adjustments could be necessary to accommodate the interests of countries like India in agriculture and the Asian LDCs for better DAC treatment in NAMA. But these would not be deal-breakers. However, the entire agreement is contingent upon what happens in NAMA and the DDA as a whole. If the DDA does not conclude, there is no need for preference erosion modalities and probably preference receiving countries will be better off as their preferences will not be affected by multilateral liberalisation. But, in the longer term, if bilateral free trade agreements proliferate because of the DDA failure, the preference receiving countries could be net losers as they would not have the safety net of the DDA modalities to shelter them from erosion for some longer time.

Endnotes

1 GATT Decision on Differential and More Favourable Treatment, Reciprocity and Fuller Participation of Developing Countries, November 1979.

2 This principle was confirmed by a Panel ruling under which differentiation can be made only on the basis of objective or multilaterally agreed criteria in the EU GSP case brought by India.

3 Alexandraki, K. and Lankes, H. P. 2004. 'The Impact of Preference Erosion on Middle-Income Developing Countries', IMF Working Paper, Policy Development and Review Department: WP/04/169.

4 Alexandraki, K. 2005. 'Preference Erosion: Cause for Alarm', *Finance and Development*, March 2005 Volume 42, Number 1:26-29.

5 Chris Milner, Oliver Morisey and Evious Zgoyu: "Preference Erosion and the Future of Preferences," *Commonwealth Hot Trade Topics*, Issue 60.

6 Comments by Ms. Kathy-Ann Brown on paper by Tangerman on Future of Preferential Trade Arrangements for Developing Countries and the Current Round of WTO Negotiations on Agriculture. FAO Papers on selected issues.

7 AIE/51 Process of analysis and information exchange (AIE) under the Committee on Agriculture.

8 The Ministerial Declaration of Doha adopted on November, 14, 2001.

9 Seventh Special Session of the Committee on Agriculture, March, 26-28, 2001.

10 Some of these proposals in the first phase of the negotiations are contained in: G/AG/NG/W/36/Rev: Note on Non-Trade Concerns (submitted by 27 countries).

11 G/AG/NG/91 by Japan, G/AG/NG/W/94 by Switzerland, G/AG/NG/W/96 by Mauritius, G/AG/NG/W/135 by Democratic Republic of Congo- G/AG/NG/W/90: EU Comprehensive Negotiating Proposal, December, 14, 2000.

12 Some CARICOM countries and Mauritius pushed in that direction.

13 A typical example of such a position could be seen in the Joint Statement on Non-Trade Concerns of Bulgaria, Chinese Taipei, Iceland, Israel, Liechtenstein, Mauritius, Norway and Switzerland in TN/AG/Gen/1, March, 14, 2003.

14 Proposal by Small Island Developing States (SIDS), G/AG/NG/W/97 of December, 29, 2000.

15 This evolution could already be seen in the Negotiating Proposals on behalf of CARICOM, G/AG/NG/W/100 of January, 15, 2001 where the switch to small developing economies was preferred to SIDS.

16 See summary report of Fifth Meeting of Special Session of CoA, G/AG/NG/R/5, March, 22, 2001.

17 G/AG/NG/W/97, December, 29, 2000, Proposals by SIDS.

18 TN/AG/R/3 of October, 01, 2002.

19 TN/AG/R/5, December, 19, 2002.

20 TN/AG/W/1, February, 17, 2003.

21 G/AG/NG/W/90 December, 14, 2000, EU Comprehensive Negotiating Proposal.

22 TN/MA/W/35/Rev 1 of August, 19, 2005, Draft Elements of Modalities in NAMA.

23 TN/MA/W/21 Add 1, July, 15, 2003, Communication from Mauritius to the Negotiating Group on Non-Agricultural Market Access.

24 See TN/Ma/W/21, January 27, 2003 and TN/MA/W/31, March 23, 2003.

25 WT/L/59, August 02, 2004 – The July Framework Agreement.

26 WT/MIN(05)/Dec, December, 22, 2005, Hong Kong Ministerial Declaration.

27 WT/L/59, August, 02, 2004.

28 The G-110 was a developing country alliance consisting of the G-20, ACP, African Group, G-33, NAMA-11 and the SVEs.

29 The author was the coordinator of the ACP Group and of the G-90 and a Member of the SVEs. He was among the initiators of that change in strategy both at the level of the ACP, G-90 and the SVEs and is talking from that vantage point.

30 ACP paper on Vulnerability Index, Job(05)/301 of November, 18, 2005.

31 Job(07)/126 of July 17, 2007, Draft NAMA Modalities. The explanation of how the Chair arrived at the list was given in a technical document issued by the Secretariat entitled "Assessing the Scope of the Problem of Non-Reciprocal Preference Erosion" dated October, 25, 2007.

32 Modalities text of December 2008.

33 Hong Kong Ministerial Declaration – Annex F, WT/MIN(05)/Dec.

34 First ACP preference list at 4 digit level.

35 Communication from Chairman of CoA-SS, Second Instalment, May, 25, 2007.

36 Draft Modalities in Agriculture TN/AG/W/4/Corr.1, August, 16, 2007.

37 ACP Job Submission of November 2007.

38 Note that the Chair himself made this confession in his covering note to his Rev.4 Modalities text of December 2008 TN/AG/W/4/Rev 4.

39 Communication from Chairman, Second Instalment, May, 25, 2007.

40 Proposal from the ACP Group regarding modalities with respect to longstanding preferences and preference erosion to replace paragraph 140 in the revised modalities for agriculture of July, 10, 2008 (TN/AG/W/4/REV.3) Internal ACP document, July, 29, 2008.

41 The July Package: See South Centre Analytical Note, October 2008.

42 The author in his capacity as the ACP Coordinator was the chief negotiator for the G-90 in these "walk-in-the-woods" and other bilateral negotiations.

43 The concern of India particularly was that some major lines which are exports were excluded from the tropical lists because they were preference products like rice and tobacco. They would be doubly penalised. Moreover, all these countries could not agree that they would know only at scheduling phase what is the list of tropical products bilaterally agreed with the EU and the US.

44 Revised Draft Modalities for Agricultures TN/AG/W/4/Rev 4 of December, 06, 2008.

45 The EU did not want to expose itself to a vulnerable position whereby having accepted the deal on bananas and rebound its banana tariff in the WTO, the TPG then seeks to include it in the Tropical list and claim additional tropical treatment on such rebound tariffs.

10 Dispute Settlement Understanding – Proposals for Reform

Manuel A.J. Teehankee
Former Ambassador and Permanent Representative of the Philippines to the WTO

The life of the law has not been logic: it has been experience. The felt necessities of the time, the prevalent moral and political theories, intuitions of public policy, avowed or unconscious, even the prejudices which judges share with their fellow-men, have had a good deal more to do than the syllogism in determining the rules by which men should be governed. The law embodies the story of a nation's development through many centuries, and it cannot be dealt with as if it contained only the axioms and corollaries of a book of mathematics. In order to know what it is, we must know what it has been, and what it tends to become. We must alternately consult history and existing theories of legislation. But the most difficult labour will be to understand the combination of the two into new products at every stage. The substance of the law at any given time pretty nearly corresponds, so far as it goes, with what is then understood to be convenient; but its form and machinery, and the degree to which it is able to work out desired results, depend very much upon its past. – Oliver Wendell Holmes, Jr.[1]

The objective of this chapter is to provide developing country negotiators with a historical overview of the dispute settlement issues in the Doha negotiations. The basic Ministerial mandate that any negotiator must know well first and foremost as set forth in paragraphs 30 and 47 of the November 14, 2001 Doha Ministerial Declaration provides (emphasis supplied):

> We agree to *negotiations* on improvements and clarifications of the Dispute Settlement Understanding[2] … based on the work done thus far as well as any additional proposals … and aim to agree … not later than May 2003 …
>
> With the exception of the improvements and clarifications of the Dispute Settlement Understanding (DSU), the conduct, conclusion and entry into force of the outcome of the negotiations shall be treated as parts of a single undertaking.

As one examines this mandate with the benefit of hindsight, immediately one word stands out, and this affected the intended work of legal and procedural refinements. The use of the word "negotiations" perhaps had an unintended impact (conceivably, ministers could have simply said that they agree to improvements and clarifications to the DSU). Negotiations and bargaining make sense in the economic and market access fields, such as in the tradition of GATT tariff-cutting rounds, but not necessarily in the context of legal and procedural rules, where timeframes are much more extended and necessities for changes evolve with experience in the application of the rules and procedures.

In addition, the exception provided in paragraph 47 seems to have been completely forgotten. By entwining the DSU negotiation process with the most ambitious market access and development trade round ever launched, in the eyes of many it created an opportunity to negotiate reforms (as opposed to clarifications and refinements) to the DSU as part and parcel of the undertaking.

A Step Back, the Uruguay and Marrakesh Mandates

The Doha mandate contains a vague qualification: that improvements or refinements to the DSU "should be based on the work done thus far." This directly relates to the DSU review process that had been undertaken pursuant to a ministerial invitation in the final GATT-era Trade Negotiations Committee meeting in Geneva in 1993 for a review of the DSU by the new WTO Ministerial Conference sometime in 1999. The Decision of Ministers, GATT TNC taken on December 15, 1993 in Geneva states:

> *"Ministers, Invite* the Ministerial Conference to complete a full review of dispute settlement rules and procedures under the World Trade Organization within four years after the entry into force of the Agreement Establishing the World Trade Organization, and ***to take a decision on the occasion of its first meeting after the completion of the review, whether to continue, modify or terminate*** such dispute settlement rules and procedures."[3]

This decision to "invite" a review of the WTO dispute settlement system is not incorporated into the covered agreements of the WTO and has doubtful legal status in terms of binding effect. It presumably was intended to provide comfort to members for an experiment then to be launched, a kind of escape clause, that, should the DSU provisions on binding panel rulings prove too politically compromising, there might yet be a way out.[4] Both the WTO and the DSU represented a continuum of the progressive transition from a negotiating member-controlled forum that was the GATT to a more legalised and adjudicatory formal organisation that became the WTO.[5]

The GATT Contracting Parties had wrestled for years with the problem of legal compliance with GATT rulings that could not be adopted owing to the need for consensus for a ruling to be binding. Strengthening the legal nature of the GATT dispute settlement system was a core objective of the Uruguay Round, and this was set out in very clear terms in the Ministerial Declaration launching the Uruguay Round. The GATT, Punta del Este Ministerial Declaration of September, 20, 1986 set forth the following objectives (emphasis supplied):

> Dispute Settlement
> To assure ***prompt and effective resolution of disputes*** to the benefit of all contracting parties, negotiations shall aim to ***improve and strengthen the rules and procedures of the dispute settlement process,*** while recognising the contribution that would be made by ***more effective and enforceable GATT rules and disciplines.*** Negotiations shall include the development of adequate arrangements for overseeing and monitoring of the procedures that would ***facilitate compliance with adopted recommendations***.

The importance of the DSU accomplishing the mandate for a more predictable and legalised dispute settlement mechanism was highlighted when it received top billing in the Marrakesh Ministerial Declaration, ahead of recognising gains in market access and disciplines, paragraph 1 of the Marrakesh Ministerial Declaration of April, 15, 1994 provided (emphasis supplied):

> Ministers salute the historic achievement represented by the conclusion of the Round, which they believe will strengthen the world economy and lead to more trade, investment, employment and income growth throughout the world. In particular, they welcome:
>
> - *the stronger and clearer legal framework they have adopted for the conduct of international trade, including a more effective and reliable dispute settlement mechanism*;
>
> - the global reduction by 40 percent of tariffs and wider market-opening agreements on goods, and the increased predictability and security represented by a major expansion in the scope of tariff commitments; and
>
> - the establishment of a multilateral framework of disciplines for trade in services and for the protection of trade-related intellectual property rights, as well as the reinforced multilateral trade provisions in agriculture and in textiles and clothing.

The clarity of the purposes of negotiations relating to dispute settlement negotiations in Punta del Este and the recognition of their attainment in Marrakesh contrasts sharply with the absence of any policy guidelines in the Doha Ministerial Declaration.[6]

As discussed above, this is perhaps because the Doha mandate for negotiations was rooted, albeit perhaps mistakenly, in the belief that it was a continuation of the review process that GATT ministers in Geneva had invited their future WTO counterparts to conduct, mainly as a political safety valve or opt-out from the binding dispute panel rulings that were achieved by the reverse consensus rule.[7] In this context, while the review could arguably be said to contain an option to modify the DSU, its ultimate purpose was mainly to permit either a termination or continuation of the DSU system by the 1999 Ministerial Conference, and not for purposes of generating substantive amendments or incorporating new ideas.

Be that as it may, with the ministers in Doha rightly or wrongly mandating negotiations to amend the DSU as a continuum of the earlier review process, DSU negotiators, particularly developing country delegates, ought then to be able to look back to the Marrakesh and the Punta del Este Declarations mentioned above to provide the missing policy guide and frame for the ongoing DSU negotiations. This way, any proposed DSU amendment must be judged or measured against the declared purposes for which the rules and procedures were established, namely, whether they contribute to

- increasing the promptness, effectiveness, and reliability of the dispute settlement system;
- facilitating compliance with adopted recommendations; and
- promoting more effective and enforceable rules and disciplines.[8]

The DSU Review (1996 to 1999)

As of October 1999, in just four years of operation of the DSU, 183 disputes were submitted to the WTO. This represented a major success and utilisation of the system, as well as an affirmation of the continued functioning of the old GATT dispute settlement system in its new structure.

Of these disputes, the US had the largest number of complaints (totalling 60) followed by the EU (51), and other members of the OECD presenting collectively 47 WTO complaints. India and Brazil, major participants in the GATT dispute system as well, presented nine and six complaints, respectively. A large number of the disputes were settled in the consultation stage, while a good number had reached the implementation and final decision stage.[9] In sum, the DSU system was working well, although there were procedural issues that required some clarification.

The post-Seattle period showed an increasing utilisation of the DSU, with another 240 complaints filed, and with the largest number of complaints now coming from the Group of Latin American and Caribbean countries (GRULAC) and Asian regions, and the US and Europe dropping off the top slots. An updated status of complaints and countries using the system through March 2011 is reflected in Table 1.

The preparatory briefing notes for the Ministers in Seattle stated:

> The DSU is the legal text that spells out the rules and procedures for settling disputes in the WTO. It contains 27 articles, is a legally binding negotiated agreement among all the WTO member governments, and is the ultimate means of enforcing the WTO's trade rules. *That makes it the backbone of the multilateral trading system.*
>
> Ministers at Seattle are expected to take a decision whether to continue, modify or terminate the DSU, although ***termination is not considered a likely option***. The decision will be based on the **review** of how the DSU has operated during the period January 1995-July 1999. The review has been conducted by the DSB of the WTO which is made up of all WTO member governments and handles all disputes.[10]

Table 1: WTO DSU Complaints Filed Pre- and Post-Seattle 1995 to March 2011 - DS1 to DS183; DS184 to DS423			
	Pre-Seattle Review (October 1999)	*Post-Seattle Complaints (through March 2011)*	*Total (March 2011)*
Total By Major Users	173	172	345
US	60	37	97
EU	51	40	91
Other OECD countries (Australia, Canada, Japan, Korea Mexico, New Zealand, Switzerland)	47	58	105
India	9	10	19
Brazil	6	19	25
China	In Accession	8	8
	1995 to October 1999	*1999 to March 2011*	*Total*
Total by Groups/ Regions	201	252	453[11]
US	60	37	97
European Region	54	50	104
Asian Region	32	59	91
GRULAC	31	81	112
Other Developed/OECD (Australia, Canada and New Zealand)	24	23	47
LDCs and SVEs	0	2	2
African Region	0	0	0

Source: See Seattle Briefing Papers, Disputes Settlement Facts and Stats, http://www.wto.org/english/thewto_e/minist_e/min99_e/english/about_e/19dis2_e.htm, and WTO Website Dispute Settlement Gateway at http://www.wto.org/english/tratop_e/dispu_e/dispu_status_e.htm, http://www.wto.org/english/tratop_e/dispu_e/dispu_by_country_e.htm

The review revolved mainly around the statistical data and an analysis thereof, and it focussed on three themes, namely, the participation of developing countries and ensuring their access to the system; identification of implementation issues, such as procedural gaps or inconsistencies; and systemic issues of balancing confidentiality and transparency.[12]

Towards the end of the mandated four-year period, in October and November 1998, a flurry of activity was triggered by the call of the Chair for proposals in preparation for the review deadline. The process somehow changed from a factual and statistical review aimed at assisting the Seattle conference of ministers in forming a general view on whether to continue, modify or terminate the dispute settlement system, into one that sought legal expert views and detailed textual proposals for adoption as amendments to the DSU. These proposed amendments were meant to correct perceived flaws as well as to address issues of access to the system for developing countries and LDCs, which were perceived as being under-represented in dispute settlement.

This is an important point to lawyers engaged in treaty law. A review for Ministerial action as a safety valve is one thing but an expert review for legal reform is quite another. As mentioned above, the purpose of the original invitation by GATT-era ministers was to allow the post-GATT ministers an opportunity to make a political decision after four years to terminate or continue the new WTO dispute settlement rules. It was certainly not to engage in a technical debate to make amendments to the system that had just then started to operate.

In any event, by December 1998, the last month for the so-called review process, along with the review of the operation of the system from 1995 to 1998, 17 members had presented expert and technical proposals to improve the DSU.[13] No consensus was reached for any proposed Ministerial action on these proposals and some delegations expressed views that an extension of the deadline was appropriate.[14]

The pre-Seattle Effort

With the lapse of the review period, in 1998, there was an attempt in 1999 to present specific amendments for adoption in Seattle. This was spearheaded by the EU and Japan and covered sequencing of the compliance procedures under Articles 21 and 22. Dubbed *the Suzuki Text*, after the Deputy Permanent Representative of the Japanese Mission who had shepherded the drafting group,[15] this effort did not yield consensus and also could not be discussed by ministers given the Seattle debacle.

What could have resulted from Seattle will remain a mystery. Based on the documentary briefings and members' views at the time, the general perspective was that the DSU was the cornerstone of the WTO system and that it was working well and should continue. The WTO dispute settlement cases were also attracting positive assessments from legal and policy scholars. By default, WTO ministers and members had decided that the binding DSU system for the settlement of trade disputes was there to stay.

The Doha Round Negotiations

With the launch in Doha of a new round of negotiations in November 2001, the first WTO-era TNC was formed, and it decided that the DSB, sitting in Special Session, would conduct the negotiations with its own chair, different from the chair of the regular DSB.

The 1995 to 1998 DSU review had been conducted by the regular DSB; it is not clear from my readings why the special session was established given that the legal improvements to be agreed was to be delivered in May 2003 and not to become part of the single undertaking of the Doha Round negotiations.

The Balas Process (2002 to 2003)/Chair-Driven Structured Process

The TNC early in 2002 elected Mr Peter Balas, Ambassador of Hungary to be the first chair of the DSU Negotiations. Keeping in mind the May 2003 timeline and the mandate calling for work to be based on the progress made so far, Ambassador Balas invited members to submit, or re-submit, their proposals for DSU reform.

A broad array of proposals affecting all areas of the dispute settlement procedures were presented, including, the re-submission of the 17 pre-Seattle ideas for improvement of the DSU.

This period was marked by an ambitious work programme driven by the chair. Negotiators recall with fondness the efforts of the chair to ensure that benchmarks were in place to allow preparation of an outcome document by the May 2003 deadline, while allocating enough time for transparency and engagement.[16] The chair process involved, first, general discussions on conceptual proposals, then structured issue-based discussions, and, finally, text-based discussions.

Ambassador Balas recalls the diversity of topics, ranging from relatively simple procedural changes, or developing countries wishing to have more access to the system, to more substantive changes that could affect the rights of members, such as those involving new features relating to transparency and referral and remand procedures. There were also completely new ideas relating to the means by which compliance could be encouraged or assured.[17] The process euphemistically was without focus, and in another manner of speaking, was out of control. Ambassador Balas has commented that there was "no clear direction, not even in respect of the issues to be looked at."[18] The absence of a clear objective and a very limited timeframe along with a certain element of tactical hostage-taking in relation to the Doha Round in general led to a very difficult situation for the chair.

Given the mandate to reach agreement by May 2003, and absent a consensus from the members, Ambassador Balas was left with no choice but to come up with a draft text on his own responsibility.[19] This resulted in the Balas composite text of May, 16 and 28, 2003.[20] Predictably, many proponents whose proposals were not reflected (because they did not have a potential for consensus) criticised the draft text. As recounted by some authors who were negotiators at the time, the text failed to generate consensus not because of what it contained but rather because of what it did not contain:

> … there were no substantive disagreements on the three main issues it covered: i.e. detailed rules on sequencing, enhanced third-party rights and remand procedures. Rather, the main problem was that several delegations insisted on a broader package that would include some of the issues that had been left out of the chairman's text. So the May 2003 deadline was missed.[21]

The DSB informally agreed to one more year of negotiations to deliver an outcome to no avail.[22]

The 2004 to 2005 Spencer Process

From 2004, Mr David Spencer, Ambassador of Australia, became the chair. During the Spencer period (2004 to 2005), the DSU negotiations became irretrievably intertwined with the Doha Round and its target for conclusion was to be by the next Ministerial conference in Hong Kong.

The period of Ambassador Spencer's chairmanship was characterised by allowing more of the initiative to come from the members, particularly the proponents or groups of proponents. This gave rise to several initiatives brought forth by groups of developing countries, such as the Group of 7, the Like-Minded Group (LMG) and the Mexico off-campus group. Their contributions to the negotiations, as they subsist till today, will be discussed in more detail in the next section.

In December 2005, the Hong Kong Ministerial Declaration, paragraph 34, simply noted:

> ...the progress made in the DSU negotiations as reflected in the report by the Chairman of the Special Session of the DSB to the TNC and direct[ed] the Special Session to continue to work towards a rapid conclusion of the negotiations.

The Spencer period is also known for the increased use by developing countries of the DSU system. In 2004, Bangladesh became the first LDC to bring a request for consultations and eventually was able to gain a mutually agreed solution.[23] Antigua and Barbuda, an SVE, successfully obtained a panel ruling against the US in WTO Dispute number 285 (the panel Report was circulated on November 10, 2004 and the Appellate Body Report on April 07, 2005).[24]

With developing countries' increased participation in the system (see also Table 1 above showing an updated tally of dispute settlement complaints filed post-Seattle), they also increased their engagement and involvement in the DSU negotiations.

The Post Hong Kong Saborio Process (2006 to present)

Beginning early 2006, a new chair was elected in the person of Mr Ronald Saborio Soto, Ambassador of Costa Rica. Under the chairmanship of Ambassador Saborio, which continues to the present, the negotiations evolved to a sort of middle ground between the Balas process that involved the active leadership of the chair and the Spencer process that gave the impetus to members to take responsibility to move the process forward.[25] The Saborio process involves concentric circles of members and allows for in-depth discussions among proponents and experts depending on the specific issue or set of proposals.

The methodology of concentric circles involves the chair meeting in small group sessions with proponents. The next level is an intermediate process involving interested delegations numbering anywhere from 30 to 40 (also called a Room E process or the G-40). Ultimately, there is the open-ended session with the wider membership. With this structure of concentric circles and variable formats, the process assures various levels of negotiations while ensuring faithfulness to the principles of transparency and inclusiveness.

This has resulted in the negotiations reaching their most mature stage, enabling the chair to table a draft legal text in the form of a revised DSU as contained in JOB (08)/81 (July, 18, 2008) which also provides an overview of the 12 topics that are the subjects of members' proposals.[26] As the Chair stated in TN/DS/24 (March, 22, 2010):

> [In] December 2008, I had informed the TNC that Members had endorsed as basis for our future work the consolidated draft legal text contained in the document that I had issued under my own responsibility in July 2008. I had also reported, at that time, that delegations were also in support of continuing our substantive consultations in a format comparable to our previous work, involving a combination of consultations in various formats and open-ended informal meetings for transparency.

Also of importance was the seminal work of the Mexican delegation in providing an analysis of the objectives and statistics relevant to the DSU negotiations. Entitled "Diagnosis of the Problems Affecting the Dispute Settlement Mechanism," TN/DS/W/90 (July, 16, 2007) originally prepared in 2003 (Job(08)/208 November, 10, 2003), the document provided a fulcrum for the holding of open-ended discussions outside the WTO premises by the Mexico off-Campus Group that numbered over 40 delegations.[27] This academic and objective approach outside the official WTO building allowed, according to many negotiators involved at the time, a spirit of brainstorming among negotiators and more intensive discussions of the merits or problems of specific proposals without having to feel wedded to official negotiating positions.

In 2011, the chair updated his report in TN/DS/W/21, April 2011.

For purposes of giving structure to our discussion of the specific proposals presented by developing country negotiators, the chair's 12 identified reform themes can be grouped into 2 groups, (i) the first relates to legal and procedural improvements and corresponds to the first 9 of the 12 themes presented by the chair in his July 2008 report,[28] and (ii) the second group relates to more substantive changes or new features of the DSU, such as improving access to the DSU and more effective remedies. In this section, we will attempt to illustrate with examples from the two general categories the perspectives of developing country proponents.

First Group of Proposals – Legal and Procedural Improvements

Among the proposals by developing countries are (i) the proposal to improve panel selection procedures, such as the Thai proposal to have a permanent roster for panel chairs,[29] (ii) enhancement of third-party rights, and (iii) the notification of mutually agreed solutions.

On third-party rights, a group of developing and developed countries, the *Group of 7* (Argentina, Brazil, Canada, India, Mexico, New Zealand, and Norway)[30] presented their ideas in JOB (05)/19 (January 2005, rev.1 March, 17, 2006).[31] At the crux of the debate is the view of some that disputes before the DSU could impact on the rights of other members and that enhancing third-party participation in various stages of a dispute would improve the system and also improve transparency. The contrary view is also well developed to the effect that the focus of the DSU should remain with allowing the parties to a dispute all the flexibility and the opportunity to settle their dispute or to seek an adjudication thereof without unnecessarily involving other members, and that the current third-party rules strike the right balance.[32]

As regards mutually agreed solutions, we have an example where an alliance of developing countries, the LMG (membership of which was not constant, in this matter the group was composed of Cuba, Egypt, India, Malaysia, and Pakistan) presented a joint submission with Switzerland in 2008 that seeks to improve Article 3.6 of the DSU as follows:

> Each party shall notify detailed terms of mutually agreed solutions with respect to matters raised . . . in writing and submitted within 10 days of reaching the solution. Any Member may raise any point relating to the solution in the DSB and the relevant Councils and Committees.[33]

The joint submission built on prior versions of the LMG proposals that were among the more important and well-discussed proposals intended to bolster developing country systemic concerns of transparency and the prompt disclosure of mutually agreed settlement terms. In the discussions, it was noted that the current Article 3.6 of the DSU already requires members to notify the DSB and other relevant WTO bodies of any mutually agreed solutions in respect of matters formally raised during consultations but lacks any provisions prescribing any time-period by which such solutions should be notified or the details that the notification should contain.

Unlike the topic of third-party rights, there seems to be general convergence and cooperation that this proposal would strengthen and improve the current DSU disclosure requirement.

On sequencing, post-retaliation, and remand, there had been extensive work since the first review process, the Balas Text, and the pre-Seattle 1999 efforts of the EU and Japan.[34] The delegation of Mexico had hosted numerous brainstorming sessions on these topics both in the off-campus format and in the Group of 7 format.

The sequencing problem had its roots in an apparent conflict between Articles 21.5 and

22.2 of the DSU rules, which had been highlighted when the EU claimed compliance with the final report's recommendations in the EC Bananas III Case[35] while the US claimed otherwise and sought authority to retaliate under Article 22.2, which sets a deadline of 20 days after the expiry of the reasonable period of time set for compliance. The EU insisted that the US should abide by the Article 21.5 procedure for settling disagreements on whether compliance has been accomplished. Most current disputes avoid this conflict by mutually agreed procedures among the parties to the dispute, specifying that an Article 21.5 procedure precede an application for authority to retaliate, thereby suspending or prolonging the period set in Article 22.2. The current proposals seek to codify the practice that has evolved to sidestep this lacuna in the rules and to assure proper sequencing, i.e., that an Article 21.5 panel ruling must first be sought before retaliation procedures are commenced under Article 22.5.[36]

After much progress had been made towards convergence, the *Group of 7*, minus Mexico, tabled their joint proposal,[37] which through to today, along with the proposal of the EU and Japan, has served as the basis for the consolidated text of the chair. The joint proposal of the G-7 also contains the suggested improvements relating to procedural gaps relating to remand procedures by the Appellate Body and post- retaliation and post-compliance procedures.[38]

Second Group of Proposals – Improving Access and More Effective Remedies

This group of proposals emphasises, not refinements of the current rules, but rather new features intended to enhance greater access to, and effectiveness of, the dispute settlement system. As shown in Table 1 above the Africa Group has filed no dispute settlement cases to date. The Africa Group therefore took the initiative in TN/DS/W/92 (March, 05, 2008) to propose a 'Fund on Dispute Settlement' as a new Article 28 of the DSU. The proposal builds on their earlier submission tabled in 2002,[39] which raised the issue of cost constraints faced by many developing countries or LDCs.[40] The LMG also proposed, *inter alia,* awarding legal costs to developing countries.[41]

Collective Retaliation

On promoting more effective remedies, the Africa Group had proposed in 2002 and 2008,[42] that developing countries be allowed to request authority to collectively retaliate against a non-compliant developed-economy member. The proposed amendment contained in TN/DS/W/92, March 05, 2008[43] reads:

> Where it is demonstrated that the suspension of concessions or other obligation would have negative consequences on the economy of a member that is a developing or least-developed country, the DSB may, upon request, authorise a Member or a group of members to suspend concessions on behalf of the affected members.

Collective retaliation was considered early in the GATT years,[44] and its revival by the African Group goes to the basic issue of the disproportionate impact or ability of smaller countries to utilise retaliation effectively under any circumstances against a larger trading partner. Many questions on operability and how to measure the level of nullification and impairment *vis-à-vis* the retaliatory compensation also date back to the GATT years.[45] However, with the increased use of regional integration agreements, there may be continuing debate on this proposal and its feasibility in the context of allowing regional or customs unions to collectively retaliate against an offending large trading partner or a large customs union may provide further room for discussions in the negotiations.

Automatic Cross-Retaliation

Another developing country alliance proposal, presented by the LMG, would establish an easier retaliation procedure for developing countries by allowing them automatic cross- retaliation rights. This would be achieved by removing the requirements of Article 22.3(b) and (c) for cross-sector retaliation. The amendment contained in TN/DS/W/47, February 11, 2003[46] as proposed reads:

> Article 22. 3*bis* of the DSU:
> Notwithstanding the principles and procedures contained in paragraph 3, in a dispute involving a developing country Member as complaining party and a developed country Member as a party complained against, the complaining party shall have the right to seek authorisation for suspension of concessions or other obligations with respect to any or all sectors under any covered agreements, if the party complained against fails to bring its measures into compliance with the rulings and recommendations of the DSB or a covered agreement.

Among the outstanding questions raised on automatic cross retaliation include the consequences to the system of making this provision applicable only against developed countries rather than neutrally across all categories of WTO members. Issues of fairness, proportionality, and necessity arise as in the case where a small developed or developing country may need to utilise the same automaticity against another large developed or developing country, or the lack of necessity of such automaticity if the developing country member's economy is large enough to find an effective same-sector or same-agreement retaliation option as required by the current DSU Article 22.3(b) and (c).

Retroactivity and Transferable Remedies

Again rooted in ideas during the GATT years was one relating to enhancing the value of remedies and correspondingly making it more costly for a member to fail to comply. Mexico in TN/DS/W/23 (November, 04, 2002) suggested the retroactive determination of compensation rights to a time when the measure was first introduced, which would allow a greater level of retaliatory rights. Also, in this same proposal, Mexico had floated the idea of permitting a developing country to transfer or sell its retaliatory rights to a third party in the event it was unable to find a sector or agreement that it could suspend to engender compliance by the offending member.[47]

Most of these enhancements of remedies in the current DSU negotiations have not yet been fully discussed, or discussions thereof have been avoided for not feasibly obtaining consensus. However, it appears from the GATT histories and the objective of ensuring or facilitating compliance through appropriate remedies, that these issues will remain important to developing countries, and negotiators will need to continue to engage in debate on these ideas.

Conclusion

The history of the DSU negotiations and the examples discussed above of developing country proposals hopefully provide new negotiators with an introduction to the range of issues and ideas in play in the DSU negotiations.

With the achievement in the WTO of a more reliable and effective DSU, the importance to developing countries of the negotiations relates to their interest in preserving the system of greater legal certainty. At the same time the increasing legalisation of the system leads to negotiations that will increasingly involve highly specialised legal experts, a process that often will be dominated by members who are frequent users of the DSU system.

This does not have to be a disadvantage to developing country negotiators, provided the objectives of the negotiations are clearly focussed on achieving more efficient and reliable dispute settlement system that serves all members, large and small alike, and the thrust remains increasing the objectivity and neutrality of the system. In this way, WTO members will ensure that the DSU remains the backbone and jewel in the crown of the WTO System.

In keeping vigilant, one noted author's assessment and caution should be kept in mind:

> The WTO legal system serves a reluctant government clientele. It is a clientele that has made great strides toward law-respecting behaviour in the last forty years, but that still has many reservations about obedience to legal rulings. An agreement adopted with this much reluctance will almost certainly encounter a bias against making its enforcement pressures stronger. To the contrary, one can expect governments to look for ways to cut back on its rigor whenever they can.[48]

Endnotes

1 Oliver Wendell Holmes Jr., The Common Law, Introduction (1881).

2 The DSU or Dispute Settlement Understanding is the short form reference to the Understanding on Rules and Procedures Governing Dispute Settlement adopted as one of the WTO covered agreements on April, 15, 1994 in Marrakesh.

3 Decision on the Application and Review of the Understanding on Rules and Procedures Governing the Settlement of Disputes adopted by the GATT Ministers at the Trade Negotiations Committee, December, 15, 1993.

4 Read, R. 2005. 'Dispute Settlement, Compensation and Retaliation Under the WTO', in Gaisford and Kerr (eds.), Trade Policy Handbook, Cheltenham: Edward Elgar; Balas, P. 2006. 'Chairing the DSU Negotiations: An Overview', in Georgiev, and van der Borght (eds.), Reform and Development of the WTO Dispute Settlement System, London: Cameron May, pp. 15-35. While references abound to the full review of the DSU, in legal terms, the decision to invite the Ministerial Conference to act was merely an invitation. It could not have permitted member states and economies to discontinue the DSU, given the prevailing rule of consensus whereby any member would be able to block such a decision to terminate the DSU system. In the absence of a legal clause in the DSU itself or the WTO *covered agreements* for suspension or termination of the DSU, the phraseology in the decision appears to have no legal effect.

5 *Ibid.* See also more discussion by leading authorities on the progressive transition to a rules-based and more adjudicative type of system akin to the judicial branch of domestic political systems, and a lessening of member control and sovereignty, Cottier, Thomas 2006, 'DSU Reform: resolving underlying balance of power issues' in Sacerdoti et al. (eds.) *The WTO at Ten: The Contributions of the Dispute Settlement System* pp. 259-265; Jackson et al. 2008. *Legal Problems of International Economic Relations 5th edition.* USA: Thomson West at 256, 261.

6 Many commentators have noted this lacuna. See e.g., Balas 2006, at p.17. See also the Mexico Analysis, Job(08)/208 November 10, 2003, reissued as TN/DS/W/90 July, 16, 2007, which noted this absence of clear objectives for the negotiations and therein attempted to frame the negotiations with suggested objectives.

7 Article 16, DSU. See discussion of this in Jackson et al 2008, at 274; See also Croome, John 1998. *Reshaping the World Trading System, a history of the Uruguay Round.* The Hague: Kluwer, e.g. at 126, 224.

8 Punta del Este Ministerial Declaration, September 20, 1986, Marrakesh Ministerial Declaration, April 15, 1994.

9 See Press Pack, WTO 3rd Ministerial Conference (issued November, 28, 1999), at 50-51 (also available from http://www.wto.org/english/thewto_e/minist_e/min99_e/english/about_e/01intr_e.htm).

10 Part 1, Review of the Dispute Settlement Understanding, briefing notes for the Seattle Conference, http://www.wto.org/english/thewto_e/minist_e/min99_e/english/about_e/19dis_e.htm. However, it should be noted that the capacity of the DSB conducting the review is among those where members have expressed some legal reservation as the Marrakesh Decision clearly states that the Ministerial Conference is the body invited to conduct the review; more accurately perhaps the WTO through the auspices of the DSB Secretariat and the DSB have provided a report to the Ministers detailing the factual statistics and comments relating to the operation of the system to assist the Ministers in the conduct of their review.

11 The cases tallied refer to DS 1 to 183 for the pre-Seattle period, and DS 184 to 423 for the post-Seattle period through to 3 March 2011. The numbers reflected in the table are slightly higher than the actual case numbers (423) due to certain cases having multiple complainants, and certain cases (like those for LDCs and SVEs) being also counted in their geographic groupings. See also, Huerta-Goldman, Jorge A. 2010. 'Mexico in the WTO and NAFTA in a Nutshell: Litigating International Trade Disputes' Journal of World Trade 44, no. 1 2010: 173-202.

12 See note 10.

13 Diego-Fernandez, M. 2006, 'Memoirs of a DSU Negotiator' in Georgiev and Van der Borght, (eds.) *Reform and Development of the WTO Dispute Settlement System*. See also Compilation of Comments Submitted by Members Rev. 3, JOB No. 6645 (December, 07, 1998).

14 See DSB MINUTES DECEMBER,08, 1998 (WT/DSB/M/52, issued February, 03, 1999), specifically regarding the extension of the review period to the end of July 1999 and the legal reservations expressed by Hong Kong, China and the Philippines. In addition, it was an open legal question how the DSB could be reviewing the operation of the DSU when the GATT-era TNC Ministerial Decision was only an invitation to the future Ministerial Conference of the WTO to conduct the review, and not the DSB, especially since the DSB is the body in charge of operating the DSU.

15 This was named after the Deputy Permanent Representative of the Japanese Mission who acted as host and chair of the discussions leading to the draft. See Diego-Fernandez, M. 2006 'Memoirs of a DSU Negotiator' in Georgiev and Van der Borght, (eds.) *Reform and Development of the WTO Dispute Settlement System* pp. 109-122 at 112. The Suzuki text provided a joint EU and Japan solution to the sequencing problem. See also Suzuki, Y. 2006 'Sequencing and Compliance' in Georgiev, and Van der Borght, (eds.) *Reform and Development of the WTO Dispute Settlement System* pp.367-391.

16 See e.g., Diego-Fernandez, M. 2006, 'Memoirs of a DSU Negotiator' at 115-116.

17 Balas, P. 2006, 'Chairing the DSU Negotiations: An Overview' in Georgiev and Van der Borght (eds.) *Reform and Development of the WTO Dispute Settlement System* pp. 15-35 at 27-30.

18 Balas, P. 2006, 'Chairing the DSU Negotiations: An Overview' at 17.

19 *Ibid,* at pages 31–34.

20 JOB (03)/91/Rev.1 28 (May 2003); JOB (03)/91 (May 16, 2003).

21 Garcia Bercero, I. and Garzotti, P. 2006, 'DSU Reform What are the Underlying Issues?' in Georgiev and Van der Borght, (eds.) *Reform and Development of the WTO Dispute Settlement System* pp. 123-152 at 127.

22 Balas, P. 2006, 'Chairing the DSU Negotiations: An Overview' at 34.

23 DISPUTE DS306, India – Anti-Dumping Measure on Batteries from Bangladesh. On February 20, 2006, the parties provided notice that the measure subject of the consultations had been terminated.

24 See WT/DS285/AB/R. DS285, US – Measures Affecting the Cross-Border Supply of Gambling and Betting Services (Complainant: Antigua and Barbuda) filed March, 13, 2003, panel report issued November, 10, 2004, Appellate Body report issued April 07, 2005, Article 22.6 arbitration report issued December 21, 2007 (USD21mn in authorised retaliation).

25 Diego-Fernandez, M. 2006, 'Memoirs of a DSU Negotiatior' in Georgiev and Van der Borght, (eds.) *Reform and Development of the WTO Dispute Settlement System* pp. 109-122 at 115-118.

26 As footnoted in the March 2010 stocktaking report and contained in Job (08)/81 (July 18, 2008), the 12 thematic areas cover: third-party rights; panel composition; remand; mutually agreed solutions; strictly confidential information; sequencing; post-retaliation; transparency and *amicus curiae* briefs; timeframes; developing country interests, including special and differential treatment; flexibility and member control; and effective compliance.

27 Interviews with Mexican Delegate Jorge A. Huerta-Goldman and Indian Delegate Atul Kaushik, both of whom were participants and officers in charge of their respective DSU negotiations; see also, Diego-Fernandez, M. 2006 'Memoirs of a DSU Negotiatior' in Georgiev and Van der Borght, (eds.) *Reform and Development of the WTO Dispute Settlement System* pp. 109-122.

28 JOB (08)/81 (July 18, 2008). In 2011, the chair updated his report in TN/DS/25 (April, 21, 2011) which annexed and made public the 2008 draft text as contained in Job (08)/81.

29 TN/DS/W/31 (January 22, 2003). See also Danvivathana, P. 2006, in Georgiev, and Van der Borght, (eds.) *Reform and Development of the WTO Dispute Settlement System* pp. 87-108.

30 The *Group of 7* worked on seven topics, sequencing, remand, post retaliation, transparency, third parties, effective compliance and developing country issues. See Diego-Fernandez 2006, 'Memoirs of a DSU Negotiator' in *Reform and Development of the WTO Dispute Settlement System* at 119.

31 See note 27 above.

32 See Busch, M. L. and Reinhardt, E. 2006. 'Fixing What Ain't Broke? Third-Party Rights, Consultations and the DSU' in Georgiev and Van der Borght, (eds.) *Reform and Development of the WTO Dispute Settlement System* pp. 73-85 also available http://www9.georgetown.edu/faculty/mlb66/DSU.pdf.

33 JOB (08)/40 (May 26, 2008); earlier versions were subject of TN/DS/W/47 (February 11, 2003) and TN/DS/W/18 (October 07, 2002); and interview with Pakistan Delegate Shandana Gulzar-Khan.

34 See Suzuki, Y. 2006 'Sequencing and Compliance' in Georgiev, and Van der Borght, (eds.) *Reform and Development of the WTO Dispute Settlement System* pp.367-391.

35 DISPUTE DS27 European Communities — Regime for the Importation, Sale and Distribution of Bananas, Panel Report, May 22, 1997, Appellate Body Report, September 09, 1997.

36 Hughes, V. 2006 'The WTO Dispute Settlement System- from initiating proceedings to ensuring implementation: what needs improvement' in Sacerdoti, Yanovich, and Bohanes, (eds.), *The WTO at Ten: the Contribution of the Dispute Settlement System* pp. 193-234.

37 Job (04)/52 /Rev.1 (March 14, 2007), updating JOB (04)/52 (May 19, 2004); see also JOB (05)/71/Rev.1 (March 16, 2007) from the EU and Japan.

38 *Ibid.*; see note 34. See also Mavroidis, P. C., Berman, G. A., and Wu, M. (eds.) 2010. *The Law of the World Trade Organisation: Documents, Cases and Analysis.*

39 TN/DS/W/15 (September 25, 2002).

40 See also the LDC proposal, TN/DS/W/17 (October 09, 2002); Francois, Horn and Kaunitz 2008. *Trading Profiles and Developing Country Participation in the WTO Dispute Settlement System.* Geneva: ICTSD Issue paper no.6, December 2008.

41 TN/DS/W/19, October 09, 2002.

42 TN/DS/W/92, March 05, 2008; TN/DS/W/15, September 25, 2002, Proposals by the Africa Group.

43 See also South Centre Trade Analysis, October 2005, SC/TADP/TA/DS/1. The WTO Dispute Settlement System: Issues to consider in the DSU Negotiations. Plasai, V. 2007. Compliance and Remedies against Non-Compliance under the WTO System. Geneva: ICTSD, Issue paper no. 3, June 03, 2007.

44 See Hudec, R. E. 2000. 'Broadening the Scope of Remedies in WTO Dispute Settlement' in Weiss and Wiers (eds.) *Improving WTO Dispute Settlement Procedures*, pp. 345-376 (also available at: http://www.worldtradelaw.net/articles/hudecremedies.pdf).

45 *Ibid.*

46 As updated in the Communication from India on behalf of Cuba, Dominican Republic, Egypt, Honduras, Jamaica and Malaysia, repeating an earlier proposal in TN/DS/W/19, October 09, 2002, presented by Cuba, Honduras, India, Indonesia, Malaysia, Pakistan, Sri Lanka, Tanzania and Zimbabwe.

47 TN/DS/W/23, November 04, 2002, Proposal by Mexico.

48 See Hudec, R. E. 2000, 'Broadening the Scope of Remedies in WTO Dispute Settlement'. in Weiss and Wiers (eds.) *Improving WTO Dispute settlement Procedures*, pp. 345-376 (also available at: http://www.worldtradelaw.net/articles/hudecremedies.pdf at 8)

Developing Country Coalitions

11 G20 – Combining Substance with Solidarity and Leadership

Ujal Singh Bhatia
Former Ambassador of India to the WTO

Introduction

As the Doha Round enters its tenth year, several analysts have expressed doubts about its successful conclusion, and by extension, about the future of the WTO. At the heart of the present impasse in the negotiations are the changes in the political economy of the organisation since the conclusion of the Uruguay Round. In previous Rounds, under the aegis of the GATT, developed countries played the pre-eminent role in agenda setting as well in shaping the final outcomes. Developing countries while active in varying degrees were not always sufficiently well organised to translate their interests and concerns in key areas into negotiated outcomes. However, the Doha Round has witnessed unprecedented engagement of developing countries, both in their individual capacity, as well as through their various coalitions. This engagement began even before the Doha Round was launched in 2001, and it was in order to take on board the concerns of developing countries that the Round was termed a Development Round with its mandate, the DDA.

The participation of developing countries in the Doha Round negotiations has been facilitated by strong coalitions, which have not only held firm on their interests in the various areas of the mandate through cohesive and determined interventions, but also significantly moulded the outcomes through well-crafted technical submissions.

The active engagement of developing country coalitions in the negotiations has changed the dynamics of the WTO's deliberative processes and lent greater credibility to the negotiations. But the changes in the negotiating dynamic have also implied that no single country or group holds sway in deciding outcomes. Arriving at outcomes that accommodate the key concerns of all players is a difficult and time-consuming task. In a sense, this highlights the central dilemma of the WTO today - rapid changes in the global trading system require quick and agile responses from the WTO in terms of rule making. However, with the greater involvement of its members in its deliberative processes, it is more difficult for the WTO to arrive at quick outcomes.

A number of developing country coalitions have been playing an active role in the Doha Round negotiations. While these coalitions are active in all areas of the mandate, it is the agriculture negotiations that have witnessed the most concentrated activity for reasons that are not difficult to understand. In most developing countries, agriculture provides sustenance and livelihoods to the bulk of the population. In many developing countries, agricultural products provide the bulk of export revenues. The well-being of this sector is closely linked with the issues of development, poverty alleviation and food security. The Doha mandate speaks of "the long-term objective referred to in the Agreement to establish a fair and market-oriented trading system through a programme of fundamental reform encompassing strengthened rules and specific commitments on support and protection in order to correct and prevent restrictions and distortions in world agricultural markets."[1] While all members are committed to progress on this issue, for most developing countries, given their dependence on this sector, it is crucial that this objective is translated into a negotiated outcome.

Developing country coalitions active in the agriculture negotiations include the Africa Group, the ACP, the C4, the LDC Group, the G-33, the G-20, the SVEs, the RAMs and the NFIDCs. Each of these coalitions has played an important role on behalf of its members in pushing their interests into the outcomes so far. However, no coalition has attracted more attention than the G-20. When it was formed in 2003, few anticipated the decisive role it would come to play in the Doha Round. There were many who predicted its early collapse due to what they perceived as internal contradictions. The G-20, through its dexterity and maturity in dealing with the diverse and sometimes conflicting interests of its members, has proved the sceptics wrong and has been able to maintain a high degree of cohesion through its constant search for consensual approaches. It is these qualities that are responsible for its continuing success and longevity.

This chapter examines the historical context in which the G-20 came into existence, how it came to play such a powerful role in the negotiations, and its role so far in contributing to a development outcome in the agriculture negotiations. The chapter also examines the role played by the G-20 in promoting developing country solidarity in the negotiations and concludes with some comments about its possible role in the future. The chapter is organised in the following manner: of its six sections, the first deals with the historical context and briefly recounts how agriculture was dealt with in the GATT up to the Uruguay Round. Section II describes the initial phase of agriculture negotiations in the Doha Round and elaborates on the events leading to the formation of the G-20 in 2003. Section III provides details about the formation of the G-20 with its first submission in August 2003, the content of that submission and the immediate impact it had on the negotiations, especially in the Cancun Ministerial Conference in September 2003. Section IV assesses the subsequent activities of the G-20 through its various submissions and their impact on the outcomes so far as detailed in the Draft Modalities text of December 2008. Section V provides a broad assessment of the role that the G-20 has played in the Doha Round negotiations so far, including its contribution to developing country solidarity. Section VI makes a few concluding comments including on the prospects of the G-20 in the future.

The Historical Context – Agriculture in the GATT till the Uruguay Round

Before the Uruguay Round, negotiations in the GATT had tiptoed around the issue of agriculture. This was for good reason. Given the power structure of GATT at that time, each of the majors had reasons to keep agriculture out of the negotiations. In the US, farm subsidy programmes had been a feature since the New Deal in 1933, when the Agricultural Adjustment Act was enacted. The Act established an important federal role in the planning and management of the agricultural sector of the economy, which continues today. In Europe, the establishment of the CAP was an integral part of the creation of the Common Market in 1956. The understanding on the CAP enabled the Common Market countries to focus on integrating their economies to compete better with the rest of the world, while securing protection for their sensitive agricultural sectors. In Japan, the cultural and economic sensitivities around agriculture played a very important role in the government's approach to the sector. Despite its stupendous success in modernising the economy, Japan had to contend with the fact that its highly protected agriculture was viewed by its people as an integral part of the Japanese way of life.

Despite its high level of support to its farm sector, the US was aggressive in pushing for market opening for its agricultural exports. This led to frequent friction with the EU and a number of disputes in the GATT dispute settlement process, especially on the domestic and export subsidies being paid to European farmers under CAP. In fact, 60 percent of all trade disputes submitted to the GATT dispute settlement process between 1980 and 1990 were concerned with agriculture.[2] The understanding between the US and the EU that the frequent tensions between them could be better addressed if agriculture was mainstreamed into the GATT was an important factor that paved the way for the inclusion of the sector in the mandate of the Uruguay Round. Another important contribution was made by agriculture-exporting countries (developed and developing) that had an interest in well-functioning markets in agricultural products and had been pushing for inclusion of agriculture in the negotiating agenda. These countries later took the lead in forming the Cairns Group.

The high level of protection enjoyed by agriculture in developed countries led to serious consequences for farmers and consumers around the world. According to the OECD, in 1986-88, domestic support to producers accounted for about 60 percent of the value of production in OECD countries. The distortions caused by such high levels of domestic support and border protection led to increasing amounts of surplus production, which could be disposed of in world markets only with export subsidies.[3] The weakening of market signals led to price instability and high export subsidies depressed world prices leading to an implicit tax on farmers in non-subsidising countries.

In the negotiations on agriculture in the Uruguay Round, predictably, the US and the EU played the dominant role. While the US was keen to open agricultural markets and reduce protection under the CAP, the EU was more defensive and keen on reaching an understanding with the US so that the CAP programmes could be enshrined in the

GATT. The Cairns Group played a supporting, albeit minor, role in pushing for liberalisation. Developing countries in general did not play an important role. The fact that it was the Blair House Accord between the US and the EU in November 1992 that paved the way for the conclusion of the negotiations in agriculture tells its own story.

The AoA that emerged from the Uruguay Round was only modestly successful in integrating the sector into GATT disciplines and left much to be done in this area. Nevertheless, the tariffication of non-tariff barriers, the extension of the concept of bindings to domestic support and export subsidies, and the recognition that domestic agricultural policies by leading to distortions are valid subjects for multilateral negotiations were positive developments. Much less impressive was its success in reducing actual levels of support. The realisation that the AoA was mainly successful in creating a multilateral framework for reform rather than leading to substantial liberalisation is obvious in the so-called continuation clause of Article 20 of the AoA, and that is why further negotiations were mandated after five years and were indeed launched in early 2000. However, when it was realised that stand-alone negotiations on agriculture may not yield the expected liberalisation and reforms without trade-offs in other sectors, the rationale for a larger round was created. Once the Doha Round was launched, the agriculture negotiations mandated in Article 20 of the AoA were subsumed into the mandate of the Doha Round along with other issues.

The Doha Round – Initial Phase

It was against this background that the Doha Round negotiations took up the baton. However, there was a crucial difference in the context: the Doha Round was to be a Development Round and the negotiating agenda was termed the DDA. The Ministerial Declaration launching the Doha Round recognised that the majority of WTO members are developing countries and that "international trade can play a major role in the promotion of economic development and the alleviation of poverty."[4] While the central preoccupation in the agriculture negotiations continues to be "to establish a fair and market-oriented trading system through a programme of fundamental reform encompassing strengthened rules and specific commitments on support and protection in order to correct and prevent restrictions and distortions in world agricultural markets,"[5] the concerns of developing countries have received much greater attention than in the past.

The beginning of the agriculture negotiations in the Doha Round in 2002 witnessed a polarisation of positions among members along the three pillars of market access, domestic support and export subsidies. Developed members, like the EU, Japan, Norway, and Switzerland, which had defensive interests in all the three pillars, stressed the multi-functionality of agriculture and argued for a gradual process of reform. The members with aggressive interests in liberalisation were led by the Cairns Group.[6] Even though the US is a major subsidiser, it supported the Cairns Group on most of its demands. The position of developing countries with defensive interests in agriculture was more nuanced. In such countries, the bulk of the population typically depended on agriculture for livelihoods and the sector is associated with issues of poverty and food security. While this group of countries was in favour of an effective reduction in distortions in developed countries, they were hesitant to accept ambitious outcomes in terms of reduced protection in developing countries. The initial skirmishes were inconclusive because the fault lines between the US and the EU remained the same as before the Round: the US demanded a sharply harmonising Swiss formula for tariff reduction, while the EU with its fundamental problems in market access, proposed the much gentler Uruguay Round approach of average tariff reduction with a minimum reduction in each line. On domestic support too, the US favoured a harmonising approach for reductions, while the EU, with its higher support levels, favoured straight-line reductions. On export subsidies, the US favoured their elimination while the EU, the major user of such subsidies, opposed the demand, arguing in favour of their reduction. [7]

The draft modalities paper released by Ambassador Stuart Harbinson, the Chairman of the Agriculture Negotiating Group, on February, 17, 2003 was unable to reconcile the differences between the EU and the US. The EU and some other developed members attacked it for being too ambitious while the US criticised it for being too modest in its market access proposals. The impasse in the agriculture negotiations threatened to derail the Ministerial Conference to be held in Cancun, Mexico in September 2003. It was in this context that the US and the EU released a joint proposal on August, 01, 2003 as a restricted, unofficial document.[8] The proposal was in the nature of a framework for resolving key issues on which the US and the EU were divided and did not address issues important for developing countries, like the special treatment to be given to them in the context of their development needs. Many developing countries quickly concluded that the proposal was an effort by the US and the EU to address each other's concerns while reducing the overall ambition of the negotiations and giving short shrift to the concerns of developing countries. Moreover, the proposal appeared to target market access in developing countries for products that would continue to be subsidised in the EU and the US. This was the spur that led to the formation of the G-20.

The Formation of the G-20 and its Immediate Impact

The run up to the Cancun Ministerial Conference scheduled for September, 10-14, 2003 witnessed much activity among developing countries, with new coalitions being formed on specific issues. These coalitions included the Core Group on Singapore Issues, the C4, the Group on Strategic Products and Special Safeguard Mechanism (later transformed into the G-33) and the G-20.[9] The common thread in these efforts was the realisation among developing countries that the conversion of the development promise of the Round into a negotiated reality required concerted and united action by them. This was a remarkable change from the Uruguay Round, when the developing countries had a much smaller say in the negotiations and clearly demonstrated that developing countries were coming into their own in the WTO. The remarkable contrast between the decisive role played by the Blair House accord between the US and the EU in the Uruguay Round and the rejection of a similar initiative by them in the Doha Round speaks volumes about the significant change in the power structure of the WTO in the space of a few years.

The joint proposal of the US and the EU created widespread disillusionment among a range of developing countries. Among them, those with export interests had hoped that the US would ensure that the Cairns Group positions were safeguarded while those with defensive interests had presumed that the EU would look after their interests.[10] At the end, however, they came to the conclusion that the US and the EU were only seeking to consolidate their policies into the Doha Round outcome, while at the same time seeking greater market access into developing countries. The agreement accommodated both the offensive and defensive interests of the US and the EU at the cost of the interests of developing countries – including both competitive agriculture producers and those with concerns about the livelihoods of small family farm holders. Their total insensitivity to the negotiating positions of all groups of developing countries and the unabashed pursuit of their self interest was instrumental in bringing developing countries together. It was with this shared understanding that Brazil and India responded to the EU-US joint proposal with a counter proposal and invited other developing countries to join them. The proposal was co-sponsored by 22 countries.[11] The initial document was circulated as a JOB document (JOB (03)/162) on August, 20, 2003. It was later circulated as WT/MIN (03)/W/6 dated September, 04, 2003.

The G-20 paper accepted the concept of harmonisation of support levels in the AMS by seeking deeper cuts in higher levels of support. However, an important innovation was its demand for product specific cuts, aimed at preventing shifting of support across products. It did not accept the modifications in the Blue Box proposed in the EU-US paper and instead sought its elimination. It also proposed tighter disciplines in Green Box payments, including through capping. In the context of S&D treatment of developing countries, it proposed the enhancement of the Article 6.2 provisions as well as maintaining the *de minimis* support levels in developing countries.

On market access, it sought crucial changes in the EU-US approach to tariff reductions. The paper flayed the blended formula approach to tariff cutting suggested by the EU and the US and described it as a fundamentally flawed approach. It proposed equal straight line cuts for all tariff lines for developed countries, along with the concept of total average cuts across the board. It also proposed expansion of tariff-rate quotas, reduction of in quota tariffs and appropriate treatment for tariff escalation. It sought the discontinuation of the SSG for developed countries. These elements were not addressed in the EU-US proposal. The proposal envisaged that developed countries would provide duty-free access to all tropical products and some other products of export interest to developing countries. It also highlighted the problem of preference erosion and proposed that it be suitably addressed. Given the differential development situation of developing countries, the G-20 paper proposed a different tariff reduction approach for them. The proposal envisaged a Uruguay Round approach with average cuts and a minimum cut for each tariff line. It also envisaged the need for some products to be treated as SPs under conditions to be determined. Such products would merit gentler treatment in terms of reduction commitments. It also proposed the establishment of a SSM for the use of developing countries. The paper also flagged the particular concerns of RAMs and LDCs and asked that they be effectively addressed.

On export competition, the G-20 paper proposed a complete elimination of export subsidies within the implementation period of the agreement. However, it recognised that some products may require longer phase outs. Regarding "officially supported export credits, guarantee and insurance programmes,"[12] it asked for disciplines to be implemented through a rules-based approach, without prejudice to existing disciplines. For developing countries, it proposed the continuation of the S&D treatment agreed to in the Uruguay

Round through Article 9.1(d) and (e) of the AoA, which enables developing countries to extend support for marketing costs and internal transport and freight charges of export shipments.

As the developments in the Cancun Ministerial Meeting demonstrated, the G-20 proposal was a major watershed in many ways. It was possibly the first time some developing countries had come together to provide their views on the elements of an integrated development outcome in the crucial area of agriculture negotiations. The proposal was remarkable in that it did not seek to push the agenda of only a section of developing countries, but covered the interests of the entire range of developing countries. It correctly recognised the locus of distortions in global agriculture trade in developed countries and submitted detailed technical proposals to further the mandated agenda of long-term reform. At the same time, it recognised that a balanced outcome required the development needs of developing countries to be considered. Specifically, the livelihood and food security interests of hundreds of millions of poor farmers in developing countries need to be addressed. In strategic terms, it can be argued that it was the first time the hegemony of the EU and the US in agenda setting and in deciding outcomes was so effectively challenged. With the emergence of the G-20, the Cairns Group suffered a sharp diminution in its influence in the negotiations.

The response to the emergence of the G-20 was quick and not entirely welcoming. The G-20 became the main interlocutor for developing countries in the Cancun Ministerial Conference with meetings being held between the EU-US and the G-20 on agriculture issues. But, there were no real negotiations and the resulting standoff on agriculture was an important contributor to the failure of the conference. The US in particular reacted quite aggressively, and Bob Zoellick, the USTR, put a lot of pressure on some G-20 members, especially the smaller Central American and Latin American countries, to disassociate themselves from the group. This resulted in Colombia, Costa Rica, El Salvador, Guatemala and Peru leaving the group. The major causes of the frustration of the US were twofold. First, G-20 opposition to the EU-US proposal meant that it could not be used as the basis for negotiations. It may be recalled that the Blair House Accord between the two had served that purpose in the Uruguay Round. Second, with major exporters among developing countries, like Argentina and Brazil, joining the G-20, it would become all the more difficult for the US to prise open the markets of emerging countries, like China and India. This was a major objective for the US in the agriculture negotiations.

Making a Difference

The various submissions of the G-20 have focussed on furthering the reform process in all three pillars of agriculture negotiations - domestic support, market access and export competition. These submissions have had a significant impact in the negotiations and have led to outcomes that (in varying degrees) reflect the perspectives and concerns not only of G-20 members, but also of developing countries in general. This section examines the G-20 position on various issues in the three pillars and the extent to which these positions have been incorporated in the outcome so far, as reflected in the Revised Draft Modalities Text prepared by Ambassador Crawford Falconer, the then Chairman of the CoA-SS and released on December, 06, 2008 (hereinafter referred to as the Chair's text).[13]

In the domestic support pillar, the G-20 has pushed for substantial reduction in trade distorting subsidies through effective OTDS cuts, reduction in final bound AMS, reduction in *de minimis* levels, introduction of product-specific AMS caps, capping of Blue Box support and disciplining of Green Box criteria. The focus of the group's proposals has been not only to obtain binding commitments from major subsidisers for effective horizontal reductions in support levels, but also to install disciplines to prevent shifting of support from one box to another or from one product to another.

In its submission dated December, 19, 2007[14] the G-20 had proposed a tiered formula for cuts in OTDS based on the principle that countries with higher support levels should take deeper cuts. While the tiered subsidy reduction formula proposed by the group is broadly reflected in the Chair's text, the cuts proposed in the Chair's text still fall short of the mandate for effective reductions in support, as they do not require reductions from current levels in most cases.

Similarly, the group's proposals on AMS, which include a tiered reduction formula, additional effort for developed countries with relatively higher AMS, frontloading of the reduction commitments by developed members, S&D treatment for developing countries, and flexibility for RAMs are reflected in the Chair's text. On the issue of product specific caps for AMS, the group had sought a definition in monetary terms with the details of the caps to be included in the schedule. It had asked for the caps to be in place from the first day of the implementation period along with a phase-in of product caps where spending is higher than the caps. The Chair's text reflects the group position. However, the Chair's text provides a special dispensation for the US in terms of the base period for determining the product-specific caps.

On Blue Box subsidies, the group's view was that any changes "should be contingent upon agreement on additional criteria in order to make it substantially less trade-distorting than it is now." As part of the additional criteria to be put in place, the group introduced the concept of product-specific caps for the Blue Box [Job (07)/218] and proposed guidelines for calculation of caps on individual products. The Chair's text reflects these proposals. As proposed by the G-20, an overall ceiling of 2.5 percent of the value of agricultural production has been accepted for support in the Blue Box.

On Green Box, the G-20 suggested a restructuring to ensure that Green Box programmes are not only non-trade distorting, but also take into account the legitimate concerns of developing countries. The group also suggested putting in place a monitoring mechanism to check the misuse of the Green Box to ensure that 'box shifting' is minimised. A major focus of the G-20's proposals on the Green Box was on the need to accommodate the requirements of developing countries to make appropriate interventions for poverty alleviation and rural development.

The Chair's text has proposed a number of changes to the Green Box to incorporate developing country programmes on the lines suggested by the G-20. These include:

- general services programmes typically operated by developing countries for promoting rural development and improving rural livelihoods;
- acquisition of food stocks with the objective of supporting low-income or resource-poor producers not to be accounted for in the AMS; and
- acquisition of foodstuffs at subsidised prices when procured generally from low-income or resource-poor producers with the objective of fighting hunger and rural poverty, to be considered compatible with Green Box principles.

However, the proposals of the G-20 related to eligibility norms for direct payments to producers and decoupled income support have been only minimally accepted. The Chair's text as it stands on these issues provides significant loopholes for bringing in trade-distorting payments into the Green Box.

The G-20 sought substantial improvements in the market access pillar for all products. An ambitious outcome on this pillar is vital for a number of G-20 members in order for the Round to deliver on its development mandate. The group has submitted a number of proposals on market access and has repeatedly stressed that the ambition in this pillar should correspond with the ambition in the NAMA negotiations. The group's submissions include specific suggestions on tiered tariff cuts with higher tariffs being subjected to deeper cuts, an additional formula to deal with tariff escalation, tariff capping, sensitive products (selection and treatment), TRQ expansion and administration, in quota tariffs, elimination of the SSG, deeper tariff cuts on cotton with an accelerated implementation of the cuts, and tariff simplification to lead to binding of all tariff lines in simple *ad valorem* terms, etc. The group proposed appropriate flexibilities for developing countries keeping in mind their development needs, including a special dispensation for LDCs, and pushed for the mandate on tropical products and preferences to be delivered.

On the issue of tariff reduction, the G-20 had proposed that in view of the different tariff structures of developed and developing countries, balance would be best achieved by tariff reduction based on tiered cuts across bands, with separate bands and cuts for the two groups. The original proposal of five bands for developed and four bands for developing countries was later modified to four bands for both developing and developed countries. Within a band the cuts were to be linear, with the tariff reduction by developing countries being less than two thirds of the reduction undertaken by developed countries. A minimum of 54 percent cut for developed countries and maximum of 36 percent cut for developing countries was proposed. These principles have been incorporated in the Chair's text.

On sensitive products, the G-20 has met with more limited success. The group had argued for the number of sensitive products to be restricted to within one percent with developing countries being allowed one half more. The G-20 had also proposed that the maximum deviation from the tiered reduction formula in final bound tariffs on products designated as sensitive product should be 30 percent. However, a number of developed countries have argued strongly for a higher allowance on sensitive products with more liberal terms. The Chair's text proposes that developed members can designate four percent of tariff lines as sensitive products, with developing countries being permitted to designate up to one third more. Deviations of one third, one half, and two thirds from the tiered tariff reduction formula are permissible for sensitive products. Developed countries, like Canada and Japan, are still pushing for higher allowances of sensitive products, and the outcome on this issue is likely to be far removed from the ambition of the G-20.

On the principles of tariff quota expansion, the G-20 had proposed a minimum new access level of six percent of domestic consumption. The Chair's text has proposed four percent as the basis when two thirds deviation is used and a lower level for lower deviations. The G-20 had proposed a differentiated capping of tariffs at 100 percent for non-sensitive products and 150 percent for sensitive products for developed countries and 150 percent and 225 percent respectively for developing countries. For developed countries, for a limited number of tariff lines, higher tariff capping would be permissible with additional substantial compensation. The Chair's text allows tariffs higher than 100 percent for developed countries if they are within the sensitive products entitlement of the member, provided the member agrees to a higher TRQ expansion. The text keeps the door open for some members to retain tariff levels on some products at higher than 100 percent even beyond their sensitive product entitlements provided they agree to higher compensation.

A major unresolved issue relates to tariff simplification. The G-20's position is that the *ad valorem* equivalent for all non-*ad valorem* duties be reflected in the member's schedule and subject to reduction under the tariff reduction formula. The *ad valorem* equivalent should be taken as a tariff ceiling and the tariff applied on imports would be the lower of the *ad valorem* equivalent and the non-*ad valorem* duty. The group has sought for 100 percent tariff simplification. However, this proposal faces opposition from a number of developed countries.

The group had argued that the SSG for the developed countries must be eliminated for all products from the beginning of the implementation period. However, the Chair's text has proposed a phase out over seven years.

The issues of special products and the SSM, which are the cornerstones of the demands of the G-33, have been somewhat problematic for the G-20. While it continues to support the demands in principle, it has not submitted any specific proposals in this regard. The special products issue has been broadly settled along the lines indicated in the Chair's text, but the SSM remains contentious within the G-20 and outside.

Regarding a special dispensation for LDCs, the group had asked for exemption of LDCs from reduction commitments and DFQF for LDCs from developed members. These provisions are a part of the Chair's text. However, the DFQF issue is hedged with the caveat that members finding it difficult to fulfil this obligation immediately provide access for 97 percent of the products from the start of the implementation period with the rest being covered in due course, "taking into account the impact on other developing country members at similar levels of development, and, as appropriate, by incrementally building on the initial list of covered products."

In the export competition pillar, the group had demanded that all forms of export subsidies in members' schedules be eliminated by 2013 and new disciplines on food aid be implemented. Regarding officially supported export credits, export credit guarantees, and insurance programmes, the group asked for new disciplines through a rules-based approach with the objective *inter alia*, of identifying and eliminating the subsidy component. It also demanded additional disciplines to prevent commercial displacement through food aid operations.

The issue of a deadline for elimination of export subsidies was finalised in the Hong Kong Ministerial Meeting, where it was agreed that developed countries would eliminate their export subsidies by 2013 (developing countries were allowed to do so by 2016).This was a major victory for the G-20. This decision is reflected in the Chair's text. The text also notes:

> In accordance with the Hong Kong Ministerial Declaration, developing country members shall, furthermore, continue to benefit from the provisions of Article 9.4 of the Agreement on Agriculture until the end of 2021, i.e. five years after the end-date for elimination of all forms of export subsidies."

This decision too was obtained due to the G-20's insistence.

The G-20 played an active role in designing the outcome on the other issues in the export competition pillar, and the outcome on these issues, which is largely stabilised, can be said to be the least contentious among the issues being negotiated in agriculture.

Overall, it can be said that the G-20 has had a significant impact on the structure of the negotiations through its various proposals. At the same time, however, developed countries with defensive interests have been successful in driving down the ambition considerably by insisting on flexibilities especially in market access and domestic support.

The Role of the G-20 in the Doha Round Negotiations

The preceding sections have attempted to assess the substantive contributions of the G-20 in the agriculture negotiations so far. The technical quality of its various submissions has distinguished its contribution from that of other coalitions in the past. These submissions have consistently provided the development perspective to the various issues under negotiation in the three pillars of domestic support, market access and export competition. Their high technical quality and innovativeness have ensured that they are taken seriously by other members. However, perhaps the most important factor that has lent credibility to the group's submissions is the composition of its membership. Given the diverse agricultural situations of the G-20 members, the pre-submission stage for every paper requires a detailed discussion and debate among the members.

The normal routine for the preparation of a G-20 submission involves a three-stage process: at first, there is a broad, conceptual discussion among the G-20 Ambassadors through which the general approach is agreed and the technical experts are charged with drafting the submission. The technical group then works on a first draft, which goes through a number of iterations based on the comments of various members. The final draft is then circulated among the members who are invited to send in their comments preparatory to a formal meeting of G-20 Ambassadors. In this meeting, the Ambassadors either approve the draft for submission or suggest some changes, which are then debated. Based on this discussion, the draft is finalised and sent to the WTO Secretariat. This elaborate process ensures that all relevant considerations are dealt with in a consensual manner.

This approach has two merits. First, as the G-20 is fond of saying, the G-20 membership represents a microcosm of the WTO membership. Its members include countries with aggressive export interests and countries with very defensive interests. Therefore, once the matter has been debated extensively within the group, the final outcome usually reflects the broad middle ground, which other WTO members should not normally find difficult to accept. Second, the internal debate within the G-20 usually ensures that the concerns of all sections of developing countries are taken on board. Therefore, the final submission normally obtains concurrence from other developing countries who are not members of the G-20. It is for these reasons that the G-20 positions have commanded so much respect in the negotiations.

The nature of its deliberative processes and its compulsive search for the middle ground on all issues has contributed enormously to the G-20's status as a leader in the negotiations. Another factor that has contributed to the unique status the G-20 enjoys among developing countries is its unstated adherence to the principle that G-20 positions should not adversely affect any section of developing countries. This has enabled the G-20 to play a leadership role in building a larger platform for developing country solidarity in the WTO.

The WTO Ministerial Conference in Seattle in 1999 witnessed the beginnings of a new phase of cooperation among developing countries for achieving a greater say in the decision-making process in the WTO. In this meeting, rather than attempting a broad front of developing countries on all issues, the focus of the coalitions was on specific issues. This trend was intensified in the Cancun Ministerial Conference in September 2003, which saw a range of developing country coalitions actively pushing for their specific concerns. This included the Core Group of developing countries resisting the Singapore issues, the C4, the Coalition on Strategic Products and SSM (which soon thereafter evolved into the G-33), along with the newly formed G-20.[15] While these coalitions were primarily interested in pushing the immediate concerns of their members, there was an underlying common interest in their positions - that developing countries should have a greater role in the governance of the global trading system.

On the issue of agriculture, while the developing country coalitions had substantial differences among their groups, owing to their various economic situations, there were the beginnings of consensus around the contours of a broad developing country position. This incipient consensus was based on the shared view that the distortions in global trade in agricultural products were largely due to the practices and policies in major developed countries and, therefore, the greater responsibility for reform in agriculture lay with them. At the same time, there needs to be greater accommodation of the interests and concerns of developing countries, where the bulk of the population depends on agriculture for subsistence. The specific elements of this understanding were:

- increased market access in developed countries;
- elimination of export subsidies;
- substantial reductions in trade-distorting domestic support in developed countries; and
- special provisions to protect the interests of poor farmers in developing countries.

In the run up to the Hong Kong Ministerial Conference, the developing country coalitions made conscious efforts to accommodate each other's concerns. A good example of this is how the G-20 formed its positions on the issues that most concern the smaller developing countries. The concerns of the G-90 (African Group, ACP, and LDCs) were reflected in their joint declaration:

> ...greater market access, reduction of tariff peaks and escalating tariffs, a programme to improve the supply capacity of agricultural products in these countries; a solution to the issue of non tariff barriers; free access (without tariffs or quotas) for products of the LDCs; and the ability to choose special products themselves.[16]

The issue of tariff preferences was of vital interest to the G-90 and they demanded that these preferences be continued with flexible rules based on development needs, along with compensatory mechanisms against preference erosion in agriculture. Similarly, the issue of trade distortions in cotton was of great importance to some African cotton-producing countries. On export subsidies, the G-90 supported the European proposal to eliminate export subsidies on products of interest to the African countries. On each of these issues, the G-20 moved toward common ground with the G-90. On export subsidies, the G-90 moved to the G-20 position.

The G-20 also moved towards gradual accommodation with the G-33 on its demands for special products and the SSM. While the special products issue has broadly stabilised after the July 2008 Mini Ministerial meeting, the G-33 demand for an easy to use SSM remains problematic for a number of G-20 members. The major challenge is to design an effective SSM that is not used frequently to deny legitimate market access. The exporting members in the G-20 are also concerned about the possibility that the SSM may enable the members who invoke it to breach the Uruguay Round bindings, as this, in their view, would be regressive. Given the nature of the differences, the G-20 has not discussed it formally in its meetings. The implicit understanding guiding this approach is that a wider political process within the WTO will be necessary to resolve the issue. This approach has enabled the G-20 to continue its work on other issues in a consensual manner.

The Hong Kong Ministerial Conference in December 2005 witnessed a new development in developing country solidarity with a joint statement being issued by a number of developing country coalitions. This joint statement issued by the so-called G-110 (the G-20, the G-33, the ACP, the LDCs, the African Group, and the SVEs) on December, 16, 2005 was a seminal event, as it was the first time such a large number of developing countries had gotten together on the same platform to articulate their expectations from the Doha Round. The meeting was coordinated by the G-20 and clearly reflected the credibility that it had begun to command with other developing countries as well as its leadership position among developing countries. The G-20 now regularly invites other developing country coalitions to its meetings and maintains close coordination with them.

Conclusions

It can be said that the G-20 has been remarkably successful so far not only in providing a developing country perspective to the agriculture negotiations, but also in spearheading coordination among developing country groups with the objective of ensuring that the development mandate of the Round is delivered. In the agriculture negotiations, barring a few knotty issues like the SSM, the bulk of the substantive, technical work on the various issues under negotiation has been completed. What remains is to muster the combined political will to take the Round to a conclusion. What will be required at that final stage to ensure a development outcome will be the maintenance of the solidarity that has been so carefully nursed in the past few years. Issues like the SSM will test this solidarity. But, given the maturity and political vision that has guided the efforts of the G-20 since its inception, it can be expected that the G-20 will continue to play a constructive and effective role when the time comes to clinch the deal.

While the success of the G-20 on many fronts is clear, it is not without its critics. The critics recognise the G-20's role in highlighting the interests and concerns of developing countries in the agriculture negotiations, but point to the modest outcomes in terms of effective reductions in domestic support and the much flexibility provided to developed countries in market access in particular. The actual reductions in OTDS being negotiated (with the tacit support of the G-20) provide substance to this criticism. The G-20 began with a demand for the elimination of the Blue Box but had to settle for much less in the negotiations leading to the Framework Agreement in July 2004. In fact, it had to agree to an accommodation of the US demand for a new Blue Box that would allow it to place its countercyclical programmes in the Box. Similarly, according to critics, the Green Box provisions as they stand provide a number of opportunities to subsidising members to shift their trade distorting support to the Green Box. The *quid pro quo* for this appears to have been the agreement to eliminate export subsidies, which was important for Brazil and the decision to include special products and the SSM as part of the S&D for developing countries, which was vital for India. Similarly, on sensitive products, a key demand for several developed countries, the G-20 has moved far away from its original position. While the G-20 had demanded that this entitlement be restricted to one percent of the tariff lines, the present proposal is to allow four percent. Not satisfied with this, Canada is demanding six percent and Japan, eight percent. There is a strong possibility that these demands will be conceded. The same is true of the G-20's original position that no fresh TRQs should be created. The discussion has now moved to the terms for fresh TRQ creation. Critics argue that the TRQ mechanism favours the most competitive exporters and the smaller developing countries, including the smaller G-20 members, have little to gain from this.

The underlying issue behind this criticism is the co-option of Brazil and India, the two leading G-20 members, into the "new quad" which includes the EU and the US. This has now been expanded to the G-5 by including China. The G-5 presently constitutes the informal clearing house for moving the negotiations forward. While most members are quite comfortable with this arrangement, a number of them question the rationale of the group in a member-driven organisation as well as the ability of its members to represent the diverse interests of all members, especially the small ones. Such criticism puts added pressure on Brazil, China, and India to be seen at all times to be representing the broader developing country interests, rather than merely their own interests.

A major challenge to solidarity within the G-20 and between the developing country coalitions comes from the efforts of some developed countries, especially the US, to designate, at least informally, a separate category of emerging countries as distinct from other developing countries and to demand additional concessions from them. This demand, along with the negotiating fatigue greatly in evidence among members, will put more pressure (as it is meant to) on leading members of the G-20, like Brazil, China, and India and, to a lesser extent, Indonesia and Mexico. These members will have to work harder to maintain the unity that has characterised the functioning of the G-20 so far.

In this effort, the G-20 will also keep in mind the fact that while the Doha Round will make an important contribution toward the objective of long-term reform in agriculture, this is decidedly a work in progress and further negotiations after the Doha Round will be necessary to fully integrate trade in agriculture with the principles that guide global trade in other merchandise sectors. For these reasons, the G-20 would need to continue its efforts even after the Doha Round is concluded. It is this longer-term vision that hopefully will guide the efforts of the G-20 in the near future.

Endnotes

1 WT/MIN(01)/DEC/1, November 20, 2001- Doha Ministerial Declaration of November 14, 2001.

2 FAO Corporate Document Repository - The implications of the Uruguay Round Agreement on Agriculture for Developing Countries.

3 FAO, 2000. Multilateral Trade Negotiations On Agriculture: A Resource Manual.

4 Doha Ministerial Declaration, WTO document WT/MIN(01)/DEC/1, November 20, 2001.

5 Doha Ministerial Declaration-ibid.

6 The Cairns Group is a group with strong interests in exports of agricultural products. It is led by Australia and its members include Argentina, Bolivia, Brazil, Canada, Chile, Colombia, Costa Rica, Guatemala, Indonesia, Malaysia, New Zealand, Pakistan, Paraguay, Peru, the Philippines South Africa, Thailand and Uruguay.

7 Aggarwal, R. 2005. Dynamics of Agriculture Negotiations in the World Trade Organisation, Journal of World Trade, 39(4): 741-762.

8 US-EU: JOB(03)/157 (restricted), circulated on August, 13, 2003

9 Narlikar, A. and Tussie D. 2004. The G20 at the Cancun Ministerial: Developing Countries and their Evolving Coalitions in the WTO. *World Economy* 27 (7): 947-966.

10 Narlikar, A. and Tussie, D., ibid.

11 G–20 or G–22 (Argentina, Bolivia, Brazil, Chile, China, Colombia, Costa Rica, Cuba, Ecuador, Egypt, El Salvador, Guatemala, India, Mexico, Nigeria, Pakistan, Paraguay, Peru, Philippines, South Africa, Thailand, Venezuela): JOB(03)/162 (restricted), August, 20, 2003; re-circulated as WT/MIN (03)/W/6, September 04, 2003; also WT/MIN (03)/W/6/Add.1, September 09, 2003, and WT/MIN (03)/W/6.Add.2, September 30, 2003.

12 WT/MIN (03)/W/6, September 04, 2003.

13 TN/AG/W/4/Rev.4, December, 06, 2008.

14 Job (07)/218.

15 Narlikar, A. and Tussie, D. ibid.

16 Quoted in Sant'Ana Lima. L. 2006. *Developing country alliances in the WTO: South-South solidarity at a crossroads after the Hong Kong Conference* available at www.*eldis.org/fulltext/Sant'Ana%20Lima%20Article%20010506.pdf.*

12 The Group of 33 – Navigating in Turbulent Waters

Dian Triansyah Djani
Ambassador of Indonesia to the UN, WTO and Other International Organisations in Geneva

Erwidodo
Ambassador/Deputy Ambassador in charge of WTO Indonesia Mission in Geneva

Deny Wachyudi Kurnia
Negotiator, Indonesia Mission to WTO

Introduction

The Group of 33 (G-33) is a group of developing countries that form a negotiating bloc within the WTO. The primary objective, or *raison d'être*, of the G-33 is to ensure that the developing world concerns on food security, livelihood security and rural development, are taken into account during WTO negotiations, and effectively and operationally incorporated in the Agreement on Agriculture (AoA).

Despite the name of the grouping, the G-33 membership stands at 46 and includes a diverse array of large countries, small island states, and LDCs.[1] The coalition is coordinated by Indonesia, which also acts as the spokesperson for the Group. The G33 meets on a regular basis at the technical, ambassadorial and ministerial levels.

The development of the agricultural sector is a key priority for the G-33 member countries, and issues of agricultural import rules in the form of the concept of SPs and SSMs continue to present major obstacles in trade negotiations between the G-33 and the WTO agricultural exporting countries.

Agriculture accounts for a large proportion of the gross domestic product (GDP) of many developing countries and is an important source of employment, income and livelihoods. Therefore, the G-33 countries have a strong interest in developing their farming communities and to defend them from unfair and subsidised foreign competitors that often create unstable international market conditions. Indeed, as former Indonesian Ambassador to the WTO (2003-2008), Gusmardi Bustami, expressed in a 2006 letter to World Bank President Paul Wolfowitz, "In an environment of highly distorted agricultural markets... the Group's mandate and concern is precisely poverty prevention and alleviation."

The G-33 coalition is united in its belief that the current international trade rules are inequitable and often detrimental to farmers in the developing world. The Group is driven by its Mission statement to ensure that the issues of food security, rural livelihood and rural development become an integral aspect of international trade negotiations and provisions to operationalise an effective S&D[2] treatment for developing countries can be agreed.

In this era of globalisation and free trade, the G-33 member countries are increasingly finding themselves in a position to compete with subsidised foreign competitors in their own domestic markets. This issue of agricultural subsidies,[3] which create distortions in the market and undermine the livelihood of millions of poor farmers in developing countries, remains a key point of contention in the Doha Development Round negotiations[4] and will determine the equitability of the international agricultural trade post the Doha round.

Thus, in summary, the G-33 alliance is primarily motivated by a common interest to protect the economically weaker agricultural sectors and farming communities from what they deem to be inequitable global trade rules. Defending and voicing the interests of small resource poor farmers at the international level has become a matter of prime importance for the Group.

Beginnings and Evolution

The G-33 evolved from a grouping previously known as the Alliance for Strategic Products[5] and Special Safeguard Mechanisms (SP and SSM Alliance) whose origins can be traced back to the early years of post-Uruguay Round agriculture negotiations. Its formation was an evolutionary exercise started by a large number of developing countries at the beginning of the deliberations in the WTO COA-SS (Committee on Agriculture Special Session) in light of the need to confront the challenges of trade liberalisation and their national development needs. The group was born out of a concern that the Uruguay Round AoA was benefiting only certain countries, while the needs and concerns of many developing countries were not adequately addressed or reflected much to the detriment of their agricultural sectors.

The statements made by a number of developing countries and the negotiating proposals that some of these countries submitted during the COA-SS meetings of 2000-03 pointed to a direction that implementation of the AoA – aimed at a long-term objective "to establish a fair and market-oriented agricultural trading system" through "substantial progressive reductions in agricultural support and protection sustained over an agreed period of time"[6] – had become increasingly problematic. For some developing countries with "special nature" of their agricultural sectors, the imbalance of rights and obligations resulting from the AoA undermine their balance of payments and reduced the size of their agricultural sectors. The Uruguay Round is not considered to have been able to equitably balance the interests of both developed and developing countries as well as those of exporting and importing countries.[7] In the words of Oxfam International, the WTO agricultural trade rules established by the AoA "are clearly biased against the interests of two-thirds of the WTO membership and 96 percent of the world's farmers."[8]

Indonesia, a member of the group of agricultural exporting countries known as the Cairns Group,[9] also realised that the ambitious agenda to further liberalise the agricultural sector was in fact putting developing countries with underdeveloped agricultural sectors under a lot of pressure. Steadfast in its belief that the agricultural sector in developing countries merited special consideration, the Indonesian statement in the 4th meeting of the COA-SS, November 2000, highlighted food security and rural development as an important "non-trade concerns" dimension of the AoA. Stressing the strong linkage between food security and political and economic stability, the Indonesian delegation defines food security as "the ability to produce our own food needs." It calls for policies and instruments to address the issue of national food security to be exempted from WTO trade disciplines (to treat it within the GATT Article XXI). It also demands for the creation of a Development Box with policy instruments aimed at, *inter alia*, protecting and enhancing developing countries' domestic food production capacity and "stop the dumping of cheap, subsidised imports on developing countries."[10]

As a result, the SP and SSM Alliance developed. The name came from the fact that SP and SSM are the two most important concepts that these countries want to get from the Doha Development Round negotiations. By early 2003, members of this movement had intensified coordination of their positions. On July, 18, 2003, the SP and SSM Alliance made a statement at the COA-SS, asserting that trade liberalisation had "mistakenly focussed only on tariff elimination and been blind to economic and social development." The Alliance proposes that provisions of SP and SSM be put in place to defend developing countries from trade distortions and volatility in the global marketplace.[11]

This coalition gained further momentum and recognition during the Fifth WTO Ministerial Conference in Cancun, Mexico in September 2003, following the submission of a ministerial communiqué by Indonesia's Minister of Industry and Trade, Rini Suwandi. Released on behalf of the developing countries of the SP-SSM Alliance, the communiqué stressed that "the Alliance's proposal for an SP and SSM mechanism should constitute an integral part of any special and differential treatment for developing countries."[12] This communiqué would later become the foundation for the G-33's position in the subsequent Doha Round negotiations.

Following the Cancun Ministerial Conference, membership of the SP and SSM Alliance continued to expand. By March 2004, this fledgling alliance had already embraced 42 member countries, including two of WTO's largest developing country members – China and India. By this time the group would call itself the G-33.[13] Expansion of the Group's membership continued until 2006, during which period the newest of the G-33 members were admitted (Botswana, El Salvador, Guatemala and Bolivia).

Advocating the SP And SSM

The Development Significance of the G-33's Issues of Interest

As has been explained above, since the onset of the Doha Development Round negotiations, the main concern of the G-33 relates to the modalities for implementation of SP and the SSM for developing countries. These are the instruments they consider to be the backbones that support developing countries' quest for food security, livelihood security and rural development. The kinds of SP and SSM they seek are those that will be effective in defending the agricultural sectors of developing countries against developed countries' trade distorting subsidies and volatility in the global markets.

Against continuing opposition from developed and exporting countries, the G-33 highlighted the development significance of the two concepts. First, the SP and SSM were put forward to satisfy the mandate set forth in the 2001 Doha Declaration.[14] Paragraph 13 of the Declaration stipulates that, with respect to negotiations in agriculture, "special and differential treatment for developing countries shall be an integral part of all elements of the negotiations and shall be embodied in the schedules of concessions ... so as to be operationally effective and to enable developing countries to effectively take account of their development needs, including food security and rural development."

Second, the development significance that underpins this ongoing demand of the G-33 can also be explained by other moral and political factors as have partly been mentioned above. The G-33's *raison d'être* is to support the basic development of the agricultural sector in developing countries and protect the livelihoods, food security and rural development of the most vulnerable sectors of society. The Group strives to fight the inherent inequalities created by the AoA and the Uruguay Round. The G-33 does not see it as fair when their farmers have to compete with subsidised foreign competitors in their own domestic markets and demands that this situation be urgently reviewed and addressed.

In the Ministerial Communiqué of September 2003, the G-33 notes that Annex 2 of the AoA[15] had heightened distortions in agricultural trade and said this explained why WTO Members – especially the rich countries – had increased rather than decreased the level of government subsidies. The communiqué reiterated the statement made by 11 developing country members during the COA-SS meeting of 2000 that the two largest agricultural exporters, the US and the EU, channel "their domestic support programmes away from the disciplined AMS and into the indisciplined Green Box, hence avoiding the need to make real domestic support reductions."[16]

On the moral rationale of its demand, a G-33 political document released in January 2010 emphasised the "objective reality of agriculture in most parts of the developing world where the central preoccupation of the hundreds of millions of people engaged in agriculture is that of survival, not trade." Citing the UN General Assembly document (A/HRC/9/23 dated September, 08, 2008), this G-33 document estimates that 1.1 billion agricultural workers and about 1.5 billion food-insecure people have to live on millions of subsistence agricultural holdings of less than 2 hectares. They are "deeply mired in the vicious cycle of low investment and growth ... and such agriculture is also deeply connected with issues of poverty alleviation as about 75 percent of the world's poor live in areas where agriculture is the main economic activity."[17]

The moral ground for helping the developing world to respond to a distorted world agricultural trading system was also acknowledged by the Cairns Group, the club of world's important exporting countries. The Group conceded that "distorted world markets for agricultural products penalise countries which have liberalised and discourage countries from implementing further liberalisation" as these countries "cannot compete against heavily and unfairly subsidised producers in other countries." The Cairns Group therefore saw "the need of small and subsistence farmers to have appropriate tools to help them adapt to change, and to cushion the impact of the reform process" through "the preservation of the current special safeguard for developing countries."[18]

All in all, the development significance that the G-33 put forth justifies its demand for S&D treatment in the multilateral trading system (MTS), including the request for SP and SSM. This derives from the fact that developing countries are at very different stages of economic, financial and technological development. It was argued that developing countries had a limited capacity to take up too much in multilateral commitments and that S&D treatment should therefore be an acceptable part of the MTS rather than an exception to the general rule. This sentiment was echoed, among others, by a proposal paper of 2001,[19] which also stated that: "Real, effective and operational S&D Treatment in agriculture is considered critical because of the special place that the agricultural sector has in most developing countries' economies."

In the Ministerial Communiqué of September 2003, the G-33 continued to highlight rural and agricultural populations in developing countries, which were facing increasingly difficult circumstances and impoverishment. It said that the agricultural systems of the developing countries were being damaged by the existing inequalities of the international trading environment and that trade distortions and other types of barriers had prevented them from enjoying market access benefits even in their own markets.[20]

In the eyes of the G-33, the onset of the issue of food price surge (in 2008 and 2011) and the 2008-09 economic crisis provided further justification to advance the S&D treatment especially in the form of effective SP. For the G-33, the resulting exacerbation of hardship and poverty in the developing world clearly exposed the vulnerability of agricultural systems and of poor farmers in the face of unforeseen food price volatility and global financial shocks. Such damaging global factors would be added up to weigh the argument that policy instruments, such as the SSM, are crucial for the protection of the food security and livelihood of small-scale producers and of the rural poor in developing countries. Citing the World Bank calculation, the G-33 reveals that "due to high food and oil prices in 2007 and 2008, the number of people living in extreme poverty may have increased by 130-150 million."[21]

How the G-33's demands differ from the multi-functionality concerns

The G-33's call for S&D treatment in the DDA agriculture negotiations has used, as its entry point, the concept of "non-trade concerns," which is embodied in the AoA. This "non-trade concerns" is also the escape clause that developed countries use to shield themselves from the otherwise powerful force of the AoA stipulation regarding the establishment of "a fair and market-oriented trading system through a programme of fundamental reform" and the DDA mandates that WTO Members negotiate "substantial improvements in market access; reductions of, with a view to phasing out, all forms of export subsidies; and substantial reductions in trade-distorting domestic support."[22]

Under the same banner of "non-trade concerns," in the early period of post-Uruguay Round agricultural negotiations, a few developing countries worked with their more developed counterparts to explore the concept of non-trade benefits in greater detail. Included in this concept is the multi-functionality issue.[23] This exploration led to the submission of a Note (WTO Document G/AG/NG/W/36/Rev.1) that attached six papers arising from a Conference on Non-Trade Concerns in Agriculture in Ullensvang, Norway, July 01-04, 2000.[24] The Note maintained that every country had the right to address non-trade concerns – including rural development and food security as well as environmental and cultural diversity – and that "market forces alone could not address these."[25]

Prior to the submission of this Note, the concept of multi-functionality was introduced by the delegation of European Communities (EC) in the First Session of the COA-SS, on March, 23-24, 2000. Discussing the issue as its non-trade concerns, the EC said that its objective was "to ensure that means can be found which will enable agriculture to continue to fulfil its multi-functional role in the context of a more liberalised trading environment" and argued that trade liberalisation could be supported as long as the "multi-functional role of agriculture" was recognised.[26]

At a later stage, however, it was realised that the objectives of food security, livelihood security and rural development as pursued by the developing countries were different from the multi-functionality concept as presented by their developed country counterparts. It turned out that such a concept, if applied at all in the developed countries, entails a perpetuation of subsidies underpinned by trade-distorting agricultural policies. The very existence of subsidies that causes imbalances in the global agricultural trading environment later became one of the factors to justify the G-33's demand for SP and SSM instruments.

On the issue of subsidies, the G-33's position is in line with majority of the developing world. This is a factor that would otherwise aggravate tensions between the Group and the G-20[27] as well as the developing country members of the Cairns Group. In the eyes of the agriculture exporters of the developing world, the effects of these subsidies were "frequently associated with the depression of international prices, the lowering of the non-subsidised farmer income, the displacement of competitive exports, the use of environmentally unsustainable methods of production, and … the perpetuation of rural poverty in developing countries."[28]

In line with the general resistance to subsidies in the developed world, a group of developing countries calls for cessation of the Green Box[29] entitlement for the developed countries while pressing for the establishment of a Development Box[30] to address developing countries' rural development and food security needs. These countries argued that the Green Box has provided legitimacy for higher rather than lower overall OECD domestic support levels, has opened up possibilities for misuse, is non-transparent and has met the non-trade concerns of the developed rather than the developing countries.[31]

Key Elements of the G-33 Position on the Issues

The G-33's main objectives in the Doha Development Round negotiations were broadly outlined in the ministerial communiqués. More detailed explanations of the Group's issues of interest have been elaborated in various G-33 proposals, statements and communications throughout the years.

The key elements of the G-33's areas of interest summed up in the Ministers' Cancun Communiqué of 2003 were (1) a fundamental reform of world agricultural trade to address the current imbalance and achieve the development objectives of the DDA, (2) operable S&D treatment for developing countries to enable them to effectively take account of their development needs, including food and livelihood security, as well as rural development, and (3) SP and SSM must constitute an integral part of the S&D treatment of developing countries, and therefore should be included into the new AoA."[32]

The ministerial communiqué agreed in Jakarta on June, 12, 2005 reiterated these ultimate goals and set the stage for further detailed explanation of the G-33 areas of interest and its preferences on the format of negotiations.[33] In requesting more meaningful and operational S&D treatment for developing countries, the communiqué demands that the agriculture modalities[34] to be agreed upon by WTO Members during the DDA negotiations must faithfully reflect the integrity of the developmental mandate of the Doha Declaration. It states that effective and operable SP and SSM instruments are the prerequisite for the operationalisation of S&D treatment that addresses food and livelihood security as well as the rural development needs of developing countries.[35]

In light of the WTO plan to finalise agriculture modalities by the Hong Kong Ministerial Meeting (December 2005), the Jakarta Communiqué noted the mandate of the July 2004 Framework,[36] which allows developing countries to designate an appropriate number of SPs on the basis of food security, livelihood security and rural development needs. Due to the complex nature of these concepts, however, the communiqué does not agree with the idea of establishing a universal criterion for selecting SPs and designating an appropriate number of SPs. Instead, self-selection of SPs should be made with full appreciation of: (a) the domestic policy context and circumstances of the individual developing countries concerned, (b) the assessment of individual countries regarding the importance of specific products for food and livelihood security, and rural development, and (c) the domestic circumstances of the developing member concerned, while being supportive of the overall development policy established by the said member. The communiqué also rejects the idea of treating SPs within the overall treatment of tariff reductions formulas or provisions related to TRQs, while requesting that these SP products shall be guaranteed access to SSM.[37]

On SSM, the 2005 communiqué highlights the G-33 demand that it should be an operationally effective remedy for developing countries against import surges and price depressions, respond to the needs and the particular circumstances of individual developing countries and LDCs, and take into account their institutional capacities and resources and thus be simple, effective and easy to implement. It also requires that, in accordance with the July 2004 Framework, this instrument be available to all developing countries, be applicable to all agricultural products and give the developing countries right of recourse to both volume and price-triggered SSM. [38]

Within the context of meaningful and operational S&D treatment, the 2005 communiqué expects no concessions to be made by developing countries in exchange for these SP and SSM flexibilities. They should be de-linked from negotiations regarding the level of tariffs reduction formulas (the tiered approach). Furthermore, it requests that the said tiered formula take into account the different tariff structures of developing country members and must therefore avoid tariff lines of developing countries being subjected to excessive tariff cuts.[39]

On the issue of domestic support, the G-33 communiqué rejects the call to reduce developing countries' *de minimis*[40] support, considering its importance as a fundamental policy instrument in supporting small and resource-poor farmers, and in addressing food security, livelihood security and rural development.

G-33 Strategies to Advance Its Interests

In advancing its interests, the G-33 adopts a few strategies commonly found in multilateral negotiations. First, it aims to forge internal coordination in order to ensure the necessary level of unity and solidarity among members and to enhance the quality of negotiating postures that it will bring. Second, it tries to shape and strengthen further the quality of the G-33's negotiating ability by working closely with outside partners. To advance its interest, the G-33 has built up stacks of submissions, statements and declarations to back up its demands for SP and SSM.

Internal coordination has always been the important feature that helps to maintain solidarity and unity within the group. This is also one of the imperatives, considering the large numbers of the membership and the diversified characteristics of the members. The G-33 includes the two largest emerging economies – China and India – but also comprises many SVEs and LDCs. As a result, the positions of the G-33 would normally require backing of the SVE and LDC groups.

Coordinated by Indonesia, the Group holds regular meetings at the technical and heads of delegation (ambassadors) levels in Geneva, as well as meetings at the ministerial level, depending on the intensity of negotiations. Meetings at the technical level have as their predominant role to look into producing drafts for both purposes of political statements and technical papers. Many of these "technical coordination" meetings start from small or very small-group formats before the draft products are ready for readings and acceptance in a wider group.

At the ambassadors' level, the Group addresses political issues, makes decisions on the day-to-day conduct of the G-33 and approves drafts prepared by the technical group. At the ministerial level, the Group addresses political issues, makes decisions and produces communiqués/statements to navigate the G-33 negotiating positions. As explained above, the G-33's main issues of interest have been set by the first two ministerial communiqués

(2003 and 2005), and the follow-up G-33 negotiating course of action guidance has also been shaped by the 2007 and 2009 communiqués.[41]

The work of the G-33, including at the technical level, relies not only on the inputs received from national focal points of capital cities of the G-33 members concerned, but also from works and studies conducted by various international think tanks. Short of financial capacity and research infrastructure, members would use their international networks to develop working relationships with external establishments to shape up G-33 technical work and negotiating finesse. In the early years of existence, the Group relied on the South Centre for much of its work.

The survival of the G-33 owes also in no small measure to its success in maintaining bonds and relations with other caucuses in the WTO, notably its fellow developing countries' groupings. As mentioned above, the G-33 maintains close coordination with the SVE and LDC groups – mainly through the chairs of each group – every time there are statements or negotiating proposals to be released. This practice has had a firm political basis since the beginning, when the 2005 Jakarta Ministerial Communiqué called for a strengthened close cooperation between the Group and other developing country groupings such as the ACP, the African Group, the LDCs and the G-20. The ministers believed that "it is only through the collective spirit and close cooperation among developing countries that the development dimension of the Doha Declaration can be effectively achieved."[42]

Indeed, events since the Cancun Ministerial Meeting suggest the prevalence of a certain degree of coordination between the G-33 and several developing-country groupings. The G-33 has had a few occasions to release or to participate in the release of joint statements (including "G-110" or "G90" statements) involving configurations of groupings that include the G-20, the African Group, the ACP, the SVEs or the LDCs.

Among these developing countries' groupings, the G-33 relationship with the G-20 would be rather problematic. This is because several G-20 members are important producers and exporters of agricultural products, and by nature they would be interested in the degree of S&D treatment the G-33 importing member countries will get from SP and SSM flexibilities. Nevertheless, in the early years of DDA negotiations, it was apparent that close contacts between members and coordinators of the G-33 and the G-20 – including among Ministers of Brazil, China, India and Indonesia, – may have helped the two groupings share some degree of common position. The two grouping are bound by the fact that almost half of the G-20 members are also members of the G-33 (Bolivia, China, Cuba, Guatemala, India, Indonesia, Pakistan, Peru, Philippines and Venezuela).

The end result was that formal declarations and statements by the G-20 through the years reflected a degree of coordination among developing country groupings. The G-20 Sao Paolo Ministerial Communiqué of June, 12, 2004 acknowledged the need to take into account food and livelihood security and rural development and endorsed SP and SSM proposals for developing countries. The G-20 Ministerial Meeting in Dalian of July, 12, 2005 agreed to make operational the provisions on S&D treatment for developing countries, in particular SPs and SSM.[43] In Bhurban, Pakistan, September, 09-10, 2005, the G-20 Ministers reassured that SP and SSM "are integral elements of the negotiations," and they welcomed the G-33 initiative "to which the G-20 is prepared to contribute, to develop a list of indicators for the designation of SPs based on the criteria of food security, livelihood security and rural development needs."[44]

In the aftermath of the 6th WTO Hong Kong Ministerial Conference of 2005, the G-20 continued to take on board the concerns of the G-33 regarding SP and SSM. Its June 2006 press statement sanctified the Hong Kong Ministerial Declaration (HKMD) that developing countries shall have the flexibility to "self-designate an appropriate number of SPs" and have "the right to have recourse to a SSM based on import quantity and price triggers."[45] This same statement, however, underscored a S&D treatment that take into account "the interests of all developing countries," implying that in pursuing SP and SSM, the developing countries should not negate the development needs of some other developing countries that have export interests in agriculture. This vague message reflects ambiguity within the G-20 that would later lead to more prevalent frictions among exporting and importing developing country members of the WTO on the negotiations on SP and SSM.

Apart from this tricky relationship with the G-20 (and the Cairns Group), one important factor that may have contributed to the weight of the G-33 is the existence of LDC and SVE members among its members. The moral standard of the Doha negotiations pointed to the fact that LDCs as well as SVEs should be the main beneficiaries of any S&D treatment and development dividends of the Round. Recognising the importance of the voices of these groupings, the G-33 had also made several joint statements that show its association with these groups.

How Has the G-33 Position Been Taken Into Account?

The paragraphs above on the relationship between the G-33 and the G-20 explain that, despite the seemingly general willingness among WTO members to discuss the concepts of SP and SSM, the G-33 has faced a long, uphill battle in advancing its interests during the course of DDA negotiations. In addition, when it comes to proposals for S&D treatment, the richer nations within the WTO tend to be reluctant to accept what would become operational and effective mechanisms. When it relates to the issue of SP and SSM in particular, the net agricultural exporters from both developed and developing countries will join forces to halt progress on any meaningful proposals for the G-33.

The G-33 describes the difficult situation of negotiations on SSM up to 2010 as follows:

> Recent discussions on the SSM have highlighted the gulf that persists in perceptions on the rationale, structure and design of the instrument. The proponents of the SSM have highlighted the need for an effective, easy-to-operate instrument which addresses their development needs, in line with the mandate in paragraph 13 of the Doha Ministerial Declaration. However, some members have focussed on its possible disruptive impact on trade flows. Based on this, they have sought to circumscribe the functioning of the SSM by proposing disciplines which would prevent it from disrupting 'normal trade'.[46]

Negotiations are about achieving objectives that do not work in a vacuum. The efforts of G-33 members to attain the best possible results in terms of issues of interest often confront opposition from opponents. The end results often point in the direction of compromise. Even since the beginning of the undertaking, the G-33's insistence on the use of the term "strategic products" had to face the reality of too much opposition; thus, a more moderate, broadly acceptable name, "special products," was finally used. The G-33 preferred the term "strategic products" to reflect their merits to qualify for exemption from any tariff reduction.[47]

When the G-33 (the SP and SSP Alliance) was formed in 2003, the main item on the table was the first draft framework for establishing agriculture modalities released by the Chairman of COA-SS, Stuart Harbinson. The Draft contains paragraphs that laid down very preliminary language on SP, and especially, on SSM.[48] When the G-33 Ministers in the September communiqué echoed the level of dissatisfaction their ambassadors had made in Geneva against the drafting of SP and SSM that they are "far short of adequately addressing developing countries' food and livelihood security and rural development problems, as well as ensuring the survival of the small vulnerable resource-poor farmers."[49] History would show that the G-33's offensive made a dent in the process of negotiations.

The 2003 ministerial communiqués have certainly laid down firm positions on several issues of SP and SSM in response to the situation of negotiations. The ensuing G-33 statements and submissions delivered in the "Geneva process" also did their part to influence the course of negotiations on revising the draft modalities text. The G-33 statements would become one of the main features of the CoA-SS meetings after 2004, other than the statements frequently delivered by the G-20, Cairns Group, ACP, LDCs, SVEs and the African Group. And submissions of G-33 negotiating proposals began to enrich collections of WTO documents.[50]

In general, the advent of the G-33 coalition was able to make a difference in the way the proposed modalities were drafted. The hard work the G-33 and its member states did during the course of CoA-SS negotiations has certainly helped to shape the evolution of the Draft Agriculture Modalities, reaching its 4th Revision (December, 06, 2008).[51] Other than this, the regular G-33 statements delivered during TNC and General Council (GC) meetings – and the few ministerial communiqués that agreed during G-33 ministerial meetings – would also have had their particular influence on the political trends that shape the DDA process and the ensuing mandates written to guide the post-Cancun negotiations.

As a result, what has originally been the Doha Ministerial mandate of 2001 that S&D treatment for developing countries "shall be embodied in the results of the Doha Development Round," the subsequent DDA political guidance – the 2004 July Framework and the 2005 Hong Kong Ministerial Declaration (HKMD) – made important strides in determining how the SP and SSM should be negotiated. The July Framework envisioned that developing countries "will have the flexibility to designate an appropriate number of products as Special Products" and that a SSM "will be established for use by developing countries." The HKMD gives the developing countries the flexibility to "self-designate" an appropriate number of tariff lines as SP, makes reference to SPs being fully exempt from any new market access commitment (entitled to zero cut treatment) and having automatic access to SSM, and gives the developing country members "the right to have recourse to a Special Safeguard Mechanism based on import quantity and price triggers."[52] The wordings on SP and SSM, in the HKMD had been tilted to the benefit of the G-33. This is two years after the Group was established.

The final judgment as to whether the existence of the G-33 has increased the bargaining position of its members and given value-addition to the goals of food security, livelihood security and rural development remains to be pronounced. The final assessment and ruling still have to wait until the final modalities of agriculture are agreed. As far as the Draft Agriculture Modalities TN/AG/W/Rev. 4 are concerned, the texts that explain the treatment of SP (Paragraph 129-131) and SSM (Paragraph 132-146) have partly accommodated the demands put forward by the G-33 during the course of negotiations. The Draft has certainly not accommodated all of the demands in full.

During the negotiations that led to the current Draft Modalities, the G-33's standing should also be attributable to its two largest members, China and India. The presence of either one or both of these countries in meetings of such exclusive groups as the G-4, the G-7 and the G-5 (from 2010) brings weight to the G-33 as a grouping that aspires for the kind of SP and SSM that "serves the purpose."

Looking to the Future

Challenges the G-33 Is Facing or Is Expected to Face in the Future

Repeated calls to conclude the Doha Round negotiations as soon as possible have been made by all stakeholders, including leaders and ministers meeting in various configurations (G-20 and APEC summits, WTO Ministerial conferences, and OECD and APEC ministerial meetings). But, the reality of day-to-day negotiations in Geneva to address pending issues, including on the draft agriculture modalities, reveals a different story. There has been a dis-connect between the rhetoric of the leaders and ministers and the real political engagement in the field. This is the challenge that WTO members have to resolve, in light of the belief among developing countries' groupings that the biggest casualties of the delay in the DDA negotiations are the developing countries.

On the G-33 issues, the DDA negotiations have not been able to reach any conclusive headway. Powerful nations continue to strongly oppose many of the G-33's suggested reforms and proposed amendments to the AoA. Therefore, the future process of negotiating for the acceptable instruments of SP and SSM through the COA-SS will continue to be an extremely challenging undertaking for the G-33. The kind of SP and SSM that the G-33 is seeking are those which will be effective in protecting the agricultural sector in the developing countries against volatile situations in the global markets. This turns out to be a tough undertaking when different groups of member states adopt different meanings to translate the mandates the DDA has provided.

Substantively, the G-33 has yet to secure agreement on accepted terms and conditions of these instruments which will be the most important challenge if the Group is to remain relevant in the WTO negotiations. The G-33 will have to continue working to ensure that the ultimate goal of establishing a simple and easy way to operate SSM and self-designated SPs is reached and applied to all agricultural products.

Opposition from the major developed and exporting member countries will continue to be very tough. Since the beginning the US has said that it would not accept hindrance to further reform of global agricultural trade due to its strategic importance to the health and productivity of the country's agricultural sector.[53] Contrary to the G-33's argument, the US administration believes that strengthening food security means "further liberalisation of trade in agricultural products."[54]

To make the matter difficult for the G-33, several other agricultural exporting countries share much of the US argument. The EU has suggested that developing countries not shy away from trade liberalisation because it is important to increase the wealth of both exporters and importers.[55] A member of the Cairns Group, Argentina, said that S&D treatment shall also mean increased openness of world agricultural trade in favour of the export interest of developing countries and the "elimination of policies which distort trade and limit the development of their production capacity."[56] In a similar vein, Thailand asserts that S&D is not "a panacea to poverty eradication, rural development and economic development." It believes that "non-trade concerns are best met through programmes geared to those concerns without creating new distorting measures."[57]

The road ahead will continue to be tough for the G-33 as exporting countries become increasingly assertive about the issue of SSM, which they consider to be among the biggest causes of the WTO's inability to conclude the DDA during the July 2008 Mini Ministerial meeting. Within the G-20 - a grouping closely linked to the G-33 due to its goal of advancing S&D treatment for developing countries - a few countries do not hesitate to accuse the defensive interest of some developing countries (G-33's call for SP and SSM) to stand in the way of the export needs of the other developing countries. More and more developing country exporters speak about the increasing importance of South-South trade.

Repeatedly highlighting its need for an open global trade in agriculture in order to sustain its national income and development, Costa Rica released a paper in September 2010. The paper argues for the necessity to underscore insertion of "disciplines" or "conditionalities" into SSM paragraphs of the 4th Revision of Draft Agriculture Modalities rather than conceiving an SSM architecture that would be "simple and easy-to-operate."[58] Costa Rica emphasised the potential negative impact of an "unconstrained" SSM on South-South trade and highlighted the need to put clearly defined conditions under which the SSM could be applied so as to "avoid unjustified or arbitrary use of the mechanism."[59]

The Costa Rican paper, together with another paper previously released by Australia and Canada (JOB/AG/10 of July 2010), is also an attempt to reinforce the arguments of the agricultural exporting countries that SSM has to be "properly designed" so as not to negatively impact "normal trade" (certain level of trade growth). The Australian-Canadian paper brings out selected statistics that support the conclusion that an SSM would prove to hinder "normal trade" or export of a few products that they selected.

For the G-33, the Costa Rican demands for "export growth that support its development" pose future homework to contemplate a possible solution that will cater to the needs of the two opposing blocs of developing countries. In addition, the G-33 will have to work with the rest of WTO exporting members concerning the level of "normal trade" that has to be compromised whenever the agricultural products of these exporting countries breach the red light of developing countries' need to stop imported goods into their territory in view of protecting the goal of food security, livelihood security and rural development. Based on the "2008 Lamy Package," exporting countries, led by the US, could not accept an SSM that applies additional duty higher than its pre-Doha Round entitlement unless the volume of imports of the products in question reach 140 percent of the previous three years' average.

The G-33 will also increasingly face significant challenges in maintaining solidarity among its members. The US Administration has consistently been saying that the world has changed since the Doha Round was launched in 2001. The emerging economies have been branded the biggest beneficiaries of the latest world trade growth and economic progress. Hence, they are requested to make a commensurate contribution and assume leadership roles in the course of negotiations. This contention has put pressure on the larger members of the G-33 to avoid the allegation that they hide behind the wall of S&D treatment to escape assuming bigger WTO obligations.

From within, an effective working relationship between larger and smaller members of the G-33 has to be maintained in light of the demand that the way the G-33 negotiates will always be mindful of the need to secure a differentiated (tiered) treatment of the SP and SSM instrument, which will particularly be in favour of the LDC and SVE members.

How Can the G-33 Face these Challenges Effectively?

A conclusion of the DDA would have to include resolution of gateway issues in agriculture negotiations, which include the issues of SP and SSM. The challenge for the G-33 is to help the COA-SS resolve these remaining pending issues without necessarily losing ground on the Group's objective to establish SP and SSM instruments that serve the purpose of catering to the food security, livelihood security and rural development needs of developing countries.

To effectively confront this challenge, the G-33 would have to continue working with other WTO members so that a way out can be found. Internally, the G-33 will need to continue working on the substance and shape its arguments to support the establishment of a simple and easy to operate SSM and the self-designated SP products. In 2010, the G-33 submitted to the WTO members six papers that offer the G-33 perspective to devise and decide on the final form of SSM architecture. These papers, from the G-33's point of view could serve as the basis for WTO members to agree on closing the deal on the SSM issue.[60]

In order to be able to close negotiations, the G-33 should be able to convince WTO members that SP and SSM should not continue to be seen merely within the prism of commerce. At the end of the day, the ideal level of "normal trade" that exporters would like to see should give preference to the needs of developing countries for food security, livelihood security and rural development. The submitted G-33 papers should be able to show that the constraining elements (or "disciplines") that exporters were trying to put into the Draft Agriculture Modalities Texts – including pro-rating, seasonality and cross-checking – were contrary to the goals of establishing a simple and operable SSM.

On the issue of SP, the G-33 has accepted that what is currently on the table (draft Modalities Revision 4) is the best compromise that members could achieve so far, and therefore should be treated as stabilised and become the basis for conclusion when all other elements of the DDA negotiations fall into place.[61]

As it is also in the interest of the G-33 to see the issues of domestic subsidy and export competition concluded, it is important that the G-33 continues to support the G-20 in its quest to get the best possible terms in the agriculture modalities. Conclusion of this negotiation would reduce the scale of negative effects of this distortion of the world agricultural trading system, and the agriculture sector of the developing world would expect more relaxed competition from the heavily subsidised imported products of the developed countries.

Post-Doha - What is the Future of the G-33?

It is extremely difficult to foresee, from today's perspective, what the G-33 will look like when and if the Doha Development Round is concluded. The G-33 came out as a "rainbow" coalition of developing countries that pursued very specific issues of SP and SSM in the Doha Round negotiations.

There were occasions when voices within the G-33 spoke of certain agricultural issues other than SP and SSM. The responses coming from the members, however, did not normally point in a direction that made it possible to craft a united G-33 stance on that particular issue. In the end, the G-33 would prove able to agree only on advancing the SP and SSM.

It might, therefore, be safer to say, at least for the moment, that the future of the G-33 post-Doha Round will depend on whether a satisfactory result on S&D treatment relating to SP and SSM can be secured in the current Round and incorporated into the next round of WTO rules.

With rates of global poverty still showing no signs of improvement, issues of food security, livelihood security and rural development in the developing world will continue to feature heavily in global trade negotiations. Agriculture still forms the backbone of many developing countries and through the Doha Development Round the G-33 will continue to fight to ensure that an effective SP and SSM system is finally accepted as an integral part of WTO agricultural rules.

Endnotes

1 The G-33 member countries are: Antigua and Barbuda, Barbados, Belize, Benin, Bolivia, Botswana, China, Democratic Republic of the Congo, Cote d'Ivoire, Cuba, Dominica, Dominican Republic, El Salvador, Grenada, Guatemala, Guyana, Haiti, Honduras, India, Indonesia, Jamaica, Kenya, Korea, Madagascar, Mauritius, Mongolia, Mozambique, Nicaragua, Nigeria, Pakistan, Panama, Peru, the Philippines, St Kitts and Nevis, St Lucia, St Vincent and the Grenadines, Senegal, Sri Lanka, Suriname, Tanzania, Trinidad and Tobago, Turkey, Uganda, Venezuela, Zambia, and Zimbabwe.

2 S&D may be understood as provisions that give developing countries special rights. These may include: longer time periods for implementing agreements and commitments, measures to increase trading opportunities for these countries, and provisions requiring all WTO members to safeguard the trade interests of developing countries.

3 A governmental subsidy paid to farmers and agribusinesses to supplement their incomes.

4 The Doha Development Round is the trade-negotiation round of the WTO that commenced in November 2001 and aimed, *inter alia*, to lower trade barriers and allow countries to increase trade globally.

5 Later the name was changed into Special Product (SP).

6 The WTO's Agreement on Agriculture was negotiated in the 1986–1994 Uruguay Round and was designed to be a significant first step towards fairer competition and a less distorted sector (Source: WTO website).

7 WTO Documents that record this tone could be seen, for instance, from the statements of India (NG/W/33) the Philippines (NG/W/48 dated October 05, 2000 and NG/W/122 dated February 21, 2001), Sri Lanka (G/AG/NG/W/83 dated December 12, 2000 and G/AG/NG/W/124 dated March 01, 2001), Jamaica (G/AG/NG/W/86 dated December 06, 2000), Korea (G/AG/NG/W/98 dated January 09, 2001), Mauritius (NG/W/119 dated February 16, 2001), African Group (G/AG/NG/W/142 dated March 23, 2001).

8 An Oxfam International letter sent to Ambassador of Indonesia on April 02, 2003.

9 The Cairns Group is made up of mostly small and medium-sized agricultural exporters such as Australia, Brazil, Canada, Indonesia, Argentina, South Africa, Pakistan, Thailand, Malaysia, and New Zealand. The group pushed hard for the liberalisation of agriculture during the Uruguay Round negotiations, and are working to further liberalise the world agricultural trading system during the Doha Development Round negotiations.

10 G/AG/NG/W/13 dated June 23, 2000

11 Statement and Declaration by the SP and SSM Coalition, July 18, 2003. The WTO members listed as supporters of this statement are Cuba, Dominican Republic, Honduras, Indonesia, Jamaica, Kenya, Republic of Korea, Nigeria, Pakistan, Panama, Peru, Philippines, Senegal, Sri Lanka, Turkey, Uganda, Venezuela, Zambia and Zimbabwe.

12 The Communiqué was co-sponsored, among others, by the following members: Barbados, Botswana, Cuba, Dominican Republic, Honduras, Indonesia, Jamaica, Kenya, Mauritius, Mongolia, Nicaragua, Nigeria, Pakistan, Panama, Peru, the Philippines, Tanzania, Trinidad & Tobago, Turkey, Uganda, Venezuela, Zambia and Zimbabwe. Accounts from a few sources which were involved in the event said that the number of countries that supported the communiqué reached 33.

13 The 42 members were: Antigua & Barbuda, Barbados, Belize, Benin, Botswana, Cuba, China, Democratic Republic of the Congo, Cote d'Ivoire, Dominican Republic, Grenada, Guyana, Haiti, Honduras, India, Indonesia, Jamaica, Kenya, Korea, Mauritius,

Madagascar, Mongolia, Mozambique, Nicaragua, Nigeria, Pakistan, Panama, Peru, the Philippines, Senegal, Saint Kitts & Nevis, Saint Lucia, Saint Vincent & the Grenadines, Sri Lanka, Suriname, Tanzania, Trinidad & Tobago, Turkey, Uganda, Venezuela, Zambia and Zimbabwe.

14 The Doha Declaration was adopted at the 4th Session of WTO Ministerial Conference in 2001. It contains parameters and principles that guide the way the DDA shall be conducted.

15 Annex 2 of the AoA provides the basis for WTO Members to exempt from disciplines of restriction or reduction the amount of domestic support given to their agricultural industry.

16 WTO Document G/AG/NG/W/14 dated June 23, 2000 submitted by Cuba, the Dominican Republic, Honduras, Pakistan, Haiti, Nicaragua, Kenya, Uganda, Zimbabwe, Sri Lanka, and El Salvador.

17 G-33 reference on this issue can be inferred from WTO Document TN/AG/GEN/30 dated January 28, 2010.

18 WTO Document G/AG/NG/W/54 dated November 10, 2000.

19 Paper by Cuba, the Dominican Republic, El Salvador, Honduras, Indonesia, Kenya, Nicaragua, Nigeria, Pakistan, Philippines, Sri Lanka, Tanzania, Venezuela and Zimbabwe: Special & Differential Treatment in Agriculture "Establishing the Objectives", COA-SS May 21-23, 2001.

20 WT/MIN (03)/14.

21 G-33 reference on this issue can be inferred from WTO Document TN/AG/GEN/30 dated January 28, 2010.

22 Doha Declaration, 2001.

23 Multifunctionality in agriculture (often simply multifunctionality) refers to the numerous benefits that agricultural policies may provide for a country or region. Generally speaking, multifunctionality refers to the non-trade benefits of agriculture, that is, benefits other than commerce and food production.

24 The developing countries that co-sponsor this Note are Barbados, Burundi, Dominica, Fiji, Korea, Madagascar, Mauritania, Mongolia, Saint Lucia, and Trinidad and Tobago.

25 WTO Document G/AG/NG/W/36/Rev.1 dated November 09, 2000.

26 EC Comprehensive Negotiating Proposal G/AG/NG/W/90 of December 14, 2000.

27 The G-20 is a grouping of developing countries in WTO agriculture negotiations – consisting 23 WTO member states – which was established in the wake of 2003 Cancun Ministerial Conference. The formation of the G-20, led by Brazil, was in response to the US-EC "Joint Paper" which the Group considered would be detrimental to the interests of the developing countries. A number of the G-33 members are also members of the G-20, such as China, India, Indonesia, Guatemala, Peru, Philippines, Bolivia and Venezuela.

28 WTO Document G/AG/NG/W/38 dated September 27, 2000, submitted by Argentina, Brazil, Paraguay and Uruguay (Mercosur), Chile, Bolivia and Costa Rica.

29 "Green Box" is agriculture-related subsidies that are not restricted by the WTO agreement because they are not considered trade distorting. To qualify for the green box, a subsidy must not distort trade, or at most cause minimal distortion. Some countries are still critical

of the Green Box as it stands, arguing that it does distort trade by encouraging more production and lowering world prices.

30 Development Box is a proposal in the WTO agriculture negotiations that relates to a possible set of measures that would help agriculture in developing countries and give additional flexibility for their needs.

31 WTO Document G/AG/NG/W/14 dated June, 23, 2000 submitted by Cuba, the Dominican Republic, Honduras, Pakistan, Haiti, Nicaragua, Kenya, Uganda, Zimbabwe, Sri Lanka, and El Salvador.

32 WT/MIN (03)/14.

33 WT/L/613, dated June 22, 2005

34 A modalities document is a techno-political document containing detailed principles that WTO member countries have to agree during the course of COA-SS negotiations. Once agreed, this modalities document will define how the result of negotiations is translated into WTO legal documents (the "new" AoA) and Members' Schedules of Tariff Concessions.

35 WT/L/613, dated June 22, 2005.

36 July 2004 Framework is a package of agreements concluded by the WTO's 147 member governments that sets out an outline (or "framework") to be used as a staging point on the road to complete the "Modalities" of the DDA negotiations, including on agriculture. The Framework document includes Annex A entitled the "Framework for Establishing Modalities in Agriculture."

37 A submission of the SP and SSM Alliance to the COA-SS in Document JOB (03)/59 dated March, 20, 2003 provides more elaborated reasoning to back up this self-selection demand.

38 WT/L/613, dated June 22, 2005

39 WT/L/613, dated June, 22, 2005

40 *De minimis* is a WTO provision which allow member countries to maintain certain level of subsidy due its minimal or negligible amounts

41 Apart from the first two meetings, the G-33 Ministers have met again in Jakarta, March, 20-21, 2007 (see WTO Document WT/L/682), in New Delhi in September 2009, and in Geneva in November 2009.

42 WT/L/613 dated June 22, 2005.

43 G-20 Ministerial Communiqué, Sao Paolo, June, 12, 2004, and Press Statement of G-20 Ministers Present in Dalian, July 12, 2005.

44 Bhurban G-20 Ministerial Declaration, September 09-10, 2005.

45 G-20 Ministerial Press Statement, Geneva, June 29, 2006.

46 WTO Document TN/AG/GEN/30, dated January 28, 2010.

47 See Report by the COA-SS Chairman, Stuart Harbinson, to the WTO Trade Negotiations Committee, June 25, 2003

48 TN/AG/W/1 of February 17, 2003 and then replaced by TN/AG/W/1/Rev.1 of March, 18, 2003. On SP, paragraph 11 of the Draft – Rev.1 – said that "Developing countries shall have the flexibility to declare up to [ ] agricultural product at the [6-digit] HS level as being special products with respect to food security, rural development and/or livelihood

security concerns." With regard to the SSM, paragraph 26 of the Draft explained that "An outline of a possible new special safeguard mechanism to enable developing countries to effectively take account of their development needs, including food security, rural development and livelihood security concerns, is currently subject to technical work."

49 WT/MIN (03)/14.

50 Among the most important G-33 negotiating proposals are: JOB(05)/91, JOB(05)/92, JOB(05)/263, JOB(05)/304, JOB(06)/64, JOB(06)/143, JOB(06)/91 JOB(06)/173, JOB(06)/189, JOB(07)/35, JOB(08)/47.

51 The first draft was introduced by Chairman Crawford Falconner on August 01, 2007 (TN/AG/W/4).

52 WT/MIN(05)/DEC dated December 22, 2005.

53 WTO Document G/AG/NG/W/7 dated April 04, 2000.

54 WTO Document G/AG/NG/W/15 dated June 23, 2000.

55 WTO Document G/AG/NG/W/24 dated July 11, 2000.

56 WTO Document G/AG/NG/W/1 dated April 04, 2000.

57 Statement by Thailand, WTO Document G/AG/NG/W/31 dated July 11, 2000.

58 The G-33 released "technical documents" (JOB/AG/3, JOB/AG/4, JOB/AG/5/Rev.1 and JOB/AG/7) in the first quarter of 2010 that reject such concepts as seasonality, pro-rating and cross-check that would otherwise constrains the goal to establish "a simple and easy to operate SSM."

59 JOB/AG/13 dated September 15, 2010

60 WTO Document TN/AG/GEN/30, JOB/AG/3; JOB/AG/4; JOB/AG/5/Rev.1; JOB/AG/6; and JOB/AG/7.

61 Based on statements of G-33 members during COA-SS consultations of 2010.

13 NAMA 11 on Industrial Goods – Theory and Practice of Successful Coalitions

Faizel Ismail
Ambassador of South Africa to the WTO

Introduction

The NAMA 11 group of developing countries was formed at the 6th WTO Ministerial Conference, held in Hong Kong, China, from December, 13-18, 2005.[1] In the period since then, NAMA 11 has become a significant group in the Doha Round negotiations on industrial tariffs, playing a role similar to that played by the G-20 in the Doha Round agriculture negotiations. Other developing country groups, including the G-33 group of developing countries;[2] the LDCs; the SVEs; the ACP; and the Africa Group, have also played an increasingly assertive role in the WTO Doha Round.[3] Coalitions hence provide a rational response to the problem of unequal bargaining power in the WTO.

In a recent contribution to the theory of bargaining coalitions in the WTO, Amrita Narlikar[4] distinguishes between two types of coalitions in the WTO, namely issue-based alliances (formed around concerns about a particular issue) and bloc-type coalitions (based on shared ideas on multiple concerns). She considers two possible hypotheses for the creation of coalitions: the "defection hypothesis" and the "collective gains hypothesis." Under the defection hypothesis, the rationale for coalition formation is based on narrow individual interests where countries join a coalition to first establish their power and then to be bought off by the outside party in the form of side payments ("the prisoners dilemma"). In this scenario, each member of the coalition is fearful of being isolated in the end game where it could be the only member left adhering to the collective position after the collapse of the coalition – thus generating the "sucker's payoff".

Narlikar asserts three arguments against the "defection hypothesis" as an explanation for the primary logic of coalition formation. She argues that: countries will not cooperate if they all are aware that each is driven by this logic; the outside party too will not take the coalition seriously; and repeated defections by members will in any event result in a lack of credibility for the coalition. Instead, she argues that a more convincing rationale for coalition formation is captured by the concept of the "stag hunt," where parties recognise that their collective interests are more likely to be achieved if they cooperate.

Narlikar provides at least three recommendations to strengthen developing country coalitions and to reduce the temptation of members to defect (for example, to enter into a self-interested side agreement): a) effective agenda setting that addresses the concerns of all the members; b) larger members making side-payments to smaller members, such as via increased market access; and c) the building of a large coalition with large and smaller members that increases the reliability of such a coalition achieving its goals and providing reassurance to its own members. Narlikar also suggests that a negotiating posture that displays a willingness to negotiate - rather than a negotiating posture of simply standing firm, ("strict distributive strategy") - is more likely to generate concessions from the other side and prevent defections and collapse of the coalition.[5] Set against this theoretical understanding of bargaining coalitions, this chapter will explore the evolution of the NAMA 11 developing country group and evaluate its role in the WTO's Doha Round of negotiations.

The paper will argue that the NAMA 11 displayed the characteristics of a successful coalition. First, it consulted its members at each stage of the process and took account of the interests of all its members in formulating proposals and responding to the various chair's texts. Second, the NAMA 11 was able to formulate a negotiating position that addressed the specific situations of each of its members with the larger members supporting the interests and concerns of the smaller members. Third, the NAMA 11 succeeded in building a broad-based alliance of developing countries that enabled it to maintain the unity of the group and advance the interests of the group within the WTO. In addition, by drafting detailed proposals on each of the issues and responding to the chair's draft texts, the NAMA 11 displayed a willingness to engage and negotiate at every stage of the process.

The chapter proceeds in ten steps. The next section will set out the background of the Doha Round's NAMA negotiations and evaluate the evolution of the NAMA text through to the July 2004 Framework Agreement (Annex B). Section 3 will evaluate the development of the NAMA text and the outcome on NAMA negotiations at the Hong Kong Ministerial Conference in 2005, with reference to the birth and role of the NAMA 11 group of developing countries. Section 4 will evaluate the role of the NAMA 11 during the process leading up to and including the suspension of the Doha Round in July 2006. Section 5 will discuss the collapse of the G-4 Potsdam Ministerial meeting and the chair's first draft NAMA text in 2007.

Sections 6, 7 and 8 then evaluate the various revisions to the NAMA modalities text and discuss the role and response of the NAMA 11 to the continued imbalances in these texts. Section 9 evaluates the July 2008 "Lamy Package," particularly its NAMA provisions. Section 10 evaluates the role of NAMA 11 in the context of the hypothesis advanced by Narlikar (above) on the rationale for bargaining coalitions. Finally, in the concluding section we discuss some attempts made in 2009 and 2010 to conclude the Doha Round.

The July 2004 Framework Agreement (Annex B)

In the area of industrial products or NAMA the Doha mandate agreed to "reduce or as appropriate eliminate tariff [...] in particular of export interest to developing countries." The WTO Doha mandate set the deadline for modalities for NAMA at the end of May 2003, after the modalities on agriculture that was to be the end of March 2003. Thus the chair of the NAMA negotiating group prior to Cancun, Ambassador Girard, began work on developing these modalities. A number of countries put forward proposals for tariff-cutting formulae. The chair modified these proposals and advanced his own compromised formula and proposal – "Elements of Modalities for Negotiations on Non-Agricultural Products,"[6] – known as the Girard Proposal.

The Girard Proposal contained a number of elements, including a formula for tariff reductions, a sectoral approach, S&D treatment provisions, recognition of the particular situation of newly acceded countries, a supplementary approach that included zero-for-zero sector elimination, sectoral harmonisation and request and offer approaches, negotiations to reduce non-tariff barriers, and the provision of technical assistance to developing countries during the negotiations.

Despite being roundly criticised by both developed and developing countries, the Girard formula succeeded in providing a basis for the negotiations on modalities for NAMA. The failure to reach agreement on agricultural modalities at the end of May 2003 and the EU-US Joint Text on agriculture on August, 13, 2003 forced the WTO to lower its target from full "modalities" and instead to produce a "Framework Agreement" for the Cancun Ministerial Meeting.

Annex B of the Cancun Text, "Framework for Establishing Modalities in Market Access for Non-Agricultural Products,"[7] was criticised by developing countries for being biased in favour of developed countries. They argued further that it did not adhere to the principle of "less than full reciprocity" stipulated by the Doha mandate. In particular the Cancun Ministerial Text was criticised by developing countries for calling for a "non-linear formula"[8] and mandatory sectoral tariff reductions.[9] The Text was not adopted owing to these criticisms and this created the collapse of the Cancun Conference.

In the period up to the July 2004 Ministerial Meeting, some of the major delegations began to display flexibility in their approach to the NAMA framework. The USTR, Robert Zoellick, in his conciliatory letter to WTO ministers in January 2004, called for both ambition and flexibility. However, in the negotiations in the months before the July 2004 General Council meeting, developed countries[10] began to insist that the Cancun text – or the Derbez text as it is referred to – should not be changed at all in spite of the criticisms and objections of developing countries.

At this stage the only possibility that remained for developing countries was to ensure that the Derbez text remained open to negotiation and that the views and perspectives of developing countries could be included in the post-July negotiations for the development of modalities. Thus, Annex B of the July 2004 Package on NAMA called for additional negotiations on the elements of the Derbez text. These issues included the treatment of unbound tariffs, flexibilities for developing countries, participation in sectoral negotiations, and the issue of preference erosion.[11]

An Evaluation of the July 2004 Framework Agreement NAMA text (Annex B)

Developing countries succeeded in ensuring that the Derbez text, which was perceived to be biased in favour of developed countries, was not imposed on them. The July 2004 Framework Agreement on NAMA made it possible for the elements of the Derbez text to be further negotiated and allowed for the possibility that the outcome of the negotiations on modalities would be more balanced and take into account the interests of developing countries. The debate on the substance of the "Framework Agreement" was postponed. Developing countries were fragmented at the time of the July Framework Agreement on the approach to the formula for tariff cuts. However, they did succeed in ensuring that the opportunity to further negotiate the modalities was not foreclosed.

The Hong Kong Ministerial Conference and the Formation of the NAMA 11

In the period leading up to the Hong Kong Ministerial Conference, a group of developing countries began to work closely together on NAMA and produced a critique of the EU and other developed countries' emerging approach to the Doha Round negotiations.[12] In a paper submitted to the WTO Committee on Trade and Development this group of countries argued that developing countries "cannot be expected to pay for the much-needed reforms in the agriculture sectors of developed countries (referred to above), by overly ambitious requests of them in industrial tariffs that do not take into account the realities of their levels of economic development and their adjustment needs."[13] These developing countries called for the "development content of the round to be reclaimed" and began to unite around their common concerns in the NAMA negotiations before the Hong Kong Ministerial Meeting. The aggressive approach taken by the EU to the formula for developing countries in NAMA in its submission of October, 28, 2005 led these countries to unite on the need to defend the flexibilities that developing countries had succeeded in obtaining in the July 2004 Framework Agreement.[14]

This united front was further consolidated in Hong Kong, where Ministers of the so-called NAMA 11 presented joint proposals in the negotiations on NAMA.[15] Due to their increased bargaining power in the WTO, the NAMA 11 was able to achieve three important victories. First, the coalition successfully resisted the attempts by developed countries to force a premature agreement on modalities in NAMA ahead of any significant agreement on the main issues in agriculture. Second, these developing countries were able to confirm that the principle of less than full reciprocity would be adhered to when making reduction commitments and appropriate flexibilities would be provided to them in order to preserve their domestic policy space. Third, the group was also able to establish a strong link in the final text of the Hong Kong Ministerial Declaration between the level of ambition in NAMA and the level of ambition in agriculture.[16]

While there were no significant gains made in Hong Kong on NAMA, the formation of the NAMA 11 (representing the more advanced developing countries that were required to make formula cuts), ensured that the developing countries were able to defend themselves from undertaking more onerous obligations in NAMA. Most important, the NAMA 11 was to become an important platform to build stronger links with other developing countries in the WTO and to build alliances between the larger and smaller developing country groupings in the WTO. In Hong Kong Ministers from the NAMA 11 joined with the G-20 in building a common platform with the G-33 and the G-90 group of developing countries that sought to unite the developing countries and build solidarity on issues of concern to each of these groups, forming the G-110.

Even at this early stage of the formation of the NAMA 11, the group ensured that it was able to: a) consult intensively with its members and formulate joint positions to the WTO Green Room in Hong Kong; b) address the specific concerns of its members with the larger members, such as India and China, supporting the specific needs for additional flexibility called for by South Africa, Argentina, and Venezuela; and c) by building solidarity with a larger group of members in the G-110, the NAMA 11 was able to gain the support of the majority of developing countries for its negotiating positions.

The Suspension of the Doha Round in July 2006

This section will briefly set out the process of the negotiations up to the end of July 2006, when the Doha Round negotiations were suspended.

Ministers in Hong Kong had agreed that the deadline for modalities on agriculture and NAMA should be April, 30, 2006. Ministers of Trade, who met on the margins of the Davos World Economic Forum on January, 28, 2006, went further and proposed a deadline for the conclusion of the Round at the end of 2006.[17] The period before April 2006 was dominated by the meetings of the G-6 (US, EU, Japan, India, Brazil and Australia) culminating in a Ministerial meeting of the G-6 in London on March, 10-11, 2006. The meeting focussed on all the main issues of the DDA, including agriculture, NAMA, services, rules and development issues.

The US and the EU were reported to have questioned the need for the paragraph 8 flexibilities[18] already provided for developing countries in the July 2004 Framework Agreement. In the discussion on NAMA, the EU, the US, Japan and Australia argued that they required "real and effective market access" in NAMA, and this would mean that they would evaluate the cuts from any formula on the applied rates of developing countries, such as Brazil and India. However, both the EU and the US proposals on cuts in their domestic support to agriculture were not going to make real or effective cuts in their subsidy levels.

In the WTO, Pascal Lamy called off the proposed Ministerial meeting at the end of April as there was insufficient progress in the negotiations. He called for the negotiations to be text-based, with an intensive bottom-up process, to continue in Geneva, and to be coordinated by the chairs of the agriculture and NAMA negotiating groups. The NAMA chair presented his text on June 26, 2006.[19] The G-6 met on several occasions at the ministerial level at the end of June in Geneva and focussed on the three sides of the "Lamy triangle" – agricultural market access, agricultural domestic support, and NAMA.

On the NAMA side of the 'triangle,' Ministers Celso Amorim of Brazil and Kamal Nath of India reported to the NAMA 11 Ministerial Meeting held on June, 29, 2006 that in the G-6 Ministerial meeting the EU, the US, Japan and Australia insisted that the NAMA 11 countries undertake tariff cuts, adopting a simple Swiss formula with a coefficient of 15. Ministers Amorim and Nath rejected this proposal as it was unreasonable, too onerous, and against the Doha mandate.[20] The extent to which tariffs get reduced under the formula depends on the coefficient used. For a given tariff rate (say 10 percent) the formula results in a lower final reduced tariff rate if higher coefficient is used. Conversely, if lower coefficient is used, the resulting reduced rate would be relatively higher (see glossary for the formula). The NAMA 11 Ministerial Meeting adopted a communiqué[21] that called for the use of higher coefficient by developing countries and suggested that there should be a difference of 25 between the coefficients used by developing and developed countries. It emphasised that its approach was based on the two main principles:[22] less than full reciprocity, and the need for a comparable level of ambition in agriculture and NAMA negotiations as agreed in paragraph 24 of the Hong Kong Ministerial Declaration.

Again, the G-6 Ministerial Meeting, chaired by Lamy, held on July 23-24, 2006 in Geneva, failed to make progress on the substance of the negotiations. Lamy convened an urgent Trade Negotiating Committee (TNC) meeting on July 24, 2006 to report back to the membership. Lamy stated that the only course at that point was to suspend the negotiations across the Round, providing everybody time out to review positions. The deadlines for the other issues in the Round would now need to be revised.

Evaluation of the Suspension of the Doha Round

The EU and the US remained united, calling upon the larger developing countries to open their markets in NAMA. The then EU Trade Commissioner, Peter Mandelson, called for the outcome of the negotiations to produce "effective cuts and real trade flows." In NAMA, he stated that the EU required "real cuts that cut through the water and cut flesh." He stated that this could be done with a Swiss 15 formula for developing countries. The USTR supported this view.

Although Brazil and India did not formally represent the NAMA 11, they defended and argued the positions of the G-20 and NAMA 11 in the G-6 and reported back repeatedly to the G-20 and the NAMA 11 Ambassadors and Ministers. The strength of their negotiating position was based on the strong technical back-up and united position of these groups. In the period leading up to the suspension of the negotiations, they were able to effectively defend and advance the interests of the NAMA 11 and other developing country groups.

Thus, the NAMA 11 maintained a posture of engagement and a willingness to negotiate. At this stage of the negotiations, the NAMA 11 was also to meet the three criteria set by Narlikar above for successful coalitions. First, the NAMA 11 met regularly with Brazil and India at a technical level and at ambassadorial levels, formulating its approach to the negotiations that was to inform the positions taken by Brazil and India in their engagements with the G-6. Second, Brazil and India were to also express the specific concerns of NAMA 11 members, such as that of Argentina, South Africa, and Venezuela that required additional flexibilities. Third, the NAMA 11 held several meetings with other developing country groups, such as the LDCs, SVEs, Africa Group and the ACP to report back on the G-6 meetings and to build and maintain solidarity on issues of concern to these groups.

The NAMA Chair's First Draft Text – July, 17, 2007

In March 2007, a process of bilateral discussions between the G-4 and the G-6 began at senior official and ministerial levels, culminating in a final negotiating meeting on modalities in Potsdam, Germany. The G-4 Ministerial Meeting in Potsdam from June, 19-23, 2007 collapsed on the third day of the scheduled four-to-five-day meeting. Amorim explained that after the first day's discussions, it became clear that the EU and the US could not move significantly from their October 2005 proposals. According to Amorim, the EU and the US did not confront each other on either the reductions needed in domestic support or tariff cuts on market access in agriculture, but instead were eager to shift the discussion to NAMA and to jointly confront Brazil and India.

Both the EU and the US demanded a Swiss 18 formula cut for developing countries. Brazil and India argued that with the numbers that the EU and the US were offering on agriculture they were not willing to accept a formula cut greater than Swiss 30. The day after the collapse of the Potsdam meeting, Lamy called on the chairs to continue with the drafting process. The chairs began to draft after consultations with members and produced draft texts on agriculture[23] and NAMA[24] on July 17, 2007.

The NAMA 11 Response to the First Draft NAMA Text

The NAMA text provided a range in the coefficients of 19 to 23 for developing countries and 8 to 9 for developed countries. As the average rates of tariffs of developing countries are high compared with those of developed countries, even with the use of these higher coefficients, the formula would result in a reduction of between 57 and 62 percent in their bound rates of tariffs. At the same time, the percentage average reductions in tariffs that the developed countries would be making would be between 31 and 33 percent. On the flexibilities for developing countries the text opened the brackets of paragraph 8. For countries that did not want to use paragraph 8 flexibilities, such as Mexico, the text included a flexibility that provided for a reduced percentage cut (of b plus 3).

The NAMA 11 made statements both in the NGMA (NAMA negotiating group)[25] and the TNC[26] that criticised the chair's draft text for being imbalanced in prescribing a level of ambition for developing countries that was disproportionate to that provided for developed countries and for jumping ahead of the agriculture negotiations by proposing narrow ranges (Swiss coefficients of 19 to 23 for developing countries), while the agriculture text provided relatively wide room for further negotiations. The statements of the NAMA 11 both in the NGMA and the TNC discredited the chair's text for its many biases and for prejudicing the outcome of the negotiations for developing countries.

As a result of this pressure and in an attempt to prevent the imbalanced chair's text from being imposed on developing countries, the NAMA 11 submitted a "members' text" (on October 09, 2007 at the WTO General Council Meeting) that included the elements and principles that should guide a NAMA text. In response to this, the US stated that "the proposal could signal the end of the Doha Round," and the EU stated that "alternative texts (to the current chairs' text) are not needed."[27]

Reactions of Other Developing Country Groups

The African Group, the ACP, and the SVEs were critical of the NAMA text, since the text also increased pressure on them. For the paragraph 6 countries (those that had low binding levels in the Uruguay Round) the text had increased the binding level to 90 percent from their preferred 70 percent. The text also required the SVEs to bind their tariffs at 14, 18 or 22 percent, increasing the burden of reduction that they envisaged.

The NAMA 11 made a joint statement together with the Africa Group, the ACP and the LDC group (the G-90) on the chair's first draft NAMA text at the TNC on July, 26, 2007.[28] The joint statement called for "the substantial imbalances" in the chair's text to be addressed. These imbalances were stated to include the attempt to "presuppose the outcome in NAMA while the negotiating positions of developed countries were still preserved in agriculture"; "making developing countries pay first in NAMA and pay more than developed countries in agriculture"; "turning the principle of less than full reciprocity on its head" by requiring developing countries to make greater commitments than developed members; and "undermining the agreement reached in Hong Kong to ensure that the level of ambition in NAMA was comparable to agriculture."

Assessment of the First Draft Text

The chair's first NAMA text appeared to largely reflect and accommodate the views and interests of the EU and the US, leading to great dissatisfaction among developing countries. Moreover, the text appeared to increase the pressure on developing countries to open their markets further than developed countries were willing to open their markets in agriculture. The sustained pressure on developing countries by the EU and the US to accept the NAMA chair's efforts to continuously raise the level of ambition was immense. However, developing countries continued to resist this pressure through their coalitions. Thus, at each stage of the process one NAMA chair produced imbalanced texts against the interests of the majority of developing countries. The agriculture chair on the other hand included the views of the majority of WTO Members, developed and developing countries, in a "bottom-up" process.

The EU and the US built a high level of coordination that enabled them to maintain a united front in pressurising the major developing countries to raise the level of ambition in market access in the Doha Round's NAMA, services, and environment negotiations.[29]

On agriculture, the EU and the US appeared to maintain the basic compromise they reached in Cancun,[30] in the EU/US Joint Text to accommodate each other's concerns in agriculture. So the EU did not apply significant pressure on the US to reduce its trade distorting support, and the US did not apply much pressure on the EU to open its markets further. Thus, the major developing countries became the joint target of the EU and the US to satisfy their market access needs.

This joint effort of the EU and the US produced enormous pressure on developing countries to accept the NAMA text. However, developing countries built strong alliances to resist this pressure and assert their own demands and interests. The Joint Statement of the NAMA 11 and the G-90 at the end of July 2007 TNC meeting was unexpected by the developed countries. The united front presented by the G-90 and NAMA 11 in their joint statement on the chair's draft text was a great achievement for the NAMA 11 and developing countries in the WTO.[31] It was a testimony to the progress made in forging deeper alliances between developing countries, notwithstanding their different levels of development and interests in the WTO. This was achieved against the very strong pressure emanating from the EU and the US to prevent such unity and strong criticism of the NAMA draft text.

Again at this stage of the negotiating process the NAMA 11 adopted a posture of willingness to negotiate and satisfied the three criteria of successful coalitions set by Narlikar above. First, the NAMA 11 worked intensively at both technical and ambassadorial levels to assess and evaluate the chair's first draft text and to formulate its responses. Second, the NAMA 11 addressed the specific situations of its Members, such as Argentina, South Africa, and Venezuela in its proposals made to the chair, and Brazil and India supported these concerns in the negotiating group. Third, the NAMA 11 was able to build a formidable alliance of developing countries to strengthen its negotiating position and build confidence among its members.

The NAMA Chair's First Revised Draft Text – February 08, 2008

The First Revised texts on agriculture (TN/AG/W/4/Rev.1) and NAMA were tabled on February, 08, 2008.

The NAMA 11 Response to the Chair's First Revised Draft Text

For the NAMA 11 there were two critical issues: the formula and the flexibilities. The range in the formula (19-23) that the chair had inserted in his first draft text remained the same. In his first draft text, the chair had removed the brackets from the paragraph 8 flexibilities (permitting exclusion of tariff lines from formula cuts, or making on them less than formula cut or keeping them unbound) that were provided in the July 2004 Framework Agreement on NAMA. In his first revised text he decided to reintroduce the brackets, but remove the numbers altogether, for the percentage of tariffs that should take less than formula cuts and for the volume of trade. In a press conference subsequent to the release of the first revised text, the NAMA chair stated that he dropped the numbers in paragraph 8 owing to pressure from members and that a new paragraph 8 proposal would be negotiated. He cited the proposal of some members for a sliding scale under which developing countries seeking more flexibilities could have either a lower coefficient or conversely limited flexibilities with a higher coefficient.[32]

The NAMA 11 criticised the chair's first revised text for once again ignoring the proposals of the NAMA 11 on both the range of coefficients and the flexibilities.[33] The NAMA 11 group of developing countries pointed out that the chair in his first draft text acknowledged that the range of coefficients was his own view. In the second draft text, however, he still insisted on retaining his range. The NAMA 11 argued that its views must be incorporated in the chair's modalities text so that ministers could determine whether they met the mandates of less than full reciprocity and paragraph 24 of the Hong Kong Ministerial Declaration.[34]

Reactions of Other Developing Country Groups

The ACP reacted to the NAMA text in the NGMA by stating that although most ACP states would not be applying the formula, "the impact of the formula will be felt by all ACP states." In this regard, the statement also raised their concerns about the possible adverse impact of sectoral negotiations on the further erosion of preferences.[35]

Assessment of the First Revised Draft Text

The major developing countries began to complain of two significant imbalances between the agriculture and NAMA texts. The first related to the substantive difference in the level of ambition, and the second related to the differences in the approach of the chairs to the drafting process. Brazil's senior official, Roberto Azevedo, made a statement that compared the difference in the level of ambition between agriculture and NAMA. He argued that developed countries were calling for a large amount of policy space in agriculture and refusing to consider the same in NAMA for developing countries. He called for a balance between ambition and feasibility.[36]

The NAMA 11 continued to display a posture of willingness to negotiate and to reflect the three factors for successful coalitions suggested by Narlikar. First, the NAMA 11 coordinated its efforts by formulating joint talking points to guide their members', responses to the first revised draft texts. Second, the group maintained its solidarity with those members that required additional flexibilities, such as Argentina, South Africa, and Venezuela. Third, the group continued to build and maintain its coordination with other developing country groups, such as the ACP, the Africa Group and the LDCs.

The Second Revised Text – May 22, 2008

The second revised texts on agriculture and NAMA were published in May 2008.

The NAMA 11 Response to the Second Revised NAMA Text

The NAMA chair's second revised text retained essentially the same set of coefficients (i.e., 7-9) for developed countries (the previous text had 8-9), and for developing countries (a range of 21-23). However, the text introduced a "sliding scale" concept for developing countries. This provided a "trade off" for developing countries which could now choose between enhanced tariff reductions and more flexibilities to deviate from the full formula cuts, or less onerous tariff reductions with less flexibilities.

In its statement to the NGMA on May 27, 2008, the NAMA 11 recognised the positive aspects of the second revised text that attempted "to create an architecture that responds to the various proposals of developing countries." However, the statement criticised the chair's text for having chosen to once again "maintain a narrow range of coefficients for developing countries that predetermines the level of ambition in NAMA and ignores the positions of the NAMA 11 on the issue of the range."[37]

The NAMA 11 statement also criticised the chair's second revised text for introducing the proposed anti-concentration clause demanded by the EU and the US, while these proposals (contained in paragraph 7f) did not enjoy the support of the majority of developing countries. Similarly, the NAMA 11 stated that the "bracketed paragraph in 7i of the chair's text attempted to draw a link between the formula and the sectorals" while the chair's text later stated that "participation in sectoral initiatives is on a non-mandatory basis."

Reactions of Other Developing Country Groups

The Africa Group in its statement to the NGMA reflected its concern that the NAMA chair's revised text had more brackets than the previous one. The statement raised a number of concerns, including on the ranges of coefficients for developing countries, the binding coverage for paragraph 6 countries, the attempts to link sectorals with the formula, and the need for more adequate treatment of preference erosion.[38]

Assessment of the Second Revised Text

At this stage of the process, both the EU and the US continued to demand increased market access to the major developing countries. They called for an anti-concentration clause that would limit the flexibilities that were provided to developing countries, and they demanded that the major developing countries participate in negotiations on sectors of interest to them. Although the major developing country groups continued to resist the pressure to accept onerous cuts in their tariffs as demanded by the EU and the US, the chair of NAMA continued to bias the texts in favour of the developed countries.

The NAMA chair continued to raise the level of ambition in the NAMA text in the direction of the EU and the US. While he made some improvements to accommodate the need for additional flexibility for developing countries in the text, he included the need for the anti-concentration clause that would limit this flexibility, notwithstanding the general opposition by developing countries to this clause. Similarly, he drew a link between the sectorals and the formula as demanded by the EU and the US, even though there was no support for this among developing countries.

At the OECD meeting in Paris on the DDA, held on June 05, 2008, the USTR, Susan Schwab, and the EU Commissioner, Peter Mandelson, called for an "anti-concentration clause" to further restrict developing country flexibilities and a "top-up" in sectoral negotiations.[39] This demand was resisted by a number of developing country ministers that were present at the Paris Ministerial meeting, including Celso Amorim, the Foreign Trade Minister of Brazil, and Kamal Nath, the Commerce Minister of India.

Again, the NAMA 11 retained a posture of a willingness to negotiate and displayed the characteristics of a successful coalition proposed by Narlikar. First, the NAMA 11 worked intensively at technical and ambassadorial levels to evaluate and respond to the chair's text. Second, the NAMA 11 continued to articulate its support for the specific situations of Argentina, South Africa, and Venezuela. Third, the NAMA 11 maintained its solidarity and coordination with the Africa Group, ACP, and LDC groups.

The Third Revised Text – July 10, 2008

The chairs of agriculture and NAMA released their third revised texts on July 10, 2008.

The NAMA 11 Response to the Chair's Third Revised Text

The NAMA 11 made a statement on July 11, 2008 to the NAMA negotiating group in which it observed some progress in the attempts of the chair to capture the complexity of the issues in the NAMA modalities architecture. However, the NAMA 11 criticised this third revision for "once again" maintaining "a narrow range of coefficients for developing countries that predetermines the level of ambition in NAMA and ignores the stated positions of the NAMA 11 on the issue of the range." The NAMA 11 also "rejected any attempt to further constrain the already limited flexibilities provided in the modalities text," with reference to the so-called anti-concentration clause proposed by the EU and the US. The NAMA 11 statement stressed the need for the modalities in NAMA to adhere to the mandate of less than full reciprocity and Paragraph 24 of the Hong Kong Ministerial Declaration, which called for comparability in the level of ambition between agriculture and NAMA.

Assessment of the Third Draft Text

Ministers of the G-20 and the NAMA 11 that met in Geneva in preparation for the Ministerial meetings at the end of July 2008 were confronted with a set of highly imbalanced texts. On the one hand, the agriculture text provided significant flexibilities for developed and developing country members to address their sensitivities and development concerns. On the other hand, the NAMA text increased the ambition for developing countries and provided a narrow range of flexibilities to protect developing country development concerns that were further constrained by the anti-concentration clause.[40]

Thus, the NAMA 11 continued to reflect a willingness to negotiate. The NAMA 11 at this stage reflected the three factors for successful coalitions proposed by Narlikar and maintained a coordinated approach by consulting its members. It maintained the support for the specific situation of some of its members, such as Argentina, South Africa, and Venezuela. Finally, it continued to build its solidarity with other developing country groups.

The WTO July 2008 Ministerial Meetings and the "Lamy Package"

A large number of WTO Ministers were invited by Pascal Lamy to join the negotiation at the ministerial level at the end of July 2008 in Geneva. After two days of opening statements in the WTO TNC and Green Room, Pascal Lamy constituted the G-7 ministerial meetings (US, EU, Japan, Australia, China, India and Brazil), which was to dominate the negotiations until their collapse on July 29, 2008. During the course of the G-7 ministerial meetings Pascal Lamy produced a so-called "Lamy Package" that proposed coefficients in the middle of the NAMA chairs ranges on NAMA.[41]

Brazil and India were part of the G-7, but were unable to consult with the NAMA 11 on the deal making within the G-7. The proximate cause of the collapse of the July ministerial meetings was the failure of G-7 Ministers to agree on a special safeguard mechanism for developing countries. However, there are three underlying causes for the collapse of the July Ministerial meetings.

First, the chair of the NAMA negotiating group played a significant role in biasing the texts against developing countries and creating an imbalance between the agriculture and NAMA texts. The NAMA 11 group of developing countries that represented a significant group of emerging market economies criticised the various draft texts of the

NAMA chair that emerged in the period before the July 2008 Ministerial meeting for ignoring their views and reflecting the preferences of the chair. This position was enunciated as follows by the South African statement to the TNC on July, 22, 2008:

> Our experience in the NAMA negotiations over the last two years is that the texts that have emerged at various points have consistently ignored the positions and views we have expressed as the NAMA 11. Furthermore the statement notes that whilst the agricultural negotiations have been conducted through a carefully constructed "bottom-up" process through which the positions of all WTO Members are found in the agricultural modalities text, the NAMA modalities text is highly circumscribed and prescriptive. [42]

Second, the EU and the US consistently failed to meet the demands of the Doha mandate to substantially reduce agricultural protection in developed countries and increased the pressure on developing countries to open their markets in NAMA. Thus, South African Trade Minister, Davies was to argue that the underlying reason for the collapse of the July Ministerial meetings was due to "a more fundamental imbalance between the legitimate claims of developmental reforms to the global trading system and the frankly mercantilist commercial interests of forces benefiting from the existing unbalanced global trading system."[43]

The third reason for the collapse of the Ministerial meetings is ironically due to the "medieval process"[44] that saw the EU and the US sticking to old habits of setting up imbalanced small groups that cut the main deals, without consideration for the smaller players, and the marginalisation of their issues in the negotiations. The G-7 Ministerial meetings called by Pascal Lamy during the July 2008 Ministerial meetings failed to achieve the objective of negotiating the breakthrough in the agriculture and NAMA modalities negotiations that the Director General, Pascal Lamy, had hoped for. Some agreements reached in the G-7 on elements of the modalities – the so-called "Lamy Package" – did not have the support of all the members of the G-7,[45] and the G-7 did not enjoy the support of the majority of members that felt that their issues were marginalised in the negotiations.

While members of NAMA 11 had met before the July 2008 Ministerial meetings to formulate a coherent and united position on NAMA they were unable to meet and consult during the process of the G-7 Ministerial meetings called by Pascal Lamy. This resulted in a fragmentation of their negotiating positions. Moreover, South Africa, as the coordinator of the NAMA 11, was not invited to the G-7 Ministerial meetings. Second, the specific situations and demand for additional flexibilities of some NAMA 11 members, such as Argentina, South Africa, and Venezuela, were not discussed in the G-7 and hence the opportunity for solidarity within the NAMA 11 was lost. Third, the issues of interest to the smaller developing countries, such as DFQF treatment for LDCs and preference erosion were also not discussed in the G-7. Thus, the opportunity to maintain and strengthen the broader alliance among developing countries was also lost.

Evaluating the NAMA 11 Coalition

Reflecting on the hypothesis presented by Amrita Narlikar on the rationale for the formation of coalitions, the evaluation of the NAMA 11 in the preceding discussion provides strong evidence that the latter coalition has indeed displayed the characteristics of a "stag hunt" – where parties recognise that their collective interests are more likely to be achieved if they cooperate. The NAMA 11 has also displayed the characteristics of other successful coalitions in the WTO. The NAMA 11 has survived and succeeded through: a) a process of internal consultation and "agenda setting" to retain the support and confidence of its members; b) a willingness to recognise the particular concerns of its members (support for the cases of Argentina, South Africa, and Venezuela for country specific flexibilities); and c) providing support for the interests of SVEs and LDCs and building effective alliances with these groups.

Narlikar's hypothesis for successful coalitions has required that these coalitions display a willingness to negotiate. From its inception, at the Hong Kong Ministerial Conference, the NAMA 11 displayed a willingness to negotiate by engaging with its main interlocutors, the EU and the US, and other developed countries, providing proposals to guide the chair's texts and detailed responses to the texts of the chair. It combined this with steadfastness and an ability to stand firm on its principles and negotiating positions. Consequently, the NAMA 11 has become the main interlocutor with the EU and the US in the NAMA negotiations. The NAMA 11 has also reflected the other three factors that Narlikar has suggested for successful coalition building. These are discussed in turn.

First, the NAMA 11, coordinated by South Africa, has consistently engaged in intense consultations with its members and has taken a proactive and constructive approach to the NAMA negotiations. Since its formation at the Hong Kong Ministerial meeting, the group has presented a raft of technical proposals on each of the issues in the NAMA negotiations, after intense negotiations among its own members. These consultations have taken place at a technical level, ambassadorial level, and at various Ministerial meetings.

Second, the NAMA 11 has adopted an approach of maintaining a common stand on principles and concepts while recognising and supporting the specific concerns and situations of its members. Thus, the group, including its larger members, namely, India and Brazil, continued to support the specific needs of Argentina, South Africa, and Venezuela. Each of these countries required specific flexibilities for different reasons, and the group supported the interests of these members at each stage of the negotiations.

Third, the NAMA 11 has been consistent in addressing the concerns of the smaller developing countries and has been building effective alliances with these members. The NAMA 11 has forged relationships of mutual trust with other developing country groupings representing the LDCs, the Africa Group, the ACP, and SVEs. It has provided leadership and support to other developing country groups and taken on board its responsibility toward the poorer members, especially the LDCs and the SVEs. In Hong Kong, "developing countries in a position to do so" pledged to provide DFQF market access to all LDCs. This was a historic breakthrough. In addition, the NAMA 11 provided recognition and support for the plight of the "small, weak and vulnerable economies."

These countries, which remain an undefined category, have been urging WTO members to recognise their special situation, and that WTO rules and market access ambitions to be mindful of their different development needs and capabilities.

The NAMA 11 has recognised the concerns of these developing countries and has agreed that they should be treated differently and provided with greater flexibilities. South Africa is the coordinator of the NAMA 11. As South Africa is also a member of a customs union (SACU) it had to ensure that its positions were well coordinated with its neighbours. South Africa was also to ensure that it continued to consult and integrate the negotiating positions of the smaller economies (the Africa Group, the SVEs, and the LDCs) that shared similar concerns with its customs union partners. The NAMA 11 thus was able to maintain unity with a wide range of developing countries in the G-90 group and reduce the capacity of the developed countries to isolate the NAMA 11 (mainly larger emerging developing economies).

Some lessons can also be drawn by the NAMA 11 from the July 2008 ministerial collapse. The NAMA 11 suffered from the lack of being formally represented in the G-7 July 2008 Ministerial negotiations. South Africa is the coordinator and was not included in the G-7 negotiations and it was not consulted on the "Lamy Package." While Brazil was willing to accept the compromise language in the "Lamy Package," India had some reservations. Other members of the NAMA 11 were not consulted and were faced with a take-it-or-leave-it package. Argentina, South Africa, and Venezuela continued to negotiate for a better deal. The group will need to reflect on how to maintain its solidarity in spite of the different negotiating positions and interests of its members. An early compromise by a major member of a coalition could be perceived to be a "defection" to obtain a "side payment," thus weakening the coalition and leading to its collapse. This puts pressure on the remaining members of the coalition to ensure that they do not end up with what Narlikar refers to as a "sucker's pay-off."

Conclusion

This paper has provided a schematic overview of the formation and evolution of the NAMA 11 leading up to its formation at the Hong Kong Ministerial Conference and at each stage of the negotiating process until the July 2008 Ministerial collapse. The paper has evaluated the evolution of the NAMA 11 in terms of the factors suggested by Narlikar for successful coalition building. In the evaluation of the NAMA 11, the paper has argued that the NAMA 11 has satisfied the essential requirements proposed by Narlikar for successful coalition building, although the group still has to learn the lessons from the July 2008 collapse to prevent "defections." Finally, the paper concludes with a brief outline of the efforts that have been made in 2009 and 2010 after the collapse of the July 2008 Ministerial meetings to "re-energise" and conclude the Doha Round.

Efforts to Resume the Doha Round in 2009 and 2010

By December 2008 WTO members had failed to agree on the "Lamy Package" and the US was to reject the attempt made by the chairs of agriculture and NAMA to capture the convergences reached in July 2008. From early 2009 the new US administration went further and argued that these texts were not acceptable to its constituencies as it did not provide them with sufficient market access to the larger developing country markets.

The US called for intense bilateral meetings with the larger developing countries, such as China, India and Brazil, in an attempt to pressurise these countries to provide US exporters with increased market access in agriculture, NAMA, and services than provided for by the July and December 2008 texts.

A large number of developing countries, led by China, Brazil, India, and South Africa have opposed the attempts of the US in 2009 and 2010 to undermine the multilateral process by entering into bilateral engagements to increase market access for US exporters beyond the agreements reached in the current modalities, which are already skewed against developing countries.[46]

Developing countries have argued that the agriculture and NAMA modalities captured in the chair's draft texts (July and December 2008) are imbalanced. The level of ambition in agriculture, they argued, was reduced for developed countries and the level of ambition in NAMA has increased considerably with deep cuts to be made in developing country tariffs through the Swiss formula and a further reduction of the flexibilities granted to developing countries through the anti-concentration clause.[47] Thus, the current attempts by the US to obtain increased market access in the major developing country markets, through bilateral negotiations and sectoral negotiations, is unfair and contrary to the Doha mandate that has prioritised the exports of interest to developing countries.

Against this background, the key question for developing countries is not when, but how, the round should be concluded. The need for the US Administration to embrace the development dimensions of the round and strive to conclude it on its development mandate will be crucial. Developing countries will need to engage the new US Administration on the overall coherence of its multilateral engagement and support for development. If the US Administration is unable to withstand the pressures from its protectionist lobbies that are campaigning for greater market access in an attempt to delay and frustrate the conclusion of the round or to temper the ambitions of the major export lobbies that aim to make huge gains in market access at the expense of some of the major developing countries in the WTO, developing countries will need to strengthen their alliances, such as the NAMA 11, the G-20, G-33, the LDC group, the ACP, and the Africa Group and defend themselves from the efforts to secure an imbalanced outcome in the Doha Round.

Endnotes

1 The NAMA 11 Group of developing countries was formed in the period shortly before the Hong Kong Ministerial Conference in December 2005. Its members are: Argentina, Brazil, Egypt, India, Indonesia, South Africa, Philippines, Namibia, Tunisia and Venezuela.

2 The G-33 was formed on the eve of the 5th WTO Cancun Ministerial Conference, held in September 2003, with some 23 members representing countries with predominantly small farms, and keen to protect their rural development, livelihood and food security needs. The G-33 group had grown to about 45 members by July 2007.

3 The LDC Group, the ACP and the Africa Group have jointly become known as the G-90 Group of developing countries.

4 Narlikar, A. 2009. "A Theory of Bargaining Coalitions in the WTO", in (ed.), Narlikar, A. and Vickers, B., Leadership and Change in the Multilateral Trading System. Dordrecht: Republic of Letters Publishing/Martinus Nijhoff.

5 For a discussion of a "strict distributive strategy" see Narlikar, A., and Odell J. 2006. "The strict distributive strategy for a bargaining coalition: the Like Minded Group in the World Trade Organisation", in Odell, J. (ed.), Negotiating Trade. Developing Countries in the WTO and NAFTA, Cambridge: Cambridge University Press.

6 See WTO document TN/MA/W/35, May 16, 2003.

7 See WTO document JOB (03)/150/Rev.2.

8 See paragraph 3 of Annex B. Some developing countries argued that when this is applied to their own tariff reductions, it would create relatively significant adjustment burdens compared to that of developed countries whose tariffs were relatively low already.

9 Some developing countries were willing to entertain the possibility of sectoral negotiations but only if this were decided on a voluntary basis. They feared that the burden of adjustment for them would be relatively large, especially if the most sensitive of their sectors were targeted for sectoral tariff reductions.

10 Developed countries created an informal negotiating group to support the Derbez text called 'Friends of Ambition.'

11 See paragraph 1 of Annex B, WTO document WT/L/579, August, 2, 2004.

12 See WTO document "Statement by South Africa to the 55th session of the Committee on Trade and Development on behalf of Argentina, Brazil, India, Indonesia, Namibia, the Philippines and Venezuela", November 28, 2005.

13 WTO Document "Reclaiming Development in the WTO Doha Development Round", submission by Argentina, Brazil, India, Indonesia, Namibia, Pakistan, the Philippines, South Africa and Venezuela to the Committee on Trade and Development, WT/COMTD/W/145, December 01, 2005.

14 See WTO document "Market Access for Non-Agricultural Products. Flexibilities for Developing Countries", Communication from Argentina, Bolivarian Republic of Venezuela, Brazil, China, Egypt, India, Indonesia, Namibia, Pakistan, Philippines and South Africa, TN/MA/W/65, November 08, 2005.

15 See letter by the above countries, and Tunisia, sent to the Chairman of the Conference and the Director General at the Hong Kong Ministerial Conference. South Africa Permanent Mission to the WTO, Geneva.

16 See WTO document WT/MIN (05)/DEC, Para 24 of the Ministerial Declaration, December 22, 2005.

17 'Ministers promise to accelerate pace of Doha talks', Financial Times, January 30, 2006.

18 The WTO July 2004 Framework Agreement agreed to provide developing countries with a small percentage of flexibility to protect some tariff lines from increased cuts or to reduce these lines by a smaller percentage than the average cut specified in the agreed formula.

19 WTO document Job (06)/200/Rev.1, "Towards NAMA Modalities" Revision, June 26, 2006.

20 'Hopes for Modalities Deal Diminish As G-6 Meeting Ends Without Progress', WTO Reporter, June 30, 2006.

21 WTO document NAMA 11 Ministerial Communiqué, June 29, 2006, Geneva.

22 The WTO Hong Kong Declaration agreed that developing countries shall reduce their tariffs by a lesser margin than developed countries (Less Than Full Reciprocity) and that the depth of the tariff cuts in NAMA shall be comparable to that in Agriculture (paragraph 24).

23 See WTO document, 'Draft Modalities for Agriculture', Job (07)/128, July 17, 2007.

24 See WTO document, 'Draft NAMA Modalities', Job (07)/126, July 17, 2007.

25 WTO document, "Statement of the NAMA 11 to the NGMA, July 17, 2007", Job (07)/132, July 31, 2007.

26 WTO document, "Statement of the NAMA 11 to the TNC", July 26, 2007. See also in "Twenty Months of the NAMA 11" August 2007. South African Mission to the UN and WTO, Geneva.

27 "Developing Countries reject Doha Round plans for tariff cuts", Financial Times, October, 10, 2007.

28 See "Joint Statement of the G90 and the NAMA 11", July 26, 2007 in "Twenty Months of the NAMA 11" August 2007. South African Mission to the UN and WTO, Geneva.

29 The EU and the US still retained some significant differences in their negotiating positions on other issues such as the Rules issues, (Anti-dumping and Fishing Subsidies), and Geographical Indications.

30 Ismail, F. 2004. "Agricultural Trade Liberalisation and the Poor: A Development Perspective on Cancun", BRIDGES, January 2004.

31 See "Joint Statement of the G90 and the NAMA 11" July 26, 2007, in "Twenty Months of the NAMA 11" August 2007. South African Mission to the UN and WTO, Geneva.

32 See WTD, February 11, 2008.

33 See "Statement of the NAMA 11 to the TNC - July 26, 2007", in "Twenty Months of the NAMA 11" August 2007. South African Mission to the UN and WTO, Geneva.

34 See "NAMA 11 Talking Points for the NGMA, February 20, 2008", in "Twenty Months of the NAMA 11" August 2007. South African Mission to the UN and WTO, Geneva.

35 See "ACP Statement to the NGMA", February 20, 2008.

36 See WTO document, "Statement of Brazil to the Open-Ended Meeting on NAMA", Geneva, February 20, 2008.

37 See WTO document, "NAMA 11 Statement on the Second Revision of the draft modalities text for NAMA", May 27, 2008.

38 See WTO document, "Statement on behalf of the African Group at the NGMA", May 27, 2008.

39 See WTD, June 05-06, 2008.

40 See NAMA 11 Ministerial Communiqué, Geneva, July 20, 2008.

41 The Lamy Package adopted the proposed middle ground of the NAMA chair's, July 10, 2008 Draft Text.

42 WTO document, "South African Statement to the WTO TNC, July 22, 2008."

43 Davies, R. 2009. Reclaiming the Development Dimension of the Multilateral Trading System, Geneva lectures on global economic governance, Global Economic Governance Programme, University College, Oxford and the Graduate Institute of International and Development Studies, Geneva, March 02, 2009.

44 Pascal Lamy, after the collapse of the WTO Cancun Ministerial meeting in 2003 blamed this on the "medieval process" of the negotiations.

45 See letter by Kamal Nath, Minister of Commerce of India, to the WTO Director General, Pascal Lamy, dated September 24, 2008 and October 17, 2008.

46 See Washington Trade Daily, June 29, 2009; See Lynn, J., "Doha hopes improve amid trade data gloom", Reuters, June 24, 2009; See www.ibsa-trilateral.org/.

47 See interview with South African Minister of Trade and Industry, Rob Davies, Washington Trade Daily, May 18, 2009.

14 Asserting the Rights of Smallness – Small and Vulnerable Economies at the WTO

Sir Ronald Sanders
Former Ambassador of Antigua and Barbuda to the WTO

Introduction

Over the years between 2001 and 2010, a Geneva-based group of over 25 countries,[1] describing themselves as "small and vulnerable" gained considerable attention in the WTO and in a number of the negotiating committees in the Doha Round of trade negotiations. The group, chaired primarily by Barbados over that period, worked assiduously to take advantage of a mandate provided by the 4th Ministerial Conference, held in Doha, Qatar in November 2001, that their trade-related concerns should be addressed but without creating another sub-category of WTO members.[2] Consequently, the group's efforts have resulted in the inclusion of several provisions related to SVEs in various draft texts prepared by the Chairs of the negotiating bodies in the Round as well as in various decisions taken by WTO committees.

This chapter will review the origins, concerns, and work of the SVE group. It will discuss the objectives with which they started, how they modified those objectives in the context of a judgment of what could realistically be achieved, and the alliances they cultivated with other groups to help achieve better treatment than was on offer for them in the negotiating bodies.

It has to be recalled that the Doha Round, as adopted by Ministers at their meeting in Doha, is supposed to be a 'development' Round, based on the concept of the DDA, which recognises that "the majority of WTO members are developing countries" and that there should be efforts to "place their needs and interests at the heart of the Work Programme."[3] The SVE group, therefore, had a reasonable expectation that the Round would address the urgent development issues that confronted them.

Nine years later (at the time this chapter is being written) the SVE group, like other developing countries, have good reason to be sorely disappointed that developed countries have not fulfilled their commitment to place 'development' at the centre of the Round. And, while the SVEs are fairly satisfied with the concessions they have managed to get from the negotiating groups, many of them (particularly the smaller states from Africa, the Caribbean and the Pacific) are keenly aware that they stand to gain least from the Round because of their small share of world trade and their capacity constraints to expand it, their loss of preferential access to markets, the loss of the application of certain subsidies to promote export diversification, and simply more trade rules than they can handle.

Even so, the relative success of the SVE group in the negotiating bodies for the Doha Round is quite remarkable given the small size of its member countries and their miniscule contribution to world trade. None of them enjoy a share of total world trade exceeding 0.06 percent computed on an average of the three most recent years.

It may be precisely because their participation in world trade is so small that the group has been relatively successful in its negotiations. Except for a few countries, the majority of the world's nations see no threat from the SVE group. The SVEs have been particularly careful not to seek greater concessions than those that apply to LDCs which comprise a sub-category in the WTO, qualifying for S&D treatment.

But, even accepting that concessions accorded to the SVE group is not now perceived as posing a threat to others, this was certainly not always the case. Considerable technical and diplomatic work had to be undertaken to explain to large and small countries, and groups of countries, why greater flexibilities should be given to the members of the SVE group. This work started before 2001 and had its genesis in the creation in 1998 (at the insistence of small states and in particular, at the time, the then Prime Minister of Barbados, Owen Arthur) of a Commonwealth Secretariat and World Bank Joint Task Force on Small States to try to establish that small states suffered from inherent characteristics that were different from other states and that required them to be treated differently by the international community if they were to survive as states in economic and political terms.[4]

Small states comprise 32 of the Commonwealth's 54 members. The majority of them gained independence in the 1970s. By the late 1990s in the face of several exogenous shocks, including natural disasters and the effects of downturns in the global economy, it became evident to their leadership that while their economies had "graduated" from access to concessional lending by the World Bank because their per capita incomes placed them in a "middle income" category, the openness of their economies rendered them vulnerable to distress in the economies of their major trading partners. In addition, all of them were highly dependent on preferential access to the markets of their major trading partners – in particular the EU and the US. These preferences were disappearing with the introduction of binding WTO rules that required greater trade liberalisation, open markets, and equal competition for market share. The changes in the international trading system brought about by the implementation of the Uruguay Round Agreements and the expiration of the EU's Lomé IV Convention were cases in point.

The report of the Joint Task Force issued in April 2000 did not evince an undisputed conviction in international institutions and among a number of industrialised nations that small states should represent a special category of countries, requiring S&D treatment by the international community. It did, however, create a greater awareness that small states cannot enjoy economies of scale in production and in public administration, that they are not competitive internationally and in most cases cannot pursue an import substitution policy, and that they are particularly vulnerable both to natural disasters and economic shocks.

This acknowledgement of the need to consider small states as a special category of developing countries now permeates the work programme of the Commonwealth Secretariat. But, as a 2004 report from UNCTAD pointed out, "in the case of the World Bank, there has, in fact, not been any effective follow-up to the report except for the holding of an annual Small States Forum at which various international organisations have listed the activities they undertake – and would have undertaken anyway – in small states."[5]

Accordingly, despite the relative success of the SVE group at the WTO in securing flexibilities in their treatment in the draft texts of the negotiating groups for the Doha Round, small states proponents remain strongly of the view that 'small states' do differ from some of the economies that have come to be regarded as 'small and vulnerable' in the corridors of the WTO. They argue that:

> Small states and small island states suffer from a combination of inherited and inherent characteristics that impede their ability to integrate into the global economy. These characteristics include smallness, physical isolation from markets, dispersion of small pockets of populations and a small and high specialised human and physical resource base. These together raise the operating cost structure of small economies and render market adjustment more difficult.[6]

But, this is not an argument that has commanded widespread international support, and it has not led to an agreed definition in the WTO of what is a "small state." For instance, the WTO Secretariat has stated that:

> Whatever the criteria used to define small states, any list would include countries that are heterogeneous in some respects and can be easily criticised, since the analysis of common characteristics turns out to be difficult. Due to the considerable diversity among small states, it is hard to find that "one" aspect of smallness that is essential in the characterisation of small economies and in distinguishing them from large states. In these circumstances, it is not surprising that a unified view on small states is still missing.[7]

However, small states proponents have rebutted this argument in the negotiating groups, using, *inter alia,* the characteristic of national resilience. As an example, small states representatives have contended that when a hurricane hits a small island state, it hits the entire country, destroying all of its agricultural production and, therefore, its complete economic output in a few hours. By contrast, if a similar hurricane hits a larger country, only a part of the country and a portion of its production are affected. Further, while the large state has resources that can be employed in its rapid rehabilitation, small states whose economies are less diversified and which have extremely limited resources, have virtually no means for continued national output, and rebuilding their damaged productive sectors takes years rather than months.[8]

Despite the above-stated observations, SVE negotiators have contended that this lack of clarity in the WTO of what is a "small economy" is to their benefit "since it made it easier to maintain the position – some might say the fiction – that a new category was not being established among developing countries in the WTO."[9] Later in this chapter, we shall see how the group used the fluidity in defining an SVE to its benefit in the negotiations.

Measures of SVEs' Success

Arguably, the first achievement of the SVE group was the successful adoption of a package of proposals by the General Council in 2006 allowing the WTO to provide technical assistance to regional organisations to help their members comply with multilateral trade rules in areas related to SPS, TBT, and TRIPs.

While many non-SVE countries argued that the General Council decision was unnecessary since there was already support for these regional institutions, the decision provided the SVEs with legal certainty, and very importantly, it explicitly recognised the existence – and positions – of a group of WTO members called "Small, Vulnerable Economies" that require special support within trade rules. This decision paved the way for acceptance of more valuable outcomes in the WTO for the SVE group.[10]

Thereafter, a major accomplishment by the group was the acceptance by the NAMA Negotiating Group of criteria that defines their economies as "small and vulnerable" and, therefore, deserving of "flexibilities" in their treatment. The criteria are as follows:

> With the exception of developed members, those members having a share of less than 0.1 percent of world NAMA trade for the reference period of 1999 to 2001 or best available data as contained in document TN/MA/S/18 may apply the following modality of tariff reduction instead of the formula modality...
>
> (a) Members with a bound tariff average of non-agricultural tariff lines:
>
> (i) at or above 50 percent shall bind all of their non-agricultural tariff lines at an average level that does not exceed an overall average of 30 percent.[11]

In non-technical terms what this basically means is that the criteria for SVE treatment for NAMA contains only one indicator, namely share of world trade in industrial goods computed at the average of the years 1999-2001. Essentially, the flexibility accorded to SVEs allows them to maintain tariffs on imports of industrial goods at levels up to a maximum of 30 percent, depending on their governments' existing dependence on tariff revenues for meeting the costs of providing goods and services to their populations. The tariffs vary from country to country. Thus, the countries that have a larger share of world trade, such as Jamaica, Trinidad and Tobago, and Central American countries will be required to bind their tariffs at 27 percent while the smaller states in the Caribbean – the six members of the Organisation of Eastern Caribbean States (OECS)[12] – will be able to bind their tariffs at the highest allowable figure of 30 percent. This flexibility allows the governments of these countries time in which to develop alternative sources of revenue, including increases in income tax and value-added taxes, for which they would have to prepare their populations and that would have to be incorporated into their fiscal policies. The flexibility will have minimal effect on world trade while at the same time encouraging greater access to SVE markets through the lowering of tariffs from 50 percent and above to an average of 30 percent.

While the criteria encompasses 45 countries,[13] many of them have not joined the SVE group for a variety of reasons, including that the NAMA criteria does not apply across the board to other negotiating bodies, and some countries that qualify for SVE treatment are also LDCs which makes them entitled to special and differential treatment that is more advantageous to them.

The SVE group argued that the same criterion that was accepted by the NAMA negotiating body should be applied to them by other negotiating groups including those on agriculture and services. But, a different criterion has been accepted for agriculture and, so far, none has been accepted for services.

With respect to agriculture, the SVE group also jumped a major hurdle when they persuaded the CoA-SS to accept that SVEs are defined (and solely for the purpose of negotiations in agriculture) "as one whose average share for the period 1999-2004 (a) of world merchandise trade does not exceed 0.16 percent and (b) of world NAMA trade does not exceed 0.10 percent and (c) of world agricultural trade does not exceed 0.40 percent."[14]

There are three pillars in the negotiations on agriculture - domestic support, market access, and export competition. In the first - domestic support - there is no SVE-specific provision. However, the SVE group is divided between NFIDCs and other members. In market access, SVEs are given two options for tariff reduction. Either two-thirds of the cut for developed countries plus an additional 10 percentage points or satisfy an average tariff cut of 24 percent by designating as many agricultural tariff lines as "special products." The special product designation means that the item need not be subjected to any cut in tariff.

In addition, as developing countries, SVEs have the right to designate up to four percent of tariff lines as "sensitive products," in which case they would be required only to reduce tariffs by one third, one half, or two thirds of the reduction that is applicable to developed countries. The other aspect of the market access pillar is the SSM - the most politically sensitive issue in DDA negotiations. The additional flexibility carved out for SVEs is square bracketed, owing mainly to the group's coalition with the G33 - the group of developing countries, including China, Cuba, India, and Indonesia, that seeks to shield their domestic markets from increased liberalisation.[15] At the time of writing, this flexibility has not been fully accepted by the members of the negotiating group.

In the event, the flexibilities accorded to the SVEs in agriculture provide them time to reform their agricultural sectors to make them more specialised and more competitive in the global market.

With respect to services, there is no special criterion applicable to SVEs because services trade and market opening is on a request and offer basis. The CTS (Special Session, July 2008) has so far concluded that: "Members shall continue to give due consideration to proposals on trade-related concerns of small economies. In recognising their special situation, further liberalisation shall be in accordance with their development needs." This is regarded by some member countries of the SVE group as potentially beneficial, but they also recognise that progress in services is tied to progress in other negotiating groups and the interests of developed countries, such as the US.

It remains to be seen whether the SVEs will secure the flexibilities in services they desire. Assuredly, many of the SVEs are now highly dependent on services, and they will require better treatment than other developed economies to compensate for their loss of market access for agriculture, and, in some cases, the loss of business and revenues from their offshore financial sectors resulting from recent actions by the OECD - the so-called "rich man's club."

Against this background, it appears that, in spite of the mandate provided by the Doha Ministerial Conference that another sub-category of WTO membership should not be created, the members of the SVE group have received *de facto* concessions in the draft texts approved so far by negotiating groups that could produce that practical result if they are subsequently adopted by Ministerial Conferences in the current Round of negotiations.

According to one of the current SVE negotiators from the Caribbean, "In all spheres of the negotiations the following hierarchy of concessions has been established: LDCs; SVEs; recently acceded Members; other developing countries; Middle Group countries (such as Chile, Costa Rica, Malaysia, Singapore) and industrialised countries."[16]

In this regard, while the SVE provisions in draft texts, prepared by the chairs of the negotiating bodies, fall short of the expectations of proponents of the importance - and need - for S&D treatment for small states, they have been sufficient to place the treatment of SVEs second only to the advantageous terms that are accorded to LDCs. As far as negotiations in the Round go, this is a huge achievement.

However, the real test of benefits for SVEs from a completed Doha Round lies in the extent to which they will be able to share in the global income that it generates. This will depend not only on the extent of the flexibilities in the treatment they receive, but also on broad development assistance and new and creative domestic policies they must adopt and implement to improve and expand their productive capacity and enhance their competitiveness. Among those policies must be the deepening of economic integration arrangements within regions, such as the Caribbean, as none of the countries on its own, has the capacity to integrate successfully into the global economy.

On the latter point, the 2006 decision by the General Council, referred to earlier, to allow SVEs to use regional bodies "to provide technical support and assistance as necessary to help them implement their obligations in areas of SPS, TBT, and TRIPs and thereby facilitate their fuller integration into the multilateral trading system"[17] assumes great significance.

Beginnings and Evolution

As noted in the introduction to this chapter, the origins of the SVE group at the WTO owes much to the work of the 1998 Joint Task Force set up by the Commonwealth Secretariat and the World Bank, and the insistence by several heads of government, especially Owen Arthur of Barbados, that small states (defined by the Commonwealth Secretariat as states with populations of 1.5 million people or less with exceptions for states with larger populations but similar characteristics[18]) merited S&D treatment.

It should be noted that, at no time, did the small states in question argue that they should receive treatment that was better than or identical to that of LDCs – they always acknowledged that while they shared some characteristics with LDCs, the latter's constraints were far greater.

Small states in the WTO appear to have resigned themselves to accepting that - in order to preserve some measure of flexibility in the application of WTO rules to their economies - they have to reach an accommodation with other states who consider themselves to be vulnerable, in particular, to any treatment accorded to small states that is more favourable than the treatment they enjoy.

Indeed, the creation and evolution of a group of SVEs in the WTO was at the initiative of small states, especially Barbados and Mauritius. It arose from the recognition that, given the resistance to creating another sub-category of membership meriting S&D treatment, they had to win over the greatest antagonists to their quest for greater flexibility in the ways that WTO rules are applied to them.

The breakthrough in overcoming resistance to the idea that SVEs required, at the least, differentiated treatment came at the 4th Ministerial Conference in Doha, Qatar in November 2001. The decision of that meeting provided a mandate for negotiations on a range of subjects and other work, including the mandate to establish a work programme relating to the trade of small economies. Paragraph 35 stated:

> "We agree to a work programme, under the auspices of the General Council, to examine issues relating to the trade of small economies. The objective of this work is to frame responses to the trade-related issues identified for the fuller integration of small, vulnerable economies into the multilateral trading system, and not to create a sub-category of WTO members. The General Council shall review the work programme and make recommendations for action to the Fifth Session of the Ministerial Conference."

Despite this Ministerial mandate, it took a further three years for anything concrete to happen. Much of the intervening period was spent trying to convince non-SVEs of the merits of according special treatment to SVEs as well as seeking to tackle the notion of special treatment without creating a new category. At the August 01, 2004 meeting of the General Council the Doha mandate on SVEs was reaffirmed with the General Council agreeing that:

> "The trade-related issues identified for the fuller integration of small, vulnerable economies into the multilateral trading system, should also be addressed, without creating a sub-category of members, as part of a work programme, as mandated in paragraph 35 of the Doha Ministerial Declaration."[19]

Then, the December 2005 Declaration of the 6th Ministerial Conference in Hong Kong, China, established under paragraph 41:

> "We reaffirm our commitment to the Work Programme on Small Economies and urge members to adopt specific measures that would facilitate the fuller integration of small, vulnerable economies into the multilateral trading system, without creating a sub-category of WTO members. We take note of the report of the Committee on Trade and Development in Dedicated Session on the Work Programme on Small Economies to the General Council and agree to the recommendations on future work. We instruct the Committee on Trade and Development, under the overall responsibility of the General Council, to continue the work in the Dedicated Session and to monitor progress of the small economies' proposals in the negotiating and other bodies, with the aim of providing responses to the trade-related issues of small economies as soon as possible but no later than December 31, 2006. We instruct the General Council to report on progress and action taken, together with any further recommendations as appropriate, to our next Session".

In addition, the Declaration of the 6th Ministerial Conference also stated the following:

> NAMA Negotiations - Paragraph 21 of the Declaration
> "We note the concerns raised by small, vulnerable economies, and instruct the Negotiating Group to establish ways to provide flexibilities for these Members without creating a sub-category of WTO Members."
>
> Services Negotiations – Annex C, Paragraph 8
> "Due consideration shall be given to proposals on trade-related concerns of small economies."

While these references to SVEs were not ideal for the small states, they worked hard to negotiate them into the texts of the decisions as the best alternative to the creation of a special category for small economies that would enjoy S&D treatment second only to the treatment accorded to LDCs. In effect, they opted to forgo the battle for recognition as a special category of membership in the WTO and, instead, to secure the maximum flexibilities they could get from the negotiations. The calculation was that the forces against the idea of awarding small states any S&D treatment were sufficient to block any such agreement.

In ordinary circumstances, it is quite probable that the industrialised countries – the G-7 - would have agreed to a negotiated category for small states in the WTO. They recognise that if S&D treatment were accorded to small states, their own circumstances would hardly be affected. But, their greater concern is access to the markets of some developing countries that regard the establishment of such a category as a threat to their capacities to compete in certain sectors. The industrialised nations are keen to open up these medium-sized markets and dare not risk resistance to market liberalisation based on the argument that a special category for small states in the WTO would put them at a disadvantage. So, small states have been sacrificed on the altar of the industrialised nations' ambition and the unresponsiveness to their inherent difficulties by other developing countries that regard differentiated WTO treatment for their neighbours as a threat.

Concerns of the SVE Group

As far back as 2005, the SVE group articulated clearly its concerns about the issues being negotiated in the Doha Round. And, it did so against the reality of "the insignificant share of small, vulnerable economies in international trade as well as their limited capacity to participate in the WTO negotiations."

The forum for formal arguments and presentations by the SVEs was the CTD, but they also promoted the message informally in bilateral meetings with other groups and to the Director-General and Secretariat of the WTO.

They made it clear that they had substantial interest in the negotiations on NAMA, agriculture, trade facilitation, services, and subsidies.

With respect to NAMA, the SVE group's primary concern was that SVEs should not be required to reduce tariff lines so drastically and quickly that they had little or no time to prepare their populations for revenue-generating measures to replace revenues lost from lower tariffs on imports. They were also concerned that they should have enough time to reduce tariffs and introduce new revenue measures in a gradual manner and so guard against inflationary and other trends that would disrupt their economies.

With respect to services, trade facilitation and subsidies, they were concerned that special priority should be accorded to the services and products of export interest in which they had the real potential to increase their exports while, at the same time, market access for service suppliers of sectors and modes of interest to them should be opened by developed countries so that they could contribute more substantially to employment creation, revenue generation, and overall growth.

With respect to subsidies and countervailing measures, they were very keen that decisions should be taken to allow them to cater to the needs of their small business sectors both in their domestic markets and globally. In terms of fisheries subsidies, the SVEs recognised the need for flexibility to protect their fishing industries and to guard their right to increase and exploit their natural fisheries resources in the future.

And, on trade facilitation, they were deeply concerned that the negotiations should respond to the specific needs of SVEs, in particular the landlocked SVEs and those with inherently high transportation and operating costs relative to the volume of goods processed.

They also signalled their concern about administrative capacity, an issue that will become increasingly vexed within the WTO now and in the future. The SVEs pointed to their limited administrative capacity to comply with all the detailed and complex WTO rules and the need to take advantage of some avenues open to all WTO members. As examples, they emphasised (a) using the provisions of the Understanding on Rules and Procedures Governing the Settlement of Disputes (DSU) and (b) enforcing the decisions of the DSB. They called for special attention to be given to these matters.[20]

Consolidation of the SVE Group

It was against this background that small states – particularly small Commonwealth States that had worked together in the Commonwealth and at the World Bank and the UN to try to establish a unique identity meriting S&D treatment[21] – elected to broaden the membership of their group in the WTO to include "vulnerable" economies. This brought Central American countries and non-Commonwealth Caribbean countries, such as Dominican Republic into the fold and, eventually, states such as El Salvador, Mongolia, and Paraguay.

The group of countries - identified in the introduction to this chapter – has worked collectively and closely to advance its case to the CTD and in the Negotiating Groups of the Doha Round.

Barbados and Mauritius were the two most vigorous proponents of the SVE cause, and it is no surprise that Barbados has held the chairmanship of the SVE group for more than eight years, a position it has maintained even when its ambassadors changed.

It should be noted that some of the states that form the core group of SVEs do not have resident missions at the WTO in Geneva, and consequently the burden of the work falls on the few that are represented there. However, the Caribbean members of the SVE group have the possibility of receiving support from the Office of Trade Negotiations of the Caribbean Community and Common Market (CARICOM) Secretariat, which bases a technical support officer in the Permanent Delegation of Jamaica.

But, the core of Commonwealth small states in the SVE group (principally from the Caribbean and Pacific) could not have advanced without the weight of the Central American countries. Each sub-group needed the others to overcome the obstacles it faced in achieving, at the least, differentiated treatment.

Not all countries that fall under the two objective and different SVE criteria in NAMA and agriculture associate themselves with the SVE cause. As one example, Costa Rica falls under the criteria of an SVE, but it has long been an opponent of the SVE work programme. Only time will tell if Costa Rica will eventually elect to benefit from treatment won by the SVEs or to maintain its opposition. Another example is Armenia, which also qualifies as a RAM and might prefer to benefit from the more moderate obligations required of new members. Similarly, there are countries that qualify for both SVE and LDC treatment, and these will rightly opt for more advantageous benefits as LDCs.

Since the start of the Doha Work Programme, SVEs have tabled more than 30 different proposals in the areas of NAMA, agriculture, services, fisheries, TRIPs, SPS and TBT, trade facilitation, accession, and (even though it is not formally on the Doha Round Agenda) aid for trade.

As pointed out in the introduction to this chapter, a major accomplishment by the SVE group was the acceptance by the NAMA Negotiating Group of criteria that define their economies as small and vulnerable" and, therefore, deserving of flexibilities in their treatment. An equally important achievement was the acceptance by the Negotiating Group on Agriculture of criteria that define an SVE.

An earlier achievement in 2002 related to the Agreement on Subsidies and Countervailing Measures (SCM) adopted at the end of the Uruguay Round in 1994. Article 3 prohibited WTO members (except LDCs or certain other low-income countries) from applying "subsidies contingent in law or in fact ... upon export performance." In the provisions of Article 3, an eight-year grace period for adherence was stipulated, but it was subsequently extended in 2002 for a further period of five years, to 2007. As former Jamaican Ambassador to the WTO, Ransford Smith, explained:

> This particular Article has been of considerable concern to a large number of developing countries, but especially so to small economies in the Caribbean and Central America. As a consequence of their sustained advocacy and activism on this issue, the grace period has now once again been further extended, this time for another eight years, to the end of calendar year 2015.[23]

Barbados was the lead negotiator for the SVEs on the SCM and actually negotiated on behalf of a number of non-SVEs that had traditionally opposed special treatment for SVEs, such as Costa Rica and Uruguay. The decision was vital to all of the Caribbean countries and many countries in Central America and the Pacific,[24] because of the importance of the concessions offered under the export subsidies to attract investment to the offshore financial services sectors that had been developed as part of the diversification of their economies and to the tourism industry. In many of the Central American SVEs these subsidy programmes bolstered employment for a large number of persons, particularly women.

In all this, the SVEs fought an uphill battle of Sisyphean proportions particularly in the face of arguments by those who opposed differentiated treatment for them on the basis that none of the characteristics and problems identified by the SVEs "can by itself be assumed to be unique to small, vulnerable economies."[25]

Building Alliances For Success

Building alliances with other groups in the WTO by way of constant explanations, backed up by sound arguments, was the foundation on which the SVEs constructed their relative success. This called for careful diplomatic work, allaying the fears of those who felt their interests might be threatened and bolstering those who saw no prospect of success.

An important factor in the evolution of the SVEs' work was the sympathetic stance of the WTO's current Director-General, Pascal Lamy. Without the empathy of the WTO Secretariat, it is unlikely that the SVEs would have gotten very far. A second factor is the supportive position of the CTD. Its membership has been very open to discussion, in large measure owing to the active role of SVE members on the Committee who laboured hard to persuade their colleagues of the rightness of their positions.

For instance, the CTD took particular note at its Ninth Dedicated Session in March 2005:

> Chairman Ambassador C. Trevor Clarke (Barbados) presented a proposal which tried to find solutions to the trade-related problems of small economies. He proposed considering the use of characteristics to identify what could be accepted as small, vulnerable economies, without naming any group of countries. He then proposed considering the trade-related problems which could reasonably be attributed to those characteristics, without naming any group of countries. A third step was to frame responses to those trade-related problems, without naming any group of countries.[26]

The objective of the SVEs, through Clarke's presentation, was two-fold: first, to dispel any fears that might have been harboured by LDCs that their special concessions would be eroded by similar concessions to the SVEs; and second, to work within the mandate that no new category of membership would be created. In this respect, the SVEs adopted a pragmatic and issue-specific approach to the question of special treatment.

Representatives of the SVEs also sought out other groups to explain and justify their request for flexibilities in their treatment. They secured support from larger developing country groups, such as the ACP group of States (in which the Commonwealth Caribbean and Pacific small states shared membership), the G-33 and the LDC group. Indeed, the SVEs have now established firm linkages with these groups.

But, the SVEs were also careful to consult regularly with larger countries, such as the US, the EU, Japan, China, India, and Brazil – the major players in the current negotiations. They encountered no road blocks from the latter three countries, and the attitude of the powerful developed countries was to encourage the SVEs to justify their need for flexibilities and to provide a road map of how long such flexibilities would run and when they would be terminated.[27]

The greatest step forward in fending off antagonists to the proponents of the SVE group came when Colombia, Costa Rica, Chile, Ecuador, Peru, and Uruguay were persuaded to drop their opposition to granting flexibilities to the group. Their initial opposition arose from their concern that flexibilities given to the Central American members of the SVE group would place them at a comparative disadvantage, and it took considerable diplomatic and technical work to convince them that they had little to fear. Indeed, as it turned out, both Ecuador and Uruguay fell within the designated SVEs criteria agreed by the Negotiating Group on Agriculture.[28]

Looking to the Future

The SVE group is perfectly aware that the relative successes they have achieved in securing favourable language and criteria in the texts on Agriculture and NAMA cannot be regarded as fixed in stone. Thus, the representative of Barbados, speaking on behalf of the group to the CTD on December 08, 2010, made the following observation:

> We believe that whilst great progress has been made in agriculture, greater effort and leadership, particularly among the larger players, is needed to complete the agricultural negotiations. SVEs are of the view that any future discussions need to be based on progress made to date and that *there should be no backtracking on any of the previously stabilised issues* (emphasis added).

And, on the NAMA negotiations, the SVEs argued:

> We continue to believe that any future progress should be based on our achievements to date, specifically in relation to the treatment of SVEs in the tariff treatment in these negotiations. There should be no attempts to undermine any progress attained thus far, which could lead to an unravelling of the careful balance that we have worked hard over the last few years to realise.[29]

The question still persists as to whether the SVEs should seek recognition as a separate subgrouping within the membership of the WTO in order to achieve the extent of differentiated and favourable treatment they need. Strong advocates of the importance of being recognised as a special subgroup argue that it is "hard to surmise how execution of the paragraph 35 mandate (of the Doha Ministerial Declaration) requiring the framing of trade-related responses to the problems of smaller vulnerable economies can occur without the logical first step of defining and clarifying what a small vulnerable economy is."[30]

This argument will not go away. It will end only if the SVEs secure sufficient flexibilities in all priority areas of the negotiating agenda of the Doha Round to justify abandoning the struggle for a special category of membership. Thus far, NAMA and Agriculture have dominated the Round. Services and rules - areas of serious concerns to many of the SVEs whose economies have become reliant on services and fisheries - are yet to be tackled in a meaningful way.

Nonetheless, the SVEs have achieved commendable success and have won important concessions. If their success continues in the Round, the argument for recognition as a special subgroup will fall away, because they will achieve their ends without forcing a disruption to the structure of WTO membership.

Given the track record so far and the level of support won from other groups, the SVEs could achieve even more success provided they: (a) retain their unity of purpose; (b) ensure that concessions they have secured in various draft texts are not clawed away; and (c) they remain cohesive in insisting that developed countries stick to their commitment that the Round must be focused on 'development' and that they, and other developing countries must be accorded concessions by the world's industrialised nations.

It should be recalled, as two renowned developed-country economists have told the global community, that in the Round:

> "First, there has been little progress on the issues of interest to developing countries (especially agriculture, labour mobility, and labour-intensive manufactures and services). Second, the new issues on the agenda, the so-called 'Singapore Issues', primarily reflect the interests of the advanced industrial countries and have been strongly opposed by many developing countries. Third, the domestic and bilateral actions of several OECD countries have led to questions about their commitment to the multilateral development agenda. Finally, there has been only limited reform to the culture and procedures of the WTO."[31]

The SVE group has shown that it is very aware of the 'development' shortcomings of the Round, and in the statement to the CTD on December 08, 2010 it set out the group's concerns in clear terms:

> ... it is vital that the development dimension of the Doha Development Agenda, be the axis around which the "successful, ambitious, comprehensive and balanced conclusion"[32] of the Round is fulfilled. With a share of less than 0.1 percent of world trade, and facing the attendant challenges of inherent small size, the extent to which our development objectives are realised, will be the true test of how successful, how ambitious, how comprehensive and how balanced the conclusion of the Round may be assessed.[33]

Many of the small states (those classified by the Commonwealth as small) in the SVE group will become basket cases and sink to LDC status if their current economic and environmental conditions continue without the assistance they need from the international community and unless they implement crucial policy decisions, such as (a) new and creative domestic policies to improve and expand their productive capacity and enhance their competitiveness, and (b) deepen regional economic and political integration among themselves in order to build much-needed administrative trade capacity and facilitate the integration of their productive sectors through amalgamation. They will have only nominal sovereignty and very restricted space for national policymaking. Moreover, their cultural identity will erode as their skilled and managerial people migrate and cultural penetration follows economic engulfment by larger and richer states.

The other "vulnerable" economies will most likely survive better, but they too will lose a significant measure of their autonomy, giving over their prosperity or poverty to the level of paternalism of their wealthier and more powerful neighbours.

Maintaining Cohesion in the Round

For the time being, however, if the SVEs want a successful conclusion to the Doha Round on their terms, they would be well advised to maintain their solidarity and to try to develop their group further as a strong, mutually supportive instrument that will continue to bargain together. Their cohesion – on the basis that "none shall be left behind" – is the key to such success. Strengthening that cohesion will call for political will and determination from each of their governments at the highest level.

Crucial issues of vital concern to SVEs remain to be discussed and resolved in 'development' terms. They include non-tariff barriers, intellectual property, migration, and unskilled intensive services. As these issues gain prominence in the current and possibly future negotiations, the SVE group will need to be even more unified and firm in its collective bargaining than it has been to date.

In immediate terms, as negotiations in the Round progress, the SVEs should ratchet up the level of active participation by ministers, and where possible, their heads of government to guard against any reversal of the gains they have achieved, and to put a political stamp on their ambitions for the negotiations. It would be in the interest of the SVEs, which are a disparate geographical group, to give their cause in the WTO a higher profile and greater political input by holding their own Heads of Government Conference on the Doha Round to which they invite the Director-General and the chairs of the negotiating groups.

Should they hold such a conference, it would be the first time that the SVEs assert themselves at the highest level of government, crossing the political divides of a colonial past and building a bridge of cooperation of their own design.

An SVE Agenda Post Doha

At the end of this Round, they should hold the group together to do two things: (i) monitor the implementation of the DDA agreements and champion the cause of any of the SVEs where implementation fails either because of a lack of capacity or a reneging of commitments by others; and (ii) take on new negotiations when the DDA is over. Among new issues for negotiation may be reform of the dispute settlement system in the WTO and the now pressing issue of climate change and its effects on trade.

The dispute settlement system has proved to be extremely costly, and its remedies often cannot be implemented by SVEs that achieve WTO panel decisions in their favour. The case for reform is urgent.

The classic 'David and Goliath' case is the dispute between the US and the small twin-island state of Antigua and Barbuda over access to the US market for Internet gaming services provided from Antigua.[34] Despite a 2004 panel decision, which found that the US had breached its commitment under the GATS, and a 2005 appellate report in its favour, Antigua and Barbuda was forced to take the US to Arbitration in 2007 since it (the US) had failed to comply with the rulings and recommendation of the DSB. The Arbitrator determined that the annual level of nullification or impairments of benefits accruing to Antigua is US$21mn and that Antigua may request authorisation from the DSB to suspend obligations under the TRIPs Agreement at a level not exceeding US$21mn annually. But, neither the original recommendations in the 2004 panel decision nor the recommendation of the arbitrator are practical remedies for Antigua and Barbuda. The first - increased tariffs on US goods and services - would have imposed higher costs for goods and services imported from the US (Antigua and Barbuda's primary source of imports) thus raising the cost of living to the Antigua and Barbuda population, and the second is virtually impossible to implement without massive investment by non-Antiguan companies. None would be willing to take on the high risk of such an investment.[35]

The point is that, at great financial cost, Antigua and Barbuda won a favourable ruling through the dispute settlement system of the WTO, but it has proved to be worthless, so far, since six years later the country has received no form of compensation or remedy although its economy has been damaged. SVEs are unlikely to secure any beneficial change to the system unless they maintain cohesion and build strong alliances with other developing countries to insist on reform.

Climate change has also become a crucial issue for small states – threatening the entire existence of some of them and threatening to erode coastal areas and displace people in others through sea level rise. These things have grave implications for the capacity of these countries to trade. Inevitably, in any post-Doha Round, climate change will become an important feature of the negotiations. Therefore, maintaining solidarity and a strong negotiating capacity for even greater flexibilities in their treatment as well as assistance for adaptation to, and mitigation of, the already evident ravages of climate change will be vital to the SVE group.

These will be the major challenges that will severely test the durability of the SVE group and its capacity to hold together, for others with a different agenda are sure to try to divide them through inducements to their individual members. But, given the successful cooperation so far, the SVE group has a solid foundation on which to continue its alliance beyond the current Round and into the next, growing stronger in its own interest.

Endnotes

1 The SVE countries are: Antigua and Barbuda, Barbados, Belize, Bolivia, Cuba, Dominica, Dominican Republic, El Salvador, Fiji, Grenada, Guatemala, Guyana, Honduras, Jamaica, Mauritius, Mongolia, Nicaragua, Papua New Guinea, Paraguay, Suriname, Solomon Islands, St. Kitts and Nevis, St. Lucia, St. Vincent and the Grenadines, Tonga, and Trinidad and Tobago.

2 World Trade Organisation (2001) Doha Ministerial Declaration; Geneva: WTO, WT/MIN(01)/DEC/1, pp. 7-8.

3 *Ibid.*

4 Report of a Joint World Bank/Commonwealth Secretariat Task Force. 2000. 'Small States: Meeting Challenges in the Global Economy'. London. The author was an adviser to the Task Force.

5 UNCTAD. 2004. "Is Special Treatment for Small Island Developing States Possible?".

6 Grynberg, R. and Remy, J. Y. 2003. 'Small Vulnerable Economy Issues and the WTO', in Mbirimi, Chilala, Gryberg (eds). From Doha to Cancun: Delivering a Development Round. London: Commonwealth Secretariat, pp. 269-290.

7 WTO Secretariat Note in document WT/COMTD/SE/W/4, July 23, 2002, pp 2-3.

8 Elliott Paige, former Chargé d'affaires of the OECS Technical Mission in Geneva in correspondence with the author.

9 See: Smith, R., former Ambassador for Jamaica to the WTO. 2009. 'WTO Doha Round Small Economies and their Interests', London: Commonwealth Trade Hot Topics, Issue 55. Also interview with Matthew Wilson, former SVEs Expert Coordinator and First Secretary of the Permanent Mission of Barbados to the United Nations and Other International Organisations in Geneva.

10 *Ibid,* and OECS Secretariat 2006. 'Small Vulnerable Economies Achieve Milestone at WTO Level. Accessed December 27, 2010, http://www.oecs.org/news-a-events/81-newstrade/219-small-vulnerable-economies-achieve-milestone-at-wto-level.

11 WT/COMTD/SE/W/22/Rev.5, November 25, 2010.

12 The six independent member states of the OECS are: Antigua and Barbuda, Dominica, Grenada, St Kitts-Nevis, St Lucia, St Vincent and the Grenadines.

13 Among the forty-five countries are: Armenia, Georgia, Jordan, Kenya, Mongolia, and Zimbabwe.

14 WT/COMTD/SE/W/22/Rev.5, November 25, 2010, p.18, para. 157.

15 Junior Lodge, Technical Co-ordinator, WTO Negotiations, Office of the Trade Negotiations of the Caribbean Community (CARICOM) in correspondence with the author.

16 *Ibid.*

17 WT/COMTD/SE/5.

18 Among these are: Jamaica with a population of 2.2 million and Papua New Guinea with a population of 5 million.

19 Paragraph 1(d) in the August 01, 2004 General Council Decision in document WT/L/579.

20 WT/COMTD/SE/W/13/Rev.1, May 27, 2005.

21 The small states core were from permanent missions at the WTO for Barbados, Jamaica, Trinidad and Tobago, and Mauritius, with support from states with non-resident missions such as Antigua and Barbuda, Dominica, Grenada, Guyana, St Kitts-Nevis, St Lucia and St Vincent and the Grenadines and the Pacific States.

22 See Note 12 for the list of OECS members.

23 *Supra* Note 9.

24 The lead negotiator was Matthew Wilson former SVEs Expert Coordinator and First Secretary of the Permanent Mission of Barbados to the United Nations and Other International Organisations in Geneva.

25 WT/COMTD/SE/W/20, February 09, 2006.

26 WT/COMTD/SE/4 November 17, 2005.

27 Discussion between Matthew Wilson, former SVEs Expert Coordinator and First Secretary of the Permanent Mission of Barbados to the United Nations and Other International Organisations in Geneva, and the author.

28 See Table in Document WT/COMTD/SE/W/22/Rev.5 at pages 20 and 21.

29 WT/COMTD/SE/W/24, December 13, 2010.

30 *Supra* Note 6.

31 Stiglitz, J. and Charlton, A. Undated. 'Initiative for Policy Dialogue: The Development Round of Negotiations in the Aftermath of Cancun'. A report for the Commonwealth Secretariat. London.

32 The SVEs quoted the reference from The Seoul Summit Document contained in TN/C/W/57, November 26, 2010.

33 *Supra* Note 30.

34 The author was Ambassador to the WTO for Antigua and Barbuda and led the country's representations on this matter that culminated in a favourable 2004 Panel decision.

35 See: http://www.wto.org/english/tratop_e/dispu_e/cases_e/ds285_e.htm for Summary of Dispute DS285, US -Antigua and Barbuda: Measures Affecting the Cross Border Supply of Gambling and Betting Services.

15 African Group and DDA – Maintaining Solidarity of a Large Coalition

Arsene M. Balihuta
Senior Presidential Advisor on Public Private Partnership in Uganda
Former Ambassador of Uganda to the WTO

Introduction

The WTO African Group is an informal group of African missions represented in Geneva. The Group was founded in 1995 to promote the development issues of interest to African countries; to overcome the non-representation of most African countries in Geneva and the lack of capacity of those that were represented; and to form a multi-nation vehicle that would carry issues of individual African countries into the open WTO fora, where such issues would not otherwise be heard by the more powerful members of the WTO.

Independent and technical, the African Group works closely with the African Union Mission in Geneva, the Economic Commission for Africa and other technical support institutions, such as the South Centre, the ICTSD and the UNCTAD. The African Group is coordinated by one of its members selected to service a six-month term on a renewable basis. The Coordinator calls meetings of the Group to discuss issues of interest to the Group, and specifically to enable the members to harmonise their positions in the WTO negotiations. The Coordinator also makes formal statements of the position on behalf of the Group in the various WTO negotiation fora, including the Green Room. In preparation for a Ministerial meeting the Coordinator oversees the intensive preparatory activity by the African countries' experts in Geneva and in capitals and briefs his Minister who acts as the spokesperson of the Group during the Ministerial.

The Group works closely with the WTO Secretariat, which has a dedicated Officer who assists in scheduling the Group's meetings, the availability of meeting rooms in the WTO building, and the availability of interpreters. Working closely with the Coordinator, the WTO officer also assists the Group in scheduling meetings with chairs of negotiating groups and other key consultations as well as guest speakers from WTO member countries and other multilateral institutions.

The current membership of this Group is shown in the table below. Some of the members of the Group also belong to other WTO groups such as the ACP; the LDCs; the largest cotton growing countries in Africa (C4), which consists of Benin, Mali, Chad and Burkina Faso; the G-20 and the G-33. All members of the African Group are members of the G-90.

Table: WTO African Group Member Countries

1. Angola	15. Gabon	29. Namibia
2. Benin	16. Gambia	30. Niger
3. Botswana	17. Ghana	31. Nigeria
4. Burkina Faso	18. Guinea	32. Rwanda
5. Burundi	19. Guinea Bissau	33. Senegal
6. Cameroon	20. Kenya	34. Sierra Leone
7. Cape Verde	21. Lesotho	35. South Africa
8. CAR	22. Madagascar	36. Swaziland
9. Chad	23. Malawi	37. Tanzania
10. Congo Brazzaville	24. Mali	38. Togo
11. DRC	25. Mauritania	39. Tunisia
12. Côte d'Ivoire	26. Mauritius	40. Uganda
13. Djibouti	27. Morocco	41. Zambia
14. Egypt	28. Mozambique	42. Zimbabwe

Source: World Trade Organisation

Beginnings and Evolution

Although several African countries were signatories to the GATT, and most of them had acceded to membership in the WTO by 1995, their participation in WTO negotiations remained quite limited due to the following factors:

i) inward-oriented development strategies followed by most countries in Africa in the 1950s and 1960s and during the GATT era, which gave these countries the view that they had little to gain from export trade and hence their limited participation in international trade negotiations at the time;[1]

ii) exclusion from the GATT of agricultural and textiles products that are of most interest to developing countries and the fact that most of these countries were beneficiaries of trade preferences, such as the Cotonou Partnership Agreement for ACP countries;[2]

iii) limited representation of African countries in Geneva and the inadequate capacity of most African Missions that were present in Geneva;

iv) lack of appreciation of the importance of WTO negotiations and laws on African national economies by some African leaders;

v) poor communication of African country Missions with their line ministries in capitals; and

vi) lack of institutional development and negotiation capacity within most of the African countries' governments.

The above factors notwithstanding, and in order to contribute to the increased participation of the African countries in WTO matters, the WTO African Group was founded in 1995 on the initiative of the representatives of Egypt, Senegal, South Africa and Tunisia, among others. At the beginning, the Group was strong and vibrant, making effective interventions as illustrated by its influence in making the DDA a development Round, as well as by its influence at the 2003 Cancun Ministerial meeting, where, working with the G-20, it became possible to reduce the hegemony of the US and the EU in the DDA negotiations and expunge the Singapore issues from the Round. Thereafter, particularly with the DDA settling into a long drawn stalemate, the Group's influence has wafted and waned depending on the charisma of the Ambassador coordinating the Group and, his or her technical knowledge and understanding of WTO and DDA issues, as well as the support the coordinating Mission gets from its capital.

However, despite the shortcomings as well as the ups and downs, the Group still wields strong influence in the WTO, especially when the members of the Group speak with one voice on an issue. This effect is even greater when they add their united voice to that of the other Groups within the G-90. For example, their strong support for the cotton issue continues to play an important role in keeping it on the DDA negotiations agenda.

Although the Coordinating Ambassador usually comes from the Ministry of Foreign Affairs of his or her country, in WTO matters she or he usually works with and reports to the Minister of Trade in his country. Where the country has capacity, it is the representatives/technical experts from the Ministry of Trade that should handle WTO trade negotiations. Where such capacity does not exist, it is career diplomats/technical experts that handle the WTO negotiation issues. But, at all times they usually work with their Ministry of Trade counterparts in their respective capitals. The authority to negotiate WTO issues, therefore, emanates from the respective Ministries of Trade.

An ideal Group Coordinator would constantly bear in mind the interests of the Group country members from the respective Ministries of Trade. These would normally actualise as country ideas coming in the form of country draft proposals or instructions to support already existing proposals. The role of the Ambassador Coordinator is to schedule meetings of colleague ambassadors who then mandate the Group of Experts to craft the ideas into proposals or appropriate WTO negotiations language. A structure of the African Group is represented in the figure below. This has remained more or less the same since the founding of the Group.

Unlike the other African Groups in the UN, concerned with Human Rights and other issues, the WTO African Group is a technical group whose mandate emanates from the Ministries of Trade in the African Group member countries and not from positions arrived at jointly at African Union deliberations. Meetings for the African Union Ministers of Trade are regularly organised to review the WTO African Group positions on various issues and these are adopted by the Ministers, which then transform the issues into African Union trade negotiation issues.

Figure: Organisational Structure of the African Group

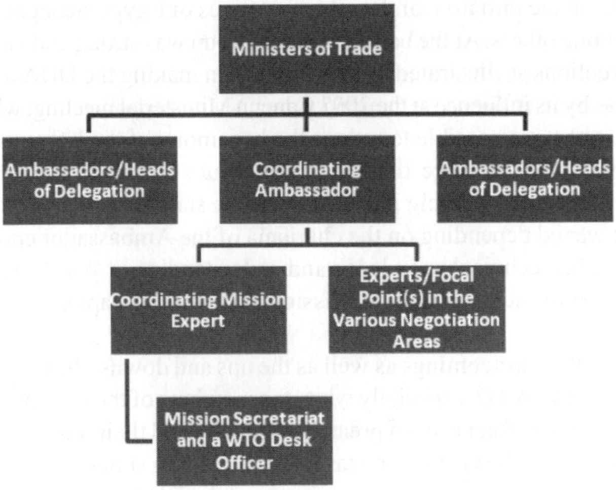

Source: Author

Issues of Interest for the African Group

Although the primary focus of the African Group is the promotion of the development issues in the DDA, the Group also promotes all DDA issues that are of interest to all its members. This means that, since the Group includes countries as diverse as South Africa on the one hand, and Burundi on the other, the Group tries to engage in the DDA negotiations in such a way that it advocates for the interests of each of its Members as much as possible, and in every negotiation forum whenever opportunity arises. Needless to say, this is quite a challenging task because some members' interests may be diametrically opposed to some other members' interests. The challenge can become quite daunting when two members happen to be in the same regional grouping.

An example is the effect of the proposed treatment of Paragraph 6 countries that include Kenya, a developing country, which is a member of the African Group and the EAC alongside Burundi, Rwanda, Tanzania and Uganda, which are LDCs. One of the proposals by the Paragraph 6 countries was that these countries should be exempt from the application of the formula proposed for developing countries in NAMA and instead be allowed to bind 70 percent of their tariff lines at a maximum tariff of 28.5 percent. If this proposal were to be accepted in the DDA negotiations, this would mean that Kenya would bind some of its tariff lines at 28.5 percent, and this would imply that its LDC partners in the EAC would also be obliged to follow suit, although for them, as LDCs, they are not obliged to make any tariff reduction commitment in the DDA.

Diversity notwithstanding, the African Group has always championed clear and distinct interests for its member countries. By and large, these interests are handled as follows:

- a member country or a combination of some member countries of the Group with a similar negotiation issue would bring the issue to the attention of the Coordinator of the Group;

- the Coordinator would convene an Ambassador level meeting of the Group to discuss the issue, among others;
- the Ambassadors would mandate the Group Experts to discuss the issue further and formulate the issue into a WTO compatible proposal;
- the Coordinator of the Group Experts would then convene a meeting of experts to meet and discuss the issue, among other issues that may have been pending until then;
- the experts would then approach the Coordinator of the Group to call a meeting of Ambassadors to consider the issue further;
- if the meeting of Ambassadors is satisfied with the state of the draft proposal, they mandate the experts to forward the draft proposal to the WTO Secretariat;
- at an appropriate time, the Coordinator of the Group is then given an opportunity to read the proposal on the floor of the Negotiation Group Meeting in the Council Hall of the WTO;
- other delegations would then support or oppose the proposal in such a meeting in accordance with how they view the proposal to be in furtherance or hindrance of trade interests; and
- the proposal then becomes a formal negotiations Group proposal that eventually finds its way into the language of the relevant Negotiation Group Chair's text.

Much as the African Group has specific issues of interest that it pursues, all the negotiation issues in the DDA will affect its member countries sooner or later. It is, therefore, of the utmost importance that the African Group pronounces itself on all DDA issues, particularly those that have a bearing on the present or future development of the African economies. For example, the African Group was regularly reminded that while it was legitimate for it to focus on the DFQF issue, it should steer clear of the subsidies issue since most of its members would not in any case be obliged to make any commitments on subsidies. Therefore, the African Group could not have a clear negotiation position on subsidies. However, in 2007 the Group members agreed to take clear positions on each of the DDA negotiation issues. With the support of the African Union, the Economic Commission for Africa, UNCTAD, ICTSD and the South Centre, an attempt was made by the Group, through a series of well organised and well attended workshops by the Group delegations, to rigorously organise all the DDA negotiations issues in a matrix form indicating the position of the African Group for each of the issues in the DDA negotiations.

This suggestion was initially resisted by some members of the Group on the grounds that this would lead the African Group to lay their "negotiating cards" on the table, which would in turn weaken the negotiation position of the Group. But another unspoken reason was that some members of the Group did not wish to antagonise their powerful country allies who were meant to undertake deep cuts in their domestic support. After some debate, the proposal was adopted and consequently the Group held a series of intensive workshops during which the Group Experts were facilitated by technical persons from the institutions mentioned above. The sessions were chaired by Ambassadors from the respective Missions. The result of these intensive sessions was a bold statement in a matrix form showing African Group positions on each of the negotiation issues, particularly those of development concern to the African countries. These issues are discussed in the following paragraphs.

Domestic Support

The African Group came out clearly and proposed that the US reduce its overall domestic agriculture subsidies to between US$10-12bn per annum; the EU and Japan should reduce their subsidies by 80 percent from their current levels; while the developing countries that have such subsidies should reduce them by lower amounts than the reductions undertaken by the EU, Japan and the US and that the affected developing countries should also be given longer periods to implement the reductions. This position did not go down well with the delegation of one of the powerful WTO member countries, which through the WTO Secretariat, unsuccessfully put pressure on the then Coordinator of the African Group to reverse the Group's position on domestic support. The Coordinator was adamant because it has been proved that domestic support by the developed countries has in many cases ruined agricultural industries in some African countries. For example, the cotton industry in the C4 countries; the rice growing industry in Ghana and the chicken farming industry in Benin have been negatively affected by massive subsidies in some developed countries. The issue of subsidies is therefore of importance to the members of the African Group.

The African Group was in agreement with the position of the Agriculture Negotiating Group Chairman that export subsidies should be phased out by the developed countries by 2013. The Group was also of the view that there should be:

- special consideration for LDCs and NFIDCs;
- longer implementation periods for developing countries; and
- strict disciplines on both volume and value.

The negotiation issue revealed, perhaps more than any other, the precarious negotiation position of the African Group. Whereas many LDCs and developing countries with plentiful food supplies and high potential for the development of the food supply sectors would have liked to see an end to the export subsidies from the developed countries and some advanced developing countries, they found themselves going along, in solidarity, with countries that have a considerable food deficit and, therefore, need food aid for the foreseeable future. Thus, although it was generally agreed in principle that export subsidies for agricultural products destroy the agricultural sectors of some countries, as illustrated by the negative impact of US and EU subsidised agricultural exports on the agricultural sectors of some West African countries, care had to be taken to preserve the positive impact of subsidised food aid to a considerable number of food deficit countries, particularly those with great numbers of refugees. This situation also illustrates the fact that WTO issues cannot be driven by trade considerations alone. A fair treatment of some African countries' negotiations concerns must be cognisant of humanitarian issues as well.

Much time was, therefore, spent by the African Group negotiation experts in discussing the issues of food aid until quite clear language was developed by the experts. This was then reflected almost entirely in the Agricultural Group Negotiation Text of July 2007. This text provided that food aid should be:

- needs driven and the needs should be decided by those recognised agencies responsible for the needs assessment and the emergency appeal and the definition of the World Food Programme should be taken as a reference;

- untied from commercial exports of goods and services and not linked to market development objectives of the donor member country;
- in fully grant form;
- open to a member, at any time, to seek advice from relevant UN/international humanitarian agencies in the event that there is no autonomous advice;
- based on needs assessment conducted by a recognised agency such as the UN or the Red Cross;
- targeted to an identified vulnerable population;
- provided to address specific developmental objectives or nutritional requirements;
- more flexible concerning the terms applicable to the self-financing period, minimum interest rates, premiums and risk-sharing provisions; and
- based on the understanding that a sovereign government or, in exceptional circumstances, the UN Secretary General should be the ones to declare a situation as an emergency that requires food aid.

Market Access for Agricultural Products

When looked at from the perspective of capitalist efficiency, it would be ideal for the most efficient producers of agricultural products to specialise in the production of food and other agricultural products and then sell them to other countries whose citizens should then specialise in the production of goods for which they have the best comparative advantage. This is indeed the argument of the developed countries when it is on this basis that they are seeking market opening for agricultural products in developing countries and LDCs.

But agricultural products, particularly food, are more than mere tradables. More specifically, food is life. The way it is produced, cooked and eaten constitutes an important part of a people's culture. Therefore, suggesting to a people that they should depend on some other country to produce for them their staples, while they focus on the production of non-food items for the rest of the world, flies in the face of the desire of most peoples to have control of their capacity to provide food for themselves. It also goes to the heart of food security and independence. This could indeed be the root cause of the failure to conclude the Doha Round as scheduled. Thus, while the developed countries would, on the one hand, like developing countries and LDCs that are able to do so, to lower tariffs on their agricultural products, they themselves would like to protect what they call "sensitive" products by maintaining high tariffs on these products. Furthermore, the same developed countries are strongly opposed to what the G-33 is calling "special" products. This negotiation issue illustrates quite poignantly the mercantilist nature of the WTO negotiations.

There has been considerable discussion on this issue by the African Group at both the Ambassadorial and expert levels. The position of the African Group on this complex issue may be summarised as follows:

- With regard to the three level formula, there should be at least a 54 percent average tariff cut for developed countries, and at most a 36 percent cut for developing countries. Developed and developing countries must be accorded differential treatment on the level of thresholds. Furthermore, developing countries should undertake, at most, cuts that are two-thirds of those undertaken by developed countries.

- Since sensitive products is an instrument that bars market access for developing countries, the selection or percentage of sensitive products should be as low as possible, and developed countries wishing to avail themselves of this mechanism should compensate trading partners through substantial tariff quota expansion. Sensitive products should thus create genuine market access opportunities for these products.

- The African Group supports the G-33 proposal as the basis for negotiations. It also supports tropical products liberalisation, so long as the liberalisation does not have a negative impact on preferences.

Agricultural Preferences

With respect to agricultural preferences, the African Group position was that there should be a longer implementation period, which is not less than 10 years. It also stated that preference-giving countries should provide a package of measures to enable preference-receiving countries to diversify. This package would be monitored and reviewed on an annual basis by the GC.

Cotton

The African Group has always supported the C4 on the issue of cotton and has adopted the formula proposed by the C4. However, despite this unshakable support from the African Group, the C4 does not wish to expand the cotton issue to the rest of the African cotton-producing countries. While Uganda was coordinating the African Group, efforts were made to establish the C36 that would include all of the 36 cotton producing African countries. Although this move would have strengthened the negotiating power on the cotton issue, there was a seemingly impenetrable resistance to this initiative from the C4 and their sponsors.

Commodities

World trade in commodities is characterised by the following factors, among others: commodities predominantly flow from the LDCs and the developing countries to the developed countries; low and unstable prices and value addition on these commodities within the developed countries. The end result of these factors is that the preponderant proportion of surplus from the production of these commodities has been accruing to the developed countries during the past three centuries.

In order to contribute to a resolution of this problem under the auspices of the WTO DDA negotiations, the African Group submitted a comprehensive proposal for the establishment of modalities on commodities.[3] The proposal, made under the mandate of the WTO Hong Kong Ministerial Declaration, attempted to clarify export restrictions and other measures, which although not consistent with the rules of GATT would be undertaken by developing countries participating in commodity agreements made up only of commodity dependent producing countries. It was also aimed at clarifying and improving existing WTO rules so that developing countries that export agricultural commodities are explicitly allowed to form or take part in commodity agreements solely between commodity producers or between consumer and producer countries. Furthermore, the proposal also wanted the WTO to re-affirm that commodity-trading developing countries and LDCs should be allowed to impose export restrictions and taxes in pursuance of such agreements.

In addition to the above proposed provisions, the Group also proposed that:

i) modalities should be established to ensure satisfactory reductions in tariff escalation and the elimination of non-tariff measures affecting trade in commodities; and
ii) technical and financial assistance should be provided to enable the affected countries to implement supply management schemes for the commodities.

The Peace Clause

Concerned with the negative effects of export credits, domestic subsidies and dumping of developed countries' agricultural products on African countries' agricultural sectors, the African Group does not accept the extension of the Peace Clause and has submitted a proposal to that effect.

Non-agricultural Market Access (NAMA)

The limited participation in the NAMA negotiations by the African Group is quite telling. Since the majority of the African countries have limited participation in world trade owing to supply side constraints, they are not as engaged in the NAMA negotiations as they are in agriculture. Nevertheless in NAMA the Group supports the simple Swiss formula with double coefficients. In most other areas of NAMA the Group has sought analytical studies from institutions such as the Economic Commission for Africa (ECA) to guide the African Group decisions on such issues. However, if it were not for the lack of foresight and capacity, the African countries should also be actively participating in the NAMA negotiations because the decision that will be agreed upon in this negotiation group will surely become binding on the African countries once they have successfully crossed the Rubicon of development.

Trade-Related Aspects of Intellectual Property Rights

Accumulation of wealth under capitalism has become a remarkably life-threatening phenomenon in some instances. A situation has arisen, and is increasingly arising, in which the thirst for intellectual property is encroaching on life forms whose genuine origin cannot be invented by any stretch of imagination. Take for instance the basmati rice case patented by some firm in the US. Suppose the Indians and Pakistanis had patented their basmati rice, the firm in the US would not have had such an easy access to the germplasm of the basmati rice in the first place. To take another example, suppose the ancient Chinese had patented the art of writing: probably there would be more illiterate people in the world today. More recently, there have been cases of misappropriation of genetic resources and traditional knowledge of the peoples in the LDCs and developing countries that have resulted in registration of patents in developed countries.

To contribute to the solution of this problem, the African Group presented a proposal to the TRIPs Council that put forward comprehensive possible modalities on the treatment of patenting of life forms, *sui generis* systems for protecting plant varieties and protection of traditional knowledge. The Group re-emphasised its position that:

- The TRIPs Agreement should be amended to prohibit patents on all life forms, because such patents are contrary to the moral and cultural norms of many societies.

- The requirement to protect plant varieties should not in any way undermine but support members' rights to public goals such as food security and poverty elimination.

- The WTO should adopt a decision on traditional knowledge that would establish a WTO Committee on traditional knowledge and genetic resources to oversee the protection of traditional knowledge and enforcement of rights of WTO members.

- The non-commercial use of plant varieties and the system of seed saving and exchange as well as selling among farmers are rights that should be ensured as matters of important public policy to ensure food security and preserve the integrity of rural or local communities.

- While the legitimate rights of commercial plant breeders should be protected, these should be balanced against the needs of farmers and local communities.

- Any *sui generis* system should enable members to retain their right to adopt and develop measures that encourage and promote the traditions of their farming communities and indigenous peoples in innovating and developing new plant varieties and enhancing biodiversity.

- TRIPs, CBD and ITPGR should be implemented in a mutually supportive and consistent manner, so that members retain the right to require within their domestic laws the disclosure of sources of any biological material that constitutes some input in the inventions claimed and proof of benefit sharing.

- Traditional knowledge and inventions of local communities should be protected and genetic resources and traditional knowledge should be documented to assist searches and examining novelty and inventive step. There should be TRIPs obligations requiring every member to prohibit and prevent misappropriation of genetic resources and traditional knowledge, through requirements for disclosure of the source of the resources and knowledge involved in the claimed inventions and a demonstration of compliance with domestic procedures in the member country where the resources and knowledge originate.

- There should not be a possibility, within TRIPs, of patents on micro-organisms as well as on non-biological and microbiological processes for the production of plants and animals.

- The distinction drawn in Article 27.3(b) for microorganisms and for non-biological and microbiological processes is artificial and unwarranted and should be removed from TRIPs, so that the exception from patentability in paragraph 3(b) covers plants, animals and microorganisms as well as essentially biological, non-biological and microbiological processes for the production of plants and animals.

- The TRIPs Council should adopt a decision on protecting traditional knowledge, which the African Group annexed with its proposal. The draft decision stated that the existence of traditional knowledge in any form shall defeat the novelty and inventiveness requirements of patents under any laws of all members.

- Article 29 of the TRIPs Agreement should be modified to contain these rights and obligations by including the requirement for equity, disclosure of the community of origin and demonstration of compliance with domestic procedures for all such patent applications.

In addition, the African Group supported a proposal submitted by Brazil and India and including Bolivia, Colombia, Cuba, Dominican Republic, Ecuador, Peru, and Thailand to amend the TRIPs Agreement so that patent applicants are required to disclose the country of origin of genetic resources and traditional knowledge used in the inventions, evidence that they received "prior informed consent" (a term used in the CBD) and evidence of "fair and equitable" benefit sharing.

While many developing countries supported the African proposal, Switzerland made a more or less counter proposal, which suggests that national patent laws should require the declaration of the source of genetic resources and traditional knowledge in patent applications by amending the regulations under the Patent Cooperation Treaty of WIPO. Thus, Switzerland is of the view that WIPO is the primary forum to deal with the issue of IPRs and traditional knowledge and that TRIPs and CBD can be implemented without conflict and there is no need to modify the provisions of either. In addition, this country has derailed serious consideration of this issue by proposing parallel negotiations on geographical indications. Similarly, several developed countries, such as Japan and Canada said that WIPO has technical expertise in this area, and the TRIPs Council should wait to see what emerges from the WIPO.

For its part, the US was of the view that traditional knowledge should be removed from the agenda in the TRIPs Council since TRIPs was not a suitable instrument to ensure disclosure, prior informed consent and benefit sharing as proposed by Brazil, Cuba, Ecuador, India, Peru, Thailand and Venezuela. Rather, contracts would be more effective to resolve the issue, and the WIPO should be the lead agency on the matter. The US was also of the view that the TRIPs Agreement was functioning well, only that some developing countries had not yet notified their laws to the WTO under the TRIPs Agreement.

Although the EC welcomed the Swiss and African Group proposals, it wanted to leave open the question of whether mandatory disclosure could be done under the WTO or the WIPO. It was also among a group of WTO members that in July 2008 called for a "procedural decision" to negotiate three intellectual property issues in parallel: two geographical indications issues and the "disclosure" proposal (see document TN/C/W/52 of July, 19, 2008). Although the EC used some Machiavellian arm-twisting tactics on some of the developing country negotiation group coordinators, members remain divided over this idea.

All the issues discussed above have an important bearing on the economic development of the member countries of the African Group. Take for instance the issues of subsidies and cotton. The cotton industry and indeed, the agricultural sectors in most African countries will flourish with difficulty as long as developed countries continue to pour money into their agricultural and cotton-growing sectors. Consider also the issue of patenting life forms that are uniquely found in tropical LDCs/developing countries. By the time the LDCs/developing countries develop a research and innovation capacity to patent such life forms they will find that most of these life forms have been patented by scientists in the developed countries. And yet economic growth and development is increasingly becoming a function of intellectual property accumulation and technological development. This means that the TRIPs/CBD issue is of utmost development importance to the members of the African Group.

In order to advance the interests of the Group more effectively, the Group works closely with the LDCs and the ACP. The Group members are also members of the G-90. For some issues members of the Group work with selected individual developed member countries. For example, when the author arrived in Geneva in 2006 as Uganda's Permanent Representative to WTO, he was informed by the Mission's WTO Desk Officer that although Uganda had made a good proposal on trade facilitation, the proposal had not been "heard" by the WTO Members since Uganda was a small country. The author's first participation in the WTO General Council Meeting, therefore, was for the reading of the same trade facilitation proposal, but this time having worked with the US to support the proposal. After the reading of this proposal and its immediate support by the United States, the proposal was then "heard" by the WTO members who then raised their flags and supported or opposed to it in accordance with their national interests.

The WTO Secretariat and the members of the WTO have come to appreciate the importance of the African Group in the WTO negotiations. This appreciation becomes more pronounced when the Group Coordinator is charismatic and has considerable understanding and knowledge of WTO issues, particularly those issues of interest to the African Group as a whole. And when the Group works with other negotiating groups and countries within the G-90 it becomes a veritable force to reckon with as was demonstrated at the formulation of the DDA and the Cancun Ministerial Conference.

Challenges and the Future

Considering what has been said in the preceding paragraphs, the past, present and future challenges of the WTO African Group arise from the:

- diversity and lack of capacity within the African Group itself;
- lack of capacity within the African Group member countries;
- attitudes of the developed and advanced developing countries;
- structure and functioning of the WTO; and
- nature and structure of WTO negotiations.

The African Group membership is diverse because it is based on a geographical rather than economic grouping. Thus, while the WTO is a trade liberalisation organisation that focusses on trade issues, the African Group membership is centred on belonging to the African continent. These countries are quite diverse in terms of their economic development and hence their levels of participation in global trade. This explains the divergence of their positions on negotiation issues in the DDA. This also may explain why at times a coordinator of the Group gets tempted to conflate his/her national negotiation issues with those of the Group. Furthermore, while most West and North African countries are Francophone, most Eastern and Southern African countries are Anglophone. Somewhere in-between are a few Portuguese-speaking countries. This is the problem of language. The Group must, therefore, have translation for its meetings. Fortunately, the WTO Secretariat has ample capacity to provide translation for Group meetings. There is also the challenge of some Group experts getting tempted to leak negotiation information to other delegations/institutions in preparation for "greener pastures" when their tours in Geneva come to an end. For the foreseeable future, membership of the African Group is likely to be based on belonging to the African continent.

Therefore, like EU members, African Group members must come to terms with this fact and learn to smartly deal with the diversity. For instance rather than members at times wasting time developing lengthy arguments on the unavailability of translated documents from English to French and *vice versa*, they should spend their time trying to become bilingual in English and French. Similarly, the Coordinator of the Group should at all times strive to be charismatic and Pan-African in outlook.

A considerable number of African Group member countries' leaders do not seem to properly appreciate the implication of the decisions taken in WTO negotiations for their economies. For example, one African Head of Delegation/Mission obtained an air ticket and made other arrangements for his Minister of Finance to come to Geneva to attend one of the scheduled General Council Meetings at the height of the DDA Negotiations in 2008. After considerable insistence by the Head of Delegation that the Minister should come to Geneva, the Minister declined, saying that the WTO had nothing to do with his work. That experience is remarkable, given that the Minister is responsible for preparing and reading an annual national fiscal budget, which relies heavily on import taxes, and that the maximum import tariff he can set for any good was probably decided during the Uruguay and other GATT Rounds.

In addition to the appreciable lack of resources to maintain missions in Geneva, leaders' attitudes like the one illustrated above account for the lack of adequate presence of several African countries in Geneva. It also underlies the lack of development of capacity in capitals to deal with WTO issues, as well as the lack of capacity of the missions of the countries represented in Geneva. This challenge should serve as a wakeup call for the leadership within the African countries to appreciate that the decisions made in WTO negotiations go to the heart of their capacity to collect/increase import tax revenues that are so important for their economic development. Indeed, in many countries import taxes constitute the bulk of revenues used to provide development-leading infrastructure and services to the people.

Mercantilism still underlies the attitudes of most of the developed countries in terms of their participation in the WTO generally, as well as in the way the DDA negotiations are organised and conducted. Developed countries still insist on the pursuit of their narrow national interests. They use divide and rule tactics, including going as far as manoeuvring outspoken individual African Group negotiators from their posts in Geneva. This challenge, which is not likely to go away in the foreseeable future, can be effectively dealt with by African Group member governments clearly knowing what their trade interests are; unwaveringly supporting their trade negotiators in Geneva in pursuit of these interests; and building the negotiation capacity both in Geneva and in capitals.

The administrative and governance structure of the WTO, as well as the principles by which its trade rules are made renders it more amenable to greater control by a powerful Director General and the more powerful developed countries, as well as the proliferation of negotiation groups. Thus, for example, unlike the World Bank, the IMF and other intergovernmental organisations, the WTO has no Board of Directors. Instead its supreme organ is the Ministerial Conference, which should meet every two years. Currently, the WTO membership stands at 153. This implies that a Ministerial Conference would have 153 Ministers or their representatives. Moreover, since WTO decisions are made by consensus, this would mean that 153 Ministers would have to be persuaded by someone in order to come to a consensus on a single issue or a package of issues such as that contained in the DDA. This has meant that the Director General has to work with the Heads of Delegation of a few developed and the more advanced developing countries to agree on an issue or issues and then the less powerful countries get persuaded in one way or another to endorse the agreement. This is then called a consensus.

For instance, at the July 2008 Ministerial, although several ministers were invited to Geneva, most of them remained in the WTO "corridors" as those from Australia, Brazil, China, the EU, India and the US held intensive negotiations in the Green Room to agree on the most crucial issues in the DDA. Furthermore, with the exception of the EC, which is represented by one negotiator, all African Group members can be represented only by their Coordinator, even though each developed/advanced developing country is invited in the Green Room. In addition, the atmosphere in the Green Room is quite intimidating and highly technical. The African Group can meet this challenge by, among other things, insisting on selecting a bold Coordinator with a good understanding of geopolitics and international trade and who is also a good negotiator with a good grasp of DDA issues.

In terms of substance, the DDA is complex. It was meant to tackle issues left over from the Uruguay Round, including subsidies and market access for agricultural products, as well as the implementation of the Uruguay Round Agreements. It was complicated further by the demand from developing countries to include development issues. Furthermore, the agreement on all the issues in the agenda should be a single undertaking. Despite the complexity of the agenda there has been an urgent desire to complete the Round as soon as possible. One consequence of this urgency has been marathon and parallel meetings of negotiation committees/groups. Given the thinness on the ground of the African Group both in numbers and capacity, this has posed a serious challenge to the African Group members. The WTO Secretariat can contribute to easing this challenge by restructuring the negotiations in such a way that important negotiations committee sessions are held in series. However, the African Group member countries should also increase their presence and capacity both in Geneva and in their capitals.

As the DDA negotiations have progressed, more informal, smaller, issue-based alliances have emerged. These have affected the African Group to the extent that the issues championed by these emergent groups have antagonised the interests of some of the members of the Group. For instance, the emergence of the SVE Group has raised some concerns for some countries of the African Group that are also LDCs. This is because the SVEs have in some instances requested S&D treatment that was initially thought would only be enjoyed by the LDCs. Yet some of these countries, such as Mauritius, are quite economically advanced in comparison with most of the LDCs. Receiving the same market access as the LDCs, therefore, such countries could wipe out the preferential benefits that would otherwise have accrued to the LDCs.

The WTO African Group was established in 1995; that is about six years before the launching of the DDA in 2001. The Group was established to overcome some of the challenges highlighted above. Since these challenges will exist beyond the DDA, the Group's existence will also be necessary beyond the conclusion of the DDA. Indeed, the view in this chapter is that the importance of the Group should increase after the DDA, since it will have to be a major vehicle by which African WTO member countries will follow upon the implementation of the DDA agreements, particularly those related to the development aspects.

Furthermore, much as the African countries had hoped that the DDA would be a development Round, it is increasingly becoming clear that since the developed countries have a different concept of development from that espoused by the developing countries, for the expedient compromises to complete the DDA Round, ample justice may not be done to the development aspects of the DDA as expected. Therefore the African Group, in conjunction with Groups from other developing countries should prepare to re-table their development interests in a post-Doha Round. Meanwhile, the African Group member countries should consider increasing their representation in Geneva, as well as building their trade negotiation capacity both in capitals and in Geneva. Furthermore, slowly but surely, the share of African countries in global trade will continue to increase. Their power and voice will also increase concomitantly in WTO issues. Therefore, it is expected that despite the challenges, the WTO African Group will become more relevant and important in the post-DDA era.

Endnotes

1 Page, S. 2002. 'Developing Countries in GATT/WTO Negotiations', Oversease Development Institute, London, Available at http://www.odi.org.uk/resources/download/3617.pdf

2 *Ibid.*

3 Khor, M. Third World Network, Geneva, June 10, 2006.

16

LDC Group – Shared Challenges, United Responses

Dr. Matern Y.C. Lumbanga

Ambassador Extraordinary and Plenipotentiary Permanent Representative of Tanzania to the UN and other International Organisations to the WTO

Introduction

The UN began paying special attention to LDCs in the late 1960s, recognising them as the most vulnerable members of the international community. LDCs are the poorest countries in the world, characterised by low gross domestic product, poverty among their inhabitants, and low levels of economic diversification. In the latest triennial review of the list of LDCs in 2009 issued by the UN Economic and Social Council (ECOSOC), based on recommendations by the Committee for Development Policy (CDP), the criteria for determining the new list of LDCs include the following:

- **Gross national income (GNI) per capita:** a three-year average GNI per capita under USD 905 is required for inclusion in the list of LDCs and above USD1086 is required for graduation;

- **Human assets index (HAI):** LDCs have weak human resources, determined by an index based on nutrition, health, education and adult literacy indicators; and

- **Economic vulnerability index (EVI):** LDCs suffer from economic vulnerability determined by an index based on indicators of instability of agricultural production; export instability; economic importance of non-traditional activities; merchandise export concentration and economic smallness; population size; remoteness and homelessness owing to natural disasters.

Under the recommendation of ECOSOC, the UN General Assembly decides which countries are included in (or graduate from) the list of LDCs. A country can qualify for addition to the list if it meets the above three inclusion criteria. Conversely, a country qualifies for graduation if it meets at least two of the three criteria for graduation as explained above. In addition, no country with a population exceeding 75 million can be considered for addition to the list.

According to the World Bank's new poverty estimates, 1.4 billion people in the LDCs live in extreme poverty, at US$1.25 per person per day or less as compared to the poor elsewhere in the world living in moderate poverty, or USD2 per person per day.[1] Currently, a total of 49 countries are listed as LDCs. They include 33 from sub-Saharan Africa, 15 from South and Eastern Asia, and Haiti in the Americas and the Caribbean. In these countries poverty is endemic, systemic and pervasive. The causes of this situation can be summarised as pressures related to demographic make-up, physical geography, agronomic conditions, disease ecology, unfavourable economic policy/fiscal framework, cultural barriers, governance failures and geopolitical conditions.

Only two countries so far have graduated from the list of LDCs: Botswana in December 1994 and Cape Verde in December 2007. Samoa was expected to graduate in December 2010 and Maldives in January 2011. The CDP in 2009 recommended that Equatorial Guinea be graduated from the list of LDCs, given its new status as an oil exporter. This is further elaborated under the paragraph on the Genesis of LDC Group in this chapter.

Least Developed Countries: Country Profile[2]

Africa (33)			
1	Angola	18	Madagascar
2	Benin	19	Malawi #
3	Burkina Faso #	20	Mali #
4	Burundi	21	Mauritania
5	Central African Republic #	22	Mozambique
6	Chad #	23	Niger #
7	Comoros *	24	Rwanda #
8	Democratic Republic of the Congo	25	Sao Tome and Principe *
9	Djibouti	26	Senegal
10	Equatorial Guinea	27	SierraLeone
11	Eritrea	28	Somalia
12	Ethiopia #	29	Sudan
13	The Gambia	30	Togo
14	Guinea	31	Uganda #
15	Guinea-Bissau *	32	United Republic of Tanzania
16	Lesotho #	33	Zambia #
17	Liberia		
Asia (15)			
1	Afghanistan **#**	9	Nepal
2.	Bangladesh	10	Samoa *
3	Bhutan **#**	11	Solomon Islands *
4	Cambodia	12	Timor- Leste *
5	Kiribati *	13	Tuvalu*
6	Lao People's Republic **#**	14	Vanuatu*
7	Maldives	15	Yemen
8	Myanmar		
Latin America and Caribbean (1)			
1	Haiti *		

\# Also SIDS
* Also LLDCs
Source: List of LDCs, UN-OHRLLS

Genesis of LDC Group in WTO

Following the formation of the WTO in 1995, developing countries fully recognised the importance of pre-round positioning after their experience in the Uruguay Round. Coalitions were formed, most notably in preparation for the Singapore Ministerial Conference of 1996, the Seattle Ministerial Conference of 1999, the Doha Ministerial Conference of 2001, and the Cancun Ministerial Conference of 2003.

Several coalitions pursued traditional policies on special and differential treatment. The LMG was formed in 1996 in opposition to the expansion of the trade agenda to include Singapore issues (trade and investment, trade and competition, trade facilitation and transparency in government procurement). The African Group and the ACP Group, as well as individual countries also continued to call for more special and differential treatment. Some coalition activity continued in the area of services, although it was less than during the Uruguay Round. Coalitions on agricultural issues, such as the Cairns Group, continued from the Uruguay Round while others came into existence to prepare for the Seattle Ministerial Conference.

The LDC Group in the WTO was formed in 1999 and mainly raised implementation and accession issues as well as questions about participation, capacity building and technical assistance. Together with the ACP Group, the LDC Group and the African Group form the G-90, an umbrella coalition that emerged during the Cancun Ministerial Conference and opposed negotiations on the Singapore issues. The Sectoral Initiative in Favour of Cotton, a very small coalition of cotton exporters from LDCs (Benin, Burkina Faso, Chad and Niger) simply known as the C4 presented an interesting challenge during the Cancun Ministerial Meeting that cotton subsidies be abolished after a limited transition period in China, Europe and the US and that financial compensation be provided to offset the losses incurred by African cotton producers during the transition.

In the Tokyo and Uruguay Rounds, a lot of concessions for market access in textiles and agriculture had been given but had not yet materialised during the negotiation of the Doha Development Round. The MFN concessions on tariff and non-tariff measures agreed in the Uruguay Round on products of export interest to LDCs, mainly agriculture and textiles, remained unresolved until the Hong Kong Ministerial Conference when LDCs were provided with DFQF market access. However, operationalisation of this provision has become a bone of contention. At the end of the Uruguay Round of world trade talks in 1994 developed countries also promised technical assistance to enhance the capacity of developing countries, particularly LDCs, to participate in the WTO and in world trade. The first WTO Ministerial Conference, held in 1996, recognised that the LDCs faced difficulties in integrating into the global economy. This led to the adoption of the WTO Plan of Action for LDCs. The following year, the WTO convened a high level meeting to discuss the specific needs of the LDCs and to formulate a programme to strengthen their trade capacities, including supply-side and market access capacities. The outcome of this meeting was what became known as the Integrated Framework (IF) for Trade-Related Technical Assistance (TRTA) to LDCs.

A number of evaluations of the IF were undertaken, and the general conclusion was that the IF provided a good framework for helping the LDCs enhance their trade development capacity and facilitating adjustment and integration into the multilateral trading system. However, it became clear that there were still significant shortcomings in the process and that IF generally failed to mainstream trade into the Poverty Reduction Strategy Papers (PRSPs) process. Furthermore, LDCs had not been provided with adequate financial and human resources to deliver the intended outcomes. The process had been slow and the success in moving from the diagnostics and priority setting of the IF to investments by donors and agencies under their permanent programmes had been relatively low. Again the issue of country ownership had been weak. All these weaknesses led to the formulation of the current Enhanced Integrated Framework (EIF) to address these challenges.

Progress of LDC Group

The LDC Group operates as a coalition within the WTO to improve its bargaining power. This coalition develops agreed negotiating positions to pursue LDCs' common interests. It is worth noting that there had been some confusion in the past over which LDC is next to take the co-ordinatorship of the Group. Reluctance to take on the position can be a manifestation of lack of capacity within the Geneva Missions. This issue and the establishment of subject-specific focal points will be expounded further under the challenges facing the LDC group. It is due to this fact that the Group adopted a system of coordination that follows the alphabetical order of country names, taking into consideration the element of capacity availability at both the ambassador and experts levels. In the early days coordination was on a rotational sixth-monthly basis and was later extended to one year, although some flexibility was allowed to take account of prevailing circumstances.

In reality, WTO negotiations proceed not by consensus of all members, but by a process of informal negotiations between small groups of countries. Such negotiations are often called "Green Room" negotiations (after the colour of the WTO Director-General's Office), or "Mini-Ministerials," when they involve a few selected ministers from some member countries. These processes, which involve 20 to 35 countries that are interested in the text being discussed, have been regularly criticised by many WTO developing country members, including LDCs, which are often excluded from these negotiations. The LDC Group coordinator is normally invited to the Green Room process. This process has been contested as it favours the major powers, and it is one of the concerns that led to the collapse of Seattle and Cancun Ministerial Conferences. It should be understood that in order to ensure transparency and inclusiveness everything that has gained consensus in small negotiating groups must be brought to the TNC chaired by the WTO Director General and later to the General Council (GC), which is the highest body of the WTO, chaired by an Ambassador from a member country appointed by the whole membership.

It is important to note that the only category of developing countries formally recognised by the WTO is the LDC as further elaborated below. The LDC Group benefits from WTO Secretariat that arranges for meeting rooms in the WTO building and translation facilities. This is not the case for other negotiating groups in the WTO. That being said, the 1947 GATT Agreement did not identify developing countries as a group. The addition of Part IV on Trade and Development in 1964 mentions "less-developed members" but does not distinguish between all developing countries and the poorest of those countries. The UN created the LDC category in 1971, and in time members proposed that elements specifically benefiting "the least developed among the developing countries" should be built into trade negotiations. Later, the creation of a special group for LDCs and the possibility of special provisions for these LDCs were formally proposed. Ultimately, the Enabling Clause established the legal framework for special and more favourable treatment regarding LDCs in 1979. The WTO eventually gave an institutional home to LDCs with the creation of a Subcommittee on LDCs in 1995 as a subsidiary body of the CTD to *inter alia,* review periodically the operation of the special provisions for LDCs in the WTO Agreements and consider specific measures to assist and facilitate the expansion of LDCs' trade. In 2003, the LDC Unit was established in the WTO Secretariat to give more focus and attention to the specific problems of LDCs.

WTO agreements also recognise LDCs as a distinct group with special needs that must be addressed as a subset of S&D treatment. This has allowed for a dynamic process, enabling LDCs to better identify and formulate their needs and to negotiate and gain specific advantages as a group.

The LDCs have increased their negotiating power by forming a coalition that develops negotiating positions agreed upon in order to pursue their common interests. Prior to the Doha Ministerial Conference, LDCs had five broad major concerns that needed to be addressed by the multilateral trading system: the supply side constraints (infrastructure, human resources development, attractive investment conditions, etc.); the need to enhance the productive capacity of their economies; predictable and easy market access for their exports; problems related to the implementation of the existing WTO Agreements; and difficulties in getting accession to the WTO for those LDCs that were not yet members of the WTO. All of these issues were carefully analysed, articulated and documented by the LDC Ministers when they met in Zanzibar, Tanzania, culminating in the Zanzibar Declaration adopted by the Ministers in July 2001. It is very significant that through Paragraph 42, the Doha Conference acknowledged LDCs' concerns by making specific reference to the Zanzibar Declaration. Through Paragraph 43, the IF was also endorsed by ministers as a viable model for LDCs' trade development.

The Cancun Ministerial Conference, held in September 2003 was the first conference where the LDCs established themselves as an influential group whose views should be taken into consideration in the WTO negotiations. In addition, the growing role of Brazil, China, India and South Africa is undeniably an important development and is continuing in strength contrary to that of the industrialised economies (the G-8). These countries continue to consolidate their ability to define common goals for the groups they are leading, most notably the G-20, this means they have had a growing influence in the WTO negotiations too. Although the leadership role of large and medium-income developing countries, such as Brazil, China and India, is undeniable, it should not overshadow the steadily increasing and broadening activities of larger coalitions of weaker states, such as the African Group and the LDC Group. The last two groups (whose memberships largely overlap) accounted for two-thirds of the proposals synthesised in the Chairman's document at Cancun; while India produced only five proposals on its own and a few more as part of a coalition.

While many LDCs do not have much of an individual voice and little institutional support, this has made it difficult to organise and sustain a coalition. However, the WTO agreements have given them the opportunity to raise their profile and level of impact, as seen at the Hong Kong Ministerial Meeting in 2005. The LDC Group successfully negotiated commitments in many areas, the most important of these being the DFQF market access for products originating from LDCs from 2008 or no later than the start of the implementation period in a manner that ensures stability, security and predictability; and the elimination of all forms of export subsidies on cotton by developed countries.

Substantive Issues of Interest to LDCs with a Significant Development Impact

DFQF Market Access

Agriculture and NAMA are the most important issues of interest to the LDC Group in the WTO. Agriculture accounts for more than 80 percent of the labour force in many LDCs and 70 percent of income compared with developed countries where it accounts for less than 10 percent of the labour force. Apart from oil exporting countries (Angola, Equatorial Guinea, Sudan and Yemen), agriculture contributes more than 50 percent to GDP, and more than 70 percent of the rural population depends on it in LDCs.

Central to the current negotiations under the DDA, LDCs stress that there has to be a strong development component in agriculture and NAMA. The implementation of the DFQF market access provisions for LDCs, the accompanying Rules of Origin (RoO), and other S&D treatment provisions, all constitute this strong cross-cutting development component. In Hong Kong, LDCs accepted the 97 percent compromise position, expecting to be able to continue to work, with the rest of the WTO membership to implement the Ministerial decisions, with the intention of gradually moving to DFQF market access for 100 percent of products from LDCs. However, since Hong Kong, the attempt by LDCs to engage other members on the implementation of DFQF market access has faced strong resistance; despite the creation of one proposal on how to operationalise DFQF. Many developed country members are not using the Round to advance the development agenda, but instead are pursuing a mercantilist approach. The aim of these countries is to aggressively promote their own offensive market access positions by negotiating improvements in real market access for their farmers, industrial producers and service providers through deep cuts in tariffs. This is accompanied by an insistence on maintaining the existing defensive domestic support structures in agriculture. For the LDCs, a successful Doha Round is one that will be centred on the implementation of the Hong Kong commitment on DFQF, including simplified RoO, which ensures enough flexibility to allow the LDCs to take advantage of the market access preferences that have been provided. Capacity building measures to LDCs are equally important to enable them to implement the DFQF market access by addressing supply side constraints, as well as dealing with sanitary and phyto-sanitary (SPS) and technical barriers to trade (TBT), all of which inhibit growth of the LDCs share of global trade.

Agriculture

Under agriculture, issues of interest to LDCs include: the inclusion of provisions for LDCs to use the SSM without conditionalities or limits on the remedies in order to address import surges; a decision on food aid that is flexible enough to address crises while minimising commercial displacement; and implementation of the proposal by the C4, which includes setting up and implementing a mechanism to address cotton revenue losses resulting from price depression in international markets. In Hong Kong, Ministers directed that the cotton issue should be resolved ambitiously, expeditiously and specifically. However, to date this issue remains pending. LDCs cannot foresee any balanced and fair conclusion of the DDA Round without a satisfactory and lasting solution on cotton, which has proven to be an important issue to many cotton growers in developing countries, especially those in Africa, the majority of whom are LDCs.

The SSM mentioned above is aimed at preventing surges of imports into the domestic market. It is a formula characterised by a volume and price trigger that signals the need for protective action for the domestically produced product in the domestic market. Given that most developing countries either cannot afford subsidies, or have already committed to zero levels of trade-distorting subsidies, tariffs remain the only tool of import regulation. So this mechanism would help developing countries and LDCs in particular, to protect their producers on grounds of food security, livelihood and rural development. However, there were developed and some developing country members who wanted to link this mechanism to trade liberalisation. This was disputed by LDCs, as they are exempt from tariff reduction and therefore automatically would have locked them out of this mechanism. With the text currently on the table, it is now clear that LDCs will also be allowed to make use of the SSM, since trade liberalisation is not the only cause of import surges as evidenced in many countries. For example, Tanzania experienced import surges in the mid-1990s in poultry and dairy products, which were not only due to trade liberalisation, but also were caused by other country specific factors, such as weather variability, exchange rate movements and price de-control policies.

NAMA

During the preparatory process for the Doha Ministerial Conference, many developing countries, especially those from Africa, with two thirds of the LDCs, opposed the inclusion of non-agricultural products in the negotiations.[3] The submission stated that African countries had undergone painful liberalisation experiences under structural adjustment programmes (SAPs). This led to de-industrialisation with its attendant consequences. As such, Africa was not ready for another similar exercise. The inclusion of other issues of interest to developing countries and LDCs in the Doha Work programme acted as an incentive that encouraged them to accept negotiations on non-agricultural products as a trade off. Given that developing countries have substantially reduced their tariffs under SAPs, they expect the North to open up markets for products of export interest to them. In order to stimulate industrialisation, LDCs have been exempted from tariff cuts under the DDA.

Furthermore, the other areas of interest to LDCs have been the elimination of non-tariff barriers (NTBs) and provisions of targeted technical assistance to identify the NTBs as well as measures to address them; the correct interpretation of the concept of disproportionately affected countries, which if not handled with care has the potential of negatively impacting the economies of LDCs; a provision of special consideration to developing countries that are in customs unions with LDCs in reduction commitments as LDCs are exempted from any form of reduction commitments in agriculture and NAMA; and exclusion of LDCs from sectorals, where, in accordance with sectoral tariff negotiations, products of export interest to LDCs are not mandatory.

Services

Since the last Signalling Conference on Services in August 2008, there has been a sense of urgency from WTO members to implement the Modalities for Special Treatment of LDCs, endorsed by members in 2003, that include the 'special priority' that was hitherto seen to violate the MFN treatment clause. One of the issues of interest to the LDC Group regarding services is the implementation of a waiver to provide special priority to LDCs, including sectors and modes of supply that are of interest to LDCs in accordance with Art.IV:3[4] of the GATS and Paragraph 7 of the LDCs Modalities. Other areas of interest include creating a provision addressing targeted and effective technical and financial assistance to assist LDCs to identify their priority sectors and modes of supply and exemption of LDCs from applying any future disciplines under domestic regulations that will affect their interest, while at the same time providing technical assistance and capacity building to help LDCs build and develop their export and regulatory capacities. Most LDCs have essentially liberalised all sectors, but they have not been able to reap the full benefits of this liberalisation process owing to various regulatory and capacity constraints. Therefore, it is necessary to have specific language on technical assistance and capacity building that will ensure LDCs benefit. LDCs should also be exempted from application of the disciplines, as agreed in Hong Kong.

Trade Facilitation

Trade Facilitation (TF) first came onto the WTO agenda during the Singapore WTO Ministerial Conference in 1996 under Singapore issues. Most developing countries, including LDCs, expressed reluctance to initiate negotiations on all Singapore issues because of the failure to reach consensus on the modalities of these issues as mandated by DDA. Singapore issues were to be clarified before continuing with any negotiations. Otherwise, there were concerns that they would lead to new agreements that would commit developing countries and LDCs in particular to a range of onerous obligations. These concerns were completely ignored in Cancun, and hence the Singapore issues became one of the hot issues that led to the deadlock of the conference.

However, after Cancun, TF was the only issue among the Singapore issues that was agreed to be negotiated under the Doha Round. Some TF proposals appear to entail substantial financial costs and require considerable administrative and legislative adjustment, reform and investment. Thus, detailed cost implications, including revenue implications as compared with the presumed benefits to traders of proposed measures, should be carefully analysed.

Enhancing technical assistance and support for capacity building, as is provided in the TF modalities, remains the cornerstone of all measures and forms the fundamental objective of negotiations for developing countries, including LDCs. Some of the proposals go beyond the mandate (e.g. corruption, integrity of customs officials, fraud and obligatory use of HS nomenclature).

LDCs want to have an agreement on a comprehensive trade facilitation programme that provides additional benefits to LDCs in terms of reducing the costs of trade and providing technical assistance and capacity building to address the challenges arising from the commitments made. Therefore, allowance of flexibilities as a policy space to enable them to undertake commitments consistent with their financial means, trade needs or administrative and institutional capacities is vital. LDCs would also like to undertake mandatory commitments based on their acquisition of the necessary capacity to implement such provisions; and in the same vein urge members to exercise due restraint on the application of the dispute settlement mechanism on LDCs.

Rules

The issue of fishery subsidies to LDCs should be linked with poverty reduction and livelihood and food security concerns. The level of fishery subsidies in LDCs is not significant when compared with developed and developing countries. It is difficult to establish any causal link between subsidies and the level of production in the context of the LDCs' fisheries sector. The Draft Consolidated Text on fisheries subsidies that was circulated by the Chair of the WTO negotiating group on Rules on November, 30, 2007 lists a large number of subsidies that would be banned. Under S&D treatment, LDCs will be exempt from the list of prohibited subsidies. Although this text is not the end of the negotiating process, it is a welcome move. It has to be noted, however, that despite being exempted from subsidies, LDCs are seeking to have recourse to technical assistance and capacity building for their fishery industries.

Exemption of LDCs' exports from safeguard measures and antidumping actions is also being sought to facilitate exports from LDCs. This is in realisation for countries at a low level of development including LDCs, because the use of safeguards as a trade remedy measure is simple to use as compared to anti-dumping and countervailing measures which require a well established legal system with a sizable staffing complement outside the remit of these countries.

Trade Related Intellectual Property Rights (TRIPs)

LDCs are supporting the proposal for mandatory requirement to disclose the country of source and origin of genetic resources and associated traditional knowledge and proof of prior consent of such countries to address the misappropriation and erroneous granting of patents in order to enhance the developmental aspects of sharing benefits in favour of the LDCs. The need to devise an appropriate monitoring mechanism for the transfer of technology as stipulated under Art.66:2 of the TRIPs Agreement is also crucial for LDCs.[5] There is also need to follow up the provision on effective and targeted technical assistance required in line with Paragraph 4 of the November, 29, 2005 agreement in conformity with the decision of the TRIPs Council on the extension of the transition period under Article 66:1 of the TRIPs Agreement.

Technical Assistance and Capacity Building (TACB)

Several developing countries and LDC members consider the TACB provided by the WTO as the core of the Doha Development Round. The establishment of the Doha

Development Agenda Global Trust Fund (DDAGTF) and contributions by WTO members to the fund have been instrumental in addressing these issues. In line with the mandate to address the best endeavour nature of S&D treatment and make it precise, effective and operational; the problems with the TACB were focussed more on quantity than quality, and they lacked national ownership. It is worth mentioning that, although the IF which is solely dedicated to LDCs, is not part of the single undertaking, it was agreed to be enhanced during the Hong Kong WTO Ministerial Conference in 2005. The Aid for Trade (AfT) initiative, also outside the single undertaking principle, was launched in Hong Kong by having a Task Force to come up with recommendations on how to assist developing countries and LDCs to increase exports of goods and services, to integrate into the multilateral trading system and to benefit from liberalised trade and increased market access.

In terms of the EIF, adoption and implementation of the recommendations of the EIF, including an increase in financial resources allocated to the IF process and timely accessibility to these additional funds, are the key issues being advocated by the LDCs. While the LDCs appreciate that AfT plays a vital role in boosting their capacities to increase their trade as a necessary tool in their development endeavours, they are calling for increased levels of funding to address supply side constraints in developing countries. LDCs benefit from AfT particularly in financing those issues contained in their Diagnostic Trade Integrated Studies (DTIS) that cannot be covered under EIF, such as hard infrastructure. The AfT initiative needs to develop a system that ensures accountability of donors and recipients alike while also making sure that disbursement mechanisms in use are simplified yet transparent.

Commodities

LDC exports are predominantly made up of a few but also similar commodities. This makes LDC exports highly vulnerable to external shocks. To avert this situation LDCs have to diversify their commodities and add value through manufacturing to ensure they benefit more than is currently the case. This in turn needs increased application of appropriate technology from the more industrialised countries together with added capital and requisite trained human resources. For these and other reasons the treatment of commodities as a trade issue is an important aspect of development in LDCs as it ensures stable, equitable and remunerative export prices for primary commodities.

Accession of New Members to WTO

LDCs have been calling for the adoption of a binding mechanism to fast-track the accession of LDCs, based on a full and faithful adherence to the letter and spirit of the guidelines for LDCs accession to the WTO that were adopted by the General Council in December 2002. Members are being called upon to refrain from taking non-trade issues to acceding countries. Instead they are urged to assist in expediting the process through provision of technical assistance and capacity building to the acceding countries. This is in light of the very slow process witnessed so far where some countries wishing to join the WTO have spent many years with no conclusion in sight. According to the Report of the Director General of WTO presented to the General Council Meeting on December 14, 2010, the WTO had paid more attention to providing top-quality technical assistance to acceding governments so as to speed up the process of accession.[6] Likewise concerted efforts by the LDCs with the support of the Sub-Committee on LDC in WTO and other developing countries have helped to push this agenda in various fora. There is hope at last that some progress may be seen with Samoa, Vanuatu and Yemen acceding to WTO soon. This is particularly important at a time when positive results are essential to deal with the global economic and financial crises.

Strategies to Advance LDC Group Interests

Developing country coalitions should be seen as largely tactical groupings that emerged as a strategy to fortify their participation in the consensus-building process. Due to the low capacity of many developing countries and LDCs, the various coalitions in which they belong have improved their inclusion in consensus-building, transparency and participation in the WTO, particularly in the Green Room. However, since the conclusion of the July Package in 2004 much of the focus of consensus-building has shifted to small group discussions between the G-6 (Australia, Brazil, the EU, India, Japan and the US) and the G-4 (Brazil, the EU, India and the US), excluding the vast majority of developing countries and their coalitions, such as the LDC Group. The LDC Group has identified and worked very closely with the African and ACP groups, which are region-based groups, with common interests. The co-sponsoring of an LDC proposal on food aid by the African and ACP groups should be seen through this prism. This proposal led to the textual language seen by the LDC group to have stabilised on the issue of "monetisation."[7] This is reflected in Paragraph 12, Annex L of the Revised Draft Modalities for Agriculture (TN/AG/W/4/Rev.4, of December 06, 2008), which is seen as a basis for further negotiations. The LDC Group also works closely with issue-specific groups, such as the G-33 on the issue of SSM.

As mentioned elsewhere in this chapter, LDCs have worked as an effective group, resulting in the inclusion of a paragraph on LDCs and a reference to the Zanzibar LDC Ministerial that preceded the Doha Conference. During the WTO Cancun Ministerial Conference in 2003, LDCs organised themselves as an influential group whose views should be taken into consideration in WTO negotiations, such as the Cotton Initiative and the Singapore issues. At the WTO Hong Kong Ministerial Conference in 2005, the LDC Group continued to further develop its positive agenda in order to make effective use of the MTS by securing DFQF market access and exempting LDCs from tariff cuts in both agriculture and NAMA.

The LDC Group has continued to advocate for an increased level of political engagement by developed countries in order to translate signals of renewed commitment into flexibilities to support the conclusion of the Round. Otherwise LDCs will suffer most because of the protectionism that has emerged to counter the global economic and financial crisis. The LDC Group has also continued to advocate for maintenance of the full transparency of the DDA negotiations, inclusiveness and preservation of a bottom-up approach. In the same vein the Group has also been insisting that bilateral or plurilateral negotiations, which can indeed help reduce the existing gaps in the negotiations, should not hold hostage or replace the multilateral engagement, but preserve and build on progress achieved in the different negotiating tracks and avoid backtracking, especially with respect to agriculture and NAMA modalities and rules governing trade in services.

In line with paragraph 47 of the DDA which provides for piecemeal conclusion of certain decisions reached without having to wait for completion of the negotiations in all the negotiating areas provided such issues are doable and enjoy consensus by the Membership, the LDCs have been advocating for early harvest. This is in areas of DFQF market access, a LDCs Services waiver and the cotton issue. An early harvest in the implementation of all the decisions that have so far been made in favour of LDCs has been emphasised in the Declaration of LDC Trade Ministers in Dar-es-Salaam in 2009 and repeated by the LDC Trade Ministers during the 7th Ministerial Conference held in Geneva from November, 30 to December, 02, 2009.

Gradually this is receiving support of many delegations including the African Group, the ACP and by extension the G-90 and indeed many other delegations outside these groupings even if the latter are also advocating for a LDCs plus arrangement that will include more issues than the LDC issues, provided of course, they will enjoy acceptance of the Membership. The LDC plus issues are intended to be submitted to the Eighth Ministerial Conference (MC8) in December 2011 in realisation of the fact that the DDA cannot be concluded in 2011. LDC plus issues will provide the needed boost for negotiations to continue with more vigour but also provide something tangible to LDCs along the lines agreed since the Hong Kong Ministerial.

The LDC Group will continue to organise these Ministerial meetings in the future as part of a strategy to exchange views and consolidate its positions in terms of LDC needs, interests and concerns in the WTO negotiations. Retreats will also continue to be held at the experts and ambassadors level to help in analysing various draft texts of the issues under negotiation before LDC Group positions are taken.

Challenges Facing the LDC Group in DDA and Post DDA

Some of the key challenges facing the LDC Group and the long-term support needed by the Group are as follows:

Institutional Functioning of the Group: Role and Challenges Faced By Group Coordinator, and Issue Focal Points

The role of the coordinator of the LDC Group is fundamental to the effective functioning of the Group. The coordinating mission organises LDC Group meetings and is responsible for making sure all issue areas of relevance to the Group are covered. These meetings take place in the WTO because it is the only venue in which the facilities are appropriate, e.g. space to accommodate all members and simultaneous translation facilities. This requires LDC Group members to attend all meetings at the WTO. This becomes practically impossible due to insufficient human resource capacity to take part in (or coordinate attendance so that the Group has full coverage) at all relevant meetings that take place at the WTO, some of which take place at the same time. Although the WTO Secretariat endeavours to plan meetings so that those that may be relevant to a similar constituency do not take place at the same time, due to capacity problems within the WTO building this is not always possible. The coordinating country must also have human resource capacity to organise meetings, collate information, take meeting notes, and distribute agendas as well as other administrative duties. This can be extremely difficult when often there is only one member of the Mission covering WTO issues, or perhaps one person working part-time on WTO issues. With so many other international organisations also accredited in Geneva, the ability of LDC Missions to provide sufficient resources to cover all relevant meetings both within the WTO and other organisations becomes limited.

The coordinator normally requires additional human resources within his or her Mission to cover all relevant WTO meetings as well as provide logistical and administrative support to prepare and run meetings effectively. Engagement from capital is, therefore, essential to ensure the negotiators are familiar with the relevant topics and are able to participate in negotiations at a sufficiently technical level. Capital engagement is also important to ensure that engagement in the WTO system has high political priority at the national level, with negotiators being sufficiently empowered and supported in their positions while in Geneva. This engagement, which is vital to help bridge the gap between Geneva and capitals, is in most cases lacking owing to national budgetary constraints or low priority attached by individual countries.

In order to be an effective negotiator, the minister negotiating on behalf of the LDC Group needs to be fully engaged with the issues, understanding why a particular negotiating position is being pursued for the entire LDC Group. The Mission that takes on LDCs coordination role does receive extra staff, but often this support is insufficient and there is little or no continuity in staff when a new mission takes over. This reduces the ability of LDCs to institutionalise knowledge. Providing support to the LDCs rather than a particular mission would help to build institutional knowledge within the LDC Group.

The method of allocating the coordinator's role is not institutionalised, and lack of capacity prevents many LDCs from taking on the role, compromising the system currently in place. Support for the coordinator from donors could mitigate this problem, making the transition between coordinators more predictable. A wider range of LDC Group members are ready to take up the co-ordinatorship with donor support they normally get from WTO and DFID through TradeMark (formally through the Regional Trade Facilitation Programme).

In order to ensure ownership, inclusiveness, transparency and consistency in positions adopted, the Group also maintains a pool of focal points (drawn from among the Group's members) for each subject area, supported by alternates and a core group. Issue areas relevant to the LDCs are distributed among the LDC Group using focal points. The roles are stable and members usually stay in their positions for a number of years, allowing them to build knowledge on a particular issue. Because of this there is a strong argument also for providing technical assistance on a demand-led basis to focal points for their work, as they provide very useful inputs to the coordinator of the group.

The focal points must attend the WTO meetings that concern their respective issue areas and detail the technical work that needs to be carried out in those areas. Some focal points stay in their roles for three years and, therefore, provide stable and reliable support to the Group. The stability of these roles means that a considerable knowledge base is built up within a particular mission, which provides an opening for technical support to be provided via the focal points rather than via the coordinator.

Although focal points are responsible for covering issue areas within the realm of the WTO, they are not technical experts in those areas. When detailed technical work needs to be carried out, an expert must be brought in to supply this analysis, which can then be used to inform the negotiating position of the LDC Group. The work needs to be of extremely high quality in order for other negotiating partners to take the demands of the LDCs seriously. The number of issue areas that need to be covered by the LDCs highlights the range of expertise required.

Challenges Regarding Implementation of LDC Issues

As mentioned elsewhere, the LDC Group has consistently been calling for an early harvest in all the areas that have secured consensus, notably the operationalisation of the DFQF market access to LDCs in agriculture and NAMA, with the accompanying simplification and transparent preferential rules of origin; the implementation of decisions to address the cotton development and trade issue; as well as according special priority to services sectors and service suppliers from LDCs. These commitments have not been fully made operational particularly on the issue of cotton. The way this issue has been handled since the Hong Kong Ministerial decision does not in any way reflect the ambition, specificity and expeditious manner that was pronounced by the ministers in Hong Kong in 2005.

The delay in concluding the negotiations under the DDA has further exacerbated the situation of LDCs in the multilateral trading system. If we are to see a balanced and meaningful outcome of the trade negotiations with a development component that is going to be beneficial to LDCs, the three issues have to be concluded. However, the LDC Group remains optimistic and continues to pursue outcomes that will contribute to enhancing development and economic growth in LDCs.

Uncoordinated Support Available to LDCs from Multilateral Institutions/NGOs

There is varied support available to LDCs within Geneva and elsewhere from NGOs, multilateral institutions and other donors. For the LDC Group to take advantage of the support that is currently available and to identify where the gaps are, it is necessary to know what is being offered.

There seems to be a lot of assistance available and it is important to ensure that support to LDCs does not duplicate other support mechanisms. Where such support can be better coordinated among the donors themselves and with the recipients this can ensure increased effectiveness. Moreover, although it is meant to be helpful, the assistance is not often guided or directed by LDCs. From experience, support agencies may decide to work on some issues but not others according to their own agendas, which can leave the LDC focal points without technical support specific to their needs.

Under the current practice, the WTO's technical assistance and training activities support coalitions, such as the LDC Group, and foster connections between the organisation and participating members and groups of members. A number of programmes are regionally focussed and aim at building capacity, synergies and networking within regional groups. Some activities are specifically offered to particular coalitions. LDCs are also identified as a group and given particular consideration.

Long-term Prospects of the LDC Group in Relation to Other Negotiating Groups

The LDC Group has a long-term future and will require support regardless of whether or not the Doha Round is concluded. Plans for future support should include details of issue areas to be covered and should be designed to work on the basis of support being provided over a long period.

The LDCs feel as though they have more in common with other LDCs than single-issue groups, such as the C4, or geographically based groups, such as the African Group. The constituency of the African Group covers a diverse range of countries at different levels of development and with different interests. As the LDC Group is given priority, work of the LDCs often feeds into other groups, such as the African Group and the ACP. In this way, these other negotiating groups rarely contradict the negotiating position of the LDCs and investments in the LDC Group will also provide spill-over benefits to other groups.

The longer-term suspension of the Doha Round negotiations will not diminish the importance of the LDC Group or end its work. There are many other areas of work that are ongoing despite the stalled Doha Round. For example, the implementation of the EIF and AfT programme, though not part of the single undertaking, has always played a crucial role for developing countries.

There are very few donors apart from DFID that currently provide bilateral support directly to the LDC Group. However, there has been interest from other donors in exploring this further. Clear criteria would need to be established for any joint support including maintaining confidentiality, ensuring joint monitoring and evaluation of support and maintaining flexibility and responsiveness to ensure that the LDC Group drives this process.

Future support should aim to institutionalise relationships between the LDC Group and consultants used. Mechanisms for channelling funds should be assessed on the basis of flexibility and suitability. Donors other than DFID should be invited to coordinate support and the support should be based in Geneva so that it is available to all members of the LDC Group.

Involvement of other donors in this process is extremely important. There are many organisations that offer services to the LDC Group. These include UNCTAD; UNCTAD Virtual Institute on Trade and Development, WTO Institute for Training and Technical Cooperation (IITC), Advisory Centre on WTO Law (ACWL), South Centre, AITIC, IDEAS Centre, OXFAM International, International Centre for Trade and Sustainable Development (ICTSD), Quaker UN Office (QUNO), CSEND, Centre for International Environmental Law (CIEL), World Trade Institute (WTI) and the Commonwealth Secretariat.

It is important that support is coordinated by the LDC Group itself so that all members are aware of the resources available and to ensure that duplication in support does not occur. In the future, partners for support programmes should be selected on the basis of compatibility with LDC needs, taking into account for example the flexible and transparent administration of funding.

Establishment of LDCs Secretariat

The establishment and support of an LDC Secretariat that would build the capacity of the LDC Group, rather than just the coordinating mission, to build institutional knowledge of the LDCs has been added to the agenda recently. This idea has yet to receive any positive acceptance from the donor community. This may be explained by the inability on the part of the donors to understand exactly the requirements of the LDC Group and, therefore, the extent of their involvement. More efforts will have to be expended by the Group to sensitise the donors on this issue.

Concluding Remarks

The LDC Group has evolved from 1999 and it has achieved a great deal. The waivers from applying the WTO cardinal principle of MFN clause, such as the Preferential Tariff Treatment on Goods for LDCs waiver for 10 years adopted in 1999 and now extended for another 10 years since July 2009 has continued to give market access to LDCs under AGOA[8] and EBA[9]. The transition period of ten years negotiated a few weeks prior to Hong Kong WTO Conference and granted to LDCs to become TRIPs compliant has now been extended for another seven and a half years to 2013. Similarly, the Doha Ministerial Declaration that extended the transitional period for LDCs for implementation of the TRIPs Agreement's obligations on pharmaceuticals, from 2006 to 2016 is yet another achievement. Furthermore, the exemptions from strict compliance of obligations and commitments, such as exempting LDCs from tariff reductions in agriculture and NAMA and from liberalising the services sector and applying disciplines regarding domestic regulations obligations in services are positive landmarks in favour of LDCs. An LDC waiver on services, which so far has received some positive comments with several paragraphs in the waiver having been stabilised, is likely to be concluded soon. Greater market access through DFQF market access as provided for in the Hong Kong Ministerial, continues to be frustrated by developed country members and supply side constraints still faced by the LDCs.

Provision of TACB across all WTO Agreements to favour developing countries and LDCs in particular to build their capacity has always been emphasised. In Doha, the establishment of the Doha Development Agenda Global Trust Fund (DDGTF) after the adoption of DDA has assisted LDCs through training, seminars and workshops.

Finally as a way forward, the LDC group will continue to press for the early harvest of the implementation of all the decisions that have so far been made in favour of LDCs, namely DFQF market access, the services waiver, and the cotton initiative.

Since LDCs make up 20 percent of the WTO membership, it is suggested that their representation should be greater in the Green Room meetings unlike the current situation where LDCs are represented only by the LDC Coordinator. Where some other LDC participants join the Green Room it is because they come in their capacities as Chairs of other negotiating Groups. If the LDCs are to be effectively integrated into the multilateral trading system there is an urgent need to change the current system which apparently is based on the global trade shares of the members concerned.

Endnotes

1 Ravallion, M. and Chen, S., 2008 "The Developing World Is Poorer Than We Thought But Not Less Successful In The Fight Against Poverty: the World Bank's New Poverty Estimates," study presented in Geneva, October 01, 2008.

2 UN-OHRLLS: Least Developed Countries-Country profiles, http://www.unohrlls.org/en/ldc/related/62/ of January 10, 2011.

3 Submission by Kenya (WTO document WT/GC/W/453, November 02, 2001) on behalf of Mozambique, Nigeria, Tanzania, Uganda, Zambia, Zimbabwe and Kenya.

4 Article IV: 3 stipulates that: "Special priority shall be given to the least-developed country Members in the implementation of paragraphs 1 and 2. Particular account shall be taken of the serious difficulty of the least-developed countries in accepting negotiated specific commitments in view of their special economic situation and their development, trade and financial needs."

5 Article 66.2 of the TRIPs Agreement stipulates: "Developed country Members shall provide incentives to enterprises and institutions in their territories for the purpose of promoting and encouraging technology transfer to least-developed country Members in order to enable them to create a sound and viable technological base."

6 Report of the Director General of WTO in WTO document WT/ACC//14, December, 08, 2010 presented to the GC on December 14, 2010.

7 Para12: Monetisation of in-kind food aid in non-emergency situations shall be prohibited except where it is in conformity with the provisions of paragraph 11 above and, as a means to meet direct nutritional requirements of least-developed and net food-importing developing country members. It is necessary to fund the internal transportation and delivery of food aid to, or the procurement of agricultural inputs to low-income or resource-poor producers in, those members. Monetisation shall be carried out within the territory of the recipient least-developed or net food-importing developing country. In addition, commercial displacement shall be avoided

8 African Growth Opportunity Act (AGOA) is a US initiative for preferential market access, which covers eligible countries from sub-Saharan Africa where the majority are LDCs.

9 Everything But Arms (EBA) is an initiative by the European Communities to provide duty free market access to all products from all LDCs except arms.

Bibliography

Books

Barton, J. H., Goldstein, J. L., Josling, T. E. and Steinberg, R. H. 2006. *The Evolution of the Trade Regime: Politics, Law and Economics of the GATT and the WTO.* Princeton, NJ: Princeton University Press. Available at http://www.bsos.umd.edu/gvpt/lpbr/subpages/reviews/barton1006.htm, accessed on May, 15, 2011

Bown, C. P. 2007. *China's WTO Entry: Antidumping, Safeguards, and Dispute Settlement.* Brandeis University. Available at http://www.nber.org/books_in_progress/china07/bown8-13-07.pdf, accessed on May, 17, 2011

Croome, J. 1998. *Reshaping the World Trading System: A history of the Uruguay Round.* The Hague: Kluwer

Finger, M. and Nogués P. (eds.). 2006. *Safeguards and Anti-dumping in Latin American Trade Liberalization - Fighting Fire with Fire.* Washington D.C.: The World Bank and Palgrave Macmillan

Georgiev, D. and van der Borght, K. (eds.). 2006. *Reform and Development of the WTO Dispute Settlement System.* London: Cameron May

Jackson, J., Davey, W. and Sykes, A. 2008. *Legal Problems of International Economic Relations - Cases, Materials and Texts,* 5th Edition. USA: Thomson West

Mattoo, A. and Payton, L. (eds.). 2007. *Services Trade and Development: The experience of Zambia.* Washington D.C.: The World Bank

Mattoo, A., Stern, R. M. and Zanini, G. (eds.). 2008. *A Handbook of International Trade in Services.* Oxford: Oxford University Press. Available at http://www.iadb.org/intal/intalcdi/PE/2008/01285.pdf, accessed on March, 15, 2011

Mavroidis, P., Berman, G. and Wu, M. 2010. *The Law of the World Trade Organization: Documents, Cases and Analysis.* USA: Thomson West

Sacerdoti, G., Yanovich, A. and Bohanes, J. (eds.). 2006. *The WTO at Ten: The Contribution of the Dispute Settlement System.* Cambridge: Cambridge University Press

Sáez, S. (ed.). 2009. *Trade in Services Negotiations: A Guide for Developing Countries.* Washington D.C.: The World Bank. Available at http://siteresources.worldbank.org/INTRANETTRADE/Resources/239054-1248204247129/Negotiating_Trade_in_Services.pdf, accessed on March, 15, 2011

Shaffer, G. C. and Ortiz, R. M. (eds.). 2010. *Dispute Settlement at the WTO.* Cambridge: Cambridge University Press

Sutherland, P. *et al.* 2004. *The Future of the WTO: Addressing Institutional Challenges in the New Millennium. Report by the Consultative Board to the Director-General Supachai Panitchpakdi.* Geneva: The World Trade Organisation

Van den Bossche, P. 2008. *The Law and Policy of the World Trade Organisation.* Cambridge: Cambridge University Press

Von Moltke, A. (ed.). 2010. *Fisheries Subsidies, Sustainable Development and the WTO.* Oxford: EarthScan and UNEP

World Bank and FAO. 2008. *The Sunken Billions: The Economic Justification for Fisheries Reform.* Washington, D.C.: The World Bank

Journal Articles

Aggarwal, R. 2005. 'Dynamics of Agriculture Negotiations in the World Trade Organisation', *Journal of World Trade*, 39 (4): 741-762

Alexandraki, K. 2005. 'Preference Erosion: Cause for Alarm', *Finance & Development,* March 2005 Volume 42, Number 1: 26-29. Available at http://www.imf.org/external/pubs/ft/fandd/2005/03/pdf/alexandr.pdf, accessed on June 10, 2011

Huerta-Goldman, J. A. 2010. 'Mexico in the WTO and NAFTA in a Nutshell: Litigating International Trade Disputes', *Journal of World Trade,* 44, No. 1/2010: 173-202

Low, P. and Santana, R. 2009. 'Trade Liberalisation in Manufacturers: What is left after the Doha Round?', *Journal of International Trade and Diplomacy,* 3(i) (Spring 2009)

Milner, C., Morisey, O. and Zgoyu, E. 2009. 'Preference Erosion and the Future of Preferences', *Commonwealth Hot Trade Topics*, Issue 60

Narlikar, A. and Tussie, D. 2004. 'The G20 at the Cancun Ministerial: Developing Countries and their Evolving Coalitions in the WTO',*World Economy,* 27 (7): 947-966

Pauwelyn, J. 2000. 'Enforcement and Countermeasures in the WTO: Rules are Rules – Toward a More Collective Approach', *American Journal of International Law,* 94: 335-337

Skeen, R. 2004. 'Will the WTO Turn Green? The Implications of Injecting Environmental Issues Into the Multilateral Trading System', *Georgetown International Environmental Law Review*

Smith, R. 2009. 'WTO Doha Round: Small Economies and Their Interests', *Commonwealth Trade Hot Topics,* Issue 55

Chapters in an edited volume

Adlung, R. 2000. 'Services Trade Liberalisation from Developed and Developing Country Perspectives', in Sauvé and Stern (eds.), *GATS 2000: New Directions in Services Trade Liberalisation.* Washington D.C.: Brookings Institution Press, pp.112-131

Balas, P. 2006. 'Chairing the DSU Negotiations: An Overview', in Georgiev and van der Borght (eds.), *Reform and Development of the WTO Dispute Settlement System.* London: Cameron May, pp. 15-36

Busch, M. L. and Reinhardt, E. 2006. 'Fixing What "Aint Broke"? Third Party Rights, Consultations and DSU', in Georgiev and van der Borght (eds.), *Reform and Development of the WTO Dispute Settlement System.* London: Cameron May, pp. 73-85. Available at http://userwww.service.emory.edu/~erein/research/DSU.pdf, accessed on April, 7, 2011

Cottier, T. 2006. 'DSU Reform: Resolving Underlying Balance of Power Issues', in Sacerdoti, Yanovish and Bohanes (eds.), *The WTO at Ten: The Contribution of the Dispute Settlement System.* Cambridge: Cambridge University Press, pp. 259-265

Danvivathana, P. 2006. 'Is it Beneficial to WTO Members to Reform the Panel System?', in Georgiev and van der Borght (eds.), *Reform and Development of the WTO Dispute Settlement System.* London: Cameron May, pp. 87-108

Diego-Fernandez, M. 2006. 'Memoirs of a DSU Negotiator', in Georgiev and van der Borght (eds.), *Reform and Development of the WTO Dispute Settlement System*. London: Cameron May, pp. 109-122

Feketekuty, G. 2000. 'Improving the Architecture of the General Agreement on Trade in Services', in Stephenson, S. (ed.), *Services Trade in the Western Hemisphere: Liberalisation, Integration and Reform*. Washington D.C.: Brookings Institution Press, pp. 20 – 42

Garcia Bercero, I. and Garzotti, P. 2006. 'DSU Reform: What are the Underlying Issues?', in Georgiev and van der Borght (eds.), *Reform and Development of the WTO Dispute Settlement System*. London: Cameron May, pp. 123-152

Grynberg, R. and Remy, J. Y. 2003. 'Small Vulnerable Economy Issues and the WTO', in Mbirimi, Chilala, Gryberg (eds.), *From Doha to Cancun: Delivering a Development Round*. London: Commonwealth Secretariat, pp. 269-290

Hudec, R. E. 2000. 'Broadening the Scope of Remedies in WTO Dispute Settlement', in Weiss and Wiers (eds.), *Improving WTO Dispute Settlement Procedures*. Cambridge: Cameron May, pp. 345-376. Available at http://www.worldtradelaw.net/articles/hudecremedies.pdf

Hughes, V. 2006. 'The WTO Dispute Settlement System – From Initiating Proceedings to Ensuring Implementation: What needs Improvement?', in Sacerdoti, Yanovich and Bohanes (eds.), *The WTO at Ten: The Contribution of the Dispute Settlement System*. Cambridge: Cambridge University Press, pp. 193-234

Karsenty, G. 2000. 'Assessing Trade in Services by Mode of Supply', in Sauvé and Stern (eds.), *GATS 2000: New Directions in Services Trade Liberalisation*. Washington D.C.: Brookings Institution Press. pp. 33-56

Narlikar, A. 2009. 'A Theory of Bargaining Coalitions in the WTO', in Narlikar and Vickers (eds.), *Leadership and Change in the Multilateral Trading System*. Dordrecht: Republic of Letters Publishing/Martinus Nijhoff

Narlikar, A. and Odell, J. S. 2006. 'The Strict Distributive Strategy for a Bargaining Coalition: The Like Minded Group in the World Trade Organisation', in Odell (ed.), *Negotiating Trade: Developing Countries in the WTO and NAFTA*. Cambridge: Cambridge University Press, pp. 115-144

Read, R. 2007. 'Dispute Settlement, Compensation and Retaliation Under the WTO', in Gaisford and Kerr (eds.), *Handbook on International Trade Policy*. Cheltenham: Edward Elgar Publishing, pp. 497-508

Sáez, S. 2006. 'Keeping Animal Spirits Asleep: The Case of Chile', in Finger and Nogués (eds.), *Safeguards and Antidumping in Latin American Trade Liberalisation - Fighting Fire with Fire*. Washington D.C.: The World Bank and Palgrave Macmillan, pp. 109-135

Shaffer, G. 2002. "If Only We Were Elephants": The Political Economy of the WTO's Treatment of Trade and Environment Matters', in Kennedy and Southwick (eds.), *The Political Economy of International Trade Law - Essays in Honor of Robert E. Hudec*. Cambridge: Cambridge University Press, pp. 349-393

Suzuki, Y. 2006. 'Charing the DSU Negotiations: An Overview', in Georgiev and van der Borght (eds.), *Reform and Development of the WTO Dispute Settlement System*, London: Cameron May, pp. 15-35

Zutshi, B. K. 1998. 'Bringing TRIPs into the Multilateral Trading System', in Bhagwati and Hirsch (eds.), *The Uruguay Round and Beyond – Essays in Honour of Arthur Dunkel*, Springer: Berlin, pp. 37-50

Other articles

Adler, M., Brunel, C., Hufbauer, G. C. and Schott, J. J. 2009. 'What's on the Table? The Doha Round as of August 2009'. *Peterson Institute for International Economics Working Paper Series,* Working Paper 09-6

AITIC. 2009. 'Evolution of Proposals on GATT Article V in the WTO Trade Facilitation Negotiations'. *Trade Facilitation Brief*

Alexandraki, K. and Lanke, H. P. 2004. 'The Impact of Preference Erosion on Middle-Income Developing Countries'. *IMF Working Paper,* Policy Development and Review Department: WP/04/169. Available at http://www.imf.org/external/pubs/ft/wp/2004/wp04169.pdf, accessed on June, 10, 2011

Banga, R. 2005. 'General Agreement on Trade in Services: India's Proactive Agenda'. *UNCTAD-India Interactive Session with Regional Media December, 14, 2005.* Available at http://www.unctadindia.org/uploadFile.asp?upFile=InteractiveSessionWithTheRegionalMediaRepresentatives-14December2005_RashmiBanga.pps, accessed on March 17, 2011

Beattie, A. 2007. 'Developing Countries Reject Doha Round Plans For Tariff Cuts'. *Financial Times*, October, 10, 2007

Beattie, A. 2006. 'Ministers promise to accelerate pace of Doha talks'. *Financial Times*, 30 January 2006

Brown, K. 2002. 'Comments on the Paper by Tangerman on the Future of Preferential Trade Arrangements for Developing Countries and the Current Round of WTO Negotiations on Agriculture'. *FAO Papers on Selected Issues Related to the WTO Negotiations on Agriculture,* pp. 108-115

Bridges Weekly Trade News Digest. Volume 9, Number 40. November 23, 2005

'General Assembly Bypassed in Informal WIPO Talks on Patent Harmonisation'. *Bridges Weekly Trade News Digest,* Volume 9 Number 6. February 23, 2005. Available at http://ictsd.org/i/ip/39684/, accessed on March 15, 2011

'WIPO: India Rejects Outcome of Casablanca Patent Harmonisation Meeting'. *Bridges Weekly Trade News Digest,* Volume 9 Number 12. April 13, 2005. Available at http://ictsd.org/i/ip/39678/, accessed on March, 15, 2011

Bridges Weekly Trade News Digest. Volume 11, Number 21. June 13, 2007

Bridges Weekly Trade News Digest. Volume 13, Number 40. November 18, 2009

Chan-Hyun, S. and Junsok, Y. 2003. 'Trade Facilitation in the WTO: Implications for Developing Countries and a Roadmap to Cancun'. *KIEP Working Paper,* 03-04

Eglin, R. 2008. 'The Doha Round Negotiations on Trade Facilitation' *The Global Enabling Trade Report 2008, World Economic Forum.* Geneva: The World Trade Organisation

FAO. 2000. '*Multilateral Trade Negotiations on Agriculture: A Resource Manual'.*

Francois, J., Horn, H. and Kaunitz, N. 2008. 'Trading Profiles and Developing Country Participation in the WTO Dispute Settlement System', *ICTSD Issue Paper No. 6*, December 2008. Geneva: ICTDS

GATT. 1971. 'Industrial Pollution Control and International Trade', *GATT Studies in International Trade*

Healy, S., Pearce, R. and Stockbridge, M. 1998. 'The Implications Of The Uruguay Round Agreement On Agriculture For Developing Countries'. *FAO Corporate Document Repository*

Hong Kong Coalition of Service Industries. 2001. *New WTO Round - A Doha Daily Report.* Available at http://www.hkcsi.org.hk/reports/reports.htm, accessed on May 16, 2011

International Centre for Trade and Sustainable Development (ICTSD). 2007. 'Building Coalitions and Consensus in the WTO'. *News and Analysis,* 11(5). Available at http://ictsd.org/i/news/bridges/4131/, accessed on May 15, 2011

International Centre for Trade and Sustainable Development (ICTSD) and International Institute for Sustainable Development (IISD). 2004. 'Developments since the Cancun Ministerial Conference: Trade and Environment'. *Doha Round Briefing Series,* Vol. 3 No. 9. Available at http://ictsd.org/downloads/2008/06/v3_09.pdf, accessed on May 16, 2011

International Centre for Trade and Sustainable Development (ICTSD) and International Institute for Sustainable Development (IISD). 2005. 'Trade Facilitation'. *Doha Round Briefing Series,* Vol. 4 No 6

International Institute for Sustainable Development (IISD). 2003. 'The WTO, Trade Facilitation and Sustainable Development'. *IISD Trade and Development Brief,* No. 3, Spring 2003

Ismail, F. 2004. 'Agricultural Trade Liberalisation and the Poor: A Development Perspective on Cancun'. *Bridges,* Year 8 No.1, January 2004

Khor, M. 2003. 'Developing Countries Against Binding Trade Facilitation Rules'. *Third World Network Info Service on WTO Issues*, June 2003

Khor, M. 2004. 'Preliminary Comments on the WTO's Geneva July Decision'. *Third World Network.* Available at http://www.ifg.org/analysis/wto/MartinsComments.html, accessed on May 15, 2011

Kim, J. 2007. 'Issues of Dual Use and Reviewing Product Coverage of Environmental Goods'. *OECD Trade and Environment Working Papers,* 2007/1

Liberti, L. 2010. 'Intellectual Property Rights in International Investment Agreements: An Overview'. *OECD Working Papers on International Investment,* No. 2010/1. Available at http://www.oecd.org/dataoecd/37/52/44822901.pdf, accessed on March 15, 2011

Lynn, J. 2009. 'Doha Hopes Improve Amid Trade Data Gloom'. *Reuters*. Available at www.ibsa-trilateral.org/, accessed on March 24, 2011

Nordström, H. and Vaughan, S. 1999. Trade and Environment. *World Trade Organisation (WTO) Special Studies 4*. Geneva: The World Trade Organisation

OECD 2003. 'Trade Facilitation Principles in GATT Articles V, VII and X: Reflections on Possible Implementation Approaches'. *OECD*, TD/TC/WP (2003)12

OECS Secretariat. 2006, 'Small Vulnerable Economies Achieve Milestone at WTO Level'. Available at http://www.oecs.org/news-a-events/81-newstrade/219-small-vulnerable-economies-achieve-milestone-at-wto-level, accessed on December 27, 2010

Page, S. 2002. 'Developing Countries in GATT/WTO Negotiations'. *Overseas Development Institute London.* Available at http://www.odi.org.uk/resources/download/3617.pdf, accessed on May 15, 2011

Palmer, A. and Tarasofsky, R. 2007. 'The Doha Round and Beyond: Towards a Lasting Relationship Between the WTO and the International Environmental Regime'. London: *The Royal Institute of International Affairs*

Plasai, V. 2007. 'Compliance and Remedies Against Non-Compliance Under the WTO System'. *ICTSD Issue Paper* No. 3, June 2007. Geneva: ICTSD

Ravallion, M. and Chen, S. 2008. 'The Developing World Is Poorer Than We Thought But Not Less Successful In The Fight Against Poverty: The World Bank's New Poverty Estimates'. Study presented in Geneva, October 01, 2008

Report of a Joint World Bank/Commonwealth Secretariat Task Force. 2000. 'Small States: Meeting Challenges in the Global Economy'. London. Available at http://siteresources.worldbank.org/PROJECTS/Resources/meetingchallengeinglobaleconomyl.pdf, accessed on March 17, 2011

Santana, R. 2003. 'Commentary on the Article "Specific Trade Obligations in Multilateral Environmental Agreements and their Relationship with the Rules of the Multilateral Trading System – A Developing Country Perspective"'. *UNCTAD Trade and Environment Review 2003*

Sant'Ana Lima, L. 2006. 'Developing Country Alliances in the WTO: South-South Solidarity at a Crossroads After the Hong Kong Conference'. Available at www.eldis.org/fulltext/Sant'Ana%20Lima%20Article%20010506.pdf, accessed on March 17, 2011

Secretariat of the Basel Convention. Undated. 'Introduction to WTO Environmental Goods and Services Negotiations - Background Information for Parties to the Basel Convention'. Available online at http://www.basel.int/trade/index.html

South African Mission to the UN and WTO. 2007.'Joint Statement of the G90 and the NAMA 11, July 26, 2007'.*Twenty Months of the NAMA 11*. Geneva: South African Mission to the UN and WTO.

South Centre. 2005. 'The WTO Dispute Settlement System: Issues to Consider in the DSU Negotiations'. *South Centre Trade-Related Agenda, Development and Equity (TRADE) Analysis Series,* SC/TADP/TA/DS/1, October 2005

Stiglitz, J. and Charlton, A. Undated. 'Initiative for Policy Dialogue: The Development Round of Negotiations in the Aftermath of Cancun'. A Report for the Commonwealth Secretariat, London.

Trade Reports International Group, *Washington Trade Daily*. December 2008

UNCTAD. 2004. 'Is Special Treatment for Small Island Developing States Possible?'. Available at http://www.unctad.org/en/docs/ldc20041_en.pdf, accessed on March 17, 2011

Vossenaar, R. 2010. 'Climate-related Single-use Environmental Goods', *ICTSD Programme on Trade and Environment*, Issue Paper No. 13, September 2010

The World Bank. 2006. 'Needs, Priorities and Costs Associated with Technical Assistance and Capacity Building for Implementation of a WTO Trade Facilitation Agreement – A Comparative Study Based on Six Developing Countries'

World Trade Organisation. 1999. 'Briefing Papers for the Seattle Conference'. Available at http://www.wto.org/english/thewto_e/minist_e/min99_e/english/about_e/19dis_e.htm, accessed on March 17, 2011

World Trade Organisation. 2004. 'Trade and Environment at the WTO'. Background Document Prepared by the WTO Secretariat

World Trade Organisation. 2009. 'LDC Briefing Book on the World Trade Organisation'

Official Documents

GATT Documents

C/M/247, GATT Council, Minutes of Meeting held in the Centre William Rappard on 6 February 1991, March 05, 1991

MTN.TNC/MIN(94)/ST/100, Negotiations General Distribution, the Uruguay Round, Trade Negotiations Committee Meeting at Ministerial Level, Marrakesh (Morocco), 12-15 April 1994, Japan Statement by Mr. Tsutomu Hata, Deputy Prime Minister and Minister for Foreign Affairs, April, 14, 1994

TNC/MIN(94)/ST/92, Negotiations General Distribution, the Uruguay Round, Trade Negotiations Committee Meeting at Ministerial Level, Marrakesh (Morocco), 12-15 April 1994, Chile Statement by Mr. Carlos Figueroa Serrano, Minister for Foreign Affairs, April, 14, 1994

Documents of Ministerial Conferences

WT/MIN(01)/DEC/1, Ministerial Conference Fourth Session Doha, 9 - 14 November 2001, Ministerial Declaration Adopted on 14 November 2001, November, 20, 2001

WT/MIN(01)/DEC/2, Ministerial Conference, Fourth Session, Doha, 9-14 November 2001, Declaration on the TRIPS Agreement and Public Health Adopted on 14 November 2001, November, 20, 2001

WT/MIN(01)/17, Ministerial Conference, Fourth Session, Doha, 9 - 14 November 2001, Implementation-Related Issues and Concerns, Decision of 14 November 2001, November, 20, 2001

WT/MIN(03)/14, Ministerial Conference, Fifth Session Cancún, 10 - 14 September 2003, Ministers' Communiqué, Alliance for Strategic Products and Special Safeguard Mechanism, 9 September 2003, Cancún Mexico, Communication from Indonesia, September, 09, 2003

WT/MIN(03)/W/61, Ministerial Conference, Fifth Session Cancún, 10 - 14 September 2003, Agriculture – Framework Proposal, Joint Proposal by Argentina, Bolivia, Brazil, Chile, China, Colombia, Costa Rica, Cuba, Ecuador, El Salvador, Guatemala, India, Mexico, Pakistan, Paraguay, Peru, Philippines, South Africa, Thailand and Venezuela, September, 04, 2003, also WT/MIN (03)/W/6/Add.1, September, 09, 2003, and WT/MIN (03)/W/6.Add.2, September, 30, 2003

WT/MIN(05)DEC, Ministerial Conference Sixth Session Hong Kong, 13 - 18 December 2005, Doha Work Programme, Ministerial Declaration Adopted on 18 December 2005, December, 22, 2005

WT/MIN(09)/2, Ministerial Conference, Seventh Session Geneva 30 November - 2 December 2009, Sixth LDC Trade Minisyters' Meeting Dar Es Salaam, Tanzania 14-16 October 2009, Dar Es Salaam Declaration, October, 21, 2009

Declarations and Decisions

S/L/92, Trade in Services, Guidelines for the Scheduling of Specific Commitments under the General Agreement on Trade in Services (GATS), Adopted by the Council for Trade in Services on 23 March 2001, March, 28, 2001

S/L/93, Trade in Services, Guidelines and Procedures for the Negotiations on Trade in Services, Adopted by the Special Session of the Council for Trade in Services on 28 March 2001, March 29, 2001

WT/L/409, Zanzibar Declaration, Meeting of the Ministers responsible for trade of the least developed countries, August, 06, 2001

WT/L/540, Implementation of paragraph 6 of the Doha Declaration on the TRIPS Agreement and Public Health, Decision of August, 30, 2003, September, 02, 2003

WT/L/579, Doha Work Programme, Decision Adopted by the General Council on 1 August 2004, August, 02, 2004

WT/L/613, G-33 Ministerial Communiqué, Jakarta, 12 June 2005, Communication from Indonesia, June, 22, 2005

Documents on Accession

WT/ACC/14, WTO Accessions, 2010 Annual Report by the Director General, December, 08, 2010

Documents of the Committee on Agriculture

G/AG/NG/W/1, Committee on Agriculture Special Session, First Special Session of the Committee on Agriculture 23-24 March 2000, Statement by Argentina, April, 04, 2000

G/AG/NG/W/7, Committee on Agriculture Special Session, First Special Session of the Committee on Agriculture, 23-24 March 2000, Statement by the United States, April, 04, 2000

G/AG/NG/W/13, Committee on Agriculture Special Session, Agreement on Agriculture: Special and Differential Treatment and a Development Box, Proposal to the June 2000 Special Session of the Committee on Agriculture by Cuba, Dominican Republic, Honduras, Pakistan, Haiti, Nicaragua, Kenya, Uganda, Zimbabwe, Sri Lanka and El Salvador, June, 23, 2000

G/AG/NG/W/14, Committee on Agriculture Special Session, Agreement on Agriculture: Green Box / Annex 2 Subsidies Proposal to the June 2000 Special Session of the Committee on Agriculture by Cuba, Dominican Republic, Honduras, Pakistan, Haiti, Nicaragua, Kenya, Uganda, Zimbabwe, Sri Lanka and El Salvador, June, 23, 2000

G/AG/NG/W/15, Committee on Agriculture Special Session, Proposals for Comprehensive Long-Term Agricultural Trade Reform Submission from the United States, June, 23, 2000

G/AG/NG/W/24, Committee on Agriculture Special Session, Second Special Session of the Committee on Agriculture 29-30 June 2000, Statement by the European Community, July, 11, 2000

G/AG/NG/W/31, Committee on Agriculture Special Session, Second Special Session of the Committee on Agriculture 29-30 June 2000, Statement by Thailand, July, 11, 2000

G/AG/NG/W/38, Committee on Agriculture Special Session, Export Sibsidies – Food Security or Food Dependency?, A Discussion Paper presented by Argentina, Brazil, Paraguay and Uruguay (MERCOSUR), Chile, Bolivia and Costa Rica, September, 27, 2000

G/AG/NG/W/36/Rev.1, Committee on Agriculture Special Session, Note on Non-Trade Concerns, Revision, November, 09, 2000

G/AG/NG/W/54, Committee on Agriculture Special Session, WTO Negotiations on Agriculture, Cairns Group Negotiating Proposal Market Access, November, 10, 2000

G/AG/NG/W/90, Committee on Agriculture Special Session, EC Comprehensive Negotiating Proposal, December, 14, 2000

G/AG/NG/W/94, Committee on Agriculture Special Session, WTO: Negotiations on Agriculture, Proposal by Switzerland, December, 21, 2000

G/AG/NG/W/97, Committee on Agriculture Special Session, WTO Negotiations on Agriculture: Proposals by Small Island Developing States (SIDS), Communication from Dominica, Jamaica, Mauritius, St. Kitts and Nevis, St. Lucia, St. Vincent and the Grenadines, and Trinidad and Tobago, December, 29, 2000

G/AG/NG/W/100, Committee on Agriculture Special Session, WTO Negotiations on Agriculture – Market Access, Negotiating Proposal on behalf of Members of the Caribbean Community (CARICOM), January, 15, 2001

G/AG/NG/W/135, Committee on Agriculture Special Session, Negotiating Proposals by the Democratic Republic of the Congo, March, 12, 2001

G/AG/NG/R/5, Committee on Agriculture Special Session, Summary Report on the Fifth Meeting of the Special Session Held on 5-7 February 2001, Note by the Secretariat, March, 22, 2001

TN/AG/R/3, Committee on Agriculture Special Session, Summary report on Agriculture Special Session Held on 6 September 2002, Note by the Secretariat, October, 01, 2002

TN/AG/R/5, Committee on Agriculture Special Session, Summary Report on the Fifteenth Meeting of the Committee on Agriculture Special Session Held on 22 November 2002, Note by the Secretariat, December, 19, 2002

TN/MA/W/21, Negotiating Group on Market Access, Market Access for Non-Agricultural Products, Communication from Mauritius, January, 07, 2003

TN/AG/W/1, Committee on Agriculture Special Session, Negotiations on Agriculture First Draft of Modalities for the Further Commitments, February, 17, 2003

TN/AG/GEN/1, Committee on Agriculture Special Session, Joint Statement on Non-Trade Concerns of Bulgaria, Chinese Taipei, Iceland, Liechtenstein, \Mauritius, Norway and Switzerland, Statement made by Switzerland at Formal Meeting of 28 February 2003, March 14, 2003

TN/AG/W/3, Committee on Agriculture Special Session, Draft possible modalities on agriculture, July, 12, 2006

TN/AG/W/4, Committee on Agriculture Special Session, Revised Draft Modalities for Agriculture, August, 01, 2007

TN/AG/W/4/Corr.1, Committee on Agriculture Special Session, Revised Draft Modalities for Agriculture, Corrigendum, August, 16, 2007

TN/AG/W/4/Rev.1, Committee on Agriculture Special Session, Revised Draft Modalities for Agriculture, February, 08, 2008

TN/AG/W/4/Rev.2, Committee on Agriculture Special Session, Revised Draft Modalities for Agriculture, May, 19, 2008

TN/AG/W/4/Rev.3, Committee on Agriculture Special Session, Revised Draft Modalities for Agriculture, July, 10, 2008

TN/AG/W/4/Rev.4, Committee on Agriculture Special Session, Revised Draft Modalities for Agriculture, December, 06, 2008

TN/AG/GEN/30, Committee on Agriculture Special Session, Refocusing Discussions on the Special Safeguard Mechanism (SSM): Outstanding issues and concerns on its design and structure, submission by the G-33, January, 28, 2010

TN/AG/GEN/30, Committee on Agriculture Special Session, Refocusing Discussions on the Special Safeguard Mechanism (SSM): Outstanding Issues and Concerns on its Design and Structure, Submission by the G-33, January, 28, 2010

Documents of the Committee on Anti-Dumping Practices

G/ADP/AHG/W/121/Rev.4, Committee on Anti-Dumping Practices, Working Group on Implementation, draft Recommendation Concerning Conditions of Competition that may be relevant to a Decision whether a Cumulative Assessment of the Effects of imports is appropriate, Revision, February, 17, 2004

Documents of the Committee on Trade and Development

TN/CTD/W/1, Committee on Trade and Development Special Session, Special and Differential Treatment Provisions, Joint Communication from Cuba, Dominican Republic, Honduras, India, Indonesia, Kenya, Pakistan, Sri Lanka, Tanzania and Zimbabwe, May, 14, 2002

TN/CTD/W/2, Committee on Trade and Development Special Session, Special and Differential Treatment Provisions, Joint Communication from Cuba, Dominican Republic, Egypt, Honduras, India, Indonesia, Kenya, Mauritius, Pakistan, Sri Lanka, Tanzania and Zimbabwe, May, 14, 2002

TN/CTD/W/5, Committee on Trade and Development Special Session, Application of the Special and Differential Treatment Provisions Contained in the Agreements and Decisions of the WTO, Communication from Paraguay, May, 24, 2002

TN/CTD/W/6, Committee on Trade and Development Special Session, Special and Differential Treatment Provisions, Communication from India, June, 17, 2002

TN/CTD/W/7, Committee on Trade and Development Special Session, Special and Differential Treatment Provisions, Communication from Thailand, June, 20, 2002

TN/CTD/W/3/Rev.1, Committee on Trade and Development Special Session, Special and Differential Treatment Provisions, Joint Communication from the African Group in the WTO, Revision, June, 24, 2002

TN/CTD/W/8, Committee on Trade and development Special Session, Special and Differential Treatment Provisions, Communication from Saint Lucia, June, 24, 2002

TN/CTD/W/3/Rev.2, Committee on Trade and Development Special Session, Special and Differential Treatment Provisions, Joint Communication from the African Group in the WTO, Revision, July, 17, 2002

WT/COMTD/SE/W/4, Committee on Trade and Development, Dedicated Session, Small Economies: A Literature Review, Note by the Secretariat, July, 23, 2002

TN/CTD/7, Committee on Trade and Development Special Session, Report to the General Council, February, 10, 2003

WT/COMTD/SE/W/13/Rev.1, Committee on Trade and Development, Dedicated Session, Work Programme on Small Economies, An Approach to Framing Responses to the Trade-Related Problems of Small Economies, Revision, Communication from Antigua and Barbuda, Barbados, Bolivia, Cuba, Dominican Republic, El Salvador, Fiji, Grenada, Guatemala, Honduras, Jamaica, Mauritius, Mongolia, Nicaragua, Papua New Guinea, Paraguay, Solomon Islands, St. Kitts and Nevis, St. Lucia, St. Vincent and the Grenadines and Trinidad and Tobago, May, 27, 2005

TN/MA/W/65, Negotiating Group on Market Access. Market Access for Non-Agricultural Products, Flexibilities for Developing Countries, Communication from Argentina, Bolivarian Republic of Venezuela, Brazil, China, Egypt, India, Indonesia, Namibia, Pakistan, Philippines and South Africa, November, 08, 2005

WT/COMTD/SE/4, Committee on Trade and Development, Dedicated Session, Report of the Committee on Trade and Development in Dedicated session to the General Council, November, 17, 2005

WT/COMTD/W/145,Committee on Trade and Development, Reclaiming Development in the WTO Doha Development Round, Submission by Argentina, Brazil, India, Indonesia, Namibia, Pakistan, the Philippines, South Africa and Venezuela to the Committee on Trade and Development, December, 01, 2005

WT/COMTD/SE/W/20, Committee on Trade and Development, Dedicated Session, Work Programme on Small Economies: An Assessment of the Progress to Date, Antigua and Barbuda, Barbados, Bolivia, Cuba, Dominica, Dominican Republic, El Salvador, Fiji, Grenada, Guatemala, Honduras, Jamaica, Mauritius, Mongolia, Nicaragua, Papua New Guinea, Paraguay, Solomon Islands, St. Kitts and Nevis, St. Lucia, St. Vincent and the Grenadines and Trinidad and Tobago, February, 09, 2006

WT/COMTD/SE/5, Committee on Trade and Development, Dedicated Session, Committee on Trade and Development in Dedicated Session, Report to the General Council on Measures to Assist Small Economies in Meeting their Obligations under the Agreements on SPS Measures, TBT and TRIPS, October, 03, 2006

WT/COMTD/W/143/Rev.5, Committee on Trade and Development, Developmental Aspects of the Doha Round of Negotiations, Note by the Secretariat, Revision, October, 28, 2010

WT/COMTD/SE/W/22/Rev.5, Committee on Trade and Development, Dedicated Session. Work Programme on Small Economies, Compilation paper prepared by the Secretariat Revision, November, 25, 2010

WT/COMTD/SE/W/24, Committee on Trade and Development, Dedicated Session, Communication from Barbados on Behalf of Small and Vulnerable Economies (SVES) on SVE Assessment of the Doha Round, December, 13, 2010

Documents of the Committee on Regional Trade Agreements

WT/REG/W/37, Committee on Regional Trade Agreements, Synopsis of "Systemic" Issues Related to regional Trade Agreements, Note by the Secretariat, March, 02, 2000

TN/RL/W/8/Rev.1, Compendium of Issues Related to Regional Trade Agreements, Background Note by the Secretariat, Revision, August, 01, 2002

Documents of the Committee on Trade and Environment

TN/TE/W/1, Committee on Trade and Environment Special Session, Multilateral Environmental Agreements (MEAS): Implementation of the DOHA Development Agenda, Submission by the European Communities, March, 21, 2002

TN/TE/R/1, Committee on Trade and Environment Special Session, Summary Report on the First Meeting of the Committee on Trade and Environment Special Session, March, 22, 2002, Note by the Secretariat, April, 19, 2002

Reports of the CTESS Chairperson to the Trade Negotiations Committee (documents TN/TE/1 to TN/TE/19)

TN/TE/W/4, Committee on Trade and Environment Special Session, Multilateral Environmental Agreements (MEAs): Implementation of the Doha Development Agenda, Submission by Switzerland, June, 06, 2002

TN/TE/2, Committee on Trade and Environment Special Session, Statement by The Chairperson of the Special Session of the Committee on Trade and Environment to the Trade Negotiations Committee, July, 04, 2002

TN/TE/W/42, Committee on Trade and Environment Special Session, Statement by China on Environmental Goods at the Committee on trade and Environment Special session (CTESS) Meeting of 22 June 2004, July, 06, 2004

TN/TE/W/51, Committee on Trade and Environment Special Session, An Alternative Approach for Negotiations under Paragraph 3 (III), Submission by India, June, 03, 2005

TN/TE/W/62, Committee on Trade and Environment Special Session, Integrated Proposal on Environmental Goods for Development, Submission by Argentina, October, 14, 2005

TN/TE/W/72/Rev.1, Committee on Trade and Environment Special Session, Proposal for an Outcome on Trade and Environment Concerning Paragraph 31 (1) of the Doha Ministerial Declaration, Submission from Australia and Argentina, May, 07, 2007

TN/TE/INF/4/Rev.14, Committee on Trade and Environment Special Session, Committee on Trade and Environment in Special Session (CTESS) List of Documents, Note by the Secretariat, Revision, February, 17, 2010

Documents of the Council for Trade in Services

S/CSS/W/7, Council for Trade in Services Special Session, Communication from Mauritius on behalf of the African Group, October, 04, 2000

S/CSS/W/13, Council for Trade in Services Special Session, Communication from Argentina, Brazil, Cuba; Dominican Republic, El Salvador, Honduras, India, Indonesia, Malaysia, Mexico, Nicaragua, Pakistan, Panama, Paraguay, Philippines, Sri Lanka, Thailand, Uruguay, and the Members of the Andean Community (Bolivia, Colombia, Ecuador, Peru, Venezuela), November, 24, 2000

S/CSS/W/44, Council for Trade in Services Special Session, Communication from Argentina, January, 29, 2001

S/CSS/W/114, Council for Trade in Services Special Session, Communication from Cuba, Dominican Republic, Haïti, India, Kenya, Pakistan, Peru, Uganda, Venezuela and Zimbabwe, October, 09, 2001

S/CSS/W/131, Council for Trade in Services Special Session, Communication from Cuba, Pakistan, Senegal, Sri Lanka, Tanzania, Uganda, Zambia and Zimbabwe, December, 06, 2001

TN/S/34, Council for Trade in Services Special Session, Elements Required for the Completion of the Services Negotiations, Report by the Chairman, July, 28, 2008

Documents of Dispute Settlement Body

TN/DS/W/15, Negotiations on the Dispute Settlement Understanding, Proposal by the African Group, September, 25, 2002

TN/DS/W/18, Negotiations on the Dispute Settlement Understanding, Proposals on DSU by Cuba, Honduras, India, Malaysia, Pakistan, Sri Lanka, Tanzania and Zimbabwe, October, 07, 2002

TN/DS/W/17, Negotiations on the Dispute Settlement Understanding, Proposal by the LDC Group, October, 09, 2002

TN/DS/W/19, Negotiations on the Dispute Settlement Understanding, Special and Differential Treatment for Developing Countries, Proposals on DSU by Cuba, Honduras, India, Indonesia, Malaysia, Pakistan, Sri Lanka, Tanzania and Zimbabwe, October, 09, 2002

TN/DS/W/31, Contribution to clarify and improve the Dispute Settlement Understanding: Panel System, Communication from Thailand, January, 22, 2003

TN/DS/W/47, Dispute Settlement Understanding Proposals: Legal text, Communication Communication from India on behalf of Cuba, Dominican Republic, Egypt, Honduras, Jamaica and Malaysia, February, 11, 2003

WT/DS246/R, European Communities – Conditions for the Granting of tariff References to Developing Countries, Report of the Panel, December, 01, 2003

WT/DS246/AB/R, European Communities – Conditions for the Granting of Tariff References to Developing Countries, AB-2004-1, Report of the Appellate Body, April, 07, 2004

WT/DS285/AB/R, United States – Measures affecting the cross-border supply of gambling and betting services, Report of the Appellate Body, April, 07, 2005

TN/DS/W/92 , Text for the African Group Proposals on Dispute Settlement Understanding Negotiations, Communication from Côte d'Ivoire, March, 05, 2008

TN/DS/25, Special Session of the Dispute Settlement Body, Report by the Chairman, Ambassador Ronald Saborío Soto, to the Trade Negotiations Committee, April, 21, 2011

TN/DS/W/23, Negotiations on improvement and clarifications of the Dispute Settlement Understanding, Proposal by Mexico, November, 04, 2011

General Council Documents

WT/GC/W/304, General Council, Preparations for the 1999 Ministerial Conference, Trade and Sustainable Development, Communication from the United States, August, 06, 1999

WT/GC/W/442, Preparations for the Fourth Session of the Ministerial Conference, Proposal for a Framework Agreement on Special and Differential Treatment, Communication from Cuba, Dominican Republic, Honduras, India, Indonesia, Kenya, Malaysia, Pakistan, Sri Lanka, Tanzania, Uganda and Zimbabwe, September, 19, 2001

WT/GC/W/453, Preparations for the fourth session of the Ministerial Conference, Proposal on Market Access for Non-Agricultural Products, Communication from Kenya, Mozambique, Nigeria, Tanzania, Uganda and Zimbabwe, November, 02, 2001

WT/GC/W/522, General Council 15, 16 and 18 December 2003, Singapore Issues: The way forward, Joint Communication from Bangladesh (on behalf of the LDC Group), Botswana, China, Cuba, Egypt, India, Indonesia, Kenya, Malaysia, Nigeria, Philippines, Tanzania, Uganda, Venezuela, Zambia and Zimbabwe, December, 12, 2003

Documents of the Negotiating Group on Market Access

TN/MA/W/31, Negotiating Group on Market Access, Market Access for Non-Agricultural Products, Communication from Egypt, India, Indonesia, Kenya, Malaysia, Mauritius, Nigeria, Tanzania, Uganda and Zimbabwe, March, 25, 2003

TN/MA/W/35, Negotiating Group on Market Access, Draft Elements of Modalities for Negotiations on Non-Agricultural Products, May, 16, 2003

TN/MA/W/21/Add.1, Negotiating Group on Market Access, market Access for Non-Agricultural Products, Communication from Mauritius, Addendum, July, 15, 2003

TN/MA/W/35/Rev.1, Negotiating Group on Market Access, Draft Elements of Modalities for Negotiation on Non-Agricultural Products, Revision, August, 19, 2003

TN/MA/W/53, Negotiating Group on Market Access, Market Access for Non-Agricultural Products, Communication from Benin on behalf of the ACP Group of States, March, 11, 2005

TN/MA/W/86, Negotiating Group on Market Access, Market Access for Non-Agricultural Products, Communication from the NAMA-11 Group of Developing Countries, June, 08, 2007

TN/MA/W/103 Negotiating Group on Market Access, Draft Modalities for Non-Agricultural Market Access, February, 08, 2008

TN/MA/W/103/Rev.1, Negotiating Group on Market Access, Draft Modalities for Non-Agricultural Market Access Second Revision, May, 20, 2008

TN/MA/W/103/Rev.2, Negotiating Group on Market Access, Draft Modalities for Non-Agricultural Market Access, Third Revision, July, 10, 2008

TN/MA/W/103/Rev.3, Negotiating Group on Market Access, Fourth Revision of Draft Modalities for Non-Agricultural Market Access, December, 06, 2008

TN/MA/W/103/Rev.3/Add.1, Negotiating Group on Market Access, Textual Report by the Chairman, Ambassador Wasescha, on the State of Play of the NAMA Negotiations, Addendum, April, 21, 2011

Documents of the Negotiating Group on Rules

TN/RL/W/7, Negotiating Group on Rules, Implementation-Related Issues, Paper by Brazil, April, 26, 2002

TN/RL/GEN/1, Negotiating Group on Rules, Lesser Duty Rule, Communication from Brazil, Chile, Colombia, Costa Rica, Hong Kong, China, Israel, Japan, Republic of Korea, Mexico, Norway, Singapore, Switzerland, Separate Customs Territory of Taiwan, Penghu, Kinmen and Matsu, Thailand and Turkey, July, 14, 2004

TN/RL/GEN/8, Negotiating Group on Rules, Prohibition of Zeroing, Communication from Brazil, Chile, Colombia, Costa Rica, Hong Kong, China, Israel, Japan, Korea, Mexico, Norway, Singapore, Switzerland, Separate Customs Territory of Taiwan, Penghu, Kinmen and Matsu and Thailand, July, 14, 2004

TN/RL/W/171, Negotiating Group on Rules, Senior Officials' Statement, Communication from Brazil, Chile, Colombia, Costa Rica, Hong Kong, China, Israel, Japan, Republic of Korea, Mexico, Norway, Singapore, Switzerland, the Separate Customs Territory of Taiwan, Penghu, Kinmen and Matsu, Thailand and Turkey, February, 15, 2005

TN/RL/GEN/32, Negotiating Group on Rules, Proposal on mandatory Application of Lesser Duty Rule, Communication from India, March, 22, 2005

TN/RL/GEN/43, Negotiating Group on Rules, Further Submission of Proposals on the Mandatory Application of the Lesser Duty Rule, Paper from Brazil, Chile, Costa Rica, Hong Kong, China, Israel, Japan, Republic of Korea, Norway, Singapore, Switzerland, the Separate Customs Territory of Taiwan, Penghu, Kinmen, and Matsu and Thailand, May, 13, 2005

TN/RL/GEN/53, Negotiating Group on Rules, Further Submission Public Interest, Communication from Hong Kong, China, Israel, Japan, Republic of Korea, Norway, Singapore, Switzerland, the Separate Customs Territory of Taiwan, Penghu, Kinmen and Matsu and Thailand, July, 01, 2005

TN/RL/GEN/61, Negotiating Group on Rules, Sunset Reviews, Communication from Canada, September, 15, 2005

TN/RL/GEN/74, Negotiating Group on Rules, Further Submission of Proposals on Sunset, Communication from Chile, Hong Kong, China, Japan, Republic of Korea, Norway, Switzerland, Separate Customs Territory of Taiwan, Penghu, Kinmen and Matsu and Thailand, October, 17, 2005

TN/RL/GEN/85, Negotiating Group on Rules, Public Interest, Paper from Canada, November, 17, 2005

TN/RL/GEN/99, Negotiating Group on Rules, Proposals on the Mandatory Application of the Lesser Duty Rule, Paper from Brazil, Hong Kong, China, India and Japan, March, 03, 2006

TN/RL/GEN/104, Negotiating Group on Rules, Proposal on Sunset, Paper from Japan, March, 06, 2006

TN/RL/GEN/126, Negotiating Group on Rules, Proposals on the Prohibition of zeroing, Communication from Japan, April, 24, 2006

TN/RL/GEN/137, Negotiating Group on Rules, Proposals on Issues relating to the Anti-Dumping Agreement, Paper from South Africa, May, 29, 2006

TN/RL/GEN/143, Negotiating Group on Rules, Special and Differential Treatment and Technical Assistance in Trade Remedies, Submission by Kenya, June, 27, 2006

TN/RL/GEN/147, Negotiating Group on Rules, Proposals on Offsets for Non-Dumped Comparisons, Proposals from the United States, June 27, 2007

TN/RL/GEN/149, Negotiating Group on Rules, Proposal on Sunset Review, Communication from China, June, 29, 2007

TN/RL/W/213, Negotiating Group on Rules, Draft and Consolidated Chair Texts of the AD and SCM Agreements, November, 30, 2007

Documents of the Negotiating Group on Trade Facilitation

TN/TF/W/5, Technical Assistance and Capacity Building on Trade Facilitation – Note by the Secretariat, January, 14, 2005

TN/TF/W/22, Negotiating Group on Trade Facilitation, Communication from Uganda and the United States, March 21, 2005

TN/TF/W/30, Negotiating Group on Trade Facilitation, Communication from Peru, April, 27, 2005

TN/TF/W/29, Negotiating Group on Trade Facilitation, Communication from the People's Republic of China and Pakistan, April, 28, 2005

TN/TF/W/33, Negotiating Group on Trade Facilitation, Communication from the African Group, April 28, 2005

TN/TF/W/54, Technical Assistance and Capacity Building on Trade Facilitation – Note by the Secretariat, July, 21, 2005

TN/TF/W/57, Negotiating Group on Trade Facilitation, Communication from India and the United States, July, 22, 2005

TN/TF/W/59, Identification of Trade Facilitation Needs and Priorities (Paragraph 4 of the Negotiating Mandate) – Self-Assessment Questionnaire and Inventory, July, 28, 2005

TN/TF/W/63, Negotiating Group on Trade Facilitation, Communication from Pakistan and Switzerland on Development-Related Issues in Trade Facilitation, September, 19, 2005

TN/TF/W/73, Negotiating Group on Trade Facilitation, Communication from Mauritius on behalf of the ACP Group, November, 10, 2005

TN/TF/W/76, Technical Assistance and Capacity Building on Trade Facilitation – Note by the Secretariat, February, 06, 2006

TN/TF/W/95, Negotiating Group on Trade Facilitation, Communication from the African Group, May, 09, 2006

TN/TF/W/103, Negotiating Group on Trade Facilitation, Communication from India, May, 10, 2006

TN/TF/W/143, Negotiating Group on Trade Facilitation, WTO Negotiations on Trade facilitation, Self Assessment Guide, Prepared by the World Bank1 in Cooperation with the WTO Secretariat and other Annex D Organizations, April, 12, 2007

TN/TF/W/43 and revisions, WTO Negotiations on Trade Facilitation – Compilation of Members' Proposals – Revision, November, 05, 2007

TN/TF/W/154, Negotiating Group on Trade Facilitation, Communication from Canada, March, 10, 2008

Documents of the Trade Negotiations Committee

TN/C/W/57, Trade Negotiations Committee, the Seoul Summit Document, November, 26, 2010

TN/C/14, Trade Negotiation Committee, Report by the Director-General on his Consultations on NAMA Sectoral Negotiations, April, 21, 2011

Glossary[1]

ACP-EC Partnership Agreement: The "Partnership Agreement between the members of the African, Caribbean and Pacific (ACP) Group of States of the one part and the European Community (EC) and its Member States of the other part" is a framework agreement for trade and economic cooperation, signed on June 23, 2000 in Cotonou, Bénin as the successor to the Lomé Convention. On April 01, 2003 it entered into force for twenty years. The Agreement entails wide-ranging cooperation in trade-related areas including, among others, trade in services, competition policy, trade and environment and trade and labour standards.

African Group: This is a Group active in the WTO, consisting of all African countries that are members of the WTO.

Aggregate Measure of Support (AMS): The term is used in agricultural negotiations. It is the annual level of support expressed in monetary terms for all domestic support measures where government funds are used to subsidise farm production and incomes. It includes product-specific support and support given to agricultural producers in general.

Agreement on Sanitary and Phytosanitary Measures: This agreement was concluded in the WTO to set out the basic rules, rights and obligations of WTO members in measures necessary to protect human health, animal or plant life or health. Among others, they must be based on scientific principles, sufficient scientific evidence and risk assessments. Measures must not be applied in a manner which would constitute a means of arbitrary or unjustifiable discrimination between members where the same conditions prevail.

Amber box: Domestic support measures for agriculture that distort production and trade, including price support and subsidies directly related to production quantities. They may have to be reduced through the *Total Aggregate Measurement of Support* (*See also blue box and green box*).

Anti-dumping measures: Anti-dumping measures can be adopted after an investigation of the importing country, when dumping and material injury resulting there from has occurred. Anti-dumping measures may take the form of anti-dumping duties or of price undertakings. They are generally enterprise-specific duties levied on certain goods to offset the dumping margin. Anti-dumping price undertaking may be offered to exporters to avoid the imposition of anti-dumping duties.

Appellate Body: This is a standing body of seven persons established under the WTO Understanding on Rules and Procedures Governing the Settlement of Disputes to hear appeals arising from panel cases. The grounds for such appeals are confined to points of WTO law.

1. This Glossary has been prepared based on Goode, W. 2007. *"Dictionary of Trade Policy Terms – Fifth Edition"*, Cambridge University Press and Centre for International Economic Studies/ WTO.

Banana cases: The EC-Bananas Cases concern the banana import regime that the European Economic Community (EEC) had established with the inception of the EC's Internal Market in 1993.

Best-endeavour undertakings: These are conditional promises to take certain actions, or to consider the possibility of taking certain action. If they are part of a trade agreement, they are an aspect of *soft law*. In trade negotiations best-endeavour undertakings are often the first step towards more binding obligations.

Blended formula: The formula is a method for reducing tariffs proposed during the Doha Development Agenda negotiations. It entails the use of the Uruguay Round tariff reduction formula for some tariffs, the Swiss formula for others and eliminating tariffs altogether on some tariff lines. The formula used during the Uruguay Round combined an average reduction with a minimum reduction per tariff line and it permitted some measures to protect sensitive products from increasing competition.

Blue box: Agricultural supports linked to production, but subject to production limits and therefore minimally trade-distorting. They are exempt from the reduction commitments under the WTO Agreement on Agriculture.

Bottom-up approach: Preparing an agenda for trade negotiations by agreeing on negotiating subjects item by item. As agreement is reached on each item, the shape of the final agenda gradually becomes apparent.

Bracketed language: This is a section of a negotiating text put in square brackets either because the language is disputed or because its adoption will depend on agreement being achieved elsewhere in the text.

C4: The coalition on cotton is a coalition of four West African States (Benin, Burkina Faso Chad and Mali) seeking cuts in cotton subsidies and tariffs.

Cairns Group: Group of agricultural exporting nations lobbying for agricultural trade liberalisation that was established at a Ministerial Meeting held in Cairns, Australia in 1986, i.e. just before the start of the Uruguay Round.

Circumvention: These are measures taken by exporters to evade *anti-dumping measures* or *countervailing duties*. It can refer also to the evasion of *rules of origin*, etc. Circumvention consists of disguising the true origin of the product, sometimes through manufacturing operations whose sole purpose it is to provide sufficient evidence to meet the requirements of an agreement. These sometimes fall into the category of *screwdriver operations*. The *Agreement on Agriculture* seeks to prevent circumvention of commitments to rein in export subsidies. Circumvention in the textile trade refers to avoiding quotas and other restrictions by altering the country of origin of a product.

Committee on Trade and Development (CTD): The CTD was first established on November, 26, 1964 under GATT. One of its main tasks has long been the administration of Part IV of the GATT and the Enabling Clause. It is now part of various Committees under the WTO and is concerned with developing-country issues.

Common Agricultural Policy (CAP): This is the European Union's agricultural policy. Its objectives were set forth in Article 39 of the Treaty of Rome (1957). The European Community's comprehensive system of production targets and marketing mechanisms designed to manage agricultural trade within the Community and with the rest of the world.

Common market: A more developed type of customs union in which, in addition to the free movement of goods between member states, labour, capital and services can also move without restriction. Common markets lead to highly integrated economies.

Commonwealth: The Commonwealth, with roots as far back as the 1870s, was reconstituted in 1949 when Commonwealth Prime Ministers met and adopted what has become known as the 'London Declaration'. It comprises 54 independent states. Its members used to be part of the British Empire. It is administered by the Commonwealth Secretariat located in London. Among its many functions, the Secretariat runs programmes aimed at the economic and trade development particularly of developing countries.

Commonwealth of Independent States (CIS): CIS was created in December 1991. In the adopted Declaration the participants of the Commonwealth declared their interaction on the basis of sovereign equality. At present the CIS unites: Azerbaijan, Armenia, Belarus, Georgia, Kazakhstan, Kyrgyzstan, Moldova, Russia, Tajikistan, Turkmenistan, Uzbekistan and Ukraine.

Cotonou Agreement: See **"ACP-EC Partnership Agreement".**

Countervailing duties: Such duties reflect action taken by the importing country, usually in the form of increased duties, to offset subsidies given to producers or exporters in the exporting country. GATT Article VI and the WTO Agreement on Subsidies and Countervailing Measures set out the rules for imposing such duties.

Customs Union: An area consisting of two or more individual economies or customs territories which remove all tariffs and sometimes broader trade impediments between them. The members making up the area then apply a common external tariff.

De minimis: A legal term describing that something is of little or no importance in the matter concerned.

Development Round: The multilateral trade negotiations launched at Doha, Qatar, on November, 14, 2001. The work programme for this round reflects the concerns of developing countries more than any previous round.

Dispute Settlement Body (DSB): The WTO General Council, when convened to settle disputes arising between members is referred to as DSB. The DSB has the sole authority to establish panels, adopt panel and appellate body reports, maintain surveillance of rulings and recommendations and authorise retaliation in cases where its recommendations are ignored.

Dispute Settlement Understanding (DSU): This is formally known as the "WTO Understanding on Rules and Procedures Governing the Settlement of Disputes". This is one of the outcomes of the Uruguay Round. Its underlying theme is that prompt settlement of disputes is essential for the proper functioning of the WTO. The understanding, therefore, sets out in some detail the procedures and timetable to be followed in resolving disputes.

Doha Development Agenda (DDA): The sum of the issues arising from the Doha Ministerial Conference which launched a new round of multilateral trade negotiation on November, 14, 2001. Development objectives are prominent in the Doha Ministerial Declaration.

Doha Round: This is the unofficial name for the multilateral trade negotiations launched at Doha, Qatar, on November 14, 2001.

Domestic Support: This is another term for assistance, internal support or subsidy to agriculture. It includes any domestic subsidy or other measures which act to maintain producer prices at levels above those prevailing in international trade. It also refers to direct payments to producers, including deficiency payments and input and marketing cost reduction measures available only for agricultural production.

Enabling Clause: The clause is one of the outcomes of the Tokyo Round and includes: the "Decision on Differential and More Favourable Treatment, Reciprocity and Fuller Participation of Developing Countries". It allows developed WTO members to take action favouring developing countries without according the same treatment to other members. Main measures covered by it include the Generalised System of Preferences, non tariff measures covered by the GATT, regional and global trading arrangements between developing countries and special treatment for the least developed countries. The Enabling Cause was intended to promote greater participation of developing countries in the world trading system.

Environmentally Preferable Products: Products or services that affect the environment less than other products having the same purpose. Such products typically contain recycled materials, save energy and water in their production, reduce waste and minimise toxic by-products.

Escape clause: This is a provision in trade agreements which permits a party to suspend its obligations when imports cause or threaten to cause serious harm to the domestic producers of similar goods. GATT Article XIX contains the escape clause for trade in goods used by WTO members. It allows a member to suspend its obligations or to modify liberalising commitments if there are unforeseen circumstances and if any product is imported in such increased quantities likely to cause or causing harm to domestic producers.

Everything but Arms: This is the European Union initiative for duty-free and quota-free access to all products except arms originating in least developed countries. It took effect on March, 05, 2001 for most products. Sugar, rice and bananas would receive free access in stages by 2009.

Export competition: The practice of competing internationally in markets for agricultural commodities through, for example, export subsidies, subsidised export credits, state trading enterprises, differential pricing, abuse of food aid and non-transparent market support systems is referred to as export competition.

Export credits: Government financial supports, direct financing, guarantees, insurance or interest rate support provided to foreign buyers to assist in the financing of the purchase of goods from national exporters are known as export credits.

Export subsidies: Government payments or other financial contributions by governments provided to domestic producers or exporters if they export their goods or services. They are generally illegal for manufactured products under the Agreement on Subsidies and Countervailing Measures.

Formula cuts: These are tariff reductions across whole sectors done through the use of a formula, such as the ***Swiss Formula.***

Framework Agreements: This terminology is given to the four instruments which are outcomes of the Tokyo Round negotiations dealing particularly with developing-country issues: (i) the Enabling Clause, (ii) the Declaration on Trade Measures Taken for Balance-of-Payments Purposes, (iii) the Decision on Safeguard Action for Development Purposes and (iv) the Understanding Regarding Notification, Consultation, Dispute Settlement and Surveillance.

Free Trade Agreements: Contractual arrangements between two or more countries under which they give each other preferential market access, usually called free trade. In practise, free trade agreements tend to allow for all sorts of exceptions, many of them temporary, to cover sensitive products.

GATT system: This refers to General Agreement on Tariffs and Trade, an international organisation and the secretariat that administered the GATT Agreement. This has been superseded by the WTO.

Geographical Indications: Place names, or words associated with a place, used to identify products (for example, Champagne, Tequila or Roquefort), which have a particular quality, reputation or other characteristics because they come from that place.

Green box: Refers to domestic support policies for agricultural products exempt from the Uruguay Round reduction commitments and permitted without limits. Green box policies include genuine relief to farmers through a wide range of assistance measures which have a minimal impact on trade, such as disaster relief, research, disease control, infrastructure, environmental protection and food security.

Group of Negotiations on Services (GNS): The group established at the start of the Uruguay Round to handle all issues relating to trade in services.

G-10: A coalition of net food importing countries lobbying for agriculture to be treated as diverse and special in the WTO agriculture negotiations because of non-trade concerns.

G-20: A coalition of developing countries pressing for ambitious reforms of agriculture in developed countries with some flexibility for developing countries in the WTO agriculture negotiations. It is so named because it was established on August 20, 2003 and had 20 members at that time.

G-33: A coalition of developing countries in the WTO agriculture negotiations that is advocating flexibility for developing countries to undertake limited liberalisation commitments based on concerns related to food security, rural development and rural livelihoods. The coalition has emerged immediately before the Cancun Ministerial Conference in 2003 and was originally called "Alliance for Strategic Products and Special Safeguard Mechanism" ("SP and SSM Alliance" in short) as these were the two main demands of the coalition. Later the name was changed to G-33 to reflect the number of its member countries at that time though its current membership is 46.

G-90: ACP states, LDCs and Africa Group when they meet jointly in the WTO are called G-90.

The Generalised System of Preferences (GSP): An autonomous, country-specific policy that permits tariff reductions or possibly duty-free entry of certain imports from designated developing countries into a developed country.

Global System of Trade Preferences (GSTP): Initiated in 1989, GSTP aims to promote the development of economic co-operation among developing countries through the exchange of tariff preferences. Non-tariff preferences may also be exchanged. Least developed countries do not have to offer reciprocal concessions. Membership of the GSTP is open to members of the Group of 77. Negotiations are conducted under UNCTAD auspices. The GSTP has 44 participating countries.

Injury: An adverse effect on domestic industry assumed to be caused by the actions of exporters from other countries, for example, through dumping, subsidies or import surges. In the case of dumping, action can be taken if there is material injury. In safeguards, serious injury must be threatening or have occurred. Both terms allow for a subjective assessment, but serious injury is deemed to be graver than material injury. The WTO has a highly developed framework for the assessment of injury and remedial action in the case of injury or threat of injury.

Intellectual Property Protection: The safeguarding of the rights of an owner of intellectual property through national legislation and international agreements especially concerning copyright, patents and trademarks. Some commentators insist that the strength or weakness of a country's system of intellectual property protection seems to have a substantial effect on the kinds of technology firms transfer to another country.

Intellectual Property Rights (IPRs): This is the general term for the assignment of property rights through patents, copyrights and trademarks. These property rights allow the holder to exercise a monopoly on the use of the item for a specified period. By restricting imitation and duplication, monopoly power is conferred but the social costs of monopoly power may be offset by the social benefits of higher levels of creative activity encouraged by the monopoly earnings.

Intellectual Property: This term generally includes patents, trademarks, industrial designs, lay-out designs of integrated circuits, copyright, geographical indications and trade secrets (confidential information).

International Trade Centre: Refers to the ITC, originally established by the old GATT. It is now operated by the WTO and the United Nations, the latter acting through UNCTAD. ITC is a focal point for technical co-operation on trade promotion of developing countries.

July package: Refers to the WTO General Council decision of August 01, 2004 which sets out a work programme leading to the conclusion of negotiations under the Doha Development Agenda. It takes its name from the intensive negotiations during July 2004 leading up to the decision.

Lesser-duty principle: The principle in the administration of anti-dumping measures that additional duties imposed on products found dumped should be less than the margin of dumping if a lesser duty is enough to eliminate the injury.

Like-Minded Group of Developing Countries: A group active in WTO negotiations. Its core members are Cuba, Dominican Republic, Egypt, Honduras, India, Indonesia, Jamaica, Kenya, Malaysia, Mauritius, Pakistan, Sri Lanka, Tanzania, Uganda and Zimbabwe.

Margin of dumping: The key concept in dumping enquiries which determines the extent to which anti-dumping measures may be imposed. The margin of dumping is the difference between the assessment by the relevant authority of what should be considered normal value and the export price of the product exported from one country to another. Procedures to be followed in ascertaining the margin of dumping are set out in the WTO Agreement on Implementation of Article VI of the General Agreement on Tariffs and Trade 1994.

Market Access: This term is governed by provisions of the Uruguay Round Agreement on Agriculture which refer to concessions contained in the country schedules with respect to bindings and reductions of tariffs and to other minimum import commitments.

Marrakesh Agreement Establishing the World Trade Organization: This Agreement, sometimes known as the WTO Agreement, was adopted on April, 15, 1994 at the Marrakesh Ministerial Meeting. It established the World Trade Organisation. It also sets out in four annexes the multilateral and plurilateral agreements under its jurisdiction.

Most Favoured Nation: The principle of not discriminating between one's trading partners. It is required by Article I of the GATT, Article II of the General Agreements on Trade in Services and Article IV of the Agreement on Trade Related Aspects of Intellectual Property Rights.

Mini-Ministerial meeting: An informal meeting to which a limited number of ministers are invited. These meetings are normally used to seek ways to maintain impetus in negotiations or to discuss key issues in negotiations. Accordingly, the selection of ministers to be invited depends largely on the topics to be discussed.

Modalities: Ways or forms of organising work in the WTO, including trade negotiations. They set broad outlines, such as formulas or approaches for tariff reductions for final commitments.

Multifunctionality: The term is derived from the idea that agriculture has many functions in addition to producing food and fibre. These functions may be environmental protection, landscape preservation, rural employment, etc. The term appears to have originated in a communiqué issued in March 1998 by agricultural ministers from OECD countries. The recognition of the various roles agriculture can play is hardly new, but multifunctionality has quickly become one of the dividing lines of agricultural trade policy. Those who stress its importance are seen as leaning towards protectionism and those who oppose its use like to think of themselves as promoters of agricultural trade liberalisation.

Multilateral Trade Negotiations (MTN): These are also known as rounds. They aim to strengthen the rules hat ensure orderly and fair conduct of international trade and to reach mutually beneficial agreements reducing barriers to world trade. Eight rounds have been held under GATT auspices since 1947. Each round has consisted of long bargaining sessions. The eight completed rounds and the names by which they are commonly known were: Geneva (1947), Annecy (1949), Torquay (1950), Geneva (1955-56), Dillon (1960-61), Kennedy (1963-67), Tokyo (1973-79) and Uruguay (1986-94). The ninth round, the Doha Development Agenda, was launched by the Doha Ministerial Conference in November 2001.

Multilateral Trading System: The term is used to describe the non discriminatory arrangement for international trade which came into existence with the GATT in 1947 and which is now represented by the WTO system.

National Treatment: The principle of giving others the same treatment as one's own nationals. GATT Article III requires that imports be treated no less favourably than the same or similar domestically-produced goods once they have passed customs. General Agreement on Trade in Services (GATS) Article XVII and the Trade-Related Aspects of Intellectual Property Rights (TRIPs) Article 3 also deal with national treatment for services and intellectual property protection respectively.

New trade issues: Issues arising because of the emergence of new trading patterns, new products, new technologies or the confluence of trade policy and social policies. The term often simply means that there is not yet a formal multilateral trade framework in existence for dealing with relevant matters or that they have only recently been taken up within the WTO.

Non-agricultural market access (NAMA): Tariff negotiations on products other than those covered by the Agreement on Agriculture are referred to as NAMA. This term was created in the preparatory phase for the Seattle WTO Ministerial Conference.

NAMA II: Coalition of developing countries seeking flexibilities to limit market opening in industrial goods trade.

Non-reciprocal: In trade negotiations, the term refers to acceptance of the principle that an offer or undertaking by a party to do something need not be matched, either wholly or partly, by the party standing to benefit from the offer. This principal is contained, for example, in Part VI of the GATT (Article XXXVI:8) which states that the "developed contracting parties do not expect reciprocity for commitments made by them in trade negotiations to reduce or remove tariffs and other barrier to the trade of the less-developed contracting parties".

Non-tariff measures: Those government measures other than tariffs that restrict trade flows. Examples include quantitative restrictions, import licensing, voluntary restraint arrangements and variable levies. They generally now contravene the WTO rules. One of the outcomes of the Uruguay Round was an obligation to convert all non-tariff measures affecting agricultural trade into tariffs.

Non-trade concerns: The term is used in the agricultural trade negotiations as a more neutral expression than, for example, multifunctionality. The preamble of the Agreement on Agriculture specifies food security and environmental protection as examples. Also cited by WTO members are rural development and employment, and poverty alleviation.

Normal trade relations: This is the term now used by the US instead of most-favoured nation treatment particularly in the annual congressional debate on the nature of the US-China trade framework.

Nuisance tariff: A tariff that is so low that it costs the government more to collect it than the revenue it generates. It is sometimes also used to refer to any tariff without a protective effect. Some countries defend this as necessary to raise revenues.

Paragraph 6 Countries: This is a group of developing countries with less than 35 percent of non-agricultural products covered by legally bound tariff ceilings. They have agreed to increase their binding coverage substantially as their main contribution in the Doha Round while being exempted from the application of Swiss formula for tariff reductions. The group is so named because it was mentioned in paragraph 6 of the first version of the NAMA draft modalities text (appears in paragraph 8 in the latest draft modalities text).

Patent Cooperation Treaty: The treaty provides for the filing of an international patent application in member states. Filing has to be done through the patent office of which the applicant is a national or resident, and it has the same effect in member states as filing an application with a national patent office of that state. The Treaty has more than 100 members. It is administered by WIPO.

Peace clause: A provision in Article 13 of the WTO Agreement on Agriculture which says that agricultural subsidies committed under the agreement cannot be challenged under other WTO agreements, especially the Agreement on Subsidies and Countervailing Measures and the GATT. The peace clause expired on December, 31, 2003.

Plurilateral trade agreements: Those agreements under the WTO, accession to which is not a precondition for WTO membership.

Preference erosion: The disappearing margins of preference as countries reduce their MFN tariffs to levels at or below the margin of preference.

Preferential investment arrangements: Formal or informal arrangements which give better access terms to investment capital and investors from selected countries or groups of countries. This may include expedited consideration of investment proposals, permission to invest in activities closed to others, higher ceilings for foreign equity, etc. Investment chapters in free trade agreements fall in this category.

Preferential market access: Any market access conditions afforded to a trading partner that are more favourable than the non-discriminatory most-favoured-nation treatment are referred to as preferential market access. Preferential access may be reciprocal or symmetrical as in customs unions, free-trade areas, or through the now residual imperial preferences. It can also be non-reciprocal or asymmetrical, as in the case with the ACP-EC partnership agreement, the Caribbean Basin Initiative, AGOA and other such agreements.

Preferential rules of origin: A system of rules of origin to determine whether a good exported under a preferential trading arrangement, such as a free-trade area, will be admitted by another member of the arrangement under the applicable preferential rules. In most cases this would be free of customs duties. Preferential rules of origin are therefore meant to ensure that preferences given to the other members of the arrangement do not leak to third countries.

Preferential tariff: This is a tariff schedule which shows the tariff rates applicable under preferential trade arrangements. The applicable tariff is usually lower than general tariff or the most favoured nation tariff. Preferential tariffs can be contractual as in a free trade agreement or autonomous as under a GSP scheme.

Preferential trading arrangements: A group of countries that levy lower (or zero) tariffs against imports from members than outsiders. They include FTAs, customs unions, and common markets.

Price dumping: A category of dumping identified at the time of the Havana Charter negotiations which is now subject to Article VI of the GATT. It is based on the concept that the exporter sells goods abroad at a lower price than in the domestic market, and that this may have an injurious effect on industry in the importing country producing similar goods.

Price undertaking: An undertaking by an exporter to raise the export price of the product to avoid the possibility of an anti-dumping duty. A price undertaking is not expected to exceed the alleged margin of dumping, and preferably it should be at the lowest possible level that would be adequate to remove the threat of ***injury*** from domestic industry.

Processes and production method: A term used in discussions concerning trade and environment. It deals with the environmental effects of processes by which goods and services are produced. A negative effect may occur in two main ways: (a) through the transformation of the product itself and (b) through a production process that does not affect the characteristics of the finished good. Some have argued that a labelling system should be established to let the consumer know what processes have been used in the production of a good. This is the so-called PPM-labelling.

Protectionism: A climate of economic policy formulation which sees merit in preventing the exposure of domestic producers to the rigours of the international market. The basic means for achieving this are tariffs, subsidies, voluntary restraint arrangements and other non-tariff measures, with an emphasis on the less transparent measures. More complex cases can involve alleged cultural, environmental and other considerations. Protectionism can also be promoted through the vigorous use of contingent protection. In most cases, protectionism merely delays the inevitable adjustment of inefficient industries to the market.

Safeguards: Action taken to protect a specific industry from an unexpected build-up of imports, governed by Article XIX of the General Agreement on Tariffs and Trade (GATT) 1994.

Sensitive products: Those products more likely than others to encounter import restriction. Typical examples are many agricultural products, textiles, clothing and footwear, passenger motor vehicles, chemicals and, sometimes, steel. The reasons for the sensitivity surrounding these products are complex. It may be the perceived need to protect the traditional occupation of a national minority, as is the case with Japanese tanneries. In other cases, technological changes and new investment may lead to lower-cost foreign competitors and an inability by domestic producers to adjust quickly. Agriculture, as shown by the European and American examples, is particularly complicated. Traditional political power combined with a vague community perception that the rural population expresses the national spirit and must therefore be preserved, may render any reform of the rural sector a delicate matter.

Services: These include key economic activities such as telecommunications, banking, insurance, land and water transport, aviation, accountancy, law, engineering, entertainment, etc., which can be produced in their own right or as a component of some product or another service.

Singapore issues: The issues are trade and investment, trade and competition, transparency in government procurement and trade facilitation. These are so named because they entered the WTO work programme through the declaration issued by the Singapore Ministerial Conference in December 1996.

Single undertaking: This is a guiding principle in the framework of multilateral trade negotiations. The Doha Ministerial Declaration states that "... the conduct, conclusion and entry into force of the outcome of the negotiations shall be treated as part of a single undertaking." Single undertaking has also been used to refer to the requirement that WTO members must join all the agreements administered by it, except for the two plurilateral agreements.

SP and SSM Alliance: See G-33.

Small, Vulnerable Economies (SVE): This is an imprecise term sometimes used to cover economies sharing several or all of the following characteristics: (a) small domestic markets, (b) limited diversification in export structure, both in terms of products and markets, (c) vulnerability to internal and external shocks, such as natural disasters or rapid increase in prices for imported energies, (d) limited qualified human resources, and (f) shortfalls in institutional and administrative capacities.

Special Safeguard Mechanism for developing countries: Proposals made by some developing countries in the Doha Development Agenda negotiations for the creation of a special safeguard mechanism for agricultural products. It would deal with cases where import volumes of specified agricultural products are rising rapidly and import prices fall below a fixed reference price. The special agricultural safeguards would only be available to developing countries meeting some defined conditions. Increasingly, free-trade agreements seem to make use of special agricultural safeguards.

Special and differential treatment: Often also referred to as S&D or SDT. It is the concept that exports of developing countries should be given preferential access to markets of developed countries, and that developing countries participating in trade negotiations need not reciprocate fully the concessions they receive. Under S&D, developing countries also enjoy longer timeframes for phasing in new rules and lower levels of obligations for adherence to the rules.

Special Products: A proposal in the WTO by developing countries that they should be able to exempt some agricultural products from tariff reductions and liberalisation of tariff rate quotas. A ceiling would apply to the number of tariff lines that could be treated in this way, but developing countries would be able to decide what products would be included.

Special safeguards: A mechanism available under the WTO Agreement on Agriculture to members who have converted non-tariff measures to tariff protection. It allows members to impose additional tariffs on agricultural products if import volumes exceed defined trigger levels or import prices fall below defined trigger prices. Special safeguards therefore provide a safety net for importing countries that are also producers in the event of a surge in imports. They are meant to be introduced in a transparent manner.

Square brackets: Please see "**bracketed language**".

Structural adjustment: The continuous process experienced by all industries needing to adjust to new economic and commercial conditions brought about by changes in consumer preferences, technological innovation, tariff reductions, subsidy phase-outs, long-term changes in the cost of components and raw materials, etc. is referred to as structural adjustment. Since the mid-1980s, the term has also come to refer to a particular set of policy prescriptions requested of developing countries by international financial institutions such as the World Bank and the International Monetary Fund.

Sunset clause: A provision in an agreement under which a measure taken by a government expires automatically once a certain time has elapsed, or unless some specified action has been taken. The WTO agreements dealing with anti-dumping measures and countervailing duties contain sunset clauses under which relevant measures expire after five years unless a review finds that they should continue.

Swiss formula: A compromise formula for achieving linear tariff cuts proposed by Switzerland during the Tokyo Round. It was intended to reduce higher tariffs by greater proportion than lower tariffs. The formula reads:

$$Z=AX/A+X$$

X represents the initial tariff rate, and A is a coefficient to be agreed on. Z is the resulting lower tariff rate.

Systemic issues: Matters pertaining to the functioning or the broad rules of the multilateral trading system. Issues usually under this heading include, for example, dispute settlement provisions, safeguards mechanisms, transparency rules etc.

Targeted dumping: Dumping concentrated in sales to certain regions, customers, or time periods.

Tariff binding: A commitment not to increase a rate of duty beyond an agreed level. Once a rate of duty is bound, it may not be raised without compensating the affected parties.

Tariff lines: Refer usually, but not always, to a six digit entry in the Harmonised System, also known as sub-heading.

Tariff Peaks: Relatively high tariffs, usually on so-called sensitive products, amidst generally low tariff levels are referred to as tariff peaks. For industrialised countries, tariffs of 15 percent and above are generally recognised as tariff peaks.

Tariff preferences: The fundamental assumption under the agreements administered by the WTO is that countries give each other most-favoured-nation treatment in their administration of their tariff regimes. It is, however, possible under certain conditions to accord lower tariff rates or zero tariffs to selected trading partners. The principal means are preferential rates by developed countries for developing countries under GSP schemes, and zero-tariff rates between members of custom unions or free-trade areas. Developing countries may also accord each other preferential rates, for example, under Part IV of the GATT and the Enabling Clause. One occurrence of this is the GSTP.

Tariff Rate Quota (TRQ): The tariff-rate quota resulted from the Uruguay Round Agreement on Agriculture. Certain countries agreed to provide minimum import opportunities for products previously protected by non-tariff barriers. This import system established a quota and a two-tier tariff regime for affected commodities. Imports within the quota enter at a lower (in-quota) tariff rate while a higher (out- of-quota) tariff rate is used for imports above the concessionary access level.

Tariffication: Procedures relating to the agricultural market-access provision in the Agreement on Agriculture under which all non-tariff measures were converted into tariffs.

Technical Barriers to Trade (TBTs): Technical regulations, minimum standards and certification systems for health, safety and environmental protection and to enhance the availability of information about products, which may have impact on trade flows.

Third parties: In proceedings under the WTO Understanding on Rules and Procedures Governing the Settlement of Disputes, members who are not directly involved in the launch of a dispute but who participate in the proceedings because they have a substantial interest in the matter. Members wishing to become third parties must show that they have a trade interest at stake. Third parties may not appeal against panel reports or decisions. In cases where a third party considers that the subject of a dispute has adverse effects on it, it may resort to the normal dispute settlement procedures.

Trade Policy Review Mechanism (TPRM): A WTO review mechanism established in December 1988 at the Montreal Ministerial Meeting which conducted a mid-term review of the Uruguay Round. It is managed by the Trade Policy Review Body. The TPRM is aimed at a smoother functioning of the multilateral trading system through greater domestic and international transparency in the trade regime of individual WTO members. Reviews are conducted according to a fixed timetable. The frequency of reviews is related to the share of Members in world trade, with large traders being reviewed more often.

Trade policy: The complete framework of laws, regulations, international agreements and negotiating stances adopted by government to achieve legally binding market access for domestic firms is referred to as trade policy. Trade policy also seeks to develop rules providing predictability and security for firms.

United Nations Conference on Trade and Development (UNCTAD): Established in 1964 through United Nations General Assembly resolution (XIX) 1995 to promote a greater participation by developing countries in the global trading system and thereby promote their economic development.

Vulnerability Index: A concept currently under discussion in United Nations forums to permit a more objective assessment of the needs of least developed countries and their eligibility for treatment as a least developed country. Various proposals have been put forward for the construction of a vulnerability index, but none enjoy widespread support.

Waiver: A dispensation granted by WTO members to another member freeing it from the obligation to apply a particular provision to a defined aspect of its international trade is referred to as waiver. Under WTO rules, waivers must be approved by three quarters of WTO members. Once granted, they are subject to periodic review.

WTO Ministerial Conference: This conference is composed of the representatives of all WTO members at Ministerial level which is to meet at least once every two years. It has authority to take decisions on all matters under any of the multilateral trade agreements under its jurisdiction.

Zeroing negative margins of dumping: When a group of closely related products is subject to a single anti-dumping investigation, some of the individual products may show a positive margin of dumping (i.e. they are deemed to have been dumped). Others may show a negative margin of dumping (i.e. they are deemed not to have been dumped). Once the pricing of the individual products in the group has been investigated, the relevant authority has to make an assessment for the group of products as a whole. Some of the positive and negative margins will then cancel each other out. Some investigating authorities have, however, adopted the practice of allocating any negative value a zero value. This means that only positive margins count for the assessment of the extent of dumping. Obviously, the result will always err in favour of a finding of dumping. The Appellate Body has repeatedly found that zeroing violates the WTO anti-dumping agreement.

